Love in the Time of Scholarship

ROCHER INDOLOGY SERIES

Series editor: Patrick Olivelle

Widows Under Hindu Law
David Brick

Mirror of Nature, Mirror of Self
Models of Consciousness in Sāṃkhya, Yoga, and Advaita Vedānta
Dimitry Shevchenko

Love in the Time of Scholarship

The Bhāgavata Purāṇa in Indian Intellectual History

ANAND VENKATKRISHNAN

OXFORD
UNIVERSITY PRESS

OXFORD
UNIVERSITY PRESS

Oxford University Press is a department of the University of Oxford. It furthers the University's objective of excellence in research, scholarship, and education by publishing worldwide. Oxford is a registered trade mark of Oxford University Press in the UK and certain other countries.

Published in the United States of America by Oxford University Press
198 Madison Avenue, New York, NY 10016, United States of America.

Library of Congress Cataloging-in-Publication Data
Names: Venkatkrishnan, Anand, author.
Title: Love in the time of scholarship : the Bhāgavata purāṇa in Indian intellectual history / [Anand Venkatkrishnan].
Description: New York, NY, United States of America : Oxford University Press, [2024] |
Series: Rocher indology series |
Includes bibliographical references and index.
Identifiers: LCCN 2024032949 (print) | LCCN 2024032950 (ebook) |
ISBN 9780197776636 (hardback) | ISBN 9780197776650 (epub)
Subjects: LCSH: Puranas. Bhāgavatapurāṇa. | India—Intellectual life.
Classification: LCC BL1140.4.B436 V45 2024 (print) | LCC BL1140.4.B436 (ebook) |
DDC 294.5/925—dc23/eng/20240905
LC record available at https://lccn.loc.gov/2024032949
LC ebook record available at https://lccn.loc.gov/2024032950

DOI: 10.1093/oso/9780197776636.001.0001

Printed by Integrated Books International, United States of America

Contents

Acknowledgments vii

The Pulse Beneath The Page 1

1. Across the Nilgiris 33
2. The Name of God in the World of Men 85
3. Family Ties 133
4. Threads of *bhakti* 175

Conclusion 208

Bibliography 219
Index 239

Acknowledgments

When I finished my dissertation many years ago, I was most excited about writing the acknowledgments. The task seems much more daunting now, because it is not only my list of obligations that has grown, but also my sense of gratitude. Hindus traditionally begin with prayers to Vināyaka, who removes impediments, to the guru, who removes ignorance, and to Sarasvatī, who removes incoherence. To the two gods my gratitude can only be abstract; I was an unknowing recipient of their blessings: a (mostly) healthy and prosperous upbringing and a talent for language. To my gurus, however, I owe an intimate debt, for they shared their human presence with me. Thank you to my graduate mentors: John S. Hawley, for his unfailing enthusiasm, relentless advocacy, and spirited guidance; Sheldon I. Pollock, for being my *dīkṣāguru*, initiating me into the humanistic study of premodern India; Rachel F. McDermott, for exemplifying religious studies pedagogy; Lawrence J. McCrea, for being my *vidyāguru* in several Sanskrit *śāstra*s; Rosalind O'Hanlon, for insisting that even Sanskritists could be social historians; Christopher Z. Minkowski, for showing me that the lives of scholars were often more interesting than their ideas. Thank you to my teachers who prepared the path: Linda Hess, for the wisdom of poets and the silliness of sages; Bert Lain, for sparkling with mischievous glee; Mark Gonnerman, for walking and talking with everyone; Marsh McCall, for tolerating neither imprecision nor unkindness; Andrea Lunsford, for combining elegance and nobility with everyday joy and a boundless interest in students; Aishwary Kumar, for embodying the virtues of anti-imperialist liberal education: generosity, nonexclusivity, and open-heartedness; Francisco "Paco" Arévalo, for transforming high school Spanish into a laboratory for *filología*; and Sarasvati Mohan, my very first Sanskrit teacher, for believing that no one was too young or too old to learn something wondrous.

As I have become more integrated into the field of South Asian religions, I have gained many friends and well-wishers, among both my peers and my senior colleagues. Jñānēśvar says, "Like moons without blemish / or suns without withering heat / may good people be family to everyone." For your encouragement, criticism, and counsel, thank you to Dean Accardi, Michael Allen, Emilia Bachrach, Chad Bauman, Carla Bellamy, Kristin Bloomer, Joel Bordeaux, Arun Brahmbhatt, Yigal Bronner, David Buchta, Patton Burchett, Ananya Chakravarti, Indrani Chatterjee, Divya Cherian, John Cort, Whitney Cox, Amanda Culp, Lynna Dhanani, Purnima Dhawan, Arthur Dudney, Elaine Fisher, Elisa Freschi, Supriya Gandhi, Ellen Gough, Ravi Gupta, Usman Hamid, Shaman Hatley, Steven Hopkins, Ayesha Irani, Jamal Jones, Sonam Kachru, Harshita Mruthinti Kamath, Christine Marrewa Karwoski, Katherine Kasdorf, Prashant Keshavmurthy, Jon Keune, Joel Lee, Tim Lorndale, Amanda Lucia, Rembert Lutjeharms, Nabanjan Maitra, James Mallinson, Dolores Minakakis, Afsar Mohammad, the late Anne Monius, Anil Mundra, Shankar Nair, Vasudha Narayanan, John Nemec, Andrew Nicholson, Christian Novetzke, Luther Obrock, Jenn Ortegren, Parimal Patil, Jonathan Peterson, Charles Preston, Teena Purohit, Hemant Rajopadhye, Dalpat Rajpurohit, Isabelle Ratié, Jay Ramesh, Chakravarthi Ram-Prasad, Ajay Rao, James Reich, Bihani Sarkar, Anna Schultz, Jason Schwartz, J. Barton Scott, Martha Selby, Samira Sheikh, David Shulman, Simran Jeet Singh, Caley Smith, Davesh Soneji, Hamsa Stainton, Eric Steinschneider, Tony Stewart, Valerie Stoker, Shiv Subramaniam, Anand Vivek Taneja, Sarah Pierce Taylor, Drew Thomases, Davey Tomlinson, Audrey Truschke, Gary Tubb, Archana Venkatesan, Ben Williams, Richard David Williams, Tyler Williams, Samuel Wright.

Special mention is owed to a fellow traveler, my *satīrthya* and current University of Chicago colleague, Andrew Ollett. The Sanskrit literary commentator Pūrṇasarasvatī once defined the fellowship (*sāhacaryam*) that develops between co-students as "being united by an unwavering affection" (*abhaṅgurasnēhayantritatvam*). I am glad we are united by that and more.

Quentin Skinner once remarked to me that I seemed to have a "fatal attraction" to elite institutions. At least that's how I heard the comment. Many such institutions have enabled my research, and I owe my career and intellectual journey to the faculty, students, and staff of all of them: Stanford University, Columbia University, the University of Oxford, Harvard University, and the University of Chicago. Various research fellowships have also supported this project, including the Jacob K. Javits Fellowship from the U.S. Department of Education and the Asoke Kumar Sarkar Junior Research Fellowship in Classical Indology at Balliol College, Oxford.

Outside my academic field, many intellectuals and artists have shaped my thinking and offered me camaraderie. Thank you to Eman Abdelhadi, Leena

Akhtar, Gaiutra Bahadur, Vivek Bald, Field Brown, Elise Burton, Eleanor Craig, Hardeep Dhillon, Alireza Doostdar, Ganavya Doraiswamy, Chenxing Han, Matt Harris, Jovonna Jones, Kareem Khubchandani, Nikhil Krishnan, Mallika Leuzinger, Rekha Malhotra, Amulya Mandava, Wendell Hassan Marsh, Laura McTighe, Durba Mitra, Taylor Moore, Noel Blanco Mourelle, Eli Nelson, Douglas Ober, Arafat Razzaque, Takeo Rivera, Deborah Schlein, Sophie Smith, Amia Srinivasan, Joseph Vignone, Trent Walker, Cornel West, Suraj Yengde, Che Yeun, Anya Yermakova.

To my editor, Kali Handelman: this book and this world would be less bright without your deft hand, sharp eye, and caring voice. May your love for reading and for people bring many more works to fruition.

Thank you to Patrick Olivelle and the board of the Rocher Foundation for choosing to include this book in the Rocher Indology Series and for your trenchant comments along the way. Thank you to the project editors at Oxford University Press, Lauralee Yeary and Rachel Ruisard, for shepherding the manuscript to completion. Thank you also to Mukti Patel for preparing the manuscript for submission.

Friends and family, many now far-flung, have nourished me in more ways than I can list: Lyndsay, Sudha, Sam, Ron, Mustafa, Kurt, Nisha, Shahjehan, Bunty, Mohsin, Tareq, Nilesh, Niha, Alifia, Kevin, Noor, Tasneem, Zahra, Taher, Aamir, Yasmin, Raju, Vino, Dr. Bala, Arul Mami, Sekhar Mama, Akila Mami, Ganesh, Sharanya, Arvind, Kamya, Maha Athai & Ananthu Athimber, Renu Mami, Radha Patti.

Thank you to my in-laws, Zain and Munira Hamza, for accepting and embracing an intercaste, interreligious relationship; to my parents, Subramanian Venkatkrishnan and Meenakshi Subramanian, for raising me with love and warmth, caring for my fragile body, encouraging my unconventional desires, and believing in me more than I believe in myself; and, always, to Shireen, for your light, your heart, your intelligence, your creativity, your tenderness. Bhavabhūti was right:

> *akiṁcid api kurvāṇaḥ saukhyair duḥkhāny apōhati*
> *tat tasya kimapi dravyaṁ yō hi yasya priyō janaḥ.*
> you don't have to do anything—
> the little joys dispel sorrow.
> what a thing it is
> to have someone
> who loves you.

The Pulse Beneath The Page

We often talk about the life of the mind as if it were the mind that mattered, when it's really the life. This is a book about scholarly life. It is prompted by the question: What goes into a person's thinking? What draws someone to a concept, or a work of art, or a text? Where do they sit to write? What did they eat, smell, and see that day? Whom did they hear crying in the streets? These are questions about the everyday life of a scholar. In the context of this book, however, they are difficult questions to answer. For the study of intellectual life in premodern South Asia, particularly in the Sanskrit systems of knowledge, presents unique archival challenges. Even apart from the methodological difficulties, there are theoretical problems. Caught as we all are in the net of discourse and power, any appeal to inner life can only be romantic, nostalgic, or downright hagiographical. Still, I write this book from the premise that scholarly texts can tell us more about their authors than they, or we, let on. That means being open to the possibility that one can discern motivations, persuasions, irritations, hopes, and even fun in a genre of writing that attempts to erase all traces of the quotidian. This book sniffs out those traces, like the scents of past lives which may yet permeate the present.[1]

In this book, I study the reception of a Hindu scripture, the *Bhāgavata Purāṇa*, from the fourteenth to the eighteenth centuries, in order to explore how religious commitments affect scholarly writing. I propose that we can delineate features of a scholarly *habitus*—personalities, dispositions, ethical comportments—in the writings of people who worked in a language, Sanskrit, and in a genre, scholastic prose or *śāstra*, that was notoriously abstracted from the world of everyday life. These members of an educated elite, contrary to how they often presented themselves, were responsive to popular currents of thought and practice. Vernacular ways of being and

[1] See Martin Mulsow, *Knowledge Lost: A New View of Early Modern Intellectual History*, trans. H. C. Erik Midelfort (Princeton: Princeton University Press, 2022), 19: "The largely unconscious portions of bodies of knowledge and their emotional 'colors' make up another tacit aspect of life, shaping the lives of individuals. This tacit dimension reaches deeply into the ambivalences of modern life: fascination, dread, feelings of disgust—all play a role even in the apparently abstract occupations of many a scholar sitting at a desk or the researcher in the laboratory."

Love in the Time of Scholarship. Anand Venkatkrishnan, Oxford University Press. © Oxford University Press 2024.
DOI: 10.1093/oso/9780197776636.003.0001

believing could and did reshape Sanskrit intellectuality. I argue that religion is at the core of these irruptions into the scholastic domain. Recent studies of Sanskrit systems of knowledge in this time period have employed the methods of intellectual history.[2] In keeping with the priorities of that approach, these studies mostly focus on the nonreligious sciences. This book is similarly an intellectual history, but of those systems—both Vedic and non-Vedic scriptural interpretation—which not only bear on religious questions but also emerge from specific communities that shape them. Religion is not epiphenomenal to the study of Sanskrit *śāstra*.[3] Religious commitments, and the particular social worlds that nourished them, prompted some scholars to reset the terms of the intellectual disciplines in which they worked. Sometimes they generated new ways of reading old texts; sometimes these projects were aborted. In either instance, the markers of newness were not wholesale changes but subtle shifts in the registers of scholastic discourse.

Religion in this book is defined by the word *bhakti*. The historical and scholarly meanings of *bhakti* range widely: an ascetic model for social elites of turning one's life into a sacrificial activity for God;[4] the veneration of past and present teachers and their images;[5] the emotional outpouring of desire for a departed beloved;[6] the simultaneous subversion of upper-caste *dharma* and its restoration on the ground of devotion;[7] active participation in a community of worship;[8] a practice that creates publics of memory (or religious

[2] I have in mind the several essays produced between 2000 and 2010 by the NEH-funded collaborative research project "Sanskrit Knowledge-Systems on the Eve of Colonialism."

[3] On making religious ideas a topic constitutive of intellectual history, see John Coffey and Alister Chapman, "Introduction: Intellectual History and the Return of Religion," in *Seeing Things Their Way: Intellectual History and the Return of Religion*, ed. Alister Chapman, John Coffey, and Brad S. Gregory (Notre Dame: University of Notre Dame Press, 2009), 1–23. For recent work on the influence of religion in Sanskrit poetry and poetics, see Rembert Lutjeharms, *A Vaiṣṇava Poet in Early Modern Bengal: Kavikarṇapūra's Splendour of Speech* (Oxford: Oxford University Press, 2018) and James D. Reich, *To Savor the Meaning: The Theology of Literary Emotions in Medieval Kashmir* (New York: Oxford University Press, 2021).

[4] Angelika Malinar, *The Bhagavadgītā: Doctrines and Contexts* (Cambridge: Cambridge University Press, 2007), 13.

[5] John Cort, "Bhakti in the Early Jain Tradition: Understanding Devotional Religion in South Asia," *History of Religions* 42.1 (2002): 59–86.

[6] Friedhelm Hardy, *Viraha-Bhakti: The Early History of Kṛṣṇa Devotion in South India* (Delhi: Oxford University Press, 1983). Cf. Tracy Coleman, "Dharma, Yoga, and Viraha-Bhakti," in *The Archaeology of Bhakti I: Mathurā and Maturai, Back and Forth*, ed. Emmanuel Francis and Charlotte Schmid (Pondicherry: Institut Français de Pondichéry; Paris: École Française d'Extrême-Orient, 2014), 34–35.

[7] Ravi M. Gupta and Kenneth Valpey, *The Bhāgavata Purāṇa: Selected Readings* (New York: Columbia University Press, 2017), 9–13.

[8] Karen Pechilis Prentiss, *The Embodiment of Bhakti* (Oxford: Oxford University Press, 1999).

polities);[9] the poetry of prayer;[10] the construction of divine embodiment;[11] a devotional sensibility developed both in tandem with and in opposition to antinomian religious modes;[12] a way to reconcile reform and social order;[13] a "movement" of vernacular storytelling and song that imagined a nation;[14] and, in the end, an indexical term that reveals the positionality of the person making statements about it.[15] Some consider *bhakti* itself to be religion, or in its most popular sense, "heart religion . . . the religion of participation, community, enthusiasm, song, and often of personal challenge."[16] Whether or not this is the case, each of the foregoing definitions involves an account of *bhakti*'s binding or unifying power, to God, to ideals, to one another. What the religion of *bhakti* binds together in this book is local, regionally specific devotional practices and the supralocal, transregional discourse of Sanskrit scholasticism. My general interest is to understand how ideas and practices associated with everyday people, popular religious networks, and vernacular languages made their way into elite Sanskrit *śāstras*—that is, not just into permeable genres of Sanskrit, like the epics or the *purāṇas*, but into intellectual disciplines, like Mīmāṁsā and Vēdānta, that are generally viewed as impervious to the world around them. The demotic registers of *bhakti*, I argue in the chapters of this book, filtered into the forbidding world of scriptural hermeneutics, shaping the very contours of Sanskrit intellectuality.

What do I mean by the demotic, the popular, the everyday? This is a question about both the social lives of Sanskrit and the hierarchies of Hinduism. The problem of multiple Hinduisms, elite and popular, right- and left-hand, high- and low-caste, continues to shape the study of Indian religion. Even those who work against the binary of "great" and "little" traditions, which

[9] Christian Novetzke, *Religion and Cultural Memory: A Cultural History of Saint Namdev in India* (New York: Columbia University Press, 2008). On polities before publics, see Brian Hatcher, *Hinduism before Reform* (Cambridge: Harvard University Press, 2020), 73–100.

[10] Hamsa Stainton, *Poetry as Prayer in the Sanskrit Hymns of Kashmir* (Oxford: Oxford University Press, 2019); Steven Hopkins, *Singing the Body of God: The Hymns of Vedāntadeśika in Their South Indian Tradition* (Oxford: Oxford University Press, 2002).

[11] Barbara Holdrege, *Bhakti and Embodiment: Fashioning Divine Bodies and Devotional Bodies in Kṛṣṇa Bhakti* (London: Routledge, 2015).

[12] Patton Burchett, *A Genealogy of Devotion:* Bhakti, *Tantra, Yoga, and Sufism in North India* (New York: Columbia University Press, 2019).

[13] Francesca Orsini, "Tulsī Dās as a Classic," in *Classics of Modern South Asian Literature*, ed. Rupert Snell and M. P. Raeside (Wiesbaden: Harrassowitz, 1998), 126.

[14] John Stratton Hawley, *A Storm of Songs: India and the Idea of the Bhakti Movement* (Cambridge: Harvard University Press, 2015).

[15] Jon Keune, *Shared Food, Shared Devotion: Equality and the Bhakti-Caste Question in Western India* (New York: Oxford University Press, 2021), 47–66.

[16] Hawley, *A Storm of Songs*, 2.

itself reproduces a Brahmanical distinction between the scriptural and the popular, acknowledge that social inequalities are reflected in the religious domain through institutional and cultural segregation: different temples, different foods, different jokes.[17] Those who see degrees of continuity between elite and nonelite beliefs and practices posit relationships of reciprocity, contestation, and domination.[18] The problem of intellectual segregation is more acute. This problem bears on the sociology of language use. As the work of Sheldon Pollock has demonstrated, outside the Persianate cultural sphere, to do scholarship in premodern South Asia was either to write in Sanskrit or to adopt its codes and conventions.[19] An important exception to the pattern was vernacular philosophical commentary and religious poetry of *bhakti* traditions. However, according to Pollock, this exception simply confirms the historical division of labor: systematic knowledge remained the preserve of Sanskrit, the literary and spiritual the preserve of the vernaculars.[20] Meanwhile, in other circles, the very textualization of vernacular religious traditions is only evidence of their being, as it were, always already interpellated, unable to discard the normative influence of Sanskrit and Brahmanical dominance.[21] Following Christian Novetzke, I understand the vernacular both in the sense of regional language and in the sense of the quotidian, the everyday.[22] Novetzke shows how the agents of vernacularization

[17] C. J. Fuller, *The Camphor Flame: Popular Hinduism and Society in India* (Princeton: Princeton University Press, 1992), 28.

[18] See Kunal Chakrabarti, *Religious Process: The Puranas and the Making of a Regional Tradition* (New Delhi: Oxford University Press, 2001). On rethinking the distinction between folk and classical, see Fred Smith, *The Self Possessed: Deity and Spirit Possession in South Asian Literature and Civilization* (New York: Columbia University Press, 2006), 146–153.

[19] Sheldon Pollock, *The Language of the Gods in the World of Men: Sanskrit, Culture, and Power in Premodern India* (Berkeley: University of California Press, 2006).

[20] Sheldon Pollock, "The Languages of Science in Early Modern India," in *Forms of Knowledge in Early Modern Asia: Explorations in the Intellectual History of India and Tibet, 1500–1800*, ed. Sheldon Pollock (Durham and London: Duke University Press, 2011), 25. On the new vernacular sciences in medieval Kannada, see Eric Gurevitch, "Everyday Sciences in Southwest India" (Ph.D. diss., University of Chicago, 2022). On the idea of a popular or public form of literary Sanskrit, see Whitney Cox, "Reading Jalhaṇa Reading Bilhaṇa: Literary Criticism in a Sanskrit Anthology," *Journal of the American Oriental Society* 141.4 (2021): 889–890. On bridging the gap between the classicism of Indology and South Asian folklore studies, see Adheesh Sathaye, "The Scribal Life of Folktales in Medieval India," *South Asian History and Culture* 8.4 (2017): 430–447. On overcoming the opposition between "scholarly" and "popular" culture in Euro-American historiography, see Roger Chartier, "Intellectual History or Sociocultural History? The French Trajectories," in *Modern European Intellectual History: Reappraisals and New Perspectives*, ed. Dominick LaCapra (Ithaca: Cornell University Pres, 1982), 32–36.

[21] Veena Naregal, "Language and Power in Precolonial Western India: Textual Hierarchies, Literate Audiences, and Colonial Philology," *The Indian Economic and Social History Review* 37.3 (2000): 271.

[22] Christian Novetzke, *The Quotidian Revolution: Vernacularization, Religion, and the Premodern Public Sphere in India* (New York: Columbia University Press, 2016), 10–19.

in medieval Maharashtra intended to read "a nonelite audience in the field of everyday life."[23] I am interested in almost the exact inverse: how the field of everyday life, represented by the wide socioreligious domain of *bhakti*, was read by elite audiences. I think it is possible to demonstrate changes at the textual level within and across Sanskrit *śāstra*s that were motivated by local devotional practices by investigating (a) the relationship between popular religious movements and the rarefied air of scholarly pedagogy, (b) the challenges that *bhakti* posed to normative scholastic traditions, and (c) how personal religious commitments prompted Sanskrit intellectuals to think innovatively about the intellectual traditions they inherited.

Let me be clear about what I am and what I am not doing in this book. My core argument is that the emotions and motifs of *bhakti*, which spread differentially across caste, class, and language, bore directly on the scholastic writings of male Sanskrit intellectuals. I demonstrate this primarily by reading scholarly texts as worldly artifacts—in other words, philology—that responded to the influence of *bhakti* traditions in both their textual and extratextual forms. By studying diversity and discontinuity within scholarly traditions, I show that Sanskrit scholarship was polyvocal and equivocal. This is not, however, a project about the recovery of nonelite voices in elite texts. The words "local," "regional," "vernacular," and "nonelite" are not interchangeable. While the first three are on display in this book in ample detail, there is very little evidence of the last. Instead, what I have peppered throughout the book are no more than echoes of what *cannot* be recovered. There is an *in*commensurability between the text and the conditions of its production. I do not intend to explain how vernacular practices made their way into Sanskrit scholarship; I only ask questions about the traces that they left. Insofar as no scholarly culture is self-contained, we should be open to finding everyday life in the Brahmanical corpus too, in order to interrogate its sense of inviolable caste purity.

How, then, can we discern the traces of the unincorporated margin in the genre of *śāstra*? The scholars studied in this book were Brahmins who worked in Brahmanical intellectual traditions. The extent to which their writings reflected a substantive engagement with the ideas and practices of nonelite castes, particularly along the axis of *bhakti*, is a matter of debate. For some, there is a seamless integrity between the worlds of elite exegesis and everyday explication, usually moving down from on high. For others,

[23] Novetzke, *The Quotidian Revolution*, 9.

the cruelties of exclusion that constitute caste society are reflected in the history of ideas; there is no meaningful exchange between these worlds that is not appropriative and oppressive. At stake for many of these scholars is how to evaluate the phenomenon of *bhakti* in Hinduism: Is it a language of protest, of power, or of plain old poetry?[24] I do not adjudicate these questions but instead read *bhakti* from the bottom up. That is, rather than pass judgment on the ability of vernacular-language *bhakti* traditions to maintain a critical edge toward social elites, I would like to flip the script and discern the impact of *bhakti* on the Sanskrit intellectual sphere. From my perspective, all knowledge is local, even that articulated in such transregional languages as Sanskrit. For example, the Marathi poet-philosophers Jñāndēv and Ēknāth challenged the purely Sanskritic nature of public philosophy, but they went about it differently. Jñāndēv's Marathi commentary on the *Bhagavad Gītā*, the *Jñānēśvarī*, was an example of "the high cosmopolitan genre of commentary become domesticated, placed in a gendered form and a localized idiom."[25] On the other hand, Ēknāth, who is said to have edited the *Jñānēśvarī*, wrote philosophical works in Marathi that transformed local thought into the idioms and values of Sanskrit knowledge.[26] Rather than consider these works vernacular translations of classical traditions, reading from the bottom up allows us to understand them as occupying a space in between the local and the cosmopolitan, the elite and nonelite. Although Sanskrit *śāstra* spoke in a universal idiom, I argue that the presence of the local in a transregional intellectual tradition suggests the everyday dimensions of its writing.[27]

To put this argument differently, my study of scholarly life is one way of provincializing Brahmanism. Not unlike the imaginary "hyperreal" Europe in the experience of political modernity in South Asia, Brahmanism and its concepts exert a powerful hold on premodern Indian intellectual history.[28]

[24] See John Stratton Hawley, Christian Lee Novetzke, and Swapna Sharma, eds., *Bhakti and Power: Debating India's Religion of the Heart* (Seattle: University of Washington Press, 2019). Cf. Sheldon Pollock, *The Ends of Man at the End of Premodernity* (Amsterdam: Royal Netherlands Academy of Arts and Sciences, 2005), 88: "Why did *bhakti* produce so much new poetry but so little new power, at least institutionalized political power?"

[25] Novetzke, *The Quotidian Revolution*, 223.

[26] Anand Venkatkrishnan, "Philosophy from the Bottom Up: Eknāth's Vernacular Advaita," *Journal of Indian Philosophy* 48.1 (2020): 9–21.

[27] For comparative reflections on the local nature of Muslim knowledge, see A. Kevin Reinhart, *Lived Islam: Colloquial Religion in a Cosmopolitan Tradition* (Cambridge: Cambridge University Press, 2020), 121: "Cosmopolitan scholars never dwell completely removed from Lived Islam, floating above their locale like balloons."

[28] Dipesh Chakrabarty, *Provincializing Europe: Postcolonial Thought and Historical Difference* (Princeton: Princeton University Press, 2000), 39. For a provocative rethinking of Brahmanism in

One of those concepts is the ahistorical, transcendent nature of Sanskrit *śāstra*.[29] Although intellectual historians have tracked changes in a tradition's way of thinking over time, we have seldom interrogated the means by which the practice of *śāstra* becomes coded as elite, male, and otherworldly.[30] In effect, this is an argument about caste in the history of ideas. To assume that Brahmanical traditions are straightforwardly internal conversations between Brahmins, without the involvement of those outside their caste order, reinscribes the normative value of caste purity. Brahmanical thought, like Brahmin community, presents itself as simultaneously exclusive and universal.[31] But in the same way that the political history of caste in premodern India refuses to treat Brahmin ideology as social fact,[32] the intellectual history of Brahmin scholarship should refuse to take its self-sufficiency at face value. For in these ways of knowing there is always the trace of that which cannot be fully absorbed or rejected. Rather than read *śāstra* as aloof and self-contained, I am interested in how the margins constitute the center. This approach takes inspiration from Christopher Bayly's attempt to contest the claims of classical European universalism.[33] Bayly argues that the birth of the modern world was not unidirectional but global, a world in which marginal and subaltern groups played a significant

the historiography of religion in India, see Chapter 1, "Defamiliarizing the Brahmanical World," in Jason Schwartz, "Ending the Śaiva Age: The Rise of the Brāhmaṇa Legalist and the Universalization of Hindu *Dharma*" (Ph.D. diss., University of California, Santa Barbara, 2023), 129–306.

[29] Sheldon Pollock, "The Theory of Practice and the Practice of Theory in Indian Intellectual History," *Journal of the American Oriental Society* 105.3 (1985): 499–519; Sheldon Pollock, "Mīmāṁsā and the Problem of History in Traditional India," *Journal of the American Oriental Society* 109.4 (1989): 603–610. Cf. Ananya Vajpeyi, "*Śūdradharma* and Legal Treatments of Caste," in *Hinduism and Law*, ed. Timothy Lubin, Donald R. Davis Jr., and Jayanth K. Krishnan (Cambridge: Cambridge University Press, 2010), 159: "the elision of *historicity* from Sanskrit discourse is related to its repression of *subalternity*."

[30] Cf. Bonnie G. Smith, *The Gender of History: Men, Women, and Historical Practice* (Cambridge: Harvard University Press, 1998), 13, on how professionalizing historians in the nineteenth century produced "scholarly selves out of historical practices and the iteration of historical rules."

[31] See Johannes Bronkhorst, *How the Brahmins Won: From Alexander to the Guptas* (Leiden: Brill, 2016), 2: "Brahmanism insisted on the separate position that Brahmins occupy in the world and in society. To the extent that they interact with society, they find their natural place at the top of the social hierarchy. Their separate position guaranteed them the exclusive possession of spiritual knowledge and power."

[32] See Sumit Guha, *Beyond Caste: Identity and Power in South Asia* (Leiden: Brill, 2013), 39: "All of these real social and political phenomena can be understood only if we abandon the Brahman-centered model."

[33] See Ajay Skaria, "Can the Dalit Articulate a Universal Position? The Intellectual, the Social, and the Writing of History," *Social History* 39.3 (2014): 358: "Universalism, [Bayly] says, is always local; there is always constitutively the part of the margin in the centre—the margin's participation, so to speak."

role in shaping the agendas of dominant groups. I take the general point as applicable to the universalisms of the Sanskrit "cosmopolis," Pollock's term for the "transregional culture-power sphere" of political elites across first-millennium South and Southeast Asia.[34] In this book, I emphasize the local, contingent character of text traditions often valorized by their authors for their universality. One can provincialize the self-professed universality that Brahmin scholars accorded to themselves by pointing out fissures and fractures in the history of their ideas. Their disagreements with one another were not simply a result of the dialectical nature of Sanskrit intellectual culture; they were examples of real and enduring social conflict.[35] Unlike "the strategic use of everyday life to critique social inequality"[36] found in the writings of vernacular intellectuals, Brahmin scholars writing in Sanskrit drew on the idioms of *bhakti* to criticize each other. While these forms of criticism did little to destabilize the institution of Brahmanism itself, they reflected anxieties and uncertainties about the constitution of Brahmin identity.[37] Reading *śāstra* from the bottom up exposes the fault lines that wend and crack through its foundation.

Religion is a way into the lives of scholars. There are other ways, of course: reminiscences, or testimonies, or festschrifts. However, in the study of Sanskrit society and culture, these forms of evidence are scarce. Before I review the major terms and outlines of this book, some reflections on method are in order. I have introduced myself as an intellectual historian. We deal in texts and their contexts. But what happens when the text escapes context, or the context is unknown? In the following section I explore what the textual orientation of Indology may have to learn from fields of knowledge that work at the limits of the archive.

[34] Pollock, *The Language of the Gods*, 12.

[35] See Valerie Stoker, *Polemics and Patronage in the City of Victory: Vyasatirtha, Hindu Sectarians, and the Sixteenth-Century Vijayanagara Court* (Oakland: University of California Press, 2016), 106–129; Madhav Deshpande, "Will the Winner Please Stand Up: Conflicting Narratives of a Seventeenth-Century Philosophical Debate from Karnataka," in *Knowing India: Colonial and Modern Constructions of the Past: Essays in Honor of Thomas Trautmann*, ed. Cynthia Talbot (New Delhi: Yoda Press, 2011), 366–380.

[36] Novetzke, *The Quotidian Revolution*, 16.

[37] See Christian Novetzke, "The Brahmin Double: The Brahminical Construction of Anti-Brahminism and Anti-caste Sentiment in the Religious Cultures of Precolonial Maharashtra," *South Asian History and Culture* 2.2 (2011): 232–252. Cf. Adheesh Sathaye, *Crossing the Lines of Caste: Viśvāmitra and the Construction of Brahmin Power in Hindu Mythology* (Oxford: Oxford University Press, 2015), 177–207.

Social History in the Study of Indian Intellectual Cultures

The study of scholarly life is usually a matter of social and cultural history. Historians of this stripe combine different forms of documentary evidence—letters, biographies, portraits, diaries, normative manuals, literary representations, land grants, tax records, inscriptions, and other material sources—to reconstruct the social, cultural, and political context for intellectual life. "Context" is similarly the buzzword for intellectual historians. Intellectual contexts, or frameworks for discourse, enable historians of ideas to make sense of what authors of texts were doing in writing them. The range of such frameworks may vary by scale, and it is up to the intellectual historian to determine which contexts are the relevant ones for the production of and intention behind ideas in specific times and places. To illustrate the importance of context in the study of premodern scholarly life, let us take a few brief examples from Europe, the Middle East, and China. In a sweeping essay that sketches the contours of the Republic of Letters from the sixteenth century onward, Anthony Grafton notes, "It is above all in the thousands of surviving letters . . . that the outlines, highways and capitals of the Republic can be glimpsed most vividly."[38] Konrad Hirschler is similarly bullish about his arguments about medieval Muslim scholarly culture because "for the Middle Period we have a sufficient array of narrative, normative and documentary textual sources as well as illustrations that allow the study of such reading practices in some detail."[39] And in an account of China's "philological turn" in the eighteenth century, Ori Sela is able to demonstrate how the intellectual turns scholars took were connected to the social turns in their lives by delineating "the intricate social networks of scholars, unraveling the social contacts and environments that facilitated—materially, institutionally, and intellectually—the exchange, circulation, and dissemination of contemporaneous knowledge."[40] Here, too, it is the many "letters, prefaces, postscripts,

[38] Anthony Grafton, "A Sketch Map of a Lost Continent: The Republic of Letters," *Republics of Letters: A Journal for the Study of Knowledge, Politics, and the Arts* 1.1 (2009): 9.

[39] Konrad Hirschler, *The Written Word in the Medieval Arabic Lands: A Social and Cultural History of Reading Practices* (Edinburgh: Edinburgh University Press, 2012), 5. This appears to have been true of Mamluk Cairo in particular, as Jonathan Berkey confirms: "Multivolume contemporary chronicles and biographical dictionaries . . . largely concerned with the education and careers of academics, allow the social historian to reproduce the world of Muslim scholarship in the later Middle Ages in finer detail than for any other premodern period." Jonathan Berkey, *The Transmission of Knowledge in Medieval Cairo: A Social History of Islamic Education* (Princeton: Princeton University Press, 1992), 14.

[40] Ori Sela, *China's Philological Turn: Scholars, Textualism, and the Dao in the Eighteenth Century* (New York: Columbia University Press, 2018), 14.

epitaphs, and tombstone inscriptions" preserved in scholarly biographies that form valuable sources for these social networks.[41] Even the laments that pepper these studies seem like privileged complaints. Despite his energetic study of the social conditions of science research in Ottoman Turkey, Harun Küçük regrets, "We still know quite little about the professoriate in the absence of heavily contextualized statistical studies of seventeenth-century ulema biographical dictionaries, which unfortunately lack any mention of family wealth."[42] Out of these historical details come reflections on the concept of scholarly habitus, or the structures of acquired, durable dispositions that underlie particular practices, as developed by social theorists like Pierre Bourdieu, Max Weber, and Norbert Elias.[43] Scholarly self-fashioning as a subject of cultural history is enabled by the social data available for premodern institutions of learning.[44]

There have been sophisticated studies of public intellectual culture, subject formation, institutions of learning, and the authorial self in premodern India.[45] Some have begun to identify the cultural markers of Sanskrit scholarship, such as hermeneutical insincerity, affective responses to philosophical novelty, and the moods attendant upon intellectual praxis.[46] However, Sanskritists do not even dream of the resources available to their

[41] Sela, *China's Philological Turn*, 25.

[42] Harun Küçük, *Science without Leisure: Practical Naturalism in Istanbul, 1660–1732* (Pittsburgh: University of Pittsburgh Press, 2020), 105. On the sources missed by Küçük, see Nir Shafir, "The Almighty Akçe: The Economics of Scholarship and Science in the Early Modern Ottoman Empire," *Osmanlı Araştırmaları/The Journal of Ottoman Studies* 58 (2021): 251–280. On a richly documented case of scholarly precarity in Ottoman Turkey, see A. Tunç Şen, "The Emotional Universe of Insecure Scholars in the Early Modern Ottoman Hierarchy of Learning," *International Journal of Middle East Studies* 53.2 (2021): 315–321.

[43] Gadi Algazi, "Scholars in Households: Refiguring the Learned Habitus, 1480–1550," *Science in Context* 16.1–2 (2003): 13, n. 10.

[44] Richard Kirwan, ed., *Scholarly Self-Fashioning and Community in the Early Modern University* (Farnham: Ashgate, 2013).

[45] See, *inter alia*, Samuel Wright, *A Time of Novelty: Logic, Emotion, and Intellectual Life in Early Modern India, 1500–1700 c.e.* (New York: Oxford University Press, 2021); Nabanjan Maitra, "The Rebirth of Homo Vedicus: Monastic Governmentality in Medieval India" (Ph.D. diss., University of Chicago, 2021); Talia Ariav and Naresh Keerthi, "Churning Selves: Intersecting Biographies in the *Nīlakaṇṭhavijaya*," *Cracow Indological Studies* 24.1 (2022): 29–60; Elaine Fisher, *Hindu Pluralism: Religion and the Public Sphere in Early Modern South India* (Oakland: University of California Press, 2017); Whitney Cox, *Modes of Philology in Medieval South India* (Leiden: Brill, 2017); Stoker, *Polemics and Patronage*; Rajeev Kinra, *Writing Self, Writing Empire: Chandar Bhan Brahman and the Cultural World of the Indo-Persian State Secretary* (Oakland: University of California Press, 2015); Christopher Minkowski, Rosalind O'Hanlon, and Anand Venkatkrishnan, eds., *Scholar-Intellectuals in Early Modern India* (London: Routledge, 2015).

[46] See Yigal Bronner and Lawrence McCrea, *First Words, Last Words: New Theories for Reading Old Texts in Sixteenth-Century India* (New York: Oxford University Press, 2021), 11, 30, 164–170; Wright, *A Time of Novelty*, 15–18; Sonam Kachru, *Other Lives: Mind and World in Indian Buddhism* (New York: Columbia University Press, 2021), 198.

counterparts. "The Indologist," says Pollock ruefully, "gazes with a mixture of envy and self-pity on the richness of the social data for the history of seventeenth-century European thought."[47] For a variety of reasons, according to Pollock, the social record of Sanskrit intellectuals has been left "a virtual blank."[48] Responses to the relative paucity of contextual data have vacillated between despair and perseverance. Some say that it is nearly impossible to answer even primary questions about the social history of knowledge production in India.[49] Others (myself included) suggest, more optimistically, that there is more information about individual intellectuals than is commonly supposed, particularly when Sanskrit texts are paired with documentary sources in vernacular languages.[50] Still others argue that we can do more with less. The sheer proliferation of Sanskrit scholastic writing means that we can read texts as "intrasystemic interventions," effectively providing their own contexts, which are literary or intellectual in character rather than physical or sociopolitical.[51] Each of these responses appeals to the idea that context is indispensable to understanding content.[52]

What if we did things the other way around? That is, what if we allowed content to reveal context? This is a practice that I call subtextual reading. It is not very different from what philologists already do—which is to try to understand other people's minds—except that it takes the lack of contextual

[47] Pollock, *The Ends of Man*, 80, n. 136.

[48] Sheldon Pollock, "Is There an Indian Intellectual History? Introduction to 'Theory and Method in Indian Intellectual History,'" *Journal of Indian Philosophy* 36.5 (2008): 537. Some of these factors include "[t]he non-textualization of life-events (birth, marriage, death); the absence of a political absolutism whose cruel documentary invigilation over its own subjects was, in some small measure, compensated for by the archival richness left to posterity; a climate that destroyed whatever was not recopied every few generations; and, for the Sanskrit intellectual milieu, a constitutional disinclination to time-space localization and a cultural proscription of self-advertisement."

[49] Peter van der Veer, "Does Sanskrit Knowledge Exist?," *Journal of Indian Philosophy* 36.5 (2008): 635.

[50] Christopher Minkowski, Rosalind O'Hanlon, and Anand Venkatkrishnan, "Social History in the Study of Indian Intellectual Cultures?," *South Asian History and Culture* 6.1 (2015): 2. On moving from context to text, by beginning with available historical documents and moving to contemporary ideas, see Samuel Wright, "History in the Abstract: 'Brahman-ness' and the Discipline of Nyāya in Seventeenth-Century Vārāṇasī," *Journal of Indian Philosophy* 44.5 (2016): 1041–1069. Cf. Cox, *Modes of Philology*, 160: "[W]e need to account empirically for the diversity of institutional forums in which textual scholarship was practiced, in order that then—and *only* then—it may become possible to venture inferences about the wider collective or individual projects in which these practices were imbricated."

[51] Jonardon Ganeri, "Contextualism in the Study of Indian Intellectual Cultures," *Journal of Indian Philosophy* 36.5 (2008): 553–555.

[52] See Quentin Skinner, *Visions of Politics*, vol. 1: *Regarding Method* (Cambridge: Cambridge University Press, 2002). On the questionable assumptions that underwrite contextualism in the history of ideas, see Peter E. Gordon, "Contextualism and Criticism in the History of Ideas," in *Rethinking Modern European Intellectual History*, ed. Darrin M. McMahon and Samuel Moyn (Oxford: Oxford University Press, 2014), 32–55.

evidence not as a roadblock but as an opportunity. Subtextual reading means reading behind or beneath the text to elucidate what is there in spirit though not in the letter. The spirit that I am trying to invoke is the social world of the scholar, shimmering before the reader who peers through the veils of abstraction. If reading from the bottom up reorients our relation to the archive, subtextual reading works at the archive's limits. Whereas similar methods, such as reading against the grain or contrapuntal reading, uncover sublimated ideologies and resurrect excluded voices, subtextual reading is concerned with the polyphony of the normative text. The author's voice is itself plural, incoherent, and fragmented. Subtextual reading dwells in the break. As Marisa Fuentes explains, scholars who recover traces of the silenced past still rely on archival fragments to reconstruct alternative narratives:

> "Reading against the grain" is a concept that historians, feminist, literary, post-colonial and interdisciplinary scholars have drawn on since at least the 1980s. It's a method that reads official archival accounts for traces of marginalized voices and/or reading dominant voices for how they document, conceptualize and represent the subaltern. But I think it still relies on what *is* there in the document even as it offers an approach to "read between the lines." . . . I wanted to stretch the documents in order to accentuate what might not be there while still keeping intact the integrity of the documents.[53]

In her study of enslaved women in colonial Barbados, Fuentes subverts the methodological constraints of history to tell subaltern stories. I have already stated that this is not a project about the recovery of nonelite voices. However, I am interested in thinking comparatively about "what might not be there" in *śāstra* and whether it is possible to "stretch the documents" to imagine them out of the text. In order to do so, I derive the concept of subtextual reading from interdisciplinary reflections on the "analytical costs and limits of archival mandates."[54] In particular, subaltern histories and histories of sexuality offer helpful analogies to think about Sanskrit *śāstra* and its contextual difficulties. I briefly invoke ways of knowing not traditionally associated with

[53] See Emily Owens, "Enslaved Women, Violence, and the Archive: An Interview with Marisa Fuentes," AAIHS, October 4, 2016, https://www.aaihs.org/enslaved-women-violence-and-the-archive-an-interview-with-marisa-fuentes/.

[54] Anjali Arondekar, *For the Record: On Sexuality and the Colonial Archive in India* (Durham: Duke University Press, 2009), 5.

the philological basis of Indology as a gesture of gratitude. Without learning from those marginalized by the historical mainstream of academia, including by my own discipline, I would not have been attuned to those on the margins of the text.[55] In subaltern studies, for instance, the colonial legal document is an "untamed fragment" that resists the condition of contextuality, of what went before and came after it. The legal apparatus is designed for "detaching an experience from its living context and setting it up as an empty positivity outside history."[56] Like the colonial monument, the colonial document is an example of historical revisionism that tears the fabric of the past and replaces the full story with a fragment. In this I find it akin to the Sanskrit scholastic text. At the level of intellectual culture, it has been argued that the ideological effects of *śāstra* as theory are to naturalize and dehistoricize cultural practices.[57] On a formal level, too, the stylized conventions of the scholastic genre set up a social and linguistic domain abstracted from the world of everyday life, which appears only in order to supply the occasional example. More important, what the Sanskrit text shares with coloniality is the force of epistemological, physical, and psychological violence, or the inequalities of caste and gender that Pollock has called "the great absent center at the heart of classical Indian studies."[58] This form of "precolonial colonialism" wraps around itself the mantle of authority by displacing those who weave its threads to the margins. The language of erasure, silence, occlusion, and recovery likewise haunts the history of sexuality.[59] Because queerness is often transmitted covertly, its evidence is ephemeral, dappled with "traces, glimmers, residues, and specks of things."[60] Contextual evidence is similarly elusive in *śāstra*. What interests me here is the possibility that everyday life,

[55] On fractures of race and gender in the history of academic Indology in the United States, see Anand Venkatkrishnan, "Skeletons in the Sanskrit Closet," *Religion Compass* 15.5 (2021): 1–9; Anand Venkatkrishnan, "Hidden Mūrtis: The Sanskrit Students of Radcliffe College," in *Modern Sanskrit: Dialogues Across Times, Spaces, and Religions*, ed. Finnian Moore Gerety, Laurie Patton, and Charles Preston (London: Routledge, forthcoming).

[56] Ranajit Guha, "Chandra's Death," in *A Subaltern Studies Reader: 1986–1995*, ed. Ranajit Guha (Minneapolis: University of Minnesota Press, 1997), 37–38.

[57] Pollock, "The Theory of Practice and the Practice of Theory."

[58] Sheldon Pollock, "Deep Orientalism? Notes on Sanskrit and Power beyond the Raj," in *Orientalism and the Postcolonial Predicament*, ed. Carol A. Breckenridge and Peter van der Veer (Philadelphia: University of Pennsylvania Press, 1993), 115. Cf. Vajpeyi, "*Śūdradharma* and Legal Treatments of Caste," 159: "There is a complex story behind why and how Sanskrit discourses, especially those in the *śāstra* mode, achieved this near-perfect repression of subalternity or indeed alterity of any kind—in other words, what the linguistic, epistemological, and ideological features of Sanskrit discursivity are that make it so perfectly an idiom of domination."

[59] Arondekar, *For the Record*, 7.

[60] José Esteban Muñoz, "Ephemera as Evidence: Introductory Notes to Queer Acts," *Women & Performance: A Journal of Feminist Theory* 8.2 (1996): 10.

hovering on the edges of the scholastic record, may be abundant in the domain of *śāstra* even as it "might not be there." Subordinated or appropriated by the intellectual elite, the songs and stories of ordinary people leave echoes in the lineaments of their thought. To read their writing subtextually is to show that they were never alone or aloof. "[B]ehind the seductive rhythms of their prose," as Abhishek Kaicker writes of elite chroniclers in Mughal Delhi, "it is still possible to hear a distant clamor from the streets."[61]

To read subtext is a delicate endeavor. There is a long history of overreach in this regard, from Orientalists who inferred too much about social conditions from prescriptive texts, to Indologists who experimented with psychoanalytic readings, to cultural historians who claimed that sensitive readers, both past and present, could tell from the texture of a work whether or not it was meant to be read as history.[62] When I read subtext in *śāstra*, I am specifically interested in how the markers of the personal in a decidedly impersonal genre reveal the influence of and engagement with a world that is ordinarily segregated from it, socially and intellectually. This is a reading at the nexus of caste, religion, and the social in premodern India. What happens when we insist that everyday religion permeates Sanskrit *śāstra*? One consequence is a greater awareness of the porousness and impurity of Brahmanism. For instance, we may become aware of the labor of gender in Sanskrit knowledge. In early modern South India, for example, the identification of regionality with the female body made a consideration of gender central to formulating a vernacular Sanskrit.[63] In a chapter on the family in this book, I explore the writings of three generations of Brahmins who established an influential scholarly household in early modern Banaras. The genealogy that they reconstruct is entirely patrilineal, even as some of their contemporaries acknowledged the increasing visibility of women in the early modern scholarly household.[64] These examples are invitations to better

[61] Abhishek Kaicker, *The King and the People: Sovereignty and Popular Politics in Mughal Delhi* (New York: Oxford University Press, 2020), 12. Although mine is not a microhistory, I also appreciate the methodological reflections on how to account for "half-heard whispers" in Nandini Chatterjee, *Negotiating Mughal Law: A Family of Landlords across Three Indian Empires* (Cambridge: Cambridge University Press, 2020), 225.

[62] The last of these refers to the controversies around V. Narayana Rao, David Shulman, and Sanjay Subrahmanyam, *Textures of Time: Writing History in South India 1600–1800* (Delhi: Permanent Black, 2001). See the critique by Sheldon Pollock, "Pretextures of Time," *History and Theory* 46.3 (2007): 366–383, and the response by V. Narayana Rao, David Shulman, and Sanjay Subrahmanyam, "A Pragmatic Response," *History and Theory* 46.3 (2007): 409–427.

[63] Kashi Gomez, "Sanskrit and the Labour of Gender in Early Modern South India," *Modern Asian Studies* 57.1 (2023): 167–194.

[64] See James Benson, "Śaṁkarabhaṭṭa's Family Chronicle: The *Gādhivaṁśavarṇana*," in *The Pandit: Traditional Scholarship in India*, ed. Axel Michaels (New Delhi: Manohar, 2011), 105–118.

understand Brahmanism's story of itself, and the stories we have told about its systems of knowledge. As scholars of this archive, we have an obligation to annihilate its caste purity, to insist that it has always been otherwise.

To a reader who expects a historical study of religion in Sanskrit *śāstra*, topics such as provincializing Brahmanism, subtextual reading, and the limits of the archive may seem outside the scope of this book. It may seem to them that I have given an outsized importance to these matters considering that the majority of the book, as I will explain in the remainder of this introduction, carries out fairly conventional Indological work. A reader expecting those topics to be more prominently featured in the body of the text may be disappointed by this discrepancy. Let me address both readers by considering this introduction's relationship with the work in the chapters. I have written this introduction not to make large-scale methodological claims about the sociology of knowledge that I set out to prove in the book, but to attune the reader to the other things that might show up in the course of my study. These are informed guesses, not provable claims; curiosity, not ambition. My opening conceit was that this is a book about scholarly life. Although the scholarship is what I focus on in the book, it is the life that intrigues me. I emerged from the archive with questions—not answers—about what lies behind the text apart from the big-picture social and political context outside of it. What I found there matters to me beyond my disciplinary constraints. These absent presences are not central to the work at all; they are in the margins, around corners, under covers. All I would like to do is open up our reading enough to hear them. The motif of hearing is laced throughout the book, and not always as metaphor. To the best of my ability, as my translations show, I treat scholarly texts as conversations and poetry as spoken word. The reader will find me thinking constantly about what I have heard and not just read: a poet's cry, a pilgrim's song, a pen's scrape, a street's bustle. What I am trying to do with the concept of subtextual reading is not to stake a claim but to ask a question, to plant a seed, to issue an invitation.[65] For those who want to read this book as a straightforward account of the *Bhāgavata Purāṇa* in Indian intellectual history, they may do so. There may also be those who are not so occupied by the technical discoveries of my research. I invite them to think further with me about what else might be going on. Perhaps it is not only the nonelite, vernacular world that shapes

[65] On reasons as invitations, see Anthony Simon Laden, *Reasoning: A Social Picture* (Oxford: Oxford University Press, 2012), 31–38.

elite thinking. Perhaps that is the wrong subtext entirely. I suggest that it is one option. For those who have ears, let them listen.

A final note on the genealogy of subtextual reading should clarify the playfulness with which I intend to use it. It is not just a feature of the fields of knowledge mentioned here. Indians did this all the time in more and less formal ways. While premodern scholars of literature developed several theories of secondary meaning that drew on concepts of figuration, suggestion, and polysemy, some tried to show that the distinction was not between false and true or primary and secondary meaning, but between true and truer meaning. One did not have to read between the lines; the truth was in the lines, in the multiple properties and depths of language itself.[66] Others speculated about the everyday life of writers based on offhand comments in their writing. In such stories, the poet Kālidāsa took a sardonic question from his wife and turned it into three major lyric poems, the playwright Bhavabhūti cloaked an editorial critique in a seemingly innocuous comment about the amount of lime in his *paan*, the love-thief Bilhaṇa was imprisoned for having an affair with a princess, and the grammarian Patañjali hated his students.[67] The majority of this book follows the empiricist imperatives of intellectual history by supplying the greatest context possible to understand the content of texts. But here and there, I also encourage a move from the indicative to the subjunctive modality, from "what is" to "what if?" Perhaps this is less an innovation than a return to time-honored tradition.

Mīmāṁsā, Vēdānta, and the *Bhāgavata Purāṇa*

At the core of this book is an intellectual history of the *Bhāgavata Purāṇa* in India from the fourteenth to the early eighteenth century. It demonstrates how readers of the *Bhāgavata* and participants in the wider world of *bhakti* prompted reappraisals within two related systems of Sanskrit scriptural

[66] On attempts to read subtext by the seventeenth-century literary commentator Nārāyaṇa, see Andrew Ollett and Anand Venkatkrishnan, "Plumbing the Depths: Reading Bhavabhūti in Seventeenth Century Kerala," *Asiatische Studien/Études Asiatiques* 76.3 (2022): 581–622.

[67] On Kālidāsa, see M. Krishnamachariar, *History of Classical Sanskrit Literature* (Madras: Tirumalai-Tirupati Devasthanams Press, 1937), 99–100. On Bhavabhūti, see V. Narayana Rao and David Shulman, *A Poem at the Right Moment: Remembered Verses from Premodern South Asia* (Berkeley: University of California Press, 1998), 120–121, 143–145. On Bilhaṇa, see Barbara Stoler Miller, *Phantasies of a Love-Thief* (New York: Columbia University Press, 1971), 2. On Patañjali, see Kottarathil Sankunni, *Aithihyamaala: The Great Legends of Kerala*, trans. Sreekumari Ramachandran (Kozhikode: Mathrubhumi Books, 2011), 28–34.

hermeneutics: Mīmāṁsā and Vēdānta. It also argues that there was a mostly unrecognized Śaiva reception of the *Bhāgavata Purāṇa*, in contrast to its exclusive association with Vaiṣṇava religious communities. A brief account of each of these terms will provide the basis for discussing problems in their historiography.

Mīmāṁsā

Mīmāṁsā, or "investigation," was a hermeneutics of the Veda, the paradigmatic corpus of Sanskrit Hindu scripture. Scholars of Mīmāṁsā, or Mīmāṁsakas, developed sophisticated theories of sentence-meaning in order to understand the structure and function of the Veda. First articulated in the form of aphorisms in Jaimini's *Mīmāṁsā Sūtras* (200 BCE), the interpretive principles of Mīmāṁsā were later elaborated upon by Śabara (fifth century CE) and his commentators, Prabhākara and Kumārila Bhaṭṭa (seventh century CE). Through these principles, Mīmāṁsakas defended the authority of the Veda as the ritual arbiter of Brahmin life and argued that the Veda was a uniquely valid source of knowledge about *dharma*, or, simply, what one must do. They did so in response to critiques of the Veda and alternative views on *dharma* enunciated by Buddhists, Jains, and other non-Vedic groups. Mīmāṁsakas believed that the fundamental definition of *dharma* was the Vedic sacrifice. According to them, the broad Brahmanical tradition known as *varṇāśrama dharma*, a system of ritual, social, and ethical norms indexed to caste and stage of life, could be derived only from Vedic commands. In order to account for the multiplicity of Indic text traditions that accorded religious authority to themselves, Mīmāṁsakas developed a hierarchy of Sanskrit scriptural genres. At the top of the hierarchy they placed *śruti*, the unauthored, eternal Veda. Next, they approved of certain human compositions called *smṛti*, insofar as they conformed to and derived from the Veda. The genre of *smṛti* included the epic *Mahābhārata*, the prescriptive literature of *varṇāśrama dharma*, and the chronicles of ancient legends known as *purāṇas*. Finally, they ejected "divinely inspired" scriptures, like the Āgamas, outside the pale of respectable Brahmin society altogether. Languages other than Sanskrit, in their view, were simply not capable of effectively communicating truth. Mīmāṁsā was also a classically atheist tradition. It argued vehemently against the existence of an omniscient creator-god, had no time for human pretensions to supernatural perception, and asserted that the Vedic gods were nothing but linguistic constructs.[68] The Mīmāṁsā discourse of scriptural hierarchy, its sociolinguistic valorization of Sanskrit, and its atheism would be challenged by the entrance of the *Bhāgavata Purāṇa* into the scholastic domain.

Vēdānta

Another tradition of Vedic hermeneutics was called Vēdānta, also known as the "latter" Mīmāṁsā. On one level, Vēdānta simply meant the Upaniṣads, the "Veda's end." The Upaniṣads reframed, reworked, and sometimes rejected the values of Vedic ritual life. In the scholastic sense, however, Vēdānta was an exegetical tradition that attempted to extract a coherent philosophical theology from the Upaniṣads, the *Bhagavad Gītā*, and the *Brahma Sūtras*, a set of three departure points called the *prasthānatrayī*. Vēdānta was at turns continuous with and distinct from what it labeled its "prior" incarnation.[69] If the *Mīmāṁsā Sūtras* held that the Veda was fundamentally about *dharma*, ritual action performed for a particular result, the *Brahma Sūtras* claimed that the Veda sought to communicate the knowledge of Brahman, the ultimate reality, from which the whole universe came into being. According to Vēdānta, Brahman was the fundamental subject of the Upaniṣads, and knowledge of Brahman would grant liberation from the cycle of death and rebirth. Acquiring that knowledge, or *jñāna*, meant properly understanding the sentences of the Veda. This required the selective application of Mīmāṁsā principles while subverting its insistence that the complex of actions (*karma*) and results (*phala*) would lead to beneficial ends.[70]

Several schools of Vēdānta formed around the interpretation of the *prasthānatrayī*. In this book, I focus on Advaita Vēdānta, the "nondualist" tradition of Vēdānta. According to Advaita Vēdānta, the liberating knowledge

[68] See Francis X. Clooney, "Why the Veda Has No Author: Language as Ritual in Early Mīmāṁsā and Post-modern Theology," *Journal of the American Academy of Religion* 55.4 (1987): 659–684; Francis X. Clooney, "What's a God? The Quest for the Right Understanding of *devatā* in Brāhmaṇical Ritual Theory (*mīmāṁsā*)," *International Journal of Hindu Studies* 1.2 (1997): 337–385; Lawrence McCrea, "'Just Like Us, Just Like Now': The Tactical Implications of the Mīmāṁsā Rejection of Yogic Perception," in *Yogic Perception, Meditation, and Altered States of Consciousness*, ed. Eli Franco (Wien: Verlag der Österreichischen Akademie der Wissenschaften, 2009), 55–70.

[69] See Johannes Bronkhorst, ed., *Mīmāṁsā and Vedānta: Interaction and Continuity* (Delhi: Motilal Banarsidass, 2007).

[70] On the selective appropriation of Mīmāṁsā in Advaita Vēdānta, see Aleksandar Uskokov, "Deciphering the Hidden Meaning: Scripture and the Hermeneutics of Liberation in Early Advaita Vedānta" (Ph.D. diss., University of Chicago, 2018).

of the Upaniṣads was that Ātman, the self, was fundamentally not different from Brahman. More than that, any hint of plurality or differentiation in the world was a superimposition resulting from ignorance (*avidyā*), like a snake erroneously seen in place of a rope, neither wholly real nor unreal. Famously, Advaitins called this inexplicable power that simultaneously veiled nondual reality and projected the everyday world an "illusion" (*māyā*). As with the atheism of classical Mīmāṁsā, the nondualist reading of Vēdānta left little room for a personal, embodied god, possessed of attributes, who would be unsuited to the forbidding austerity of the formless, partless, undifferentiated Brahman. However, unlike in Mīmāṁsā, the range of sources for Advaita Vēdānta were broader than the Vedic canon. It is important both to distinguish and to discern the overlaps between "classical Advaita Vēdānta" and "greater Advaita Vēdānta."[71] In its "classical" sense, Advaita Vēdānta was an exegetical tradition centered around a canon of Sanskrit philosophical texts. In the "greater" sense, it included genres of poetry and prayer, vernacular works, and eclectic, nonphilosophical works that spanned languages and religions.[72] We find the *Bhāgavata Purāṇa* occupying a space in the interstices.

The *Bhāgavata Purāṇa*

The *Bhāgavata Purāṇa* belongs to the Sanskrit genre of *purāṇa*, ancient legend, usually read in tandem with the epics, or *itihāsa*. Perhaps because of their broad doctrinal scope, the *purāṇas* were significant sources of theological inspiration for different religious communities. Not only were they cited in support of different theological arguments, but also they attracted prose commentaries of their own. While Mīmāṁsakas clumped the *itihāsa* and *purāṇa* together as part of the body of Hindu texts known as *smṛti*, the *Bhāgavata* billed itself as being another Veda, or *śruti*. Written in twelve cantos over the course of the first millennium, the *Bhāgavata* was a narrative, devotional, and philosophical treatment of the life of the god Kṛṣṇa. It was subsequently translated, explicated, painted, and performed throughout the subcontinent, becoming one of the most influential Hindu scriptures

[71] Michael Allen, *The Ocean of Inquiry: Niścaldās and the Premodern Origins of Modern Hinduism* (Oxford: Oxford University Press, 2022).

[72] See the essays in the special issue "Pluralizing the Non-Dual: Multilingual Approaches to Advaita Vedānta, 1560–1847," *Journal of Indian Philosophy* 48.1 (2020).

of modern times. Although the *Bhāgavata* resembled other *purāṇas* by including tales of the creation and destruction of the universe, genealogies of kings, and stories of human desire and fallibility, it was distinguished by its poetic celebration of and philosophical meditation on Kṛṣṇa as God incarnate. The *Bhāgavata* was fascinated by the paradox of a transcendent absolute who simultaneously appeared on earth to play with his lovers. In its voluminous tenth canto, the *Bhāgavata* lavished attention on the life of Kṛṣṇa from childhood onward, endowing him with a number of qualities that would be repeated by poets and singers in many languages: his dark hue resembling dense gathering clouds, his boyish charm and penchant for leaving lovers behind, his disregard for social mores, his resistance to injustice and old ways, his inscrutable smile, and his ultimate identity with Brahman. The *Bhāgavata*'s stories served a specific purpose: to cultivate *bhakti* for God in order to relieve the suffering of ordinary life.

The legend of Kṛṣṇa had gone through multiple iterations by the time it reached the *Bhāgavata*. He played multiple roles in the epic *Mahābhārata* where he was both Machiavellian strategist and philosophical sage. While his more humble beginnings as a cowherd were narrated in the *Harivaṁśa*, an appendix to the *Mahābhārata*, he was identified with the supreme god Viṣṇu in the *Bhagavad Gītā* and the *Viṣṇu Purāṇa*.[73] Inscriptional and architectural evidence for the origins of Kṛṣṇa indicates the flourishing of a cult dedicated to Bhagavān, "the blessed one," from the early centuries CE in northern India. When it came to the Tamil South, this "Bhāgavata" tradition mingled with local religious cultures and literatures, including the poetry of the Aḻvārs, who composed devotional poetry in Tamil.[74] Evidence for the southern provenance of the *Bhāgavata Purāṇa* as a text has come from a reading of its multiple layers alongside the architectural projects of the Pallava kings, though some have contested the interpretation of this evidence.[75] Other South Indian texts dedicated to Viṣṇu include the Āgamas, scriptures of early

[73] Simon Brodbeck, *Krishna's Lineage: The Harivamsha of Vyāsa's Mahābhārata* (New York: Oxford University Press, 2019); Freda Matchett, *Kṛṣṇa: Lord or Avatāra? The Relationship between Kṛṣṇa and Viṣṇu* (Richmond: Curzon, 2001).

[74] On the ambivalent presence of Kṛṣṇa in Tamil Buddhist and Jain literature, see Anne Monius, "Dance before Doom: Krishna in the Non-Hindu Literature of Early Medieval South India," in *Alternative Krishnas: Regional and Vernacular Variations on a Hindu Deity*, ed. Guy L. Beck (Albany: State University of New York Press, 2005), 139–149.

[75] See Hardy, *Viraha-Bhakti*, 486–488. On the southern provenance, see D. Dennis Hudson, *Krishna's Mandala: Bhagavata Religion and Beyond*, ed. John Stratton Hawley (Oxford: Oxford University Press, 2010), 125–140. For a dissenting view, see Edwin F. Bryant, "The Date and Provenance of the *Bhāgavata Purāṇa* and the Vaikuntha Perumal Temple," *Journal of Vaishnava Studies* 11.1 (2002): 51–80, and Gupta and Valpey, *The Bhāgavata Purāṇa*, 13.

Pāñcarātra and Vaikhānasa ritual, cosmology, and "yogico-ascetic-cum-devotional" practices.[76] Although the Vaiṣṇava Āgamas were technically outside the Vedic canon as defined by Mīmāṁsā, they came to possess a close relationship with the Brahmanical tradition of Vēdānta. The encounter of these ritual, narrative, and philosophical traditions with the emotional poetry of the Āḻvārs would eventuate in the *Bhāgavata Purāṇa*. Together, they came to define *bhakti* as love for an embodied, enchanting God.[77]

The narratives and motifs of the *Bhāgavata* appeared frequently in both Sanskrit and regional-language *bhakti* poetry. Poets often identified themselves as Kṛṣṇa's intimate devotees with reference to legendary figures from the *Bhāgavata*. Compared to previous iterations of yogic-ascetic *bhakti*, the *Bhāgavata* described *bhakti* with intensely physical language. One could develop all kinds of emotional relationships with God: as a friend, a lover, a mother, a servant, a child, a confidant. The mere thought of this intimate presence in one's life, someone who had come only to soothe the pain of worldly life, could prompt uncontrollable outpourings of emotion and involuntary gestures. Kṛṣṇa himself explained what this form of *bhakti* entailed:

> If your body doesn't bristle, if your mind doesn't melt,
> if you're unable to weep with tears of ecstasy,
> if you don't have any *bhakti*, then how do you expect
> your heart will stand a chance of being pure?
> If your voice does wobble, if your heart does dissolve,
> if you go on crying, and then turn around and laugh,
> if you sing and if you dance shamelessly, in love with me,
> you'll be the one to purify the world.[78]

Despite its associations with Vaiṣṇavism, the *Bhāgavata*'s concept of *bhakti* overlapped significantly with Śaiva literature, in particular the Śivadharma corpus, which was dedicated to the god Śiva. The affective dimensions of *bhakti* that many scholars believed were unique to the *Bhāgavata*—hairs

[76] Gérard Colas, "History of Vaiṣṇava Traditions: An Esquisse," in *The Blackwell Companion to Hinduism*, ed. Gavin Flood (Oxford: Blackwell Publishing, 2003), 233.

[77] See Hardy, *Viraha-Bhakti*, and Adalbert Gail, *Bhakti im Bhāgavatapurāṇa: Religionsgeschichtliche Studie zur Idee des Gottesliebe in Kult und Mystik des Viṣṇuismus* (Wiesbaden: Otto Harrassowitz, 1969).

[78] *Bhāgavata Purāṇa* 11.14.23–24. For the vulgate edition of the *Bhāgavata* I use *Śrīmadbhāgavatamahāpurāṇam: Mūlamātram* (Gorakhpur: Gita Press, 1953). All translations are mine unless indicated otherwise.

rising on end, tears of ecstasy, the overwhelming experience of divine presence—were part of a language of *bhakti* shared by Śaiva and Vaiṣṇava traditions.[79] And although many readers believed that the primary message of the *Bhāgavata* was *bhakti* for the embodied Kṛṣṇa with all his attributes, the text itself bore affinities with the classical tradition of Advaita Vēdānta, representing a kind of "Advaitic theism."[80] Śaivism and Advaita Vēdānta often represent a foil for the *Bhāgavata* tradition, the first because it is not Vaiṣṇavism, and the second because it is ostensibly nontheistic. They prompt us to revisit the historiography of the *Bhāgavata* in some more detail.

A History of Reception

Although it would eventually become the scripture par excellence for Vaiṣṇava *bhakti* traditions, the *Bhāgavata* attracted little attention until well into the second millennium. Given its connections to the world of South Indian Vaiṣṇavism, one might have expected a substantive engagement with the *Bhāgavata* in the writings of Rāmānuja (eleventh century) and Madhva (thirteenth century), founders of the Viśiṣṭādvaita and Dvaita schools of Vēdānta. Both Rāmānuja, philosopher of the Śrīvaiṣṇava tradition originating in Tamilnadu, and Madhva, founder of his own Vaiṣṇava sect in western Karnataka, had ties to temple traditions centered on the ritual worship of Viṣṇu. They believed that Viṣṇu was the ultimate reality, immanent insofar as the universe was suffused with his presence, but transcendent in that, as human beings, we represent only a part of his majesty, like the sparks of a flame. The *Bhāgavata*, however, does not seem to have played a major role in the development of their theologies. According to Rāmānuja, only the *Viṣṇu Purāṇa* was "accepted without dissent by all educated people in the East, North, South, and the West because it alone is sufficient in establishing all *dharmas* and all categories of reality."[81] Even his illustrious follower Vēdānta Dēśika (thirteenth century) cared less about the *Bhāgavata*

[79] Jason Schwartz, "Caught in the Net of *Śāstra*: Devotion and Its Limits in an Evolving Śaiva Corpus," *Journal of Hindu Studies* 5.2 (2012): 210–231. Cf. V. Raghavan, "The Sūta Saṁhitā," *Annals of the Bhandarkar Oriental Research Institute* 22 (1941): 250–251.

[80] Daniel Sheridan, *The Advaitic Theism of the Bhāgavata Purāṇa* (Delhi: Motilal Banarsidass, 1986).

[81] Sucharita Adluri, "Defining Śruti and Smṛti in Rāmānuja's Vedānta," *Journal of Vaishnava Studies* 15.1 (2006): 209. See Johannes van Buitenen, *Rāmānuja's Vedārthasaṁgraha: Introduction, Critical Edition, and Annotated Translation* (Poona: Deccan College Postgraduate and Research Institute, 1956), 140, 262 (translation with my modifications).

and more about theorizing and exemplifying specifically Śrīvaiṣṇava forms of devotion. For example, Vēdānta Deśika's Sanskrit praise-poem, the *Mahāvīravaibhava*, though inspired by Tamil panegyric used by the Āḻvārs, was dedicated to Rāma in a spirit of respectful devotion, far from the erotic mood of Kr̥ṣṇa-centered *bhakti* preferred by the *Bhāgavata*.[82] As for Madhva, his essay on the *Bhāgavata*, the *Bhāgavatatātparyanirṇaya*, was a series of exemplary verses deployed to support his maverick theological vision. Madhva commented with extreme brevity on selected verses from each chapter of the *Bhāgavata* and followed these glosses with long quotations from several sources, many of which were famously "unknown" to his other Vēdānta contemporaries.[83] If the *Bhāgavatatātparyanirṇaya* had any impact on the Sanskrit intellectual world, it did not reach far beyond his own community until perhaps the synthesizing efforts of the Gauḍīya Vaiṣṇava theologian Jīva Gōsvāmī in the sixteenth century.

Conspicuously missing from this account is the role that votaries of Advaita Vēdānta may have played in the transmission of the *Bhāgavata*. There are a few reasons why this may be the case. First, the traditions of Vēdānta that affiliated themselves with Vaiṣṇava theology were historically hostile to Advaita, from those of Rāmānuja and Madhva to those of Vallabha and Caitanya in the fifteenth and sixteenth centuries, who were more directly influenced by the *Bhāgavata*. These traditions and the texts they valued, according to the logic of histories of Indian philosophy, were properly theistic in nature, in contradistinction to the necessarily nontheistic implications of nondual Advaita Vēdānta: a classic and insurmountable distinction between monotheism and monism.[84] A second reason is less philosophical than sectarian. From the fourteenth century onward in the South of India, philosophical differences between Advaitins and their opponents

[82] Ajay Rao, *Refiguring the Rāmāyaṇa as Theology: A History of Reception in Premodern India* (London: Routledge, 2015), 110.

[83] See Roque Mesquita, *Madhva's Unknown Literary Sources: Some Observations* (New Delhi: Aditya Prakashan, 2000).

[84] Some histories of Indian philosophy segregate Vaiṣṇava Vēdānta thought from Advaita Vēdānta on these grounds. See, e.g., Surendranath Dasgupta, *A History of Indian Philosophy*, vol. 4 (Cambridge: Cambridge University Press, 1961); R. Balasubramanian, ed., *Theistic Vedānta* (New Delhi: Centre for Studies in Civilizations, 2003). Cf. Andrew Nicholson, *Unifying Hinduism: Philosophy and Identity in Indian Intellectual History* (New York: Columbia University Press, 2010), 75: "[T]he Vedāntic teachings presented in the Purāṇas are generally not compatible with the teachings of Śaṅkara and, instead, have more in common with Rāmānuja and Vijñānabhikṣu. . . . It should therefore not be surprising that Advaita Vedāntins less frequently quote the Purāṇas. For Vedāntins of other affiliations, however, the Purāṇas stand side-by-side with the Bhagavad Gītā as the most important *smr̥ti* texts."

also came to be structured around Śaiva and Vaiṣṇava religious identities. The early history of the Vijayanagara Empire in medieval South India, for example, demonstrates how a new Brahmanical form of Advaita was fashioned to fit a Śaiva political regime and monastic project.[85] This regime of Advaita Vēdānta, also known as "Smārta" Brahmanism, was displaced by the Vaiṣṇava preferences of subsequent dynasties in the region and would set the stage for social and philosophical disputation in South India for the next few centuries.[86] Scholarly attempts to study Advaita Vēdānta and Vaiṣṇavism together either proclaim Advaita Vēdānta as inherently nonsectarian, downplaying its social contexts, or seek common philosophical ground between two identities defined as historically contradictory.[87]

But what are we talking about when we talk about Advaita Vēdānta? Even in its classical dimensions, Advaita Vēdānta was a shifting, splintered tradition, a sprawling banyan tree with a mesh of roots, sometimes intersecting, sometimes leading nowhere, sometimes of indiscernible origin. To restrict Advaita to "Śaṅkara's Advaita," or to use his as the model against which all else is to be measured, reduces other texts and interpreters that exhibit Advaita affinities to bit players in Advaita history, or players who are not following the rules. To the more specific problem of Advaita and Vaiṣṇavism, Śaṅkara himself probably belonged to a South Indian Vaiṣṇava milieu, as did many of the texts contested by Advaita and non-Advaita scholars, including parts of the *Viṣṇu Purāṇa* and the *Bhāgavata Purāṇa*.[88] Aleksandar Uskokov has shown that the *Bhāgavata Purāṇa* itself layered *bhakti* over the soteriology of Advaita Vēdānta, specifically the version of Advaita presented by Śaṅkara and his followers.[89] Moreover, the fact that Rāmānuja and Madhva were contending with Advaita even in their *purāṇic* exegeses leads us to infer the contemporary existence of Advaitic interpretations.[90]

85 Matthew Clark, *The Daśanāmī-Saṁnyāsīs: The Integration of Ascetic Lineages into an Order* (Leiden: Brill, 2006), 177–226. See also Maitra, "The Rebirth of Homo Vedicus."

86 See Stoker, *Polemics and Patronage*, 45–72. Cf. Fisher, *Hindu Pluralism*.

87 For the former, see T. M. P. Mahadevan, ed., *Preceptors of Advaita* (Secunderabad: Sri Kanchi Kamakoti Sankara Mandir, 1968); Krishna Sharma, *Bhakti and the Bhakti Movement: A New Perspective* (New Delhi: Munshiram Manoharlal Publishers, 1987). For the latter, see Bradley Malkovsky, *The Role of Divine Grace in the Soteriology of Śaṁkarācārya* (Boston: Brill, 2001); Lance Nelson, "Theological Politics and Paradoxical Spirituality in the Life of Madhusūdana Sarasvatī," *Journal of Vaishnava Studies* 15.2 (2007): 19–34.

88 Paul Hacker, "Relations of Early Advaitins to Vaiṣṇavism," in *Philology and Confrontation: Paul Hacker on Traditional and Modern Vedanta*, ed. Wilhelm Halbfass (Albany: SUNY Press, 1995), 35.

89 Aleksandar Uskokov, "The Black Sun That Destroys Inner Darkness: Or, How Bādarāyaṇa Became Vyāsa," *Journal of the American Oriental Society* 142.1 (2022): 63–92. Cf. Gail, *Bhakti im Bhāgavatapurāṇa*, 93: "Das BhP beweist, daß Śaṅkaras Monismus mit der Liebesidee vereinbar ist."

90 On Rāmānuja's reconstructions of Advaitic readings of the *Viṣṇu Purāṇa*, see Sucharita Adluri, *Textual Authority in Classical Indian Thought: Rāmānuja and the Viṣṇu Purāṇa* (London: Routledge,

One of the earliest and most popular commentaries on the *Bhāgavata* was written around the fourteenth century by Śrīdhara Svāmī, who lived in Orissa.[91] Seldom studied in his own right, Śrīdhara is often considered a predecessor of the Gauḍīya Vaiṣṇava tradition, which began to take shape in the sixteenth century. Inspired by the public devotional practices of the charismatic preacher Caitanya, particularly singing the name of God, Gauḍīya Vaiṣṇavas sought to reconstruct the very landscapes of *bhakti* imagined in the *Bhāgavata Purāṇa*, moving from Bengal in the East to Braj in the North to walk on the same ground where their god had once played. Gauḍīya Vaiṣṇava theologians like Jīva Gōsvāmī synthesized Caitanya's *bhakti* sensibilities with the exegetical tradition of Vēdānta. In spite of his intense dislike of nondualist metaphysics, Jīva was interested in repurposing technical language from Advaita Vēdānta. This was perhaps because the two traditions, especially in social terms, were closer than the Gōsvāmīs might have liked to let on. Scholars often distance Śrīdhara from Śaṅkara's Advaita and instead locate him halfway toward Gauḍīya Vaiṣṇava thought.[92] Śrīdhara's own version of Advaita is demonstrably different from Śaṅkara's Advaita, at least in its refusal to engage with theories of *avidyā* and *māyā*, which are held to be definitive of pure scholastic Advaita Vēdānta.[93] Jīva Gōsvāmī's own view was that Advaita is one thing and Vaiṣṇavism quite another. Therefore, he claimed, Śrīdhara was trying to move away from classical Advaita by bringing other Advaitins into the properly Vaiṣṇava fold. But the spectrum of

2015), 11. For the claim that Madhva was contending with nondualist readings of the *Bhāgavata Purāṇa*, see B. N. K. Sharma, *History of the Dvaita School of Vedānta and Its Literature* (Delhi: Motilal Banarsidass, 1961), 128–130.

[91] See P. K. Gode, "Date of Śrīdharasvāmin, Author of the Commentaries on the Bhāgavata Purāṇa and Other Works—Between c. A.D. 1350 and 1450," in *Studies in Indian Literary History*, vol. 2 (Bombay: Bhāratīya Vidyā Bhavan, 1954), 169–175. Writers in the sixteenth and seventeenth centuries claimed that classical Advaitins like Citsukha and even Śaṅkara had authored commentaries on the *Bhāgavata*. Others, however, retorted that there was little to no proof for the existence of these commentaries. See Christopher Minkowski, "I'll Wash Out Your Mouth with My Boot: A Guide to Philological Argument in Mughal-Era Banaras," in *Epic and Argument: Essays in Honor of Robert P. Goldman*, ed. Sheldon Pollock (New Delhi: Manohar, 2010), 123–124.

[92] See Daniel P. Sheridan, "Śrīdhara and His Commentary on the *Bhāgavata Purāṇa*," *Journal of Vaishnava Studies* 2.3 (1994): 45–66; Ravi M. Gupta, *The Caitanya Vaiṣṇava Vedānta of Jīva Gosvāmī* (London: Routledge, 2007), 65–84; Okita, *Hindu Theology in Early Modern South Asia*, 63–123; Ravi M. Gupta, "Why Śrīdhara? The Makings of a Successful Sanskrit Commentary," *Religions* 11.9 (2020): 1–14.

[93] See Gupta, *The Caitanya Vaiṣṇava Vedānta of Jīva Gosvāmī*, 70. Cf. Lance Nelson, "Bhakti Preempted: Madhusūdana Sarasvatī on Devotion for the Advaitin Renouncer," *Journal of Vaishnava Studies* 6.1 (1998): 71, n. 5: "Śrīdhara Swāmin (ca. 1350–1450)—nominally an Advaitin but sympathetic to devotion, was sufficiently influenced by Vaiṣṇavism to accept a plurality of souls and a more realistic interpretation of *śakti* than Śaṅkara. He therefore cannot be considered a true non-dualist."

Vaiṣṇava Advaita may well have extended from Śaṅkara through to Śrīdhara. Who Śrīdhara was cannot be determined retroactively and without a wider perspective on the *Bhāgavata*'s rise to prominence.

The *Bhāgavata* was also a source of inspiration for two scholars of the thirteenth century who worked for the Yādava court in the western Deccan: Vōpadēva and Hēmādri, authors of the *Bhāgavatamuktāphala* and *Kaivalyadīpikā* commentary on it. The *Muktāphala* is more or less a compilation of stanzas from the *Bhāgavata* interspersed with explanatory notes. Organized into four sections, the *Muktāphala* addresses the object of religious affection, namely Viṣṇu, the exalted status of *bhakti*, the material practices of worship, and the characteristics of the devotee. The work is perhaps the first of its kind to offer a typology of *bhakti* and its practitioner that was directly adapted from the *Bhāgavata*. The *Kaivalyadīpikā*, on the other hand, is a notoriously difficult and opaque work, a proper reading of which requires its contextualization in the thought-world of contemporary Maharashtra.[94] There was also a tradition of premodern philological dispute that considered Vōpadēva to have been the author of the *Bhāgavata* itself.[95] Whatever the motivations behind these accusations, the memory of the *Bhāgavata* taking shape in Maharashtra reflects a renewed emphasis on the text at this time. Like Śrīdhara, Vōpadēva and Hēmādri were Advaitins of a sort.[96] Also like Śrīdhara, they are primarily remembered for their influence on the Gauḍīya Vaiṣṇavas, in the domain of Sanskrit aesthetics (*alaṁkāraśāstra*).[97] By the second millennium, the discourse of *alaṁkāraśāstra* had begun to move from purely formal considerations to questions of content and reader-response. Beginning in Kashmir in the ninth century, theorists argued that the concept of *rasa*, or aestheticized emotion, was not simply an incidental feature of a poetic or dramatic work but its very *telos*. They included nine canonical *rasas*: the erotic (*śṛṅgāra*), comic (*hāsya*), tragic (*karuṇa*), violent (*raudra*), heroic (*vīra*), frightening (*bhayānaka*), disgusting (*bībhatsa*), wondrous (*adbhuta*), and calming (*śānta*). In their writing, Vōpadēva and Hēmādri added a tenth: *bhaktirasa*. The aesthetic

[94] For such a reading, and for a magisterial account of this thought-world, see Chapter 11, "Staging Devotional Advaita in Thirteenth-Century Maharashtra," in Schwartz, "Ending the Śaiva Age," 1763–1955.

[95] See Minkowski, "I'll Wash Out Your Mouth with My Boot."

[96] V. Raghavan, "Bopadeva," in *Ramayana, Mahabharata, and Bhagavata Writers*, ed. V. Raghavan (New Delhi: Publications Division, Ministry of Information and Broadcasting, 1978), 122–134.

[97] Neal Delmonico, "Sacred Rapture: A Study of the Religious Aesthetic of Rupa Gosvamin" (Ph.D. diss., University of Chicago, 1990), 164–175.

experience of love for God, they claimed, was not just another *rasa* but rather the paradigmatic *rasa* which could be experienced through all the other nine. In their view, the *Bhāgavata Purāṇa* exemplified *bhaktirasa*, a special delight produced in the hearts of listeners as they relished the stories of God and his lovers. Eventually, the Gauḍīya Vaiṣṇavas would develop this idea into a full-fledged theory of religious aesthetics.

But just how Vaiṣṇava was the idea of *bhaktirasa*? This brings us to the specter of Śaivism that haunts the *Bhāgavata* and its reception. I understand Śaivism here as a religion with its own corpus of scriptural revelations (*āgama* or *tantra*), practices of formal initiation (*dīkṣā*), ritual formulae (*mantra*), rules of conduct (*ācāra*), and doctrines of liberation (*mukti*), that sometimes rejected and sometimes accommodated itself to Vedic Brahmanism.[98] Most relevant for this book is the tradition of Śaiva nondualist philosophical theology known as Pratyabhijñā. Śaiva nondualism was not the same as Advaita Vēdānta. Pratyabhijñā theologians traced their thinking to non-Vedic Śaiva scriptures. Developed in tenth- and eleventh-century Kashmir by scholars like Utpaladēva, Abhinavagupta, and Kṣēmarāja, the path to salvation in Pratyabhijñā was the recognition that one was none other than the great deity Śiva, forever entwined with his partner Śakti, a dynamic, blissful presence that suffused the universe and contained all phenomena. Pratyabhijñā theology belonged to the Trika cult of goddess worship, which spread to South India by the twelfth century as the worship of the beautiful goddess Tripurasundarī.[99] With the transmission of the Śaiva and Śākta traditions of Kashmir to South India, there also came about an attempt to link Śaṅkara the classical Advaitin with their ritual and theological traditions. People began to attribute to Śaṅkara authorship of Śākta hymns like the *Saundaryalaharī* and ritual manuals like the *Prapañcasāra*, which probably date from around the thirteenth century in Orissa.[100] Some of the earliest hagiographies of

[98] For a general overview, see Alexis Sanderson, "Śaivism and the Tantric Traditions," in *The World's Religions*, ed. Stewart Sutherland et al. (London: Routledge, 1988), 660–704.

[99] See Anya Golovkova, "The Forgotten Consort: The Goddess and Kāmadeva in the Early Worship of Tripurasundarī," *International Journal of Hindu Studies* 24.1 (2020): 87–106; Douglas Renfrew Brooks, *Auspicious Wisdom: The Texts and Traditions of Śrīvidyā Śākta Tantrism in South India* (Albany: State University of New York Press, 1992).

[100] On the date and provenance of the *Prapañcasāra*, see Alexis Sanderson, "Atharvavedins in Tantric Territory: The *Āṅgirasakalpa* Texts of the Oriya Paippalādins and Their Connection with the Trika and the Kālīkula, with Critical Editions of the *Parājapavidhi*, the *Parāmantravidhi*, and the **Bhadrakālī-mantravidhiprakarana*," in *The Atharvaveda and Its Paippalāda Śākhā: Historical and Philological Papers on a Vedic Tradition*, ed. Arlo Griffiths and Annette Schmiedchen (Aachen: Shaker Verlag, 2007), 230–233.

Śaṅkara were composed around the fourteenth century in Kāñcīpuram, Tamil Nadu. These stories concluded with Śaṅkara's establishment of a *śrīcakra*, an esoteric symbol of the goddess, at the heart of the Kāmākṣī Kāmakōṭi temple. This imbrication of Śākta ritual and Advaita philosophy set the stage for the intellectual and religious alliances between the Brahmin communities and monastic institutions of Kāñcīpuram in the seventeenth century and beyond.[101]

Pratyabhijñā theologians were also interested in *bhakti* and the aesthetic theories of Sanskrit literary culture. Not only was it the case that Śaiva descriptions of emotionally intense *bhakti* mirrored the *Bhāgavata*'s own; concepts of *bhaktirasa* were incipient in the Sanskrit praise-poetry, or *stōtras*, written by Śaivas in Kashmir from the tenth century onward.[102] Although not directly linked to Sanskrit aesthetics in its early forms, the use of the term *bhaktirasa* in Śaiva poetry was ambiguous enough that Abhinavagupta felt compelled to argue against its inclusion among the canonical *rasas*. And it was precisely Abhinavagupta's position that the authors of the *Muktāphala* and *Kaivalyadīpikā* resisted. Śaiva theories of *bhaktirasa* were not just developed through readings of Śaiva texts; they also emerged from a poetic and scholastic engagement with the *Bhāgavata Purāṇa*. For some readers, the *Bhāgavata* was the nexus of many different religious, literary, and philosophical interests: Śaiva theology, Vaiṣṇava *bhakti*, Advaita philosophy, and Sanskrit aesthetics. In this book, I provide an alternative reception history of the *Bhāgavata* with attention to these relatively minor thinkers.[103]

From the fourteenth to the eighteenth centuries, Śaivas and Advaitins laid claim to the *Bhāgavata* in ways irreducible to the dominant historiographical modes reconstructed above. The paradox of nondualist *bhakti* is understood best not as a doctrinal problem but as a hermeneutical question. It reveals connections between texts and people who do not fit within the religious and philosophical boundaries assigned to them. By expanding our sense of these boundaries, by reading *bhakti* from the bottom up, we may find that Sanskrit *śāstra* was reshaped by the presence of those on its margins.

[101] Fisher, *Hindu Pluralism*, 57–98.
[102] Stainton, *Poetry as Prayer*, 231–264.
[103] On "greater" and "lesser" thinkers in the history of philosophy, see Randall Collins, *The Sociology of Philosophies* (Cambridge: Harvard University Press, 2012), 12–15.

Chapter Outline

Each chapter in this book addresses a different but related historiographical and hermeneutical problem in the *Bhāgavata* tradition. In the process, I ask questions about the textual and extratextual sources that influenced scholarly writing in the disciplines of Mīmāṁsā and Vēdānta. I find evidence for those sources both in the context of that writing and in its forms of subtext, including signature expressions, rambling asides, and unusual preoccupations. Ultimately, I argue that the religion of *bhakti* introduced subtle, differentiated, and identifiable changes in the conventions of Brahmin scholarly life.

Chapter 1, "Across the Nilgiris," reassesses the historiographical assumption that the *Bhāgavata* was primarily the purview of Vaiṣṇava religious communities. This requires a geographical reorientation. Instead of jumping from Tamil Nadu northward, as if to follow the route mapped by the *Bhāgavata Māhātmya*, a late introduction appended to the text, we move across the Western Ghats to Kerala.[104] From at least the fourteenth century, a cluster of Śaiva ascetics in north and central Kerala were reading the *Bhāgavata* as well. Influenced by the ritual, poetic, and philosophical traditions of Pratyabhijñā Tantrism, these Malayali monks believed that Vaiṣṇava *bhakti* and classical Advaita philosophy could enhance, rather than contradict, their commitments to nondualist Śaivism. The *Bhāgavata* was the perfect site for all these interests to coincide. Unlike the conflicts between Śaivism and Vaiṣṇavism that would condition much of the social and political life of premodern South India, the two traditions were far more symbiotic in Kerala. The *Bhāgavata* commentarial tradition produced on the text in Kerala attests to this mutuality. It was distinctive to the region, however, and bore little resemblance to the mainstream. This alternative history has gone virtually unrecognized, but it has implications for the later trajectories of the *Bhāgavata*.

I also argue that in Kerala, the *Bhāgavata* became the public face of private, esoteric, initiation-based practices. For the poetry and scholarship produced by the Kerala ascetics also betrayed the influence of regional contestations over temple space, caste prerogatives, and antinomian

[104] See John Stratton Hawley, "The *Bhāgavata-Māhātmya* in Context," in *Patronage and Popularisation, Pilgrimage and Procession*, ed. Heidi Pauwels (Wiesbaden: Otto Harrassowitz, 2009), 81–100.

spirituality. The premodern polities of northern Kerala involved complex negotiations of power between Brahmin, martial, and lower castes, often mediated by the ritual work of Śākta religion. The scholastic writings studied in this chapter reflect the structural correspondences and conflicts between Brahmanical and Tantric religion that cut across the caste-configured social order. The itinerary of our Śaiva ascetics suggests that they were involved in the changing relationship between elite and nonelite religious communities at this time. Their lives appear before us through both the context and subtext of their writing.

Chapter 2, "The Name of God in the World of Men," pursues the relationship between elite and nonelite *bhakti* practices by focusing on one example: singing the name of God. Instead of either positing continuity or differentiating among all modes of performing this act, I argue that we should read Sanskrit scholastic discourse on singing the name of God from the bottom up. In other words, scholarly writing on the subject was responding not only to the example of the *Bhāgavata* and other Sanskrit texts but also to the wider world of subaltern religious practice. The chapter follows the trajectory of a single book by one of the Kerala scholars, called the *Bhagavannāmakaumudī* or "The Moonlight of God's Name." It answers the following questions: How did readers of the *Bhāgavata* rethink the discourse of scriptural authority? How was the *Kaumudī* adopted by different religious communities? and Why did a scholarly monograph feature in the cultural memory of a tradition of Brahmin musical performance?

The *Kaumudī* presented a radical and unprecedented claim in the history of scriptural interpretation. Drawing inspiration from the *Bhāgavata*'s claims to Vedic status, and possibly from Śaiva discourse on authoritative speech, the author of the *Kaumudī* argued that statements in the *purāṇa* were just as valid as Vedic utterances. Although the Mīmāṁsā tradition had relegated the *purāṇas* to a supporting role, the author of the *Kaumudī* believed that *purāṇic* claims should be taken seriously in their own right, especially when they involved the power of God's name. As such, the *Kaumudī* made an important yet unrecognized intervention in Sanskrit intellectual history. Its social and cultural history was no less significant. At roughly contemporaneous moments in the sixteenth century, both Advaita Vēdāntins and Gauḍīya Vaiṣṇavas in northern India, often depicted as intractably opposed, laid claim to the *Kaumudī* as a source of theological inspiration. And only a century or so later, the *Kaumudī* made its way back down south, where the musical-performative tradition known as the *bhajana sampradāya* began to take shape during the rule of the Thanjavur Marathas. In the latter part of this chapter, I look at the diverse reception history of the *Kaumudī* for what it may reveal about the local character of a text tradition valorized for its universality. For the author and the readers of the *Kaumudī* to latch onto the name as a subject of scholastic reflection was a choice only partially inspired by the superposed ideals of a Sanskrit canon. They also called upon a vernacular practice, in both the linguistic and quotidian sense. Singing the name was one way in which the power of the quotidian could "expand beyond the parameters of its inaugurators or champions."[105] For one scholar in medieval Kerala, it would upset the very foundations of thinking about Sanskrit scriptural hierarchy. For his readers, it would affirm that there was more than one way to be a Brahmin in the early modern world.

Chapter 3, "Family Ties," seeks to understand the place of *bhakti* in Brahmin identity by reconstructing the scholarly lives of the Dēvas, a family of Maharashtrian Brahmins who lived in Banaras between the sixteenth and seventeenth centuries. Curiously for a family dedicated to upholding the caste prerogatives of Brahmin supremacy, they traced their patriline to Ēknāth, a Marathi poet-saint known for flouting caste boundaries. Influenced by the *Bhāgavata*, the *Kaumudī*, and local communities and pilgrimage networks in North India and the Deccan, the Dēvas attempted to reconcile their personal religious convictions with their public lives as scholars and teachers in a multilingual world. The Dēvas were educated in the disciplines of Mīmāṁsā and Vēdānta and wrote only in Sanskrit. However, they argued that the everyday practice of singing the name of God, especially in vernacular languages, should be respected and celebrated by Brahmins. I contextualize the intellectual impact of *bhakti* on their writings in Mīmāṁsā and Advaita Vēdānta within the social world of early modern Banaras. The relationship between the scholarly world and the larger social world in this era was also dramatized in imaginative and biographical literature. As professional scholars and amateur dramatists, the Dēvas explored the tension between piety and pedagogy in the new intellectual economy of early modern India. They criticized the materialistic excess of the very systems of patronage and networks that made them successful. I demonstrate how these tensions refracted those of the Maharashtrian *bhakti* traditions to which the Dēvas traced their heritage.

Chapter 4, "Threads of *bhakti*," revisits debates over the compatibility of *bhakti* with Advaita Vēdānta, or the problem of loving an embodied god

[105] Novetzke, *The Quotidian Revolution*, 15.

while preaching a formless absolute. The chapter argues that we should resist succumbing to the two classical fallacies of intellectual history, the "mythology of doctrines" and the "mythology of coherence." The former assumes that each classic writer in a particular system must articulate some doctrine constitutive of that system, while the latter states there is some inner coherence to a certain author's writing that it is the duty of the interpreter to reveal, despite the presence of contradictions and ambivalences.[106] In both of these mythologies, a scholar is identified by adherence to a system, any deviation from which is evidence of inconsistency. Instead, in this chapter I study scholars who recognized and resolved the tension between *bhakti* and Advaita on their own terms. I argue for the value of relatively minor thinkers in the history of philosophy and pay attention to the neglected dimensions of their writing. Nārāyaṇa Tīrtha's commentaries on the *Bhakti Sūtra*s and the *Yōga Sūtra*s demonstrate that *bhakti* brought together previously disparate fields of knowledge. Nārāyaṇa's reading of classical Advaita Vēdānta is disorienting, unintuitive, and sprinkled with esoterica from the wide world of *bhakti* and *yōga*. The chapter concludes by showing how the purportedly Vaiṣṇava *Bhakti Sūtra*s find their way into the spiritual program of the Śākta theologian Bhāskararāya in the early eighteenth century. In Bhāskararāya's pedagogical model, *bhakti* plays a key role in the formation of a religious intellectual. The specter of Śaivism thus bookends this study of the *Bhāgavata*'s reception history.

The conclusion establishes an analogy between the scholars studied in this book and those of the present by focusing on my own scholarly practice and how I came to write this book. The same methods by which one may understand the social history of Indian intellectual culture—attention to individual style, social spaces, subtextual and paratextual comments—apply to my work as well. This metatextual commentary suggests that reflecting on what goes into scholarship in the present may illuminate the past. Everyday life has always filtered into the forbidding world of academic discourse. Understanding it in the present makes its past versions seem less foreign.

[106] Skinner, *Visions of Politics*, 59–72.

1
Across the Nilgiris

Introduction

If you walk into the Rājarājēśvaran Śiva temple in Taḷipparamba, in the Kaṇṇūr district of northern Kerala, you will see many standard features: lush green lawns, old stone architecture, the occasional elephant munching on grass, low tiled roofs housing an array of deities that surround the main shrine. Having paid your respects to the various spirits and goddesses around the periphery, you proceed to the *namaskāra maṇḍapam*, the platform of obeisance, placed before the sanctum. Here things get a little strange. Before peering into the sanctum, you walk over to the large granite sacrificial altar, the *valiya balikkallu*, a few feet from the entrance. Take a close look at the two figures carved into the niches on the east side of the decorative stone. One is Śiva as Dakṣiṇāmūrti, the silent teacher, seated with one leg crossed over the other under a banyan tree. Across from him, however, is a little boy playing the flute, legs crossed in a dancing motion. Other oddities remind you of Kṛṣṇa as well. You witness the *abhiṣēkam*, the lustration ceremony, only to see that Śiva is not worshiped with *bilva* leaves but with *tulsi*, sacred to Viṣṇu. A loquacious old man seizes on your puzzled look and tells you the legend of the time when the goddess Lakṣmī came to pay her respects. She entered the shrine only to see that Śiva had disguised himself as her husband, the four-armed Viṣṇu. When she turned to leave, she found that the doorkeeper had closed the gates. She was able to slip out only when Viṣṇu distracted Śiva by dancing before him in the guise of his own son Kumāra. Some people still call the place Lakṣmī City.

Shaking your head, you walk down the road to the Tṛccambaram Kṛṣṇa temple. Here, surely, the iconography makes no mistake. The wood panels above the shrine are adorned with stories from the *Bhāgavata Purāṇa*. But then the same uncle, eager to share unsolicited information, sidles up behind you and says that this Kṛṣṇa is in *raudra bhāva*, a violent mood, having just slain the elephant Kuvalayāpīḍa before taking on his evil uncle Kaṁsa. To you this sounds much less like the sweet, seductive Kṛṣṇa of the *Bhāgavata*

Love in the Time of Scholarship. Anand Venkatkrishnan, Oxford University Press. © Oxford University Press 2024.
DOI: 10.1093/oso/9780197776636.003.0002

and more like the fierce Bhairava, a criminal god for demon devotees.[1] The incorrigible uncle points to an old tree in the compound that used to be frequented by an *atyāśramī*, often understood in a general sense as a celibate renunciant, but still the term of art in these parts for a Śaiva ascetic who deliberately flouts caste boundaries. First a Śiva who is not quite a Śiva. Then a Kṛṣṇa who is not quite a Kṛṣṇa. What is going on? And why won't Uncle leave you alone?

The worship of Śiva and Viṣṇu in premodern Kerala was symbiotic. Not only was there a synthesis of Śaiva and Vaiṣṇava ritual systems in the ritual literature of Kerala; by the thirteenth century, "the sectarianism so characteristic of Tamil *bhakti*, particularly rivalry between Vaiṣṇavas and Śaivas, was already being deliberately elided in Kerala at this early date."[2] This chapter asks how this mutuality, in both material and textual culture, might make us revisit certain historiographical commonplaces in Indian religion and philosophy. One such commonsense claim is that the *Bhāgavata Purāṇa* was the prerogative of Vaiṣṇava religious communities. I provide evidence for an alternative reception history of the *Bhāgavata* that sometimes parallels and sometimes anticipates its Vaiṣṇava adaptation. At the center of this story are three scholars who lived in Kerala between the fourteenth and sixteenth centuries: Lakṣmīdhara, Pūrṇasarasvatī, and Rāghavānanda. I locate these Malayali mavericks at the nexus of a number of philosophical, religious, and literary trends: (a) the confluence of Vedic and non-Vedic forms of nondualism, or Advaita; (b) the transitions and continuities between the Tantric goddess traditions of Kashmir and South India; (c) the proliferation of *stōtras*, or poetry of prayer, of both Śaiva and Vaiṣṇava persuasions; and (d) the discourse of Sanskrit aesthetics, *alaṁkāraśāstra*, between literature and religion. I argue that recuperating Vaiṣṇava *bhakti* in a Śaiva world was irreducible to the "nonsectarian" universalist rhetoric of Advaitins or Smārtas—the broad term for Brahmin worshipers of several deities as the supreme. While Lakṣmīdhara's relationship with Śaivism was muted, both Pūrṇasarasvatī and Rāghavānanda had clearly received initiation into Śaiva religion. Instead of subordinating Vaiṣṇava scriptures, stories, and *stōtras*, they grafted them onto a distinctive local configuration of Advaita that

[1] Alf Hiltebeitel, ed., *Criminal Gods and Demon Devotees: Essays on the Guardians of Popular Hinduism* (Albany: State University of New York Press, 1989).

[2] Rich Freeman, "The Literature of Hinduism in Malayalam," in *The Blackwell Companion to Hinduism*, ed. Gavin Flood (Oxford: Blackwell Publishing, 2003), 164. Cf. S. A. S. Sarma, "*Paḷḷivēṭṭa*, or the 'Royal Hunt,' in Prescriptive Literature and in Present-Day Practice in Kerala," *Cracow Indological Studies* 16 (2014): 290.

sought a rapprochement between the classical exegetical Vēdānta of Śaṅkara and his followers, the Pāñcarātra cosmological traditions common to South Indian Vaiṣṇavas, and the Śākta-Śaiva Pratyabhijñā tradition that moved from Kashmir to the south. I attempt to understand the local contours of Śaiva ecumenicism, one that engaged with the core texts of Vaiṣṇavism not as subordinate in a hierarchically inclusive series, or as subsumed within the universalism of Advaita philosophy, but as canonical and liberating in their own right.

What I am proposing, however, is not just a story about nonsectarianism but an account of several complex and overlapping relationships: between private esotericism and public religion, between high textual culture and antinomian ritual practice, between austere philosophical traditions and exuberant literary criticism, and between Brahmin scholars and Tantric gurus. In many ways this chapter is an intellectual history of the structural correspondences between Brahmanical and Tantric religion that characterized politics and society in medieval Kerala.[3] As Rich Freeman observes, narratives about the *bhakti* movement, issued from the perspective of upper-caste reformists of both premodern and modern stripes, have obscured these correspondences, tending to concentrate on the association of *bhakti* with medieval Śaiva Siddhānta and Śrīvaiṣṇava traditions at the expense of pan-Indian Tantrism.[4] Freeman underscores the historical importance of the steady incorporation of Śākta goddess traditions into the temple networks, ritual manuals, folk performances, possession cults, and cross-caste patronage systems of medieval Kerala. Here I look at the scholastic side of the picture in order to build toward a social history of intellectual life. While we know virtually nothing about Lakṣmīdhara, we do know that Pūrṇasarasvatī and Rāghavānanda frequented the Tṛccambaram Kṛṣṇa temple and belonged to institutional networks of local Advaita monasteries and Śākta temples up and down the Malabar coast. I approach the corpus of these Brahmin scholars, including scriptural exegeses, literary commentaries, and public stage-plays, with an eye to their relationship with the wider world of Tantric religion. I explore how the *Bhāgavata* came to play a central role in how they appropriated and accommodated it.

[3] Rich Freeman, "Śāktism, Polity and Society in Medieval Malabar," in *Goddess Traditions in Tantric Hinduism*, ed. Bjarne Wernicke Olesen (London: Routledge, 2016), 141–173.
[4] Freeman, "Śāktism, Polity and Society," 148.

On the one hand, then, this chapter revises the historiography of the *Bhāgavata* to incorporate its reception by Śaivas and Advaitins in medieval Kerala. In broader terms, it concerns the social and cultural history of intellectual life: the regional qualities of scholastic commentary, the institutional networks that facilitated distinctive ways of thinking, the stories that circulate about authors, and the social world that bubbles up and out of the text. While I provide contextual evidence for this history, I also listen to the voices in the text with occasional subtextual readings. Sometimes they announce themselves in prose style. Sometimes they pipe up in asides. And sometimes they echo in the space where the personal becomes public.

Lakṣmīdhara: Love and Literature

In the early fourteenth century, not long before Śrīdhara wrote his famous commentary on the *Bhāgavata Purāṇa*, a scholar from Kerala named Lakṣmīdhara composed a commentary called the *Amṛtataraṅgiṇī*.[5] Lakṣmīdhara wrote the following works: (a) the *Advaitamakaranda*, a short treatise in verse on the nature of the Ātman; (b) the *Bhagavannāmakaumudī*, a three-part essay on the power of singing God's name; (c) the *Amṛtataraṅgiṇī*, a commentary on the *Bhāgavata Purāṇa*; and (d) the *Nayamañjarī*, an independently circulating commentary on the so-called *Vēdastuti* or *Śrutigītā* section of the *Bhāgavata* (10.87). The *Advaitamakaranda* was being read by Advaitins as early as the mid-fifteenth century, when it was commented upon by Vāsudēva Sārvabhauma in Purī, Orissa, and cited by Brahmānanda Bhāratī in Śṛṅgērī, Karnataka.[6] As I will show in the following chapter, the *Bhagavannāmakaumudī* became influential for many different communities

[5] The mid-fourteenth century is the *terminus ante quem* for Lakṣmīdhara, when his *Amṛtataraṅgiṇī* was cited by Pūrnasarasvatī. See N. V. P. Unithiri, H. N. Bhat, and S. A. S. Sarma, *The Bhaktimandākinī: An Elaborate Fourteenth-Century Commentary by Pūrṇasarasvatī on the Viṣṇupādādikeśastotra Attributed to Śaṅkarācārya* (Pondicherry: Institut Français de Pondichéry, École française d'Extrême-Orient, 2011), 26 (henceforth cited as *Bhaktimandākinī*). For a brief account of his life and work, see P. Thirugnanasambandham, "Lakṣmīdhara," in *Preceptors of Advaita*, ed. T. M. P. Mahadevan (Secunderabad: Sri Kanchi Kamakoti Sankara Mandir, 1968), 201–205. There is no evidence that this Lakṣmīdhara was the nephew of Sāyaṇa, as claimed by Srikantha Sastri, "Advaitācāryas of the 12th and 13th Centuries," *Indian Historical Quarterly* 14 (1938): 406.

[6] *Advaitamakaranda*, ed. R. Krishnaswami Sastri (Srirangam: Vani Vilas Press, 1926). Vāsudēva Sārvabhauma's commentary is unpublished. See Rajendralala Mitra, ed., *Notices of Sanskrit Mss.*, vol. 8 (Calcutta: Baptist Mission Press, 1886), 291–292. For Brahmānanda Bhāratī's citation, see *Dṛgdṛśyavivēkaḥ*, ed. K. Achyuta Poduval, Sri Ravi Varma Samskrita Grandhavali, Vol. 6 (Tripunithura: The Sanskrit College Committee, 1958), 28.

in the sixteenth and seventeenth centuries, from the Gauḍīya Vaiṣṇavas who lived in Brindavan, to the Dēva family of Maharashtrian scholars in Banaras, to the Tamil Brahmin musicians of the southern *bhajana sampradāya*. The other two works have not been edited and survive in manuscript form mostly in southern libraries.[7] The *Amṛtataraṅgiṇī* seems to have been read only in Kerala. It was cited by Pūrṇasarasvatī in the mid-fourteenth century and reproduced verbatim by Rāghavānanda in the sixteenth century. It remained influential well into the eighteenth century, when a tutor of the Pāliyam ruling class of Kochi wrote a *Bhāgavata* commentary in which he explicitly placed Lakṣmīdhara and Rāghavānanda in the same commentarial lineage.[8]

A near contemporary of the more famous Śrīdhara, Lakṣmīdhara seems to show no awareness whatsoever of Śrīdhara's writing. He comments on stanzas and cites variant readings that are entirely unknown to Śrīdhara, and his mention of alternative interpretations suggests the existence of a local commentarial tradition. Still, some of his writings made it to Orissa, where Śrīdhara lived. On the one hand, the links between Orissa and Kerala are unsurprising. Networks of Sanskrit intellectual exchange and textual transmission had been established between these regions by the time Lakṣmīdhara began writing. Ritual manuals of goddess worship like the *Prapañcasāra* and the *Śāradātilaka* made their way from Orissa to Kerala,[9] and the erotico-religious poetry of Jayadēva's *Gītagōvinda* greeted the effusive lyrics of Bilvamaṅgala's *Kṛṣṇakarṇāmṛta* as they passed each other on

[7] For a list of manuscripts of the *Amṛtataraṅgiṇī*, see V. Raghavan, ed., *New Catalogus Catalogorum*, vol. 1, revised ed. (Madras: University of Madras, 1968), 347. On the *Nayamañjarī*, see K. Kunjunni Raja, ed., *New Catalogus Catalogorum*, vol. 9 (Madras: University of Madras, 1977), 348; K. Sāmbaśivaśāstrī, ed., *A Descriptive Catalogue of the Sanskrit Manuscripts in H.H. The Maharajah's Palace Library, Trivandrum*, vol. 1 (Trivandrum: V.V. Press, 1937), 347–348; K. Sāmbaśivaśāstrī, ed., *A Descriptive Catalogue of the Sanskrit Manuscripts in H.H. The Maharajah's Palace Library, Trivandrum*, vol. 2 (Trivandrum: V.V. Press, 1937), 649–652. In two manuscripts of the *Amṛtataraṅgiṇī*, the author appears to have the Śaiva name Jñānapūrṇa, but this could also be a reference to the copyist (*alikhaj jñānapūrṇākhyaḥ siddhō'mṛtataraṅgiṇī*). See S. Kuppuswami Sastri, ed., *A Triennial Catalogue of Manuscripts Collected during the Triennium 1916–17 to 1918–19 for the Government Oriental Manuscripts Library, Madras*, vol. 3, part 1: *Sanskrit C* (Madras: Superintendent, Government Press, 1922), 4009–4010. See also S. S. Saith, ed., *Catalogue of Sanskrit Manuscripts in the Panjab University Library, Lahore*, vol. 2 (Lahore: University of the Panjab, 1941), 139. The last reference may suggest circulation in Kashmir.

[8] S. Kuppuswami Sastri, ed., *A Triennial Catalogue of Manuscripts Collected during the Triennium 1919–20 to 1921–22 for the Government Oriental Manuscripts Library, Madras*, vol. 4, part 1: *Sanskrit C* (Madras: Superintendent, Government Press, 1927), 5431–5432.

[9] Alexis Sanderson, "Atharvavedins in Tantric Territory: The *Āṅgirasakalpa* Texts of the Oriya Paippalādins and Their Connection with the Trika and the Kālīkula, with Critical Editions of the *Parājapavidhi*, the *Parāmantravidhi*, and the **Bhadrakālīmantravidhiprakaraṇa*," in *The Atharvaveda and Its Paippalāda Śākhā: Historical and Philological Papers on a Vedic Tradition*, ed. A. Griffiths and Annette Schmeiden (Aachen: Shaker Verlag, 2007), 232.

their respective journeys southwest and northeast. It is not difficult to imagine Lakṣmīdhara's work traveling along the social networks that made this exchange possible. On the other hand, it is not clear why the *Amṛtataraṅgiṇī* did not survive the journey. Perhaps it was intellectually overshadowed by Śrīdhara. Or perhaps its more strongly Advaitic flavor, and possible Śaiva origins, made it less attractive to the *Bhāgavata* communities in Orissa, who ensured that poets and thinkers from Kerala would be remembered only for their Vaiṣṇava sympathies. We will return to the network that connected Kerala to the rest of the subcontinent. For the moment we must consider the *Amṛtataraṅgiṇī* as belonging to an alternative commentarial tradition.

To establish the alternativeness of this tradition, we may first look at the language of Advaita Vēdānta in the commentary. Scholarship on Śrīdhara has distanced him from the doctrines of classical Advaita Vēdānta. His relative disinterest in the concepts of *avidyā* or *māyā*, the primordial illusion veiling Brahman, the ultimate reality, and his positive account of Brahman's creative power have led some to claim that he was not properly an Advaitin at all, but rather halfway toward the Vēdānta of the Gauḍīya Vaiṣṇavas.[10] Whatever Śrīdhara's ultimate position, Lakṣmīdhara used the language of Advaita Vēdānta much more strongly than he did, especially where it counted, on the problem of *māyā*. Let us take an example from the very opening of the commentary. The first stanza of the *Bhāgavata* describes the cause of the universe, Brahman, as one "about whom the wise are deluded." Lakṣmīdhara offered several alternatives for how to interpret this line, each one more Advaitic than the previous:

1. If Brahman is the self of every individual, then why does it not manifest while the individual does? In response to this question comes the line "about whom the wise are deluded." . . . Here "delusion" is meant to denote primordial ignorance, and it is connected with pure consciousness. Ignorance then divides consciousness into two entities, the individual and Brahman, like an image and its counterimage. It appears to belong to the individual and have Brahman as its content, in the form "I do not know Brahman." Because it is enveloped by that delusion, Brahman does not manifest, even though it is the self.[11]

[10] Ravi Gupta, *The Caitanya Vaiṣṇava Vēdānta of Jīva Gosvāmī* (London: Routledge, 2007), 70; Daniel Sheridan, "Śrīdhara and His Commentary on the Bhāgavata Purāṇa," *Journal of Vaiṣṇava Studies* 2.3 (1994): 65.

[11] *Bhāgavata Vyākhyā (Amṛtataraṅgiṇī)*, R. No. 2795, Government Oriental Manuscripts Library, Chennai, f. 10: *athavā nanu yadi kṣētrajñasyātmabhūtaṁ brahma kim iti tarhi tasmin prakāśamānē'pi*

Here Lakṣmīdhara employs the classic Advaitic metaphor of an image (*bimba*) and its counterimage (*pratibimba*) to illustrate the relationship between Brahman and the individual human being. In this view attributed to the tenth-century Advaitin Prakāśātman, the so-called *pratibimbavāda*, pure consciousness is the basis of *avidyā*, the "delusion" denoted by the stanza to describe one's confusion about one's own true nature. The next alternative suggests a different kind of confusion regarding how the changeless Brahman can be the cause of the universe, as the opening words of the stanza state:

2. How can Brahman, which is pure consciousness and does not undergo change, be the material cause of the world, something so distinct from it? In response is the line "about whom the wise are deluded." The word "delusion" denotes a cognition belonging to the individual, neither quite real nor unreal, that objectifies Brahman *qua* creator of an illusory world. It is only creator insofar as it is the basis for the arising of another thing, like an unrecognized rope is the basis for the origin of a snake. Brahman does not transform into the world. Only an object and its actual transformation necessarily share features, not a substrate and its apparent modification.[12]

The second possible confusion introduces another Advaita concept: creation as actual transformation of an object (*pariṇāma*) or creation as only apparent modification (*vivartta*) superimposed on a real substratum. Brahman is "the cause of this universe" only insofar as the individual has misconstrued it to be a creator endowed with qualities. Ignorance here is a mistaken cognition belonging to the individual (*jīvāśrita*), perhaps a reference to the *avacchēdavāda* theory attributed to the tenth-century Advaitin Vācaspati Miśra. In truth, not only is the universe itself illusory (*mithyā*), but so is the very process of its creation. This misapprehension is neither quite real nor

na prakāśa[ta] ity āśaṅkyāha—muhyanti yat sūraya iti . . . iha mōha iti mūlājñānaṁ vivakṣitaṁ tac ca cinmātrasaṁbandhy api, caitanya[ṁ] jīvabrahmabhāvēna biṁbapratibiṁbavat vibhajya jīvāśritaṁ brahmaviṣayan tu pratibhāsatē ahaṁ brahma na jānāmīti. tēnāvṛtatvād ātmabhūtam api brahma na prakāśata iti bhāvaḥ. Henceforth cited as *Amṛtataraṅgiṇī*. My emendations are in square brackets.

[12] *Amṛtataraṅgiṇī*, f. 11: *athavā cidēkarasasya nirvikārasya brahmaṇaḥ katham atyantavilakṣaṇaṁ jagadupādānatvam iti. tatrāha—muhyanti yat sūraya iti. mohaśabdābhidhēyēna jīvāśritēna sadasadvilakṣaṇēna jñānēna viṣayīkṛtaṁ brahma mithyājagata upādānaṁ ajñātā rajjur iva sarpasya utpadyamānāśrayatvam ēvāsyōpādānatvaṁ na tadrūpēṇa pariṇamanatvaṁ prakṛtivikārayōr ēva sālakṣaṇyaniyamō nādhiṣṭhānavivarttayōḥ.*

unreal, like a snake seen in place of a rope. The rope does not actually transform into a snake, it only appears like one, but the perception of a snake cannot be wished away. This brings Lakṣmīdhara to an account of the creative power of illusion:

> 3. There is a certain impulse behind the entirety of creation whose basis is nothing but Brahman. It confuses everyday people like the audience at a magic show, but not the magician himself, for it belongs to none but him. That is the power called *māyā*, inexplicable as being either real or unreal. It is Brahman enveloped by that *māyā* that is the creator of the world, not pure consciousness by itself.[13]

Lakṣmīdhara explains how the universe can emerge from the changeless Brahman by using the analogy of a magician's trick. Because it is entirely under the magician's control, the magic is unable to affect him even as it bewilders the audience. The magic called *māyā*, however, cannot be described as being either Brahman or other than Brahman (*tattvānyatvābhyām anirūpyā*), a common formula among early Advaitins, who used similar terms, such as "inexpressible" (*anākhyēya*) or "inexplicable" (*anirvacanīya*), to describe *māyā*'s ineffability.[14] Lakṣmīdhara concludes that the only reason for positing an inexplicable *māyā* in the first place is to account for the plurality experienced by everyday people, not because Brahman has any positive role to play in creation:

> Because it makes little sense to consider God as pure consciousness being the source of people's confusion, it implies that there must be some inconceivable power on his part. It is Brahman speckled by that power, due to which individuals find themselves differentiated, that is the source of their confusion. It is not at one and the same time pure consciousness and the creator of the universe. By this line of argument we refute the concern that there can be no essential unity between Brahman, who can create the universe, and the individual, who cannot. For the

[13] *Amṛtataraṅgiṇī*, f. 11: *athavā brahmāśritaiva kācid aśēṣaprapañcaprakṛtir indrajālavidyaivaindrajālikaṁ svāśrayam avimōhayantī sāmājikān iva jīvān ēva mōhayantī. tattvānyatvābhyām anirūpyā māyā nāma śaktir asti tatsaṁvalitam ēva brahma jagatkāraṇaṁ na kēvalaṁ cinmātraṁ.*

[14] See Paul Hacker, "Distinctive Features of the Doctrine and Terminology of Śaṅkara: Avidyā, Nāmarūpa, Māyā, Īśvara," in *Philology and Confrontation: Paul Hacker on Traditional and Modern Vedānta*, ed. Wilhelm Halbfass (Albany: State University of New York Press, 1995), 71–73.

very concept of Brahman being creator of the universe is a conditioning of *māyā*.[15]

Lakṣmīdhara's reconstruction of different viewpoints in Advaita intellectual history on the locus of *avidyā*, down to the language of magic and "speckling," resembles that given by the thirteenth-century scholar Ānandānubhava, who was probably also a South Indian.[16] It is worth emphasizing here that the "inconceivable power" said to belong to Brahman bears little resemblance to the positive model offered by Śrīdhara. For Lakṣmīdhara, the universe is fundamentally illusory. Brahman remains supreme and one-without-a-second precisely because *māyā* is inexplicable.[17] Lakṣmīdhara's commentary is littered with Advaitic affinities from the very first words of his benediction. In this stanza, Lakṣmīdhara describes Kṛṣṇa with a formula we see repeated later in the writings of Pūrṇasarasvatī and Rāghavānanda: the ambrosial ocean of existence, joy, and pure, undifferentiated consciousness (*cidēkarasa-nirbhēda-sadānanda-sudhārṇava*). The term *cidēkarasa*, generally used interchangeably with *cinmātra*, signaled something to Lakṣmīdhara about the *Bhāgavata*'s version of Advaita. Consider his comment on the following stanza much later in the text (*Bhāgavata* 1.2.8*): "The truth of the Upaniṣads remains far from those whose mind doesn't melt, who don't cry tears of love, and whose hairs don't stand on end as a result of tasting the stories of God."[18]

[15] *Amṛtataraṅgiṇī*, f. 12: *atra kēvalasya cinmātrasyēśvarasya mōhahētutvānupapattēr artthāt kācid asyācintyā śaktir astīti gamyatē. tayā śabaḷam ēva brahma tayā kalpitabhēdānāṁ jīvānāṁ mōhahētur na kevalaṁ cinmātra[ṁ] jagatkāraṇam api tad ēvēti bhāvaḥ. anēna jagajjanmādisamartthēna brahmaṇā tadasamartthasya jīvasya katham ēkatvam ity ētad api pratyuktaṁ māyōpādhikatvāt jagatkāraṇatvasya.*

[16] See *Nyāyaratnadīpāvaliḥ by Ānandānubhava*, ed. V. Jagadisvara Sastrigal and V. R. Kalyanasundara Sastrigal (Madras: Government Oriental Manuscripts Library, 1961), 89–93. Ānandānubhava's reference to Bhāskara as "that blockhead from Karnataka" suggests a South Indian provenance and regional antagonism. See Patrick Olivelle, *Renunciation in Hinduism: A Medieval Debate*, vol. 1 (Vienna: University of Vienna Institute for Indology, 1986), 115, 117. Cf. Mahadevan, *Preceptors of Advaita*, 130–138.

[17] *Amṛtataraṅgiṇī*, f. 13–14. To contrast Śrīdhara on the same topic, see Gupta, *The Caitanya Vaiṣṇava Vēdānta of Jīva Gosvāmī*, 68–71.

[18] This verse is relegated to the apparatus of many modern editions of the *Bhāgavata*. In the critical edition of the *Bhāgavata*'s first canto, the verse is noted with an asterisk after 1.2.8, which is the way I have referred to it here. See *Śrīmad Bhāgavata Mahāpurāṇam*, ed. P. Radhakrishna Sarma (Tirupati: Tirumala Tirupati Devasthanam, 1989), 57: *śrutam apyaupaniṣadaṁ dūrē harikathāmṛtāt yanna santi dravaccittaprēmāśrupulakōdgamāḥ*. Śrīdhara knew of it as well, although the verse and his remarks on it are relegated to a footnote in the J. L. Shastri edition of his commentary. See *Bhāgavata Purāṇa of Kṛṣṇa Dvaipāyana Vyāsa with Sanskrit Commentary Bhāvārthabodhinī of Śrīdhara Svāmin*, ed. J. L. Shastri (Delhi: Motilal Banarsidass, 1983), 16, n. 4. The verse also found its way into the poetry anthology *Padyāvalī* (v. 39) compiled by the Gauḍīya Vaiṣṇava scholar Rūpa Gōsvāmī in the sixteenth century, with slightly different readings that more clearly contrast the content of the Upaniṣads to stories about God. Cf. *Padyāvalī*, ed. S. K. De (Dacca: University of Dacca, 1934), 17: *śrutam apy aupaniṣadaṁ dūrē harikathāmṛtāt yatra santi dravaccittakampāśrupulakōdga-māḥ.*

Lakṣmīdhara criticized those who would read into this verse a distinction between the practice of Vēdānta and the pursuit of *bhakti*:

> There are some who interpret this verse as follows: "Even the study of the Upaniṣads [*śravaṇa*] is far from—that is to say, significantly different from—hearing the stories of God, for one's heart doesn't melt, tears of love don't fall, and hairs do not stand on end while studying Brahman. There is as such an implicit reason in the sentence structure." This is unsound because the reason is not established. To the contrary, we see all these physical effects on the part of those fortunate people who are absorbed in ultimate reality, whether immersed in it in *samādhi* or upon hearing of it from their teacher. That is pure consciousness [*cidēkarasa*], a great ambrosial ocean of extraordinary joy, in which the foam, bubbles, and waves of all kinds of conceptual constructions have subsided.[19]

This passage is striking for its exuberant account of yogic absorption, or *samādhi*. Even as the waves of thought subside, the physical signs of absorption in Brahman erupt effusively. This condition can result just as easily from studying with one's teacher as in the depths of meditation. Although later readers would interpret the stanza in just the way that Lakṣmīdhara warned against,[20] Lakṣmīdhara found in it a bridge between the forbidding austerity of classical Advaita and the bubbling bliss of the *Bhāgavata*. Was there more to his use of the term *cidēkarasa*, then, than mere consciousness? I draw attention to this term because it was a staple of Śaiva-Śākta metaphysics; one of the thousand names of the Śrīvidyā goddess Lalitā Tripurasundarī, for instance, is *cidēkarasarūpiṇī*, one whose very form is pure consciousness.

Rūpa Gōsvāmī attributes this verse to Vyāsa, while Jīva Gōsvāmī cites it in the *Bhaktisandarbha* but attributes it to Caitanya (*kaliyugapāvanāvatāra*). The memory of the verse among several readers of the *Bhāgavata* but its absence in several manuscript traditions suggests that it fell out of the text somewhere along the way.

[19] *Amṛtataraṅgiṇī*, f. 36: *śrutam apīti yat yasya puṁsō harikathāmṛtād āsvādyamānāt dravaccittaprēmāśrupulakōtsavā na santi bhavanti tasyaupaniṣadaṁ brahma śrutam api dūrē parōkṣam ēvētyartthaḥ. kēcit tv ēvaṁ vyācakṣatē. aupaniṣadaṁ upaniṣatsaṁbandhi śrutaṁ śravaṇam api harikathāmṛtād dūrē harikathāmṛtasya tasya ca mahad antaraṁ yat yasminn aupaniṣadē śravaṇē dravaccittaṁ premāśrūṇi puḷakōtsavāś ca na santīty antargarbhitō hētur iti. tad ayuktaṁ asiddhatvād dhētōḥ vilīnavividha[vi]kalpaphēnabudbudataraṅgē niratiśayānandāmṛtamahārṇavē cidēkarasē paravastuny api sadgurubhyaḥ śrūyamāṇē samādhāv avagāhyamānē vā sabhāgyānāṁ rōmōdgamādidarśanāt.*

[20] Mōhana, a commentator on Rūpa Gōsvāmī's *Padyāvalī*, explicitly distances studying the Upaniṣads from listening to God's stories, for it does not provide the same degree of happiness. I am grateful to David Buchta for this information.

Classical and postclassical Advaitins who employed the term did so without much fanfare.[21] That Lakṣmīdhara placed it at the very beginning of his commentary signals to me a distinct stage of Advaitic writing. If not conclusive proof of Śaiva resonance, the term *cidēkarasa* at least merits mention given the *Amṛtataraṅgiṇī*'s later significance to the Śaivas Pūrṇasarasvatī and Rāghavānanda. It also prompts me to move from questions of philosophy to questions of literature. How did *rasa* proper, the concept of aestheticized emotion, feature in the *Bhāgavata*, and how did its early readers respond?

Writing around the tenth century, the dramatic theorist Dhanañjaya takes a sarcastic jab at moralistic art critics in the opening to his *Daśarūpaka* (1.6): "Prostrations to the idiot who turns his face from pleasure and says that poetic figures that ooze with delight are simply for moral instruction, no different from epics, etc."[22] The formula "epics, etc." (*itihāsādi*) generally included the *purāṇas*, which for most Brahmanical thinkers was functionally no different from the epics. However, the *Bhāgavata* accorded to itself a superlative quality, not only as the quintessence and culmination of all Brahmanical scripture but as the best example of *kāvya* or Sanskrit *belles lettres*. In the third stanza, the *Bhāgavata* exhorts its listeners, whom it calls *rasika*s or *bhāvuka*s, emotionally sensitive connoisseurs, to drink the *rasa*, the sweet juice, that flows from the narrator Śuka's mouth as he bites into the fruit from the tree of the scriptures. A serious project of theorizing *bhaktirasa*—the *rasa* that is love for God—took its cue from the *Bhāgavata*, first in the writings of Vōpadēva and Hēmādri in the thirteenth century, culminating in the systematized concept of *bhaktirasa* proposed by the Gauḍīya Vaiṣṇavas in the sixteenth century. So at least runs the standard historiography of *bhaktirasa*.[23] But there are other stages in the intellectual history of that concept, particularly in the Śaiva devotional poetry of Kashmir.[24]

[21] For a representative spread, see Vācaspati Miśra's *Bhāmatī* on *Brahmasūtrabhāṣya* 1.1.0, Gōvindānanda's *Ratnaprabhā* on BSB 1.3.2, 1.4.19, and 3.2.30, and Vidyāraṇya's *Jīvanmuktivivēka* 3.8.1, 3.9.2. See *The Brahmasūtra-Shānkarbhāshyam with the Commentaries Bhāshya-Ratnaprabhā, Bhāmatī and Nyāyanirṇaya*, ed. Mahādeva Śāstrī Bakre, revised ed., Wāsudev Laxmaṇ Śāstrī Paṇśīkar (Bombay: Nirnaya Sagar, 1934), 18, 207, 329, 659. Robert Alan Goodding, "The Treatise on Liberation-in-Life: Critical Edition and Annotated Translation of The *Jīvanmuktiviveka* of Vidyāraṇya" (Ph.D. diss., University of Texas, Austin, 2002), 401, 404.

[22] *The Daśarūpaka of Dhanaṁjaya*, ed. T. Venkatacharya (Madras: The Adyar Library and Research Centre, 1969), 5: *ānandaniṣyandiṣu rūpakēṣu vyutpattimātraṁ phalam alpabuddhiḥ yō'pītihāsādivad āha sādhus tasmai namaḥ svāduparāṅmukhāya.*

[23] Cf. Sheldon Pollock, *A Rasa Reader: Classical Indian Aesthetics* (New York: Columbia University Press, 2016), 285–309.

[24] See Hamsa Stainton, *Poetry as Prayer in the Sanskrit Hymns of Kashmir* (Oxford: Oxford University Press, 2019), 231–264.

Some have tried to suggest that Śrīdhara was also responsible for laying the seeds of a *bhaktirasa* theory.[25] However, apart from a stray comment on a stanza buried in the *Bhāgavata*'s tenth chapter, Śrīdhara shows no inclination that Sanskrit aesthetics is relevant to understanding the *purāṇa*. To the contrary, he does not recognize the aesthetic valence of *rasa* in *Bhāgavata* 1.1.3 at all. Lakṣmīdhara, however, not only picks up on the metaphor but also explicates it in some detail, using the technical language of Sanskrit poetics:

> This stanza is a metaphor, as it compares two similar things because of a figurative expression of non-difference. As an earlier scholar (Daṇḍin) has said: "A metaphor is nothing but a simile whose differentiating sign has been concealed." Furthermore, it is a metaphor that is at once "compounded and separate." The compounded metaphor is "From the tree that is scripture," while "The fruit that is the *Bhāgavata*" is separate (in that it is two separate words). It is a "punned" metaphor since words like "Śuka," meaning parrot or narrator, apply equally to both sides of the pun. It is also a "total" metaphor that "consists of attributes" because metaphorical identification of the text with a fruit is brought about by all the qualifiers. To wit, the fruit, hanging from a certain tree, having sweet juice and a special taste, is nibbled on by birds and drops to the ground. Once it falls on the ground, others who know its taste relish it. All that is brought about here.[26]

Here Lakṣmīdhara demonstrates a clear familiarity with the subdivisions of metaphor defined by one of the earliest literary critics, Daṇḍin, in his *Kāvyādarśa* (2.66 and following). But why does he go into such detail? The point is not only to prove that the *purāṇa* has all the requisite elements to produce *rasa* but also that that *rasa* is distinctive:

> If we read the stanza as being about a fruit, then *rasa* means passion, the desire to taste the fruit, and *rasikas* are the people who have that desire. If,

[25] Gupta, *The Caitanya Vaiṣṇava Vēdānta of Jīva Gosvāmī*, 73, n. 12.

[26] *Amṛtataraṅgiṇī*, f. 22: *sadṛśavastunōr abhēdōpacārāt rūpakam idaṁ yathōktam abhiyuktaiḥ "upamaiva tirōbhūtabhēdā rūpakam iṣyata" iti. tatrāpi samastavyastarūpakam idaṁ nigamakalpatarōr iti samāsāt bhāgavataṁ phalam iti vyastāc ca. śliṣṭarūpakaṁ ca śukādiśabdānāṁ pakṣadvayasādhāraṇyāt. saviśēṣaṇarūpakam idaṁ sakalarūpakaṁ ca sarvair viśēṣaṇaiḥ phalatvasaṁpādanāt. tathā hi phalaṁ t[k]asyacit tarōs sambandhi madhudravasaṁyutaṁ rasaviśēṣavac ca vihagair āsvādyatē nipātyatē ca bhuvi nipatitaṁ ca tad anyaiḥ rasajñair āsvādyatē tad iha sarvaṁ sampādyatē.*

> however, it is about the text itself, then that *rasa* is a certain joy, a flash of happiness that arises in the heart, whose foundational factor is a figure like Rāma, either depicted in literature by poets or depicted on stage by actors. As they say: "When there is a transformation in the heart that relies on an external object, those in the know call that a *bhāva*. The intensification of that *bhāva* is known as *rasa*."[27]
>
> The term "relying on an *external* object" only expresses a part of the whole, for we see that very same upswelling in the heart when the Ātman *within* all is described by those learned in Advaita. When it comes to this subject, too, the *rasa* is the (intensified form of the) stable emotion of love, etc., not the transitory emotions like disenchantment. As it is said in the *Daśarūpaka* (4.1): "The stable emotion, when heightened to the state of relish by means of aesthetic factors, voluntary and involuntary physical reactions, and transitory emotions, is known as *rasa*."
>
> It is a *rasa* insofar as it culminates in the manifestation of joy [*ānanda*], or else it wouldn't be something that one would want to relish. And therefore it is joy that is the fundamental *rasa*. As we hear in the Veda (*Taittirīya Upaniṣad* 2.7): "He, verily, is *rasa*. For having obtained *rasa*, one becomes joyful."[28]

According to Lakṣmīdhara, the *Bhāgavata* deals with no ordinary subject. Its topic is the Ātman, pure undifferentiated consciousness. But that ultimate reality is not only to be known, it is to be experienced. People experience the Ātman as unparalleled joy, or *ānanda*, in the same way that people who love to read literature or attend the theater experience happiness in their hearts. While their happiness is based on external factors, the joy of the Ātman is intimate and unique. The Pratyabhijñā theologian Abhinavagupta had analogized the experience of *rasa* and the experience of Brahman. However,

[27] Cf. *Bhāvaprakāśana of Śāradātanaya*, ed. Yadugiri Yatiraja Swami and K. S. Ramaswami Sastri (Baroda: Oriental Institute, 1968), 37 (2.99): *vikārō mānasō yas tu bāhyārtthālambanātmakaḥ vibhāvādyāhitōtkarṣō rasa ity ucyatē budhaiḥ.*

[28] *Amṛtataraṅgiṇī*, f. 23: *iti phalapakṣē rasō rāgaḥ phalāsvādanēcchā tadvantō rasikāḥ prabandhapakṣē tu raghunandanādiṣu kavibhir varṇyamānēṣu bharatair abhinīyamānēṣu vā tadālaṁbanaḥ kaścana manasas subhagas samullāsō jāyatē sa rasa ity ucyatē. tathā cāhuḥ "bāhyārtthālaṁbanō yas tu vikārō mānasō bhavēt sa bhāvaḥ kathyatē prājñais tasyōtkarṣō rasaḥ smṛtaḥ" iti. tatra bāhyārtthālaṁbana ity upalakṣaṇaṁ sarvāntarē 'py ātmavastuny advaitakuśalair nnirūpyamāṇē tādṛśasya manaḥprōllāsasya darśanād atrāpi ratyādisthāyī bhāvō rasaḥ. na vyabhicārī nirvēdādi. uktaṁ daśarūpakē "vibhāvair anubhāvaiś ca sāttvikai[r] vyabhicāribhiḥ unnīyamānaḥ svādyatvaṁ sthāyī bhāvō rasaḥ smṛtaḥ." tasyāpy ānandāvirbhāvāvadhitvāt rasatvaṁ anyathāsvādyatvānupapattēḥ. tataś cānanda ēva mukhyō rasaḥ "rasō vai saḥ. rasaṁ hy ēvāyaṁ labdhvānandī bhavati" iti śrutēḥ.*

Lakṣmīdhara goes beyond analogy to equivalence. The joy known as *ānanda* is the fundamental *rasa* and it is accessible to those steeped in the nondual Ātman. Note how similar this sounds to Lakṣmīdhara's account of the blissful experience of both *yōgīs* and students, absorbed as they are in the ultimate reality, flush with all the physical reactions appropriate to aesthetic pleasure. At the same time, all the supporting aesthetic factors that turn a stable emotion into a *rasa* in secular dramaturgy remain operational. Lakṣmīdhara says further on that one may even interpret the *Bhāgavata* as one would any other *kāvya*. For example, Viṣṇu is the self-possessed, exalted hero (*dhīrōdātta-nāyaka*), and the text foregrounds the *rasa* of heroism while saving plenty of space for the erotic.[29] Here and there, Lakṣmīdhara takes care to point out the poetic figures, or *alaṁkāras*, being employed in a certain verse or another.[30] Whether or not it is *kāvya* by definition, the *purāṇa* produces the experience of *rasa*, especially for those who relish absorption in the nondual Ātman.

At this juncture, Lakṣmīdhara returns to the *Daśarūpaka*, citing the stanza about boring readers with disapproval. Remember, Dhanañjaya had little patience for those who read literature the way they read the epics, that is, as sources of advice rather than sources of pleasure. Lakṣmīdhara takes offense at the "etc." in "epics, etc." Why should the *purāṇa* be lumped along with the epics as being merely a vehicle of moral instruction? For Lakṣmīdhara, the *purāṇa* was a source of *rasa* just like, and perhaps even more than, *kāvya* proper. Therefore, he says, *Bhāgavata* 1.1.3 and its call to enjoy *rasa* refutes the *Daśarūpaka*'s implicit criticism of the *purāṇa*.[31] Of course, neither *itihāsa* nor *purāṇa* was the focus of Dhanañjaya's jibe. He was instead making a point about moralistic approaches to *kāvya*. But this is exactly what Lakṣmīdhara takes to be at stake: What counts as *kāvya* and why? His intervention marks a shift in how authors familiar with the discourse of Sanskrit aesthetics understood the range of possible sources of *rasa*. And it was precisely such an extension that culminated in the concept of *bhaktirasa*, the *rasa* produced by textually determined love for God.

29 *Amṛtataraṅgiṇī*, f. 24–25.

30 See, e.g., *Amṛtataraṅgiṇī*, f. 87, commenting on *Bhāgavata Purāṇa* 1.8.25. In this stanza, Kunti famously asks Kṛṣṇa to bless her with calamities forever, so that she might always be able to see him come to the rescue. Lakṣmīdhara reads this, once again referring to Daṇḍin's typology, as "an objection in the form of blessing" (*āśīrvādākṣēpa*), a kind of implicit interdiction where the speaker wishes to prevent something about to take place. He proceeds to cite the exemplary verse given to illustrate this figure in the *Kāvyādarśa* (2.141): "Go if you must, my dear, and may your roads be safe. And wherever you end up, let me be born (again) there too." In the guise of well-wishing, a woman tries to convince her lover not to leave on a trip by implying that she will die if he does.

31 *Amṛtataraṅgiṇī*, f. 25.

There are three dimensions of this alternative commentarial tradition that prefigure the interests of Pūrṇasarasvatī and Rāghavānanda: Śaiva religion (in Vaiṣṇava texts), Advaita philosophy, and Sanskrit literary culture. The first of these is less prominent, and I have read it subtextually. Whether or not this alternative tradition was also a Śaiva one, it was certainly distinct from contemporary commentaries. Lakṣmīdhara's willingness to use the concepts of Advaita Vēdānta contrasts with Śrīdhara's relative reticence thereto. His knowledge of literary theory, and his intervention in matters internal to Sanskrit poetics, suggests a desire to read the *Bhāgavata* as *kāvya*, in a way both similar to and different from contemporary writings on *bhaktirasa*. And his interest in combining the experience of *rasa* with the language of Advaita metaphysics recalls similar efforts in the writings of the nondualist Śaivas of Kashmir, and perhaps laid the groundwork for the more elaborate confluences we find later in Kerala.

Pūrṇasarasvatī: Poetry and Prayer

The fourteenth-century litterateur and renunciant Pūrṇasarasvatī is well-known in the history of Sanskrit literature for his commentaries on exemplary works of *kāvya*. These included Kālidāsa's *Mēghadūta*, on which he modeled his own *Haṁsasandēśa*, and Bhavabhūti's *Mālatīmādhava*, which he retold in verse form in his *Ṛjulaghvī*. He was an influential if unusual figure in the history of Sanskrit literary interpretation. Belonging to two overlapping communities, the monastic order and the literary salon, Pūrṇasarasvatī was familiar with both the ostensibly secular tradition of literary criticism and the philosophical theologies of Pratyabhijñā and Advaita Vēdānta.[32] In his commentary on the *Mālatīmādhava*, for example, he not only developed creative ways of thinking about the play's thematic and affective concerns, but also believed that the playwright was a "master of *yōga* and Vēdānta" who communicated the secrets of yogic practice that one would otherwise receive from one's guru.[33] The characters of the play, in his view, were representatives of spiritual concepts. His own stage-play, the

[32] Jason Schwartz, "Parabrahman among the *Yogins*," *International Journal of Hindu Studies* 21.3 (2017): 369–374.

[33] *Mālatīmādhava of Bhavabhūti with the Rasamañjarī of Pūrṇasarasvatī*, ed. K. S. Mahādēva Śāstrī, Trivandrum Sanskrit Series No. 170 (Trivandrum: Government Central Press, 1953), 9–10, 265 (henceforth cited as *Rasamañjarī*).

Kamalinīrājahaṁsa, can be read as an allegory expressing the philosophies of Śākta and Śaiva Tantrism.[34] Śaivism permeated Pūrṇasarasvatī's writing, but it was inflected with devotion to Viṣṇu. After comparing his teacher, Pūrṇajyōti, to the form of Śiva known as Dakṣiṇāmūrti, in the next breath he describes him as Kṛṣṇa, the author of the Gītā.[35] He also wrote a commentary on a Vaiṣṇava poem of prayer, the *Viṣṇupādādikēśa Stōtra*, which describes the body of Viṣṇu from foot to head. This genre of *stōtra* encouraged a devotional experience that Steven Hopkins calls "extravagant beholding, that holds in tension together ideal visionary forms with the concrete, material reality of the individual object of love."[36] Or as Pūrṇasarasvatī deliciously put it, the body of God is an apparent transformation of the ideal Brahman, "like a congealed block of ghee" (*ghṛtakāṭhinyavat*).[37]

In his commentary, the *Bhaktimandākinī*, Pūrṇasarasvatī assigns authorship of the *stōtra* to the Advaita philosopher Śaṅkarācārya, whom he identifies as an incarnation of Śiva and author of the commentary on the *Brahma Sūtras*.[38] The *stōtra* itself was probably composed much later, given the many references to post-Śaṅkara texts. But Pūrṇasarasvatī's attribution, like all apocrypha, is historically meaningful. Not only was there a vibrant memory of Śaṅkara in his purported land of origin but also attempts to link that memory to a particular kind of *bhakti*. There is no doubt as to Pūrṇasarasvatī's Advaita affinities here. He equates visualizing God, who is nothing but Brahman as existence, joy, and pure consciousness (*cidēkarasa*), with the traditional Advaitic practice of "listening, reflection, and meditation."[39] Pūrṇasarasvatī's understanding of *bhakti* and the God to whom it is directed was derived not only from the classical tradition of Advaita Vēdānta, but also from texts that were contested between Vēdānta traditions, the *Bhāgavata* and the *Viṣṇu Purāṇa*. He quoted the former no fewer than fifty-two times and the latter seventy-five times in his commentary.[40] The *Viṣṇupādādikēśa Stōtra* was probably used as a meditative text among certain

[34] N. V. P. Unithiri, *Pūrṇasarasvatī* (Calicut: University of Calicut, 2004), 55–61.

[35] *Rasamañjarī*, 1–2. Elsewhere he compares Pūrṇajyōti to "a second Śiva, who looks through the three eyes of grammar, hermeneutics, and epistemology" (*padavākyapramāṇanētratrayanirīkṣaṇāparaparamēśvara*). *Kamalinīrājahaṁsa of Pūrṇasarasvatī* (Trivandrum: The Superintendent, Government Press, 1947), 5.

[36] Steven P. Hopkins, "Extravagant Beholding: Love, Ideal Bodies, and Particularity," *History of Religions* 47.1 (2007): 8.

[37] *Bhaktimandākinī*, 9. This is likely a reference to Śaṅkara's commentary on *Brahma Sūtra* 2.2.15.

[38] *Bhaktimandākinī*, xix–xxi.

[39] *Bhaktimandākinī*, 7–9. Cf. Schwartz, "Parabrahman among the *Yogins*," 370.

[40] Unithiri, *Pūrṇasarasvatī*, 324, 326–327.

circles of South Indian Vaiṣṇavas.[41] Usually this has meant the Śrīvaiṣṇavas of the Tamil country. If we float over and across the Nilgiris, we find another set of devotees who found the text to be a source of Advaitic meditation.

For Pūrṇasarasvatī, who enjoyed representation on the stage as much as representation of the divine, aesthetics was the bridge between religion and literature. Beyond his casual mentions of the term *bhaktirasa*,[42] Pūrṇasarasvatī justifies the whole enterprise of composing *stōtras* on account of its widespread appeal as a method of instruction for the aesthetically inclined. When an opponent objects that God's physical features have been described in simple language in the *purāṇas* and need no further representation in elaborate *stōtra* form, Pūrṇasarasvatī responds that different people have different capacities to comprehend. Some get it by hearing it just once. Some require more detail. And some just have different preferences when it comes to modes of instruction.[43] He jokingly accuses his interlocutor of misunderstanding the purpose of both science and poetry:

> It is based on the differences between people in need of instruction that such a wide range of technical treatises are laid out for study. Otherwise, if everyone could understand something that could be communicated in a few words, what would be the use of these voluminous tomes, tangled with all sorts of opinions, arguments, and concepts? If a single *mantra* could get us everything we wanted, what would be the point of this merry-go-round of all manner of *mantras* and techniques and ritual formulae? But enough of this blather, all puffed up with talk of *rasas*, *bhāvas*, and poetic figures, all

[41] Fred Smith, "Reviews: *The Bhaktimandākinī*," *Bulletin of the School of Oriental and African Studies* 76.3 (2013): 524–525. The ritual function of *stōtras* in medieval Tamil Śaiva Siddhānta provides a possible context for the interest in *stōtras* among their non-Saiddhāntika counterparts in Kerala. See Whitney Cox, "Making a Tantra in Medieval South India: The Mahārthamañjarī and the Textual Culture of Cōḷa Cidambaram" (Ph.D. diss, University of Chicago, 2006), 107: "[T]he PĀS (*Pañcāvaraṇastava*) is concerned with the projection of an aesthetically compelling picture of the basic Saiddhāntika ritual form, mapping out of the imaginative spaces of daily worship. . . . [T]hrough the poetic restaging of the essential liturgical forms through which he and every other Saiddhāntika initiate structured their religious lives, Aghoraśiva hints at the possibility of a self-consciousness, an inner depth that emerges precisely through the adherence to ritual discipline."

[42] *Bhaktimandākinī*, 47, 79, 87.

[43] *Bhaktimandākinī*, 9. In support of the idea of preference, he quotes the Pratyabhijñā philosopher Utpaladēva's *Īśvarapratyabhijñākārikā* (2.33): *yathāruci yathārthitvaṁ yathāvyutpatti bhidyatē ābhāsō'py artha ēkasminn anusaṁdhānasādhitē*. See Isabelle Ratié, "'A Five-Trunked, Four-Tusked Elephant Is Running in the Sky': How Free Is Imagination According to Utpaladeva and Abhinavagupta?," *Asiatische Studien* 64.2 (2010): 359, n. 47: "In an object that is one (*ēka*), [because it is] established through a synthesis (*anusaṁdhāna*), an [elementary] phenomenon (*ābhāsa*) can also be distinguished according to [the subject's] free will (*ruci*), a [particular] desire (*arthitva*), [or] according to education (*vyutpatti*)."

> of which are ultimately unreal (or: unphilosophical). It is well-established that this undertaking of the blessed teacher, ocean of boundless knowledge, whose every act is exclusively dedicated to giving grace to others, is purposeful in order that those who have become infused with *rasa*, and whose minds are tender and sincere, may alight upon this extremely profound subject matter.[44]

This passage is noteworthy for a few reasons. One is the gesture—a good-humored jab—toward the excesses of both Śaiva ritual and scholarly proliferation. Another is the smooth transition between the devotional and the aesthetic; *bhakti* is the prerogative of the sensitive connoisseur, someone who wants both "fun and freedom" (*bhuktimuktyabhilāṣuka*).[45] Finally there are the traces of Pūrṇasarasvatī's playful character, peeking through not only in his opinionated asides—for example, his tongue-in-cheek apology for inserting poetics into a philosophical commentary—but also in his poetic prose style. He often employs alliteration (*vikalpajalpakalpanā*), consonance (*karatalakalitam iva kanakakaṭakam*), and light syllables in quick succession (*mṛdulasarala*). The most sustained example comes when he breathlessly retells, almost entirely in short vowels, as if to the rapid beat of a drum, a story from the *Harivaṁśa* of Viṣṇu coming to the aid of the gods in battle against the demons.[46] While contemporary poets in the *stōtra* genre were experimenting with "flashy" poetry (*citrakāvya*), Pūrṇasarasvatī was becoming a flashy prose stylist. Commentary should be fun, as he said while reading the plays of Bhavabhūti.[47] Instead of being purely pedagogical, commentary can help us understand an author's affective state, especially when

[44] *Bhaktimandākinī*, 12: *vyutpādyabhēdāpēkṣayā hi śāstrāṇi vicitrāṇi vistīryantē. anyathā parimitākṣarōpadēśyēna tattvēna sarvēṣāṁ caritārthatvāt kimartha ēṣa vividhavikalpajalpaka-lpanājaṭilō granthaskandhātibhāranibandhaḥ? ēkēnaiva mantrēṇābhimatasakalārthasiddhau kiṁprayōjanā cēyaṁ bahuvidhamantratantrapāratantryayantraṇā? ity alam atattvarasabhāvāla-ṁkārataraṅgitabhaṅgipratipādanēna. sarasatām āpādya, mṛdulasaralamatīnām atigahanē'sminn arthē'vataraṇārthaṁ sārthaka ēva parānugrahaikasakalavyāpārāṇām apārajñānapārāvārāṇāṁ bhagavatām ācāryāṇām ayam ārambha iti sthitam.*

[45] *Bhaktimandākinī*, 9.

[46] See *Bhaktimandākinī*, 138–139. For example, "Coming to know this inspired compassion in his heart, and the enemy of demons then delighted the gods by revealing his own body before them as if it were ambrosia, neutralizing all sins" (*tadavagamajanitakaruṇamatir asuraripur atha nijavapur akhiladuritaśamanam amṛtamayam iva purata upadadhad amarapariṣadam aramayad*).

[47] See *Rasamañjarī*, 268, on reading a "chain of imaginative comparisons" (*utprēkṣāśṛṅkhalā*) in *Mālatīmādhava* 5.10: "What would be the fun if we interpreted them as being independent of one another? There would just be a pointless proliferation of *utprēkṣās*" (*parasparanirapēkṣatayā vyākhyānē kaś camatkāraḥ? utprēkṣābāhulyaṁ ca nirarthakam āpadyēta*).

love for God is in play. Even grammatical faults can become virtues if you read them right:

> Here, the use of particular verbs at different times, like "Protect us" or "I worship" or "I bow down" should be understood as a result of the agitation on the part of the composer. His heart is out of control in its obsession with God, swung back and forth by *bhaktirasa*. In such circumstances, the absence of grammatical order is in fact an aesthetic virtue, since it causes the sensitive listener to respond with amazement. As Vātsyāyana says (*Kāmasūtra* 2.2.31): "Manuals are only useful for people who lack imagination. But when the wheel of love starts spinning, no instructions, no direction."[48]

It is *camatkāra*, wonder, fascination, that matters for the devotee and the critic alike.[49] One version of wonder is limited to the form of poetry, while another comprehends its object. In the former, the beautiful arrangement of words prompts critics to smack their lips in appreciation. In the latter, inspiration trumps grammar, as God throws the devotee for a spin with his blinding beauty. The more marvelous and inexplicable the vision of God, the more wondrous the poetry becomes.[50]

Although the *Bhaktimandākinī*'s view of *bhakti* was relatively sedate and philosophical, this passage hints at a correspondence between the erotic and devotional moods of love. Pūrṇasarasvatī exploited the erotic motifs of *bhakti* in his *Haṁsasandēśa*, a lyric poem in the messenger genre. In the *Haṁsasandēśa*, a lovelorn woman enlists a goose to take a message to her faraway lover. At first, we know only that she is longing anxiously for a

[48] *Bhaktimandākinī*, 47: *atra ca, kadācit pāyān na iti, kadācit vandē iti, kadācit praṇaum ītyādikriyāviśēṣaprayōgō bhaktirasāvēdhēna bhagavadanusandhānē paravaśahṛdayasya prayōktuḥ sambhramavaśād iti mantavyaḥ. ēvaṁvidhē ca sthalē, prakramabhēdaḥ pratyuta sahṛdayacamatkārakārīti guṇa ēva, "śāstrāṇāṁ viṣayas tāvad yāvan mandarasā narāḥ. raticakrē pravṛttē tu naiva śāstraṁ na ca kramaḥ" iti vātsyāyanōktatvāt.*

[49] See David Shulman, "Notes on Camatkāra," in *Language, Ritual and Poetics in Ancient India and Iran: Studies in Honor of Shaul Migron*, ed. David Shulman (Jerusalem: The Israel Academy of Sciences and Humanities, 2010), 249–276. On the use of this term among Kashmiri poets and philosophers to characterize the devotee's experience of Śiva, see Stainton, *Poetry as Prayer*, 246–247, 249–251, 259–261.

[50] On the aesthetics of astonishment and wonder in the *stōtra* genre, see Stainton, *Poetry as Prayer*, 218–226. Cf. Harshita Mruthinti Kamath, "Praising God in 'Wondrous and Picturesque Ways': *Citrakāvya* in a Telugu *Prabandha*," *Journal of the American Oriental Society* 141.2 (2021): 255–271. For an account of wonder in poetry and theology alike, see Rembert Lutjeharms, *A Vaiṣṇava Poet in Early Modern Bengal: Kavikarṇapūra's Splendour of Speech* (Oxford: Oxford University Press, 2018), 273–274.

certain hardhearted heartthrob. In the tenth stanza we discover that he is none other than Kṛṣṇa, scion of the Vṛṣṇis. The forlorn woman then guides the goose through "all of the places my lover has loved."[51] The route begins in Kāñcīpuram, home to both the Vaikunṭha Perumāḷ temple that features the *Bhāgavata* in its very structural program, as well as the Śrīvidyā cult of Tripurasundarī, which will resurface in the writings of Rāghavānanda. The goose then glides over several Tamil Vaiṣṇava hotspots: Śrīraṅgam, site of the Raṅganātha temple; the Kāvērī and Tāmraparṇī rivers; and Āḻvār Tirunagari, a sacred site to Śrīvaiṣṇavas. Here, Pūrṇasarasvatī pauses to pay respects to the Vaiṣṇava poet-saint Nammāḻvār and his *Tiruvāymoḻi*:

> Bow your head to Murāri's icon
> —we call him Śaṭhakōpan—
> who revealed the meaning of scripture
> (holy waters, blissful waters!)
> by weaving it in Tamil like a necklace,
> and who relieves for all his lovers
> the pain of living in the world.[52]

After a considerable detour through Kerala, during which he visits the temples at Trivandrum and Tṛccambaram, the goose goes directly to his final destination: Vṛndāvana. The message he delivers to Kṛṣṇa locates the distress of his mistress in that particular narrative landscape created by the *Bhāgavata*. It mentions the *Bhāgavata*'s favorite stories: how Kṛṣna felled the two Arjuna trees, lifted Mount Gōvardhana, and danced with the young women of Braj. At this point, in the goose's telling, the heroine daydreams that her divine lover briefly appears and tries to go in for an embrace, only to find her arms firmly crossed over her breasts and her eyes crimson, rimmed with tears. "Your chest is splashed with saffron from all those *gōpī*s' breasts," she admonishes him. "Don't let it get pale by rubbing up against mine."[53] The

[51] *The Hamsasandeśa*, ed. K. Sāmbaśiva Śāstrī (Trivandrum: Superintendent, Government Press, 1937), 3 (v. 10c) (henceforth cited as *Haṁsasandēśa*).

[52] *Haṁsasandēśa*, 5 (v. 22):

āviścakrē nigamavacasām artham ānandatīrthaṁ
yā saṁgranthya dramiḍadharaṇībhāṣayā bhūṣayēva
tāṁ bhaktānāṁ bhavapariṇataṁ tāpam atrōddharantīṁ
mūrtiṁ mūrdhnā vinama śaṭhakōpābhidhānāṁ murārēḥ.

[53] *Haṁsasandēśa*, 16 (v. 85):

saṅkalpais tvāṁ kṣaṇam upagataṁ satvarāślēṣalōlaṁ
raktāpāṅgī stanakṛtabhujasvastikā sāsram āha

tone of intimacy, withdrawal, and intense longing that charaterizes *bhakti* poetry for Kṛṣṇa[54] comes to a stirring conclusion:

> You know how dark Draupadī,
> dragged by the devilish Kurus
> into that great hall, called out in duress:
> "Kṛṣṇa, Kṛṣṇa, KṚṢṆA!!"
> and it reached your ears so far away—
> Well I find it strange that
> you can't seem to hear
> the cries of this woman
> when you're sitting in her heart.[55]

The *Bhāgavata* was a spectral presence in Pūrṇasarasvatī's writing, but it shimmered with many kinds of love: divine, literary, everyday. Pūrṇasarasvatī appreciated the emotional tenor of *bhakti* poetry in the same way that he relished the taste of *kāvya*. *Bhakti* as poetry could give you both pleasure, *bhukti*, and liberation, *mukti*. The two were not so far apart in the Śaiva imaginary. Pūrṇasarasvatī said as much in a mischievous stanza that introduces the setting of *Kamalinīrājahaṁsa*: "In the city of Vṛṣapurī (Tṛśśūr), the courtesan of liberation pleases her suitors even without the price of non-dual awakening."[56] The double entendre of liberation as "release" and of nondualism as "coupling" would not have been lost on the play's audience. Pūrṇasarasvatī was fond of such metaphors. Later he would say that even if his language was less than perfect, the learned should regard it highly if it were about Śiva. For even "if a king's concubine becomes his

gōpastrīṇāṁ kucaparicitaiḥ kuṅkumair aṅkitaṁ tē
vakṣō mā bhūt kucaviluṭhanair luptaśōbhaṁ mamēti.

[54] Of course, emotions run high in *bhakti* poetry for Śiva as well. Cf. Hamsa Stainton, "Wretched and Blessed: Emotional Praise in a Sanskrit Hymn from Kashmir," in *The Bloomsbury Research Handbook of Emotions in Classical Indian Philosophy*, ed. Maria Heim, Chakravarthi Ram-Prasad, and Roy Tzohar (London: Bloomsbury, 2021), 239–254.

[55] I have included a third cry to Kṛṣṇa even though the word in the original is an adjective for Draupadī, because that is the sonic effect intended by the poet. See *Haṁsasandēśa*, 18–19 (v. 98):

kṛtsnadviṣṭaiḥ kurubhir adhamaiḥ kṛṣyamāṇā sabhāyāṁ
kṛcchrasthā yad vyalapad abalā kṛṣṇa kṛṣṇēti kṛṣṇā
tat tē dūraṁ śravaṇapadavīṁ yātam ētat tu citraṁ
cittasthō'pi pralapitagiraṁ yan na tasyāḥ śṛṇōṣi.

[56] *Kamalinīrājahaṁsa*, 2 (v. 7cd): *advaitabōdhapaṇabandhanam antarāpi yasyāṁ vimuktigaṇikā bhajatē mumukṣūn.*

wife, everyone comes to respect her as queen."[57] We have already seen that he was familiar with the science of sex, having quoted the *Kāma Sūtra* in the *Bhaktimandākinī*. For an ascetic, Pūrṇasarasvatī knew what it was like to let loose.

Rāghavānanda: Rapprochement and Religious Reading

Two centuries later,[58] another Śaiva renunciant named Rāghavānanda placed the *Bhāgavata* at the center of his religious, philosophical, and literary interests. There was some not inconsiderable intellectual overlap between Rāghavānanda and Pūrṇasarasvatī. Both wrote commentaries on literary *stōtras*, both found direct sources of inspiration from the *Bhāgavata*, and both sought a rapprochement between Pratyabhijñā theology, classical Advaita Vēdānta, and Vaiṣṇava *bhakti*. Their biographies also suggest a shared geography. Both frequented the Vaṭakkunāthan Śiva temple in Tṛśśūr as well as the Tṛccambaram Kṛṣṇa temple. I will return to the institutional networks that linked Pūrṇasarasvatī and Rāghavānanda later. For now, I am focusing on Rāghavānanda's body of work. His writings include commentaries on the *Bhāgavata Purāṇa*, the *Paramārthasāra* of Ādiśēṣa, the *Mukundamālā* attributed to King Kulaśēkhara, the *Viṣṇubhujaṅgaprayāta Stōtra* attributed to Śaṅkarācārya, and the *Laghustuti*, a Śākta praise-poem of Kashmiri provenance. The last of these gives us the clearest indication that Rāghavānanda

[57] *Kamalinīrājahaṁsa*, 6 (v. 16cd): *dāsī nṛpasya yadi dārapadē niviṣṭā dēvīti sāpi nanu mānapadaṁ janānām.*

[58] There is some disagreement about Rāghavānanda's date. Some have said that he lived in the fourteenth century. I argue that he lived in the sixteenth century. Rāghavānanda recognizes the patronage of King Rāghava, purportedly one of the Kōlattiri *rājas* who ruled over parts of northern Kerala and possibly lived toward the beginning of the fourteenth century. Rāghavānanda is often identified with one Kokkunnattu Svāmiyār, whose traditional dates also line up with the early fourteenth century. Rāghavānanda certainly postdates the thirteenth century, since he cites the *Saubhāgyahṛdayastōtra* (v. 5) by Śivānanda (c. 1225–1275 CE). However, he also quotes the *Kramadīpikā* (1.4) by the Nimbārkī Vaiṣṇava author Kēśava Kāśmīrī Bhaṭṭa, which pushes his date to the sixteenth century. Rāghavānanda does not cite the text by name, and at first it seems improbable that a Nimbārkī Vaiṣṇava who was closely associated with the Braj region should have influenced Śaivas in the South. But it was not unheard of. The South Indian Śākta-Śaiva Śāmbhavānandanātha quoted the *Kramadīpikā* (2.15) in his *Paramaśivādvaitakalpalatikā*. On the Kōlattiri *rājas*, see K. Kunjunni Raja, *The Contribution of Kerala to Sanskrit Literature* (Madras: University of Madras, 1980), 8. On the identification with Kokkunnattu Svāmiyār, see E. Easwaran Nampoothiry, "Contribution of Kerala to Advaitavēdānta Literature," *Vishveshvaranand Indological Journal* 22 (1984): 190–191. On Śivānanda and Śāmbhavānandanātha, see Alexis Sanderson, "The Śaiva Literature," *Journal of Indological Studies* 24–25 (2012–2013): 68, 69, n. 267. On the dates of Kēśava Kāśmīrī Bhaṭṭa, see Gérard Colas, "History of Vaiṣṇava Traditions: An Esquisse," in *The Blackwell Companion to Hinduism*, ed. Gavin Flood (Oxford: Blackwell, 2003), 253–254.

was initiated into a Śākta-Śaiva religious tradition. In a concluding stanza, he credits his teacher Kṛṣṇānanda with giving him *sannyāsa*, and instructing him in the Upaniṣads and Vēdānta. This is of a piece with his autobiographical comments in other works, but here he also records attaining the "Śaiva path" at the hands of another guru, whom he gives the title of *ānandanātha*.[59] This title is not a proper name but an appellation tacked onto a guru's initiation name in the Śrīvidyā tradition of Śākta Tantrism, originating in the Kaula cults associated with the *Matsyēndrasaṁhitā* and *Mahākālasaṁhitā*.[60] Rāghavānanda's command of the Śrīvidyā liturgical corpus, its schemes of mantric visualization, and its transgressive practices, is plainly evident in the commentary.

In this commentary, Rāghavānanda also lays out his cards as an advanced reader of Pratyabhijñā, familiar with both the Śaiva scriptures themselves and with postscriptural exegetes like Utpaladēva, Abhinavagupta, and Kṣēmarāja. At the same time, and unlike his Kashmiri predecessors, Rāghavānanda tried to meld the terms of classical Advaita Vēdānta with the cosmology and philosophy of nondual Śaivism. More surprising is how Śaiva discourse filtered into ostensibly Vaiṣṇava literature in Rāghavānanda's writing, not in such a way as to undermine the integrity of Vaiṣṇavism itself,[61] but rather in order to achieve a degree of synthesis that nevertheless preserved the particularity of each tradition. For example, let us look at Rāghavānanda's *Tātparyadīpikā*, a commentary on the *Mukundamālā*, a famous *stōtra* from Kerala. When the poem describes Kṛṣṇa as the highest reality (*paraṁ tattvam*), a Śaiva reader objects that "Kṛṣṇa" cannot literally be the highest *tattva*, for he must be identified with the "Puruṣa" *tattva*, a lower category on the hierarchy of thirty-six *tattva*s in the Śaiva Tantras. Rāghavānanda responds that there is in fact no higher principle than the Puruṣa—understood as the Supreme Person—and that all thirty-six *tattva*s inhere in him. Instead of adopting the universalist rhetoric of mainstream Advaita Vēdānta, he follows with a

[59] *The Laghustuti of Srī Laghu Bhaṭṭāraka with the commentary of Srī Rāghavānanda*, ed. T. Gaṇapati Sāstrī (Trivandrum: Superintendent, Government Press, 1917), 43 (henceforth cited as *Laghustuti*).

[60] James Mallinson, *The Khecarīvidyā of Ādinātha: A Critical Edition and Annotated Translation of an Early Text of* haṭhayoga (London: Routledge, 2007), 165–166, n. 6.

[61] The sixteenth-century scholar Appayya Dīkṣita tried to do just this by rereading the *Rāmāyaṇa* and *Mahābhārata* as Śaiva works. See Yigal Bronner, "A Text with a Thesis: The *Rāmāyaṇa* from Appayya Dīkṣita's Receptive End," in *South Asian Texts in History: Critical Engagements with Sheldon Pollock*, ed. Yigal Bronner, Whitney Cox, and Lawrence McCrea (Ann Arbor: Association for Asian Studies, 2011), 45–63. However, on Appayya's more conciliatory approach to sectarian conflict, probably as a result of different systems of patronage, see Ajay Rao, "The Vaiṣṇava Writings of a Śaiva Intellectual," *Journal of Indian Philosophy* 44.1 (2014): 41–65.

peculiar combination of Śaiva, Vaiṣṇava, and Advaita language: "The Puruṣa unfolding [*kramamāṇa*] in his very own self, pure unbroken self-reflective consciousness [*ahaṁ-vimarśa*], that is existence, joy, and pure consciousness [*cidēkarasa*], non-conceptual, eternal, stripped of all dualities, is described by the Pāñcarātras as Nārāyaṇa, and by Śaivas as Paramaśiva."[62] What we have here is not a colorless Brahman standing above squabbling sectarians but rather an appeal to a specific Śaiva notion of the Puruṣa fused with classical Advaita terms of art. Having first employed the technical Pratyabhijñā term *ahaṁ-vimarśa* to describe the Puruṣa's reflective consciousness of the entire creation as his own self, Rāghavānanda then deftly inserts *sat*, existence, into the Śaiva terminology of *cid-ānanda*, consciousness-and-joy. He refers to the Vaiṣṇava and Śaiva communities not by name but by their differences regarding the number of *tattvas*: the Pāncarātra Tantras speak of twenty-five, while the Śaiva Tantras count thirty-six. What follows is a dizzying transposition of the Śaiva hierarchy of *tattva*s and their operations onto Vēdānta metaphysics and Upaniṣad verses. For example, the various powers of Śiva (*jñāna-śakti*, *kriyā-śakti*, *icchā-śakti*), are mapped onto the three *guṇas* (*sattva*, *rajas*, *tamas*), the constituent qualities of creation that, in Vēdānta, belong to the cosmic illusion *māyā*.[63]

This passage finds a curious parallel in Rāghavānanda's commentary on the *Laghustuti*. The parallel suggests that he saw these prayers to Śakti and to Kṛṣṇa as being of a piece with one another, as sites for the exact same exegetical practice. A closer look at the *Laghustuti* passage reveals that Rāghavānanda was not cursorily interested in the Pāñcarātra tradition but actively wove together Śaiva and Vaiṣṇava theories of creation. In the middle of an account of the thirty-six *tattva* model of Śaiva cosmology, Rāghavānanda introduces concepts from Pāñcarātra when he arrives at *saṁkōca*, the "self-contraction" of the highest principle, Śiva-Śakti:

[62] *Śrīmukundamālā with Tātparyadīpikā of Rāghavānanda*, ed. K. Rama Pisharoti (Annamalainagar: Annamalai University, 1933), 43: *nirvikalpakanityanirastanikhiladvaitānuṣaṅgē sadānandacidēkarasē svātmany ēvānavacchinnāhaṁvimarśasārē kramamāṇaḥ puruṣō nārāyaṇa iti pañcaviṁśattattvavādibhiḥ, paramaśiva iti ṣaṭtriṁśattattvavādibhir varṇyatē* (henceforth cited as *Tātparyadīpikā*).

[63] *Tātparyadīpikā*, 44–45. On the homologies between Śaiva, Vaiṣṇava, and Advaita being established in medieval South India, see Whitney Cox, "Purāṇic Transformations in Cola Cidambaram: The *Cidambaramāhātmya* and the *Sūtasaṁhitā*," in *Puṣpikā: Tracing Ancient India through Texts and Traditions*, vol. 1, ed. Nina Mirnig, Péter-Dániel Szánto, and Michael Williams (Oxford: Oxbow Books, 2013), 25–48. Cf. Cox, "Making a Tantra in Medieval South India," 67: "It is essential to see the resulting eclectic synthesis not as a collision of unreconciled sources, but as a deliberate textual strategy, a harmonization of diverse materials within the text's own superordinate structure."

> This is the process of *saṁkōca*: Īśvara (the fourth of the thirty-six *tattvas*) makes this world, which only appears as if different from himself, actually separate, through his own *māyā* called Prakr̥ti, by employing her *rajas*, in a sequential order of elements beginning with *mahat*. When he does so, he becomes the Creator, Hiraṇyagarbha. When he enters into that very creation as its inner controller, by taking recourse to Prakr̥ti's *sattva*, and regulates it, then he becomes Viṣṇu. And when he himself withdraws it, using Prakr̥ti's *tamas*, then he becomes Rudra. In this way, Prakr̥ti is comprised of the three *guṇas*. When Prakr̥ti's *guṇas* are agitated [*kṣubhita*] through the power of the Lord called Parā, she creates the element *mahat*, in accordance with time and action.[64]

The first unconventional move here is to equate *māyā* with Prakr̥ti, two separate *tattvas* in the Śaiva model but equivalent in the Vaiṣṇava Pāñcarātra, which adapted the Sāṁkhya cosmology. The association of the three Hindu gods Brahmā, Viṣṇu, and Rudra with the three *guṇas* is also an older one, though not elaborated in Śaivism in exactly this way. The concept of *kṣōbha*, agitation or effervescence, had a technical meaning for Pratyabhijñā authors like Abhinavagupta, for whom it signified the state of consciousness in which creation appears, perturbing the stillness of the absolute. Here, however, Rāghavānanda draws upon the Vaiṣṇava inflection on the same concept, in which it is the *guṇas* that are disturbed and not creation itself *qua* cosmic agitation.[65] He provides intertextual resonances with the *Sātvata Tantra*, a late Vaiṣṇava scripture that centers on the figure of Kr̥ṣṇa, to describe how the elements give rise to the universe, through God's will.[66] He even describes

[64] *Laghustuti*, 33: *ayaṁ ca saṁkōcakramaḥ—yadā punar īśvaraḥ svasmāt pr̥thag iva bhāsamānaṁ viśvaṁ svamāyayaiva prakr̥tisaṁjñayā rajōguṇam avalambya mahadādikramēṇa pr̥thag ēva karōti, tadā sraṣṭā hiraṇyagarbhō bhavati. tatraivāntaryāmitvēna prakr̥tēḥ sattvaguṇam avalambyā'nupraviśya yadā niyamyati, tadā viṣṇuḥ. sa ēva prakr̥tēs tamōguṇam avalambya yadā saṁharati, tadā rudraḥ. ēvaṁ guṇatrayātmikā prakr̥tiḥ. saivēśaśaktyā parākhyayā kṣubhitaguṇā kālakarmānuguṇyē mahāntaṁ sr̥jati.*

[65] See *Viṣṇu Purāṇa* 1.2.29–31; *Bhāgavata Purāṇa* 8.3.16, 11.22.33. In Śaiva nondualist systems, agitation is creation itself (*sr̥ṣṭir ēva kṣōbhaḥ*). See André Padoux and Roger Orphé-Jeanty, *The Heart of the Yoginī: The* Yoginīhr̥daya, *A Sanskrit Tantric Treatise* (Oxford: Oxford University Press, 2013), 47.

[66] *Laghustuti*, 34: *ēvaṁ sr̥ṣṭāni mahadādīnīśvarecchayā kālakramēṇānyōnyaṁ militvā haimaṁ brahmāṇḍam utpādayanti.* Cf. *Sātvata Tantra* 1.30–31: *mahadādīni tattvāni puruṣasya mahātmanaḥ kāryāvatārarūpāṇi jānīhi dvijasattama. sarvāṇy ētāni saṁgr̥hya puruṣasyēcchayā yadā aṁśair utpādayāmāsur virājaṁ bhuvanātmakam.*

that God by one of his Vaiṣṇava epithets, the Kāraṇōdakaśāyī, one who sleeps in the waters of creation.[67]

As we have seen in the *Tātparyadīpikā*, it was not all one-way traffic. If Rāghavānanda brought Vaiṣṇava terms of art into his Śaiva-Śākta metaphysics, he returned the favor in his writings on Vaiṣṇava texts. In doing so, he was far from subsuming either Śaiva or Vaiṣṇava doctrines into the inclusivist ocean of Advaita. His was much more an act of grafting, of inserting concepts, sometimes uncomfortably, into slits in a well-rooted corpus, in the hope that each may sustain the other. In his commentary on the first stanza of the *Paramārthasāra*, a transitional text between Sāṁkhya and Vēdānta that was produced in a Vaiṣṇava milieu, Rāghavānanda describes the supreme in the Śaiva nondualist terms we previously encountered, as "existence, joy, and pure consciousness" (*sad-ānanda-cidēkarasa*).[68] In support of the notion that this undifferentiated being is able to create the world as a manifestation of his ever-luminous self, he quotes the *Śivastōtrāvalī* (20.9) by the Pratyabhijñā theologian Utpaladēva. That he regards Utpaladēva as an authority alongside more conventional Vaiṣṇava authorities is made apparent when he cites Utpaladēva's *Īśvarapratyabhijñākārikā* (1.5.2) immediately after and in support of statements made in the *Viṣṇu Purāṇa* and the *Bhagavad Gītā*.[69] The same infiltration is in effect in Rāghavānanda's commentary on the *Viṣṇubhujaṅgaprayāta Stōtra*. Commenting on the penultimate stanza, Rāghavānanda glosses the word "god" with technical terms derived from Śaiva nondualism, as "that self-luminous consciousness delighting in his very own self with the five actions: creation, preservation, dissolution, concealment, and grace."[70]

Why did Rāghavānanda feel compelled to keep the specificities of Śaiva and Vaiṣṇava discourse alive and intermingling, when, as an Advaitin in the Śaṅkara mold, he could have easily subordinated them to the universalism of mainstream Advaita Vēdānta? Let us be clear: Rāghavānanda knew his

[67] In some Vaiṣṇava traditions, the Kāraṇōdaka-, Garbhōdaka-, and Kṣīrōdaka- forms of the reclining Viṣṇu correspond to three of his four manifestations (*vyūha*) in Pāñcarātra doctrine: Saṅkarṣaṇa, Pradyumna, and Aniruddha.

[68] On the Śaiva "rewriting" of the *Paramārthasāra* by Abhinavagupta, see Lyne Bansat-Boudon and Kamalesha Datta Tripathi, *An Introduction to Tantric Philosophy: The Paramārthasāra of Abhinavagupta with the Commentary of Yogarāja* (London: Routledge, 2011).

[69] *The Paramārthasāra of Bhagavad Ādisesha with the Commentary of Rāghavānanda*, ed. T. Gaṇapati Sāstrī (Trivandrum: Travancore Government Press, 1911), 2, 16. Recall that Pūrṇasarasvatī quoted Utpaladēva's *Īśvarapratyabhijñākārikā* in his *Bhaktimandākinī*.

[70] *Viṣṇubhujaṅgaprayātastōtram*, ed. C. K. Raman Nambiar, Sri Ravi Varma Saṁskṛita Granthavali vol. 1, no. 3 (Tripunithura: The Sanskrit College Committee, 1953), 7: *hē dēva svaprakāśacinmūrtē viśvōtpādanapālanādānatirōbhāvānugrahaiḥ pañcabhiḥ kṛtyaiḥ svātmany ēva krīḍamāna.*

Śaṅkara very well, and his Surēśvara, his Sarvajñātman, and several other votaries of "classical" Advaita Vēdānta. Perhaps the answer is in the question itself. What did it mean to be an Advaitin in the Śaṅkara mold in the first place? It is now widely accepted that Śaṅkara and other authors of early Advaita probably belonged to a Vaiṣṇava environment.[71] More recently it has been argued that the *Bhāgavata* was responsible for placing *bhakti* over the value system and soteriology of the specific form of Advaita Vēdānta represented by Śaṅkara and Surēśvara, a process localizable in medieval Kerala.[72] Himself immersed in the exuberant language of Śākta-Śaiva nondualism, Rāghavānanda invokes Śaṅkara as a Vaiṣṇava poet and Advaita philosopher, as if trying to recuperate the radical roots of Vaiṣṇavism. Vaiṣṇava literature and philosophy permeated Rāghavānanda's writings because of and not in spite of the fact that he was an Advaitin, one who was trying to engage both with the wider world of embodied *bhakti* and with the internal tensions between multiple nondualisms.

It is in the service of the attempted synthesis between a forbidding, austere, firmly textual Advaita Vēdānta, and the positive, life-affirming, antinomian joy of Tantric Śaivism, that the *Bhāgavata* comes into play for Rāghavānanda. In the same way that *bhukti* and *mukti* were experienced simultaneously in nondualist Śaivism, for Rāghavānanda *bhakti* and *mukti* were one and the same. Rāghavānanda opens the *Tātparyadīpikā* with stanzas from the eleventh canto of the *Bhāgavata* that exalt *bhakti* above all other means to liberation. He then launches into a summary of classical Advaita teaching about the unity between Ātman and Brahman and the illusory nature of duality. He concludes his introduction by quoting a stanza from the *Sāmbapañcāśikā*, a *stōtra* from eighth-century Kashmir, which says that there is no difference between the agent of praise, the object of praise, and the act of praise itself. The sense of difference is a result of ignorance, as is the idea, according to the *Bhāgavata* (11.11.1), that one is either bound or liberated. If the concept of liberation is a result of *māyā*, then it is fine to employ illusory methods of differentiation like praise to achieve that desired end.[73] There is thus a close relationship between *bhakti* and *mukti*, and not simply as means to an end, as he explains while commenting on the third stanza:

[71] Paul Hacker, "Relations of Early Advaitins to Vaiṣṇavism," in *Philology and Confrontation: Paul Hacker on Traditional and Modern Vedanta*, ed. Wilhelm Halbfass (Albany: SUNY Press, 1995), 33–40.

[72] Aleksandar Uskokov, "The Black Sun That Destroys Inner Darkness: Or, How Bādarāyaṇa Became Vyāsa," *Journal of the American Oriental Society* 142.1 (2022): 63–92.

[73] *Tātparyadīpikā*, 1–3.

Even if *bhakti* and *mukti* deliver the same benefit, since both are the experience of uninterrupted joy, different people have different preferences,[74] so for the author to say (in verse 3) that he prays only for *bhakti* is not a problem. What we have to understand is this. *Mukti* is the direct, unmediated awareness of Brahman as pure inner consciousness. Brahman is pure existence, consciousness, and joy. It is the cause of the creation, preservation, and dissolution of the world. Such awareness has as its source great statements of the Upaniṣads like "That you are."

Bhakti, for its part, is a happiness in the mind never seen before, which is recognized through such signs as hairs standing on end, tears falling, and staring with mouth agape. Insofar as perfect veneration and faith in God and perfect love for the Ātman culminate in the undivided unity of Ātman and Brahman, this happiness, also known as eternal, unsurpassed love, manifests at the exact same time.

Because they have the same cause, the same time, the same locus, and the same content, they are in reality one and the same, and their difference is only conventional. It makes sense, then, that one can freely choose between them, because achieving one accomplishes the other. So says the *Bhāgavata Purāṇa* (11.2.42), a veritable Upaniṣad: "*Bhakti*, experience of God, and disdain for other things—all three appear at the same time." And it is with this in view that the revered author of the *Śivastōtrāvalī* (1.7, 20.11) proclaimed: "Lord! You alone are the self of all, and everyone loves themselves. People will really flourish if they realize that *bhakti* for you is spontaneous, in their own nature. Those who prosper with the wealth of *bhakti*, what else could they want? Those who are impoverished without it, what else could they want?"[75]

[74] The concept of *ruci-vaicitrya* was also used by Pūrṇasarasvatī to explain the appeal of the literary *stōtra*. It famously appears in Puṣpadanta's *Mahimnaḥ Stōtra* (v. 7) in a slightly different register, to show that even though people have different tastes in religion and philosophy, all culminate in Śiva, like waters in the ocean.

[75] *Tātparyadīpikā*, 14: *yadyapi bhaktimuktyōs tulyayōgakṣēmatā akhaṇḍānandānubhavamayatvāt, tathāpi puṁsāṁ rucivaicitryaniyamān mama bhaktiviṣayaiva prārthanā na dōṣāyēti bhāvaḥ. atraitad avadhēyam—muktir nāma viśvōtpattisthitisaṁhārahetutvōpalakṣitasya saccidānandaikarasamūrtēr brahmaṇas tattvamasyādimahāvākyapramāṇakaḥ pratyakcinmātratāsākṣādbōdhaḥ, bhaktiḥ punar īśvaraniṣṭhaniratiśayabahumānaviśvāsayōr ātmaniṣṭhaniratiśayaprēmṇaḥ cākhaṇḍabrahmātmaparyavasitatayā tatsamasamayābhivyajyamānō rōmaharṣāśrupātamukhavikāsādiliṅgakaḥ kaścanāpūrvadarśanō mānasōllāsō yō'sau nityaniratiśayaprītyāvirbhāvāparaparyāyō bhavatīty atō'nayōr ēkanimittatvāt ēkakālatvād ēkādhikaraṇatvād ēkaviṣayatvāc ca vastuta aikarūpyaṁ vyavahārataś ca bhēdaḥ, tenātrēcchāvikalpō yuktataraḥ anyatarasiddhāv aparasyāvaśyaṁbhāvād iti. tathā ca purāṇōpaniṣat—"bhaktiḥ parēśānubhavō viraktir anyatra caitat trika ēkakālam" ity ētad abhisandhāya ca śrīmān stōtrāvalīkāraḥ prāvōcat—"tvam ēvātmēśa sarvasya sarvaś cātmani*

In this dazzling passage, Rāghavānanda once again sews together what appear to be disparate and contradictory threads of thought. First is the relationship between *bhakti*, an emotional outpouring of love for a divine object, and *mukti*, liberation from the mistaken notion that one is finite and subject to birth and death. Rāghavānanda suggests that these two are not as different as they may appear in everyday life. The metaphysical question that generally arises at this point for nondualists and their critics is that if *bhakti* requires a lover and a beloved, and *mukti* obliterates the distinction, how can they be compatible? Rāghavānanda sidesteps this question entirely and appeals to a different kind of phenomenology. Both ultimately operate with respect to God who is the Ātman, and in both cases one becomes ec-static, thrown outside the confines of one's self. Here we find the second fascinating splice, the juxtaposition of the *Bhāgavata* with Utpaladēva's *Śivastōtrāvalī*. Utpaladēva was a key source for the reconciliation of *bhakti* and nondualist theology in the *stōtra* form.[76] His poetry tackled theoretical questions about the relationship between prayer and nondualism, and it brought together the emotional and philosophical registers of language. He thought of *bhakti* in a distinctively nondualist way, "not as a stepping stone, but as a manifestation of unity, an articulation of the final goal itself."[77] And he was one of the first to use aesthetic terminology in his devotional poetry. What is distinctive about the southerners is their incorporation of the *Bhāgavata* and other Vaiṣṇava texts in their commentarial program. Like his predecessors, Rāghavānanda cared about the literary quality of devotional poetry. Attending to the aesthetics of *bhakti* allows us deeper insight into why he considered the *Bhāgavata* so central to his intellectual enterprise.

Rāghavānanda's most ambitious project was a commentary on the *Bhāgavata* called the *Kṛṣṇapadī*.[78] Although he borrowed heavily from Lakṣmīdhara's *Amṛtataraṅgiṇī* and followed many of his readings, Rāghavānanda wrote on a much larger scale and sometimes disagreed with

rāgavān iti svabhāvasiddhāṁ tvadbhaktiṁ jānañ jayēj janaḥ. bhaktilakṣmīsamṛddhānāṁ kim anyad upayācitam ēnayā vā daridrāṇāṁ kim anyad upayācitam."

Cf. *The Sivastotravali of Utpaladevāchārya with the Sanskrit Commentary of Kṣemarāja*, ed. Rājānaka Lakṣmaṇa (Varanasi: The Chowkhamba Sanskrit Series Office, 1964), 6, 346.

[76] Stainton, *Poetry as Prayer*, 120–127.

[77] Stainton, *Poetry as Prayer*, 125.

[78] *Śrīmad Bhāgavataṁ Kṛṣṇapadīsamētam*, ed. Achyuta Poduval and C. Raman Nambiar, Sri Ravi Varma Samskrita Grandhavali no. 11 (Tripunithura: Sanskrit College Committee, 1963) (henceforth cited as *Kṛṣṇapadī*).

his predecessor.[79] In his commentary on the first stanza, he claimed that the *Bhāgavata* was the essence of all sorts of texts, genres, and doctrines: *śruti*, *smṛti*, *itihāsa*, *purāṇa*, *kāvya*, *nāṭaka*, Mīmāṁsā, Uttara Mīmāṁsā, the Sātvata Saṁhitās, the Śaiva Āgamas, and a whole host of others.[80] To regard the *Bhāgavata* as the quintessence and culmination of all scriptures, Vedic and Tantric, was not necessarily unique, though unusual for a Śaiva.[81] What is most interesting is what Rāghavānanda found most interesting about the *Bhāgavata*. Even more strongly than Lakṣmīdhara, Rāghavānanda repeatedly emphasized the literary quality of the *Bhāgavata* as its most distinguishing and superlative feature. Pūrṇasarasvatī may have been the more accomplished litterateur, but Rāghavānanda was equally versed in Sanskrit aesthetics, and it shone throughout his religious and philosophical writings.

Rāghavānanda introduces *Bhāgavata* 1.1.2 with a question seemingly straight out of the *Kāvyaprakāśa*, Mammaṭa's classic eleventh-century textbook of *alaṁkāraśāstra*: How does this poem tell us about the true nature of things? Is it as a master (*prabhu*), a relative (*bandhu*), or a lover (*kāntā*)? Each of these is already covered; the Veda commands us like a master, the *itihāsa* and *purāṇa* entreat us like a friend, and *kāvya*s like the *Rāmāyaṇa* seduce us like a lover. Rāghavānanda answers that the *Bhāgavata* is a combination of all three. The first two quarters of *Bhāgavata* 1.1.2 tell us that it can stand in for the Veda's ritual- and knowledge-oriented sections, respectively. The third quarter shows us that the *Bhāgavata* is both the essence of the epics and *purāṇa*s and distinct from them, insofar as it says that *bhakti*, the "central deity" of absolute oneness, a term that echoes Tantric notions of the primary god of a temple or a *mantra*, is the most important thing. The final quarter distinguishes the *Bhāgavata* from every other *kāvya* because its subject is God.[82] Other commentators also found embedded in this stanza a claim that the *Bhāgavata* was the essence of the Vedas and other scriptures. Rāghavānanda is the only one who frames it in such explicitly literary terms. Sequence matters; that *kāvya* comes last also means it is the best, according to some measure. Rāghavānanda pauses to ensure we understand

[79] See, e.g., *Kṛṣṇapadī*, 86, where he accuses "someone" of interpolating a stanza after *Bhāgavata* 1.4.4, which, like *Bhāgavata* 1.2.2, recalls a slightly embarrassing story about Śuka's father, Vyāsa. Rāghavānanda trashes an interpretation which matches Lakṣmīdhara's in *Amṛtataraṅgiṇī*, f. 54–55.

[80] *Kṛṣṇapadī*, 4–5.

[81] Cf. Frederick M. Smith, "Purāṇaveda," in *Authority, Anxiety, and Canon: Essays in Vedic Intepretation*, ed. Laurie Patton (Albany: SUNY Press, 1994), 97–138.

[82] *Kṛṣṇapadī*, 22–23.

this claim in detail, for it was why he considered the *Bhāgavata* so important and unique:

> Like a lover, this book instantly attracts the hearts of listeners, for the following reasons: (a) it does not have such aesthetic flaws as being harsh to the ears; (b) it contains such excellent poetic qualities as sweetness; (c) it manifests the erotic *rasa* and all the others; (d) it has ornaments of sound like alliteration and oblique speech, and ornaments of sense, like simile and imaginative comparison; (e) it reveals something unprecedented. So even people who like to have fun will attend to it with faith, and their thoughts are purified in no time. Then they use the chain of *bhakti* to lash God to the pillar of their heart.
>
> The verse emphasizes that "God is locked up in the heart in that instant" (*Bhāgavata* 1.1.2d). This is because other texts may captivate the mind of the listener (but not as quickly, for they are not as poetic). And because stories like *Kādambarī* may immediately captivate the mind, the verse stresses that it is God who is locked up in the heart. Those books only exemplify *rasas* that have external objects as their basis [*ālambana*]. Reading them only increases attachment to sense objects. But in the *Bhāgavata* the basis is God, the inner reality, so the more you read it, the less interest you have in worldly objects, and the more you get attached to the Ātman, which is not an object.
>
> Now you might say that something like the *Rāmāyaṇa* is a *kāvya* that features God, so this can't be that special. Even so, it does not "instantly" produce *bhakti* for Kr̥ṣṇa, for it tends to foreground the *rasa* of heroism, among others. Because the *Bhāgavata* was written with *bhaktirasa* at its very core, it instantly produces *bhakti* for Kr̥ṣṇa, and as such is better than everything else.[83]

[83] *Kr̥ṣṇapadī*, 23–24: *śrutikaṭutvādidōṣarahitatvān mādhuryādiguṇavattvāc chr̥ṅgārādirasavyañjakatvād anuprāsavakrōktyādiśabdālaṅkāravattvād upamōtprēkṣādyarthālaṅkāravattvād apūrvārthabōdhakatvāc cātratyā kr̥tiḥ kāntāvac chrōtr̥̄ṇām manaḥ sadya āharati. tataḥ śraddhayātraiva yatamānair bhōgibhir apy acirēṇa kālēna viśuddhabuddhibhir bhaktiśr̥ṅkhalayā bhagavān svahr̥dayastambhē badhyata iti. kr̥tīnāṁ śrōtr̥manōharatvaṁ salakṣaṇēṣu granthāntarēṣv apy astīty atō viśinaṣṭi—tatkṣaṇād iti. tatkṣanāt śrōtr̥manōhārakatvaṁ kr̥tīnāṁ kādambaryādiṣv api astīty ata uktam īśvaraḥ sadyaḥ hr̥dy avarudhyata iti. bāhyārthālambanānām ēva rasānāṁ tatrōdīraṇam iti tadabhyāsād viṣayāsaṅgābhivr̥ddhir ēva syāt. atra tu pratyaktattvalakṣaṇabhagavadālambanatvam. ata ētadabhyāsād viṣayakāmanāprahāṇēnāviṣayātmatattvāsaktir udīyāt. tēna siddhō'tiśaya iti. tathāpi rāmāyaṇādibhyō bhagavadviṣayēbhyō'sya nātiśaya ity ata uktaṁ sadya iti. rāmāyaṇādīnāṁ bhāgavatakāvyatvē'pi vīrarasādirasāntaraprādhānyān na sadyaḥ kr̥ṣṇabhaktyutpādakatā. asya bhaktirasaprādhānyēna pravr̥ttēḥ sadyas tadutpādakatvam. tēna sarvātiśātīty āśayaḥ.*

On one level we can read in this passage a classic disparagement of entertaining but frivolous literature in favor of the devotional and the soteriological. What Rāghavānanda would have us believe, however, is that the *Bhāgavata* is superlative not because it is *not* literary in that way, but because it is the *most* literary, far more so than other competing *kāvyas*. For its subject was God, the most delectable object of aesthetic pleasure, even for those "who like to have fun" (*bhōgī*). Even the *Rāmāyaṇa*, which for Sanskrit literati was the paradigmatic *kāvya* and had become a source of theological inspiration,[84] was hampered by foregrounding feelings other than love for Kr̥ṣṇa. Unlike with other *kāvyas*, as Lakṣmīdhara had pointed out, the aesthetic pleasure derived from the *Bhāgavata* was based on the most intimate of subjects, the Ātman, and not on external objects. That it took the form of literature rather than philosophical teaching was a virtue and not a flaw. Like Pūrṇasarasvatī, Rāghavānanda applied different modes of instruction to differently qualified individuals.[85] Poetry was much more likely to hold people's attention and reorient them to what really mattered. If art was the lowest form of teaching, it was because most people needed to be entertained, not because it was not edifying. To the contrary, it was desperately important to Rāghavānanda to lend overall coherence to the *Bhāgavata* as a work of literature. The *locus classicus* for this way of reading was the *Dhvanyālōka* by Ānandavardhana (ninth century), which argued that what gave a work its unity was the employment of a single predominant *rasa*.[86] As far as I know, Rāghavānanda was the only commentator to talk about the *Bhāgavata* in terms of an "inner" and "outer" *rasa*:

> Here in the *Bhāgavata*, *rasa* is of two kinds: outer and inner. The inner *rasa* is the experience of the joy of Brahman because that *rasa* has as its basis the inner truth. As the Veda says (*Taittirīya Upaniṣad* 2.7.1), "This person, having obtained *rasa*, becomes joyful." Moreover, that *rasa* is primary, both because it brings out an extraordinary eternal happiness, and according to

[84] See Ajay Rao, *Re-figuring the Rāmāyaṇa as Theology: A History of Reception in Premodern India* (London: Routledge, 2017).

[85] *Kr̥ṣṇapadī*, 4: "Scriptures offer teachings to benefit people, like a master, a friend, and a lover. It depends on the qualification of the recipient: the best, the average, and the worst" (*śāstraṁ puruṣahitam upadiśati. prabhuvad bandhuvat kāntāvac ca, uttamamadhyamādhamādhikārib hēdāt*). Cf. *Bhaktimandākinī*, 11: "There are all sorts of people in this world whose qualifications differ: some are bright, some are okay, and some are dim" (*iha khalu uttamamadhyamamandabhēdē nādhikāriṇō bahudhā bhavanti*).

[86] See Gary Tubb, "*Śāntarasa* in the *Mahābhārata*," *Journal of South Asian Literature* 20.1 (1985): 141–168.

> the Veda itself (*Chāndōgya Upaniṣad* 1.1.3): "He is the most *rasa*-esque of *rasas*." . . . Now even though this is the *rasa* that this scripture wishes to communicate, the outer *rasa* is also revealed here and there as a means to achieve it. And that is called *bhaktirasa* which is the tenth type. We consider *bhaktirasa* to be a category of *rasa* all on its own. Here it is predominant, while the other *rasa*s are subordinate to it.[87]

Over the next page, Rāghavānanda lists all the ways in which the classical *rasa*s are suggested (*vyañjita*) by the narrative and poetic features of every chapter in the first canto. On the one hand, this is an application of Ānandavardhana's theory of aesthetic unity to the *Bhāgavata*, a work similar in scope to the *Dhvanyālōka*'s examples of the *Mahābhārata* and *Rāmāyaṇa*. Rāghavānanda was influenced by Lakṣmīdhara in citing Vedic precedence and in identifying the inner Ātman, instead of external objects, as the foundation of *rasa*. What is patently new, however, is the concept of inner and outer meaning.[88] There is more than meets the eye here, clues to the lurking presence of Tantrism in the text. That it was Kr̥ṣṇa and not Rāma, the *Bhāgavata* and not the *Rāmāyaṇa*, that inspired Rāghavānanda was due to his imbrication in the Śaiva-Śākta world. We will look at the social dimensions of this further on, but in terms of intellectual history, it is possible to show that Rāghavānanda saw the *Bhāgavata* as an extension and perhaps culmination of his Tantric commitments. For he reproduced this exact concern with the aesthetic unity of the text, down to the hierarchy between primary and subordinate *rasa*s, at the end of his commentary on the Śākta poem *Laghustuti*. Aesthetic virtuosity makes the *Laghustuti* unimpeachable:

> In the Veda we hear of Śiva-Śakti, the ultimate reality-principle, as being the primary *rasa*, viz., "the most *rasa*-esque of *rasas*." That principle, together with the *rasa* of *bhakti* for it, in other words the experience of undivided joy, is suggested [*vyañjita*] throughout this *stōtra* as primary. Other

[87] *Kr̥ṣṇapadī*, 363: *iha dvividhō rasaḥ bāhyābhyantarabhēdāt. tatra brahmānandānubhavarasa āntaraḥ, tasya pratyaktattvāvalambanāt, 'rasaṁ hy ēvāyaṁ labdhvānandī bhavati' iti śrutēś ca. sa ēva ca mukhyaḥ, 'sa ēṣa rasānāṁ rasatamaḥ' iti śrutēr nityaniratiśayasukhāvahatvāc ca. . . . yady apy ayam ēva rasō'sminñ śāstrē sarvatra pratipipitsitaḥ, tathāpy ētatsiddhyaṅgatayā bāhyarasō'pi tatra tatra prakāśyatē. sa cēha bhaktirasasyāpi śr̥ṅgārādivad rasaviśēṣatvōrarīkaraṇād daśamavidhaḥ bhaktirasa ēva pradhānaḥ. taditarē tu tadapēkṣayā guṇabhūtāḥ.*

[88] On the use of the terminology of "inner" and "outer" meaning in seventeenth-century Kerala, and its possible connection with the Kūṭiyāṭṭam tradition of Sanskrit drama, see Andrew Ollett and Anand Venkatkrishnan, "Plumbing the Depths: Reading Bhavabhūti in Seventeenth-Century Kerala," *Asiatische Studien/Études Asiatiques* 76.3 (2022): 613–618.

> *rasas* have been expressed as subsidiary ornaments to it as and where appropriate. . . . Because it commences with *bhaktirasa* and concludes with *bhaktirasa*, we trust that the *stōtra* has that as its purport. Here and there we also find similes, as well as ornaments of sound like alliteration and tenderness. People in the know will also find it manifestly clear that it is a formally creative poem [*citrakāvya*], given its puzzling syntactic construals and hidden phoneme constructs. Therefore, because it has no aesthetic flaws [*nirdōṣa*], contains aesthetic virtues [*saguṇa*], and is full of *rasa* [*sarasa*], we maintain that everyone should recite it.[89]

Everything that has occupied Rāghavānanda in his survey of the *Bhāgavata* shows up here: the Vedic precedence, the centrality of *bhaktirasa*, the layers of aesthetic expression, and the proliferation of poetic devices. Moreover, the final three terms—*nirdōṣa*, *saguṇa*, and *sarasa*—are precisely the ones that appear at the end of his commentary on *Bhāgavata* 1.1.2, with the addition there of *sālaṅkāra*, hewing even more closely to the classic definition of good poetry in Bhōja's *Sarasvatīkaṇṭhābharaṇa* (1.2): to be free of flaws, to have excellent qualities, to be rich in aesthetic flavor, and to be decorated with poetic ornaments.[90] It was incumbent upon Rāghavānanda, in the end, to experience religious texts, and the truth of which they spoke, as literary. This was the way to hold earthly pleasure and transcendent joy together, more immediately than any one theological stance would offer. The *Bhāgavata* was the perfect candidate, and why not? Considering he spent much of his scholarly career reading the highlights of Sanskrit poetry, it was probably not subjective fancy that prompted Daniel H. H. Ingalls to call the *Bhāgavata*, especially its tenth book, "the most enchanting poem ever written."[91]

Rāghavānanda depicted the relationship between devotional and literary aesthetics with a flourish in his commentary on *Bhāgavata* 1.2.22, where he

[89] *Laghustuti*, 42: *"sa ēṣa rasānāṁ rasatama" iti mukhyarasatvēna śrutau śrutasya śivaśaktyātmakasya tattvasyākhaṇḍānandasaṁvidrūpasya tadbhaktirasasya ca sarvatrātra prādhānyēna vyañjitatvād anyēṣām api rasānāṁ yathāyōgam ētadaṅgatayālaṅkāratvēna vyañjitatvāc ca.... bhaktirasēnōpakramya tēnaivōpasaṁhārē tatraivāsya tātparyam iti ca pratyāyitaṁ bhavati. prathamaślokādiṣūpamālaṅkārō 'pi kvacit kvacid bhavati, anuprāsasaukumāryādayaḥ śabdālaṅkārāś ca bhavanti. gūḍhayōjanatvagūḍhavarṇatvādinā citrakāvyatā ca vispaṣṭā vipaścitām iti. tad ēvaṁ nirdōṣatvāt saguṇatvāt sarasatvāc ca sarvaiḥ paṭhanīyam ētad iti siddham.*

[90] *Kṛṣṇapadī*, 24: *nirdōṣatvasaguṇatvasālaṅkāratvasarasatvāni gamayati.* Cf. *The Saraswatī Kaṇṭhābharaṇa by Dhāreshvara Bhojadeva*, ed. Paṇḍit Kedārnāth Śarmā and Wāsudev Laxmaṇ Śāstrī Paṇśīkar (Bombay: Nirnaya Sagar, 1934), 2: *nirdōṣaṁ guṇavat kāvyaṁ alaṅkārair alaṅkṛtam rasānvitaṁ kaviḥ kurvan kīrtiṁ prītiṁ ca vindati.*

[91] Daniel H. H. Ingalls, "Foreword," in *Krishna: Myths and Rites*, ed. Milton Singer (Honolulu: East-West Center Press, 1966), vi.

compared achieving liberation to falling in love. It is possible to detect in this wedding of erotic and religious language something more than analogy, something like a tip of the hat to those in the know. For the sexual imagery sprinkled throughout this passage reflects not only the conventions of Sanskrit aesthetics but also the influence of the Kaula tradition, that most explicit fusion of sexuality and spirituality in Hindu Tantrism. Table 1.1 shows the processes side-by-side.[92]

On the face of it, we have a comparison between how the practice of *bhakti*, here portrayed in thoroughly Advaitic terms, eventuates in liberation, and how the quintessential lover in Sanskrit poetry and drama meets with his beloved. But the centrality of experience (*anubhava*), a term we have seen repeatedly in Rāghavānanda's writings, pushes us outside that frame to consider the influence of Śaiva nondualism.[93] The appeal to experience challenges the literary analogy as well. What begins as a description of love that conforms to Sanskrit aesthetic conventions, easily mapping onto as classic a tale as the story of Nala and Damayanti, quickly becomes more personal. The worldly

[92] *Kṛṣṇapadī*, 56–57: *tatra śravaṇakīrtanābhyāṁ tāvad bhagavata ānandānubhavaikarasavigrahatām asau pratipadyatē, śravaṇālōkanābhyām iva ramaṇīkumāraruciratarākāratāṁ kāmukaḥ. tataś ca yathāvagatavigrahē bhagavati samaṣṭyātmani vyaṣṭyātmani vā cirakālanirantaramanaḥpravartanātmakād dhyānāt tatsvābhāvyaṁ svayam aśnutē. yathāvagatarūpāyāṁ nāyikāyāṁ cirakālanirantaramanaḥpravartanāt tatsvābhāvyam iva kāmī. tataś cāsya bhagavati nityaniratiśayaprītirūpiṇī bhaktir āvirbhavati, kamitur iva kāminyāṁ paramā ratiḥ. tadanantaram ātmatattvāsaṅgātiśayāt tadvirōdhiṣu śabdādiviṣayēṣu naisargikō'pi kāmō nivartatē. aṅganāsaṅgātiśayāt tadvirōdhiṣu mātṛpitṛgurvādiṣv iva pūrvasiddhaḥ kāmukasya snēhātiśayaḥ. tathā ca śabdāditattvajijñāsāpraśamanād bāhyārthapāramārthikatāniścayalakṣaṇavirōdhyabhāvēna pratyaktattvaṁ brahmaiva pāramārthikaṁ vastu, tadanyad akhilaṁ tatsat tāsphūrtyadhīnasattāsphūrtikatvād anvayavyatirēkābhāvaparihārēṇa tasmin śuktau rūpyavad ajñair adhyārōpitam iti śāstrārthanirṇayō bhavati, mātrādiṣv āsthānivṛttivaśāt tatsānnidhyādirūpavirōdhyabhāvēna ramaṇasyēva yathēcchaṁ ramaṇīviharaṇam. evañ ca bāhyān śabdādīn avastutayā parityajya vastutattvē brahmaṇyēvāsya manō vilīyatē, svairaviharaṇavaśād ramaṇasya viṣayāntaram apahāya ramaṇyām ēva manōvilayavat. tataś cākhaṇḍānandānubhavātmakaṁ brahmātmabhēdēna yōginaḥ sākṣāt prakāśatē niratiśayasukham ivātmasaṁbhinnatayā bhōginaḥ. tadā vigaḷitasakalasāṁsārikaduḥkhatadupādhibandhō nirmuktanikhilasandēhaḥ kṛtakṛtyaś ca bhaktō bhavati. yathāpūrvanidhuvanasukhānubhavē mahatō duḥkhāt priyālabdhisandēhāc ca vinirmuktaḥ kṛtārthaś ca yōṣitsaṅgī bhavati, tadvad iti.*

[93] The dissertation on how *anubhava* enters the domain of classical Vēdānta has yet to be written, but we may at least make a note of its relative novelty. While some have argued that *anubhava* was used to refer to the experience of nonduality in Śaṅkara's own writings, its mention is admittedly scattered, equivocal, and inconclusive. Others say that this attribution was largely a result of modern scholarship on Śaṅkara. Neither party, however, considers the influence of Śaiva nondualism, where personal experience, whether of possession or of intuitive gnostic insight, held a more prominent place than anywhere else in Indian philosophy. On the debate about *anubhava* in Advaita Vēdānta, see Arvind Sharma, "Is Anubhava a Pramāṇa According to Śaṅkara?," *Philosophy East and West* 42.3 (1992): 517–526; Anantanand Rambachan, *Accomplishing the Accomplished: The Vedas as a Source of Valid Knowledge in Śaṅkara* (Honolulu: University of Hawaii Press, 1991), 1–14. On the scripturally determined rhetoric of experience in Tantric Śaivism, see Christopher D. Wallis, "To Enter, to Be Entered, to Merge: The Role of Religious Experience in the Traditions of Tantric Shaivism" (Ph.D. diss., University of California, Berkeley, 2014).

Table 1.1 *Kṛṣṇapadī* on *Bhāgavata* 1.2.22

Falling in Love with God	Falling in Love with a Woman
By hearing and singing the stories of God, one learns that God is the pure experience of ecstasy [*ānandānubhav-aikarasa*].	In the same way, a lover learns from laudatory accounts that his beloved is a sweet tender youth.
When he understands God to be like that, whether in the universal or particular, he himself comes to experience God's nature through meditation, a long and uninterrupted mental exercise.	In the same way, a lover experiences his beloved as he has previously understood her to be, by obsessing about her in his mind for a long time and without interruption.
Then manifests for him *bhakti*, in the form of permanent, extraordinary love for God.	In the same way, a lover comes to possess extreme attachment to his darling.
As a result of excessive attachment to the Ātman, his instinctive desire for anything contradictory to that, namely the objects of sense, fades away.	Just like a lover, who is head over heels for his woman, loses the love he used to have for his mother, father, teacher, and others who get in his way.
Once he is no longer interested in learning about material objects, and since there is no longer any basis for the contrary understanding that external objects are real, he understands the meaning of scripture: that the inner truth, Brahman, is the only reality; that all things seem to exist because of its existence; and that everything other than it has been superimposed by the ignorant, like seeing silver where there is a shell.	In the same way, the lover delights in his beloved as he pleases, because he is no longer in the proximity of people like his mother, for he no longer has any faith in such people.
Having cast aside external sense-objects as being unreal, his mind is dissolved in nothing but the true reality, Brahman.	In the same way, once he has abandoned everything else, a lover's heart dissolves in his beloved alone, because he is no longer restricted in his pleasure-seeking.
For the *yōgī*, Brahman, the experience of undivided joy [*akhaṇḍānandānubhava*], appears directly before him as nondifferent from himself.	As for the *bhōgī*, the man who continues to relish everyday pleasures, it appears distinct from his self, like an extraordinary joy.
Then the *bhakta*, one who is in love with God, becomes fulfilled, having been released of all doubts and stripped of all the sorrows of birth and death and their conditionings.	In the same way, the woman's lover becomes fulfilled, freed from sorrow and from the uncertainty of not reaching the beloved, in the unprecedented experience of sexual pleasure [*apūrvanidhuvanasukh-ānubhava*].

lover, like the ideal renunciate, leaves all attachments to family and friends; like the ideal *yōgī*, he dissolves himself in the other; and like the ideal devotee, he relishes the blissful experience of union. Even more telling is the juxtaposition of the *yōgī* and the *bhōgī*, the *bon vivant*, who has been mentioned more than once by both Pūrṇasarasvatī and Rāghavānanda. One is reminded of a similar juxtaposition in the *Kulārṇava Tantra* (2.23): "They say that if you're a *yōgī*, you can't be a *bhōgī*, and vice versa. That's why, my dear, the Kaula, comprised of *bhōga* and *yōga*, surpasses all."[94] If we were left with any doubt as to what constitutes *bhōga*, the final comparison embellishes the point in a way that leaves little to the imagination. The subtext of Rāghavānanda's language is that *bhakti* engenders a union that would be familiar to participants both in public religion, mediated by orthodox systems of philosophical theology, and in private esoteric practices, mediated by ritual initiation.

Pūrṇasarasvatī and Rāghavānanda weave together several strands of religion, philosophy, and literature in their commentaries. They juxtapose Vedic and non-Vedic scriptures, Śaiva and Vaiṣṇava theologies, classical and greater Advaita, the poetry of prayer and the poetry of literature, and *yōga* and *bhōga*. Having fun was serious business for these two. *Bhakti*, being in love with God, was the bridge between the worldly pleasures of literature and the ascetic rigors of philosophy, between *bhukti* and *mukti*. A single consonant can make all the difference. How their example makes us reconsider the *Bhāgavata* as an exclusively Vaiṣṇava text is the least of the historical questions they raise. What was the social and political context in which such convergences seemed not only possible but necessary? What were the institutional networks that facilitated this distinctive form of thinking? How can we trace that world in the text? Is a social and cultural history of intellectual life even possible?

Caste, Religion, and the Social in Premodern Kerala

For Pūrṇasarasvatī and Rāghavānanda, the answer to the last question is partially yes. We can reconstruct two primary contexts for their intellectual production: the existence of local Advaita Vēdānta monasteries and the sociopolitical influence of Śākta religion in medieval Kerala.[95]

[94] *Kulārṇava Tantra*, ed. Tārānātha Vidyāratna (Delhi: Motilal Banarsidass, 1965), 146.
[95] See Olga Nowicka, "Local Advaita Vēdānta Monastic Tradition in Kerala: Locating, Mapping, Networking," *The Polish Journal of the Arts and Culture* 1 (2019): 27–51.

General hagiographies of the Advaita philosopher Śaṅkara credit him with establishing four monastic centers in different corners of the Indian subcontinent. According to local accounts in Kerala, however, Śaṅkara founded all four monasteries in a single city, Tr̥śśūr (Skt. Vr̥ṣapurī). These institutions were the Northern Monastery (Vaṭakke Maṭham), the Middle Monastery (Naṭuvil Maṭham), the Between Monastery (Iṭayil Maṭham), and the Southern Monastery (Tekkē Maṭham). Shortly after establishing these centers, Śaṅkara attained liberation at the adjacent Śaiva Vaṭakkunāthan temple. Three of the four monasteries survive in the city today. According to the Nampūtiri Brahmins who populate the institution, renunciation is possible only for Nampūtiris from a few families, all Vaiṣṇava in their orientation.[96] Most interesting for our purposes is the Vaṭakke Maṭham. Though transformed into a school for Vedic learning in the seventeenth century, its ascetic lineage is said to continue in northern Kerala, in the Iṭanīr Maṭham in the Kasaragod district, close to the Karnataka border. The temple of both the Iṭanīr and Vaṭakke Maṭham is dedicated to two deities: Dakṣiṇāmūrti and Gōpālakr̥ṣṇa. The Iṭanīr Maṭham is said to have its own branch in Taḷipparamba in the nearby Kaṇṇūr district to the southeast, in close proximity to the Tr̥ccambaram Kr̥ṣṇa temple. The head of the Iṭanīr Maṭham, who is not a Nampūtiri but a Śīvaḷḷi Brahmin from Karnataka, makes the journey to the Taḷipparamba branch once a year during the festival held at the Tr̥ccambaram temple.[97]

It starts to become clear how the itinerary of our Malayali monks mapped onto these institutional networks. Pūrṇasarasvatī wrote his stage-play, the *Kamalinīrājahaṁsa*, to be performed during the spring festival at the Vaṭakkunāthan temple in Tr̥śśūr.[98] He depicted his guru simultaneously as Dakṣiṇāmūrti and as Kr̥ṣṇa, the deities of the Vaṭakke and Iṭanīr monasteries and, not incidentally, the same two figures carved into the granite altar of the Rājarājēśvaran temple in Taḷipparamba. Finally, he ensured that his goose-messenger would linger over the Tr̥ccambaram Kr̥ṣṇa temple. Rāghavānanda was probably born near Tirunāvāya in the Malabar region (in his own words, "on the banks of the Nilā River"), home to a famous Kr̥ṣṇa temple and a Śrīvaiṣṇava pilgrimage spot. However, his education took him along the same route as Pūrṇasarasvatī: his guru, Kr̥ṣṇānanda, held classes near the Vaṭakkunāthan temple and spent his final days at the Tr̥ccambaram

[96] Nowicka, "Local Advaita Vēdānta Monastic Tradition," 29, 33.
[97] Nowicka, "Local Advaita Vēdānta Monastic Tradition," 35–37.
[98] *Kamalinīrājahaṁsa*, 2.

temple.[99] The cultural prominence of each of these temples and of the Nilā River basin by the fifteenth century is evident from the *Kōkilasandēśa* by Uddaṇḍa Śāstrī,[100] a Tamil Brahmin transplant to Kerala who is said to have received scholarly recognition at the Rājarājēśvaran temple. All of these people were Brahmin men steeped in the propagation of Brahmanical systems of knowledge. Nevertheless, the institutions they inhabited had complex relationships with the caste-configured religious order of medieval Kerala, imbued as it was with varieties of local and universal Tantrism.

The subject of caste crops up in curious ways in legends about Rāghavānanda. For example, he received the title of *atyāśramī*, one who disregards the boundaries of *varṇāśramadharma*, as a pejorative nickname from other Brahmins who were upset that he would accept food from anyone regardless of caste. The term *atyāśramī* was used more generally to refer to a renunciant who had crossed beyond the normative strictures of Brahmanical society.[101] But the term in its original usage bore close association with a group of Atimārga Pāśupatas, Śaiva Brahmin ascetics whose search for liberation prompted them to engage in severe bodily mortification and antisocial behavior.[102] The Atimārga was theoretically confined to Brahmins in texts like the *Pāśupata Sūtra*, even as its practices, such as those of the Lākula sect, became increasingly heterodox, including "wandering, carrying a skull-topped staff (*khaṭvāṅga*), skull begging bowl, a garland of human bone, and covered in ashes, with matted hair or shaven head in imitation of their Lord Rudra."[103] Cremation-ground asceticism of the Pāśupata variety was closely connected with non-Vedic, non-Brahmin possession cults and, its appropriation by Śaiva Brahmins notwithstanding, would continue to feature in subaltern religious life in parallel with the high textual culture of Tantric Śaivism.[104] This was nowhere more evident than in Kerala. Other legends say that Rāghavānanda was later known as the fearsome and enigmatic *yōgī* Śivāṅṅaḷ, "a name that no one uttered aloud

[99] Kunjunni Raja, *The Contribution of Kerala to Sanskrit Literature*, 7.

[100] See Rajendran Chettiarthodi, "A Scholar Poet from the Neighbouring Land: Uddaṇḍa Śāstrin's Perceptions of Kerala," *Cracow Indological Studies* 22.1 (2020): 73–94.

[101] Patrick Olivelle, *The Āśrama System: The History and Hermeneutics of a Religious Institution* (New York; Oxford: Oxford University Press, 1993), 222–234.

[102] Elaine Fisher, "Public Philology: Text Criticism and the Sectarianization of Hinduism in Early Modern South India," *South Asian History and Culture* 6.1 (2015): 57.

[103] Gavin Flood, "Śaiva and Tantric Religion," in *An Introduction to Hinduism*, ed. Gavin Flood (Cambridge: Cambridge University Press, 1996), 157.

[104] On the mutual flow of ideas about spirit possession between educated elites and popular cultures in Kerala, see Fred Smith, *The Self Possessed: Deity and Spirit Possession in South Asian Literature and Civilization* (New York: Columbia University Press, 2006), 544–578.

or used even in jest."[105] Śivāṅṅaḷ occasionally intervened in disputes between fractious Brahmins in Taḷipparamba but preferred to live alone in the jungle. After being cursed with leprosy due to his sexual assault of a Dalit woman, the *yōgī* sought relief by meditating beneath a tree adjacent to the Tr̥ccambaram temple, only to be pelted by its fruits.[106] In another story, Rāghavānanda's *atyāśramī* status and appearance seems to have confused orthodox Nampūtiri Brahmins. Upon a visit to the Kūṭallūr Māna, a center of Sanskrit learning, Rāghavānanda asked the scholars there for a copy of Śrīdhara's commentary on the *Bhāgavata*, only to be turned away on the basis that he was an outcaste (*avarṇa*).[107] Stung by this rejection, he wrote his own commentary, which would become the *Kr̥ṣṇapadī*.[108] This case of "mistaken" identity points not so much to Rāghavānanda's ambiguous caste status as it does to the status of caste itself in a world where Brahmin, martial/royal, and lower castes together participated in a complex, connected, and differentiated network of social life, all within the scope of Tantric religion.[109]

This brings us to the second context for knowledge production, the wide social significance of Śāktism in the political and religious culture of medieval Kerala. The textually trained anthropologist Rich Freeman has explored how the various Śākta traditions that flourished in Kerala, such as the Trika, the Kubjikā, and the Krama, exhibited influence both on and from their regional, vernacular contexts. He situates the powerful and popular Śākta complex, one that cut across the caste-configured religious order, at the nexus of local possession cults, temple networks, patronage from major royals and minor chieftains, and the sexual politics of Brahmin liaisons with martial and other lower-caste consorts. Freeman primarily focuses on the institutions of northern Kerala, that is, Malabar, under the purview of the Kōlattiri *rājas*,

[105] Vāṇidās Eḷayāvūr, *Vaṭakkan Aitihyamāla* (Kottayam: Current Books, 1996), 120: *śivāṅṅaḷ—ennŭ āruṁ annŭ uccattil paṟayāṟilla. kaḷiyāyi ā padaṁ upayōgikkāṟilla.*

[106] Vanidas Elayavoor, *Lore and Legends of North Malabar: Selections from the Vadakkan Aitihyamala*, trans. Ashvin Kumar (Kottayam: DC Books, 2016), 368–372. This shocking account of sexual violence and retribution likely draws upon a memory of Tantric conjugality, which involves sexual rituals with low-caste women but explicitly prohibits abuse. See Csaba Kiss, "A Sexual Ritual with Māyā in *Matsyendrasaṁhitā*," in *Śaivism in the Tantric Traditions: Essays in Honor of Alexis G. J. S. Sanderson*, ed. Dominic Goodall et al. (Leiden; Boston: Brill, 2020), 426–450.

[107] That the practice of excluding all non-Brahmins, including wealthy Nairs, from the Kūṭallūr Māna continued well into the twentieth century is attested by Kalāmaṇḍalam Gōpi, an exponent of the Kerala style of dance-drama known as *kathakaḷi*, who was nevertheless allowed to train in the art form at this Nampūtiri stronghold. See "Koodallur Mana, Childhood Memories," YouTube, accessed August 10, 2021, https://www.youtube.com/watch?v=yAq8RzCvPlk.

[108] For the stories about Rāghavananda the *atyāśramī*, see Rama Varma, "Introduction," in *Sreemad Bhagavatam 10th Skandha Part I, with the Commentary of Raghavananda Muni*, ed. M. B. Sankaranarayana Sastri (Tripunithura: Sanskrit College Committee, 1949), i–ii.

[109] Freeman, "Śāktism, Polity and Society in Medieval Malabar," 147.

who were probably Rāghavānanda's patrons. He demonstrates that narratives of the goddess in Sanskrit *purāṇas* and in Malayalam folk performances share in incorporating Śākta esoterica—especially concerning the wild, blood-drinking, antinomian, violent, and powerful Bhadrakāḷī—into the architectural programs and oral liturgies of the temple cult. While discussing the Teyyam, or the dance of ritualized spirit-possession, pertaining to the goddess at the temple of Mannampuṟattu Kāvu along the Malabar coast, Freeman notes the imbrication of non-Brahmin folk practices and Sanskrit rites under the rubric of Śākta Tantrism and royal patronage: "The spirit-possessed Teyyams have offerings of huge *kalaśams* (pots) of toddy and cock-sacrifices offered to them outside the temple, while traditionally, the Cāmuṇḍā inside had blood-sacrifice and liquor offerings, as well. So as a simultaneous orchestration what we see, both at Mannampuṟattu Kāvu, and the Kōlattiri's royal shrines (and the others through northern Malabar), is an inner temple-cult of Śākta, Sanskritic rites, and an outer cult of possessed folk-worship coordinating the martial and lower castes all under royal patronage, and framed in local, historical versions of Kerala-wide Puranic charters of conquest and divinely sanctioned rule."[110]

The Mannampuṟattu Kāvu is of particular interest to us because according to local memory, the *Laghustuti* was composed there by one Laghu Bhaṭṭāraka, who belonged to the Piṭārar caste of Śākta ritual officiants.[111] The Piṭārars were like Nampūtiri Brahmins in that they were invested with sacred threads, studied and taught Sanskrit systems of knowledge, and even maintained sexual relationships with temple-servant castes. They were, however, avowedly Śākta in conducting the worship of the goddess with flesh, liquor, and similar offerings. The Śākta installation, liturgy, and priesthood of the Mannampuṟattu Kāvu was replicated in several other temples patronized by the Kōlattiris, including the Māṭāyi Kāvu a little further south. The Bhadrakāḷī of the Māṭāyi Kāvu also features in the outer compound of the Rājarājeśvaran temple in Taḷipparamba, where we began this chapter.[112] Most versions of Bhadrakāḷī's story in Kerala involve her domestication into the outer precincts of a temple. Crazed with blood-lust after killing the

[110] Freeman, "Śāktism, Polity and Society in Medieval Malabar," 155.

[111] Freeman, "Śāktism, Polity and Society in Medieval Malabar," 155–156. "Piṭārar, as a contemporary caste-title for a Śākta officiant no doubt derived from Bhaṭṭāra(ka), as a title for Śaiva officiants, but was also closely associated with the feminine Bhaṭṭāri(kā), as a term for the Śākta or assimilated folk-goddesses whom they served, convergent with the pan–South Indian Piṭāri and her cult."

[112] S. Jayashanker, "Śree Raajaraajeśwara Temple, Thaḷipparamba," in *Temples of Kaṇṇoor District* (Delhi: Controller of Publications, 2001), 134.

demon Dāruka, she advances to attack the temple itself, only to be pacified by Brahmins and temple servants.[113] But in Taḷipparamba, the peace did not last long. Legend has it that, frustrated with the lack of blood sacrifice, she fled the temple to live on her own in Māṭāyi. She is still periodically delivered the evening *naivēdyam*, or leftover offerings, from the Rājarājeśvaran temple, but probably finds it unappetizing.

This latter twist to the story gestures toward the eventual marginalization of Śākta teaching and practice by the hegemony of Brahmanical orthopraxy.[114] But in the time of our scholars, Brahmin attention to the varieties of Śākta religion was alert, if appropriative. Rāghavānanda's commentary on the *Laghustuti* takes on a new sheen in light of the social history of Śāktism in medieval Kerala. And it returns us to those stories about his mistreatment at the hands of orthodox Nampūtiris, who denied him access to scholastic texts for appearing to them like an untouchable, and who called him *atyāśramī* in order to denigrate his freewheeling disregard for caste boundaries. Could these stories be directing us toward the actual history of social and political contestation between transgressive Śākta *yōgī*s and locally established Brahmins of the Malabar region? Freeman shows that certain classes of Brahmins actually patronized Teyyam performances, such as the liturgy of Poṭṭan, an "untouchable tantric gnostic" who humbles Śaṅkarācārya by turning his Advaita language against him.[115] Some Teyyam liturgies also told of powerful Śākta householder *yōgī*s called Gurukkaḷ, themselves often drawn from lower castes, who moved south into Malabar from Karnataka and Tamil Nadu.[116] These *yōgī*s belonged to esoteric cults that worshiped the fierce Bhairava, cured Kōlattiri kings with blood rites, and courted the ire of the region's Brahmins.[117] Competition between all these parties for royal patronage prompted the Malabar rulers to endow both

[113] Freeman, "Śāktism, Polity and Society in Medieval Malabar," 153. "We could hardly ask for a clearer set of parallels to the ambivalent relations of martial servitude, connubium, and hybridly popular rituals by which, from the Brahman perspective, the dangerously violent and impure, yet necessary, matrilineal military castes were incorporated in the temple cult under the person of their goddess."

[114] Freeman, "Śāktism, Polity and Society in Medieval Malabar," 161.

[115] Rich Freeman, "Untouchable Bodies of Knowledge in the Spirit Possession of Malabar," in *Images of the Body in India*, ed. Axel Michaels and Christoph Wulf (New Delhi: Routledge, 2011), 130–138. Cf. Abraham Ayrookuzhiel, "Chinna Pulayan: The Dalit Teacher of Sankaracharya," in *The Emerging Dalit Identity: The Re-assertion of the Subalterns*, ed. Walter Fernandes (New Delhi: Indian Social Institute, 1996), 63–80.

[116] For local tales about individual Gurukkaḷ, see Elayavoor, *Lore and Legends of North Malabar*, 302–308 (Kūṭan Gurunāthan), 309–311 (Paliyēri Eḻuttaccan), 380–382 (Maṇakkāṭan Gurukkaḷ).

[117] Freeman, "Śāktism, Polity and Society in Medieval Malabar," 157–160.

Smārta and Śākta temples, and explains some of the curious convergences between them. Freeman concludes, "[O]n both the domestic front, as well as in public fora, the Śaiva-Śākta mendicants and lineages that entered South India posed considerable challenges to the region's Brahmans. The latter met these challenges in the texts and practices we find today. . . . The ultimate triumph of an (admittedly transformed) Smārta orthodoxy further explains the survival of much of the original impetus and content of Śāktism in the folk-religion of Malabar."[118]

We can see traces of this tension in the institutional histories reconstructed above. The Vaṭakke Maṭham's sudden transformation from an Advaita monastery with ties to secular literary culture and Śaiva-Śākta theology to a Vedic school for Nampūtiri Brahmins only may have been a reactionary response to the combination of elite and popular thought and practice. Legend has it that the Vaṭakke Maṭham was originally headed by a Śīvaḻḻi Brahmin, but due to caste conflict with the Nampūtiri heads of the other Tr̥śśūr monasteries, he left for Malabar and established the Iṭanīr Maṭham at the request of a local pastoral community.[119] As for parallels to the narrative of *yōgī*s moving south, Rāghavānanda's own teacher, Kr̥ṣṇānanda, roamed into Kerala on pilgrimage from the mysterious city of Nāgapura, named after the king of serpents, Śēṣa, who also incarnated as the grammarian Patañjali.[120] Where should we place Pūrṇasarasvatī and Rāghavānanda along this spectrum? Did their intellectual attempts to effect a rapprochement between Brahmanical and Śākta Advaita, between Śaiva and Vaiṣṇava theology, and between worldly pleasure and ascetic philosophy refract this broader social struggle between multiple orthodoxies? Were they aware—indeed, were they a product—of the complex caste configurations that characterized these interesting times?

For an intellectual historian, answering in the affirmative would require that our subjects have made these issues textually explicit. But Sanskrit commentators held their cards close and seldom referred to the world outside the text except as examples. This means we frequently grasp at hints, traces, and glimpses. While one is loath to build arguments from near silence, I have suggested that this form of subtextual reading is a virtue. For instance, anxieties about caste recur now and again in Rāghavānanda's writing,

118 Freeman, "Śāktism, Polity and Society in Medieval Malabar," 167.
119 Nowicka, "Local Advaita Vēdānta Monastic Tradition in Kerala," 36.
120 Kunjunni Raja, *The Contribution of Kerala to Sanskrit Literature*, 7, n. 34.

and not always in the same tone. In *Bhāgavata* 1.1.8, the sages of the Naimiṣa Forest casually remark that "gurus even teach secrets to devoted students." Rāghavānanda takes this, quite unprompted, as a reference to the addressee, Sūta, who narrates the frame story: "How would the sages have revealed the truth to me, Sūta, who am of mixed 'against-the-grain' parentage and not a renunciant? Well, if a devoted student has the desire to know, gurus explain even hidden meanings in clear fashion. The primary cause here is devotion to the teacher and the desire to know, not belonging to the highest caste or stage of life."[121] Similarly, in the *Tātparyadīpikā*, Rāghavānanda insists that lovers of God should only take recourse to the religion of love and not obey the strictures of *varṇāśrama dharma*, the social and ethical norms appropriate to one's caste and stage of life:

> If you think that someone who desires *bhakti* should not abandon his *varṇāśrama dharma*, and instead continue to practice it, then that is idiotic. All the scriptures you have mobilized to that effect only concern external practices. But the simple phrase "Abandon your own *dharma* and worship God's lotus feet" (*Bhāgavata* 1.5.17) is a commandment to take up *bhakti*'s inner workings. . . .
>
> People who identify with *varṇa* and *āśrama* simply cannot be lovers of God. As the *Bhāgavata* (11.2.51) says: "The beloved of God is one who has no sense of 'I' with respect to his body, as a result of his birth, deeds, caste, or stage of life." You can't say that such a statement only means that one should only let go of *identification* with *varṇa* and *āśrama*, but not its obligations and signs. For that would conflict with what we find elsewhere in the same text: "Whether one is detached, established in knowledge, or loves me without relying on anyone else, one should give up *āśramas* and their external trappings, and roam about freely, not subject to commands" (*Bhāgavata* 11.13.28).[122]

[121] *Kṛṣṇapadī*, 35: *nanu mama vilōmajātēr asamprāptōttamāśramasya [em. *āśrayasya] ca munayas tattvaṁ kathaṁ prakāśayēyur iti tad āha—snigdhasya bhaktasya śiṣyasya jijñāsōḥ guravaḥ guhyō gōpanīyam apy artham uta spaṣṭaṁ brūyuḥ. ācāryabhaktatvaṁ jijñāsutvañ ca param atra kāraṇam, na mukhyavarṇāśramitvādiḥ.*

[122] *Tātparyadīpikā*, 7, 9: *tasmāt bhaktikāmēna varṇāśramadharmō na tyājyaḥ pratyutānuṣṭhēya ēva iti cēt—tan mandam. uktavacanānāṁ bahiraṅgasādhanatatparatvāt "tyaktvā svadharmaṁ caraṇāmbujaṁ harēr bhajann" iti vākyasya tadantaraṅgasādhanavidhāyakatvāc ca. . . . . varṇāśramābhimāninānāṁ bhaktatvāsampratipattēḥ. tathā ca purāṇōpaniṣat—"na yasya janmakarmabhyāṁ na varṇāśramajātibhiḥ sajjatē'smin ahaṁbhāvō dēhē vai sa harēḥ priyaḥ" iti. na ca tatra varṇāśramābhimānatyāga ēva bhaktasyōktō na tatkarmaliṅgatyāga iti vācyam. "jñānaniṣṭhō viraktō vā madbhaktō vā'napēkṣakaḥ saliṅgān āśramāṁs tyaktvā carēd avidhigōcaraḥ" iti vākyāntaravirōdhāt.*

Like his comments on *Bhāgavata* 1.2.22, we find an equivalence between the passionate lover, whose beloved in this case is God, and the unattached *yōgī* or renunciant, who is beyond the pale of *varṇāśrama*.[123] Rāghavānanda draws a distinction between the "external trappings" of *varṇāśrama dharma* and the "inner workings" of *bhakti*. But his endorsement was not wholesale. Commenting on *Bhāgavata* 1.1.14, which says that singing God's name will instantly bestow liberation, Rāghavānanda is more circumspect:

> You might say that, in everyday life, one does not see people of low birth being delivered from *saṁsāra* by reciting the name of God just once. But what is meant here is that the name leads to liberation by means of getting rid of sins. Now we cannot see that process, so even if previous and future sins are wiped out, the residue of karma being worked out from previous lives prompts one to act just as before until the body dies. Even so, you might reply, repeating the name cannot lead to liberation in this very life for such people, because they cannot study Vēdānta. True, but it allows them to be born in an (upper-caste) family that is eligible to do so and thereupon leads to liberation....
>
> As for those who say that singing the name directly leads to liberation, they are in contradiction with scriptural teachings that say that knowledge alone leads to the absolute. Reciting the name does not give rise to knowledge, for that would contradict injunctions that say "listening," etc. are the means to knowledge. So we're the ones who have it right.[124]

Here Rāghavānanda plays the role of the classical Advaita Vēdāntin, for whom knowledge derived from hearing the Upaniṣads is the only means to liberation. Hearing the Upaniṣads, however, is restricted to upper castes eligible for Vedic learning. Practices like singing the name of God, then, work for non-upper castes only in stages: first they get rid of sins, then they allow one to be reborn in an upper-caste family and then to study Vēdānta. The

123 Rāghavānanda would speak of the true renunciant as an *ativarṇāśramī*, perhaps where he got his nickname. See *Kṛṣṇapadī*, 334–337. Cf. Olivelle, *The Āśrama System*, 227–228.

124 *Kṛṣṇapadī*, 37: *nanu pāpayōnīnām api sakṛnnāmōccāraṇāt saṁsāranivṛttir ity anubhavaviruddham iti cēn na; pāpōpaśamadvārēṇaivātra nāmnō muktihētutvasya vivakṣitatvāt, pāpōpaśāntēś cāpratyakṣatvāt pūrvōttarapāpānām asattvē'pi prārabdhakarmaśēṣavaśād ādēhapātaṁ pūrvavadācaraṇōpapattēś ca. tathāpi tasmin janmany ēva na muktir vēdāntaśravaṇābhāvād iti cēt satyam, tathāpi janmāntarē tadanuṣṭhānayōgyakulajatvēna saṁbhavaty ēvāsya muktir ity avirōdhaḥ . . . yē punar nāmasaṅkīrtanasya sākṣān mōkṣahētutvam āhuḥ, tēṣāṁ jñānād ēva kaivalyam ityādiśāstravirōdhō vācyaḥ. na ca nāmōccārāj jñānōtpattiḥ, śravaṇādīnāṁ tatsādhanatvavidhivirōdhāt. atō'smad abhihitaiva rītiḥ.*

eradication of sins does not fundamentally change one's behavior. Like student debt, the deeds of the past carry over for lifetimes and must work themselves out in everyday life. This is far from the radical rejection of *varṇāśrama* we have seen in previous passages.[125] The privileging of unbridled passion over Brahmanical norms was, of course, a common motif of *bhakti*. The extent to which this exhortation was rhetorical rather than real—as if the two were necessarily opposed—has occupied much writing on *bhakti*, in order to judge whether it is a language of protest or a retrenchment of power.[126] What we find here instead could be a third angle, an allusion to the ambivalent role of caste in Tantric Śaivism.[127] On the one hand, scriptural texts and postscriptural exegetes exposed the artificiality of caste distinctions; on the other hand, initiates into the religion were expected to maintain outward observances appropriate to their caste, while engaging in transgressive practices in secret. Thus we have a famous dictum in the Pratyabhijñā tradition: "internally a Kaula, externally a Śaiva, and in social practice a follower of the Veda."[128] This would certainly describe Rāghavānanda. His *Laghustuti* commentary demonstrates his familiarity with Kaula teaching. His references to Pratyabhijñā thinkers like Utpaladēva show his Śaiva credentials. And his knowledge of Vēdānta and Brahmin supremacy clinches his Vedic education. Interestingly, the redaction of this verse in the *Kulārṇava Tantra*

[125] Caste hierarchy is reinforced in even starker terms in Rāghavānanda's commentary on *Bhāgavata* 1.6.25, where he wonders, not without some frustration, why the Veda would set strict caste-bound customs and practices if the uneducated son of a working single mother (i.e., Nārada) could attain liberation in this lifetime. See *Kṛṣṇapadī*, 130.

[126] Cf. John Stratton Hawley, Christian Lee Novetzke, and Swapna Sharma, eds., *Bhakti and Power: Debating India's Religion of the Heart* (Seattle: University of Washington Press, 2019). For the Marxist view that temple-centered *bhakti* was employed by ruling castes and classes in order to achieve both ideological and socioeconomic domination, see Kesavan Veluthat, "Religious Symbols in Political Legitimation: The Case of Early Medieval South India," *Social Scientist* 21.1–2 (1993): 23–33. Cf. Kesavan Veluthat, "Making the Best of a Bad Bargain: The Brighter Side of Kaliyuga," *Indian Historical Review* 41.2 (2014): 173–184. On the limits of this historiographical framework, see Jason Schwartz, "Ending the Śaiva Age: The Rise of the Brāhmaṇa Legalist and the Universalization of Hindu *Dharma*" (Ph.D. diss., University of California, Santa Barbara, 2023), 101–102, n. 51.

[127] See Alexis Sanderson, "The Śaiva Age: The Rise and Dominance of Śaivism during the Early Medieval Period," in *Genesis and Development of Tantrism*, ed. Shingo Einoo (Tokyo: Institute of Oriental Culture, University of Tokyo, 2009), 292–297; Alexis Sanderson, "How Public Was Śaivism?," 34–36, 39–41; Csaba Kiss, "The Bhasmāṅkura in Śaiva Texts," 83–105; Nina Mirnig, "'Rudras on Earth' on the Eve of the Tantric Age: The *Śivadharmaśāstra* and the Making of Śaiva Lay and Initiatory Communities," 471–510, all in *Tantric Communities in Context*, ed. Nina Mirnig, Marion Rastelli, and Vincent Eltschinger (Vienna: Austrian Academy of Sciences, 2019); John Nemec, "Innovation and Social Change in the Vale of Kashmir," in Goodall et al., *Śaivism in the Tantric Traditions*, 299–305.

[128] Nemec, "Innovation and Social Change in the Vale of Kashmir," 292. Cf. Alexis Sanderson, "Tolerance, Exclusivity, Inclusivity, and Persecution in Indian Religion during the Early Medieval Period," in *In Honoris Causa: Essays in Honour of Aveek Sarkar*, ed. John Makinson (London: Allen Lane, 2015), 178.

(11.83b) replaces "a follower of the Veda in social practice" with "Vaiṣṇava when among people" (*janamadhyē tu vaiṣṇavaḥ*). Such a person, in other words, moved about in the world as if they were a Vaiṣṇava but continued Śākta practices in secret. Rāghavānanda may have had something of the sort in mind when he described Śuka, the primary narrator of the *Bhāgavata*, as "woke" (*unnidra*), following *Bhāgavata* 1.4.4: "He has woken up from a false dream, namely the illusions of caste, class, life-stage, family, lineage, and name. For that very reason he 'walks about as if foolish' among people, while 'concealed' in the trappings of *varṇa* and *āśrama*."[129]

Perhaps the *Bhāgavata* was the site where Śaiva, Śākta, and Vaiṣṇava came together in Kerala, a textual site of public reckoning with private religion. Rāghavānanda's Vaiṣṇava commentaries had much wider circulation than the *Laghustuti* commentary, suggesting that it was intended for privileged confidantes aware of its antinomian content. Pūrṇasarasvatī was less explicit but more playful, toeing the line between "fun and freedom." If we can take anything from the series of winks and nudges scattered throughout the commentaries of these Brahmin scholars, it is a more provocative understanding of how the cross-caste socioreligious networks of medieval Kerala impacted writing in the most elite exegetical registers.

The *bhakti* Network

Neither Pūrṇasarasvatī's nor Rāghavānanda's writings circulated outside Kerala, and no other Śaivas seem to have taken up the *Bhāgavata* cause. However, the provinciality of this mode of engagement with the *Bhāgavata* is a virtue and not a flaw, for the point of alternative or minority histories is to show that the history we narrate is not nearly as comprehensive as it claims. Nevertheless, there are interesting reverberations of this local tradition in the subcontinent at large. First, Pūrṇasarasvatī and Rāghavānanda did not emerge from or write into a vacuum, least of all in the rich multilingual literary world of premodern Kerala. On the vernacular side, the poet Ceṟuśśēri composed his *Kṛṣṇagāthā* in the fifteenth century, "the most extreme example of the medium of Malayalam and the poetics of Sanskrit

[129] *Kṛṣṇapadī*, 85: *jātivarṇāśramakulagōtranāmabhrāntilakṣaṇamāyāsvapnād utthita ata ēva gūḍhaḥ gṛhītavarṇāśramaliṅgaḥ tēna mūḍha iva ajña iva janānām īyate gamyatē.*

cohabiting the same genre."[130] The *Kṛṣṇagāthā* was ostensibly an adaptation of the *Bhāgavata* but included the idioms and themes of Malayalam courtesan literature, fusing *bhakti* with a secular eroticism. The complex social context of *bhakti* literature in Kerala, expressed differently across and between caste communities and linguistic registers, would continue into the sixteenth century and beyond.

Consider Pūntānam Nampūtiri, a Brahmin who translated the popular Sanskrit *stōtra Kṛṣṇakarṇāmṛta* into Malayalam at the behest of his non-Brahmin friend, and whose *Jñānappāna* was "an independent treatise that casts an advaita and bhakti fusion into the simple song-form of the *pāna* chant."[131] Or take Pūntānam's contemporary Tuñcattu Eḻuttaccan, a low-caste poet and scholar who lived in Tīrūr, close to Rāghavānanda's birthplace, and composed the *Harināmakīrtanam*, a similar fusion that simplified Vēdānta for a regional audience, an incipient nonbourgeois Hinduism, if you will.[132] No doubt it was works such as these that set the stage for other versions of the *Bhāgavata* in Kerala, most recognizable among which was the Sanskrit *Nārāyaṇīyaṃ* by Mēlputtūr Nārāyaṇa Bhaṭṭatiri in the late sixteenth century.[133]

It was only around the sixteenth century, and largely under the Mughal aegis, that the *Bhāgavata* became instrumental in the formation of Kṛṣṇa-centered religious communities in northern India, specifically the Vallabha Sampradāya and the Gauḍīya Vaiṣṇavas. Inspired by the charismatic Bengali saint Caitanya Mahāprabhu, several Gauḍīya Vaiṣṇavas, led by Rūpa Gosvāmī and his nephew Jīva Gōsvāmī, provided a sophisticated theologico-aesthetic framework for Caitanya's ecstatic proclamations and practices. As they moved westward, they also fashioned the region of Braj as a sacred landscape, where Kṛṣṇa's fabled exploits in the *Bhāgavata* were said to have taken place.[134] The Vallabha Sampradāya coalesced under the guidance of

[130] Rich Freeman, "Genre and Society: The Literary Culture of Premodern Kerala," in *Literary Cultures in History: Reconstructions from South Asia*, ed. Sheldon Pollock (Berkeley: University of California Press, 2003), 469.

[131] Freeman, "Genre and Society," 483–484.

[132] Cf. Brian Hatcher, *Bourgeois Hinduism, or the Faith of the Modern Vedantists: Rare Discourses from Early Colonial Bengal* (Oxford: Oxford University Press, 2008).

[133] Nārāyaṇa Bhaṭṭatiri's grammar teacher, Acyuta Piṣāraṭi, belonged to a non-Brahmin temple-servant caste that was highly learned in Sanskrit. The name Piṣāraṭi probably derived from the Piṭārar caste of Śākta officiants discussed earlier. See Freeman, "Śāktism, Polity and Society in Medieval Malabar," 156–157. Cf. Kunjunni Raja, *The Contribution of Kerala to Sanskrit Literature*, 122–125.

[134] Barbara Holdrege, *Bhakti and Embodiment: Fashioning Divine Bodies and Devotional Bodies in Kṛṣṇa Bhakti* (London: Routledge, 2015), 228–270.

Vallabhācārya (fifteenth century), who wrote the *Subōdhinī* commentary on the *Bhāgavata*, and his son Viṭṭhalnāth. Their community, which spread over northern and western India, would come to be called the Puṣṭi Mārga, a sect of Kṛṣṇa *bhakti* patronized by a variety of wealthy royals and laypeople well into the twentieth century.[135] The followers of Vallabha and Caitanya were perhaps most responsible for mobilizing the *Bhāgavata* to serve the exegetical purposes of clearly bounded Vaiṣṇava religious communities.

But just how Vaiṣṇava were the influences upon these Vaiṣṇava communities? Our study of the Śaiva *Bhāgavata* in Kerala reveals affinities between this local history and the more well-known trajectory of the *Bhāgavata* in northern India. One of the most popular *stōtra* composers in Kerala at the nexus of Śaivism, Vaiṣṇavism, and Advaita Vēdānta was the fourteenth-century poet Līlāśuka Bilvamaṅgala.[136] His two *stōtras*, the *Bilvamaṅgalastava* and *Kṛṣṇakarṇāmṛta*, quickly spread through the South. That Bilvamaṅgala was, like our subjects in this chapter, a Śaiva in love with Viṣṇu can be inferred from his confession in *Kṛṣṇakarṇāmṛta* 2.24:

> I'm a Śaiva for sure, there's no doubt about it,
> devoted to chanting the five-letter *mantra*,
> yet my heart dwells on the milkmaid's son
> with the smiling face and dark as the *atasī* flower.[137]

Elsewhere in the *Kṛṣṇakarṇāmṛta*, Bilvamaṅgala invokes his guru Sōmagiri (1.1) and Īśānadēva (1.110), both plainly Śaiva names.[138] He was also an Advaitin of a strangely familiar stripe, as he says in the *Bilvamaṅgalastava* (2.2):

[135] Shandip Saha, "Creating a Community of Grace: A History of the Puṣṭi Mārga in Northern and Western India, 1493–1905" (Ph.D. diss., University of Ottawa, 2004).

[136] Frances Wilson, ed., *The Love of Krishna: The Kṛṣṇakarṇāmṛta of Līlāśuka Bilvamaṅgala* (Philadelphia: University of Pennsylvania Press, 1975) (henceforth cited as *Kṛṣṇakarṇāmṛta*).

[137] *śaivā vayaṁ na khalu tatra vicāraṇīyaṁ*
pañcākṣarījapaparā nitarāṁ tathā'pi
cētō madīyam atasīkusumāvabhāsaṁ
smērānanaṁ smarati gōpavadhūkiśōram.

[138] Frances Wilson argues that the verses to Rāma and Śiva in the companion collection, the *Bilvamaṅgalastava*, are part of the original. Moreover, *Bilvamaṅgalastava* 2.4, 2.100, and 3.32 establish the identity of Kṛṣṇa and Śiva. See Frances Wilson, ed., *The Bilvamaṅgalastava* (Leiden: Brill, 1975), 4–6.

We'd set out to travel on Advaita Road
initiates at the throne of our own inner joy,
when a trickster forced us to be his slaves,
the one seducing the farmers' wives.[139]

The mention of initiation (*dīkṣā*) and inner joy (*svānanda*) reminds us of Śaiva forms of nondualism. The poem dramatizes Bilvamaṅgala's captivation with and capture by a visually entrancing Kr̥ṣṇa. Unlike the exegetical efforts of Pūrṇasarasvatī and Rāghavānanda, these poems did not stay in Kerala. By the early decades of the sixteenth century, Bilvamaṅgala's poems and character, now largely shorn of their Śaiva origins, found their way northeast to Caitanya and the Gauḍīya Vaiṣṇavas as a result of Caitanya's alleged travels to the South.[140] Bilvamaṅgala also features in the *Sampradāyapradīpa* by Gadādhara Bhaṭṭa, a member of the Vallabha Sampradāya. There he is said to have been waiting hundreds of years for Vallabha's incarnation, in order that people's attraction for the worship of Śiva may cease and that they may return to "God's path."[141] Bilvamaṅgala's poetry would also go on to influence the visual arts. In the late fifteenth or early sixteenth century, a Gujarati patron financed a set of paintings to illustrate the *Bilvamaṅgalastava*, also known as the *Bālagōpālastuti*.[142] These paintings, which exhibit the influence of Jain representational styles, capture the vivid imagery of the poems themselves, whose celebration of the visually entrancing form of Kr̥ṣṇa is likewise prevalent in the temple cultures of northern India.[143]

Finally, there is Lakṣmīdhara. Although his *Bhāgavata* commentary remained in Kerala, his *Advaitamakaranda* and *Bhagavannāmakaumudī* quickly spread to the North and the East. If the commentarial tradition that he participated in was suffused with the language of Advaita Vēdānta,

[139] *The Bilvamaṅgalastava*, 88:

advaitavīthīpathikāḥ pravr̥ttāḥ
svānandasiṁhāsanalabdhadīkṣāḥ
śaṭhēna kēnāpi vayaṁ haṭhēna
dāsīkr̥tā gōpavadhūviṭēna.

[140] John Stratton Hawley, *A Storm of Songs: India and the Idea of the Bhakti Movement* (Cambridge: Harvard University Press, 2015), 210–211.

[141] Hawley, *Storm of Songs*, 208.

[142] See Dominik Wujastyk, "The Love of Kr̥ṣṇa in Poems and Paintings," in *Pearls of the Orient: Asian Treasures from the Wellcome Library*, ed. Nigel Allen (London and Chicago: Serindia Publications, 2003), 87–105.

[143] See Cynthia Packert, *The Art of Loving Krishna: Ornamentation and Devotion* (Bloomington: Indiana University Press, 2010).

could it also have been a Śaiva tradition? I am willing to raise the possibility because I keep finding strange, many-headed creatures: Śaiva Vaiṣṇavas, Advaitic devotees, southerners from the North. If they seem fantastic and mysterious and inexplicable, perhaps it's because we've been asking the wrong questions, looking in the wrong places. For all his considerable erudition, the great Friedhelm Hardy was disappointingly general when it came to the early reception history of the *Bhāgavata Purāṇa*. Except for one important study of the possible links between South Indian *bhakti* and Bengali Vaiṣṇavism, Hardy repeated what has become a conventional understanding of the *bhakti* movement, associating the proliferation of Vaiṣṇava traditions of Vēdānta with structural similarities between vernacular *bhakti* poets.[144] But the historiography of *bhakti* has moved on to include Jains, Sufis, *sādhus*, and Sanskrit poets. Perhaps if Hardy had lived long enough he might have turned his attention to the Śaivas that lined the road, captivated by a dashing highwayman with a flute and a smile on his lips. But his absence, like the early afterlife of the *Bhāgavata*, leaves a gap in history that is difficult to fill.

In this chapter, I have tried to situate the *Bhāgavata* at the crossroads of a number of intellectual currents that are often at odds in the historiography of Indian religion and philosophy: Śaivism and Vaiṣṇavism, *bhakti* and Tantra, upper-caste and lower-caste practices. I offer an alternative history of the reception of the *Bhāgavata* through the writings of three scholars in medieval Kerala who worked at the intersection of poetry, poetics, and philosophy. I pay attention not only to their texts but to their subtexts—hints, traces, and inklings—which reveal a thought-world of remarkable energy and playfulness. I pair this intellectual history with a reconstruction of the complex and overlapping socioreligious networks of the region. Finally, I suggest that this local history was far from self-contained and that it helped shape some of the more recognizable religious communities that organized themselves around the *Bhāgavata*. Next I consider how the *Bhāgavata* impacted the world of *śāstra*, the very constitution of certain Sanskrit intellectual disciplines. The following chapter studies the *Bhāgavata*'s meteoric rise to prominence through the intellectual history of a single text, Lakṣmīdhara's *Bhagavannāmakaumudī*. The

[144] Friedhelm Hardy, "Mādhavendra Purī: A Link between Bengal Vaiṣṇavism and South Indian *Bhakti*," *Journal of the Royal Asiatic Society of Great Britian and Ireland* 1 (1974): 23–41; Friedhelm Hardy, *Viraha-Bhakti: The Early History of Kṛṣṇa Devotion in South India* (Oxford: Oxford University Press, 1983), 556–558.

Bhagavannāmakaumudī changed the way that premodern scholars would come to think about the authority and power of the *Bhāgavata Purāṇa*. That it also influenced a wide range of scholarly and religious communities, who did not always intersect or see eye-to-eye, further highlights the need to study the *Bhāgavata* and its text traditions from unlikely angles. Therein lies the promise of writing histories in the plural.

2
The Name of God in the World of Men

Introduction

Once upon a time, there was a man named Ajāmila. He used to be a pious man, but he lost his way. He left his wife and children to shack up with another woman. But he loved his youngest son. He loved to watch him play ball and eat snacks and dribble milk down his lips. Before he knew it, Ajāmila's time had come. His fate was certain. As he saw the messengers of Death coming to take his soul to hell, he cried out for his son one last time: "Nārāyaṇa!" At once, the servants of God appeared to block Death's emissaries. "We are owed this life," the demons protested. "He has strayed from the righteous path and deserves to be punished for his actions." God's servants replied, "We don't care how many lifetimes of sins he has committed. He had God's name on his lips as he was dying. That wipes out everything. Intentional or not, in jest or not, in disrespect or not, in contempt or not, all that matters is that he uttered the name." Hearing that he'd been given a second chance, Ajāmila resolved to become a better man.

This story from the sixth canto of the *Bhāgavata Purāṇa* illustrates a common motif of *bhakti*: just sing the name of God and all your sins will be purified. Forget the commands and prohibitions of *dharma*, forget its labyrinthine systems of punishment and expiation. All you need is the name of God. The practice of singing or repeating the name has a marked presence in South Asian religions, from Hindus and Jains to Sufis and Sikhs.[1] Scholars such as V. Raghavan argued that the presence of this motif across Sanskrit *stōtra*s, Marathi *abhang*s, Hindi *pad*s, and Telugu *padam*s proved that the "*bhakti* movement" was a cultural phenomenon that presciently mapped the nascent nation-state.[2] In a famous essay delivered as the Sardar Vallabhbhai Patel memorial lecture in 1964, Raghavan described *bhakti* saints and

[1] See the essays dedicated to this subject in the *Journal of Vaishnava Studies* 2.2 (1994).
[2] John Stratton Hawley, *A Storm of Songs: India and the Idea of the Bhakti Movement* (Cambridge: Harvard University Press, 2015), 19–28.

Love in the Time of Scholarship. Anand Venkatkrishnan, Oxford University Press. © Oxford University Press 2024.
DOI: 10.1093/oso/9780197776636.003.0003

singers as the "great integrators" of India who bridged the gap between elite theology and popular religion.[3] In other complementary essays he developed the idea of a *Nāmasiddhānta*, a nationwide tradition of scholarship and storytelling that fused the theory and practice of singing the name of God.[4] Raghavan thought that the *Nāmasiddhānta* was inherently capacious, mirroring the Indian nation-state itself, with room for every scholarly antinomy: abstract philosophy and everyday practice, Sanskrit and the vernacular, knowledge and devotion. However, steeped in the Brahmin sensibilities that profess to include even as they implicitly exclude, Raghavan suppressed the caste- and class-bound character of the traditions he believed to be universal.[5] The power of the sacred name did not grow naturally in the religious soil of the subcontinent, but was indexed to specific historical moments and agents. Differences of power mattered too: "Whole swaths of the South Asian population, including many of those to whom Raghavan specifically alluded, have historically been excluded from realms in which *bhakti* is celebrated."[6] Still, Raghavan's provocation raises for me a question that inverts his own top-down view of affairs: How did vernacular ways of being and believing make their way into the Sanskrit scholastic record? What could have been the relationship of a Sanskrit ideal from the *purāṇas* with regional-language devotional poetry, or Tantric practices of *mantra* repetition, or Sufi notions of the divine presence in language? How might Sanskrit scholastic writings have participated in a broader "cult of the divine name" that moved between communities: Śaiva and Vaiṣṇava, Sanskrit and vernacular, Hindu and Muslim?[7] Can we revisit Raghavan's idea of the *Nāmasiddhānta* as a transregional phenomenon even as we resist its cultural-nationalist implications?

[3] V. Raghavan, *The Great Integrators: The Saint-Singers of India* (New Delhi: Publications Division, Ministry of Information and Broadcasting, 1966).

[4] V. Raghavan, *The Power of the Sacred Name* (Bloomington: World Wisdom Press, 2011).

[5] See Davesh Soneji, "The Powers of Polyglossia: Marathi *Kīrtan*, Multilingualism, and the Making of a South Indian Devotional Tradition," *International Journal of Hindu Studies* 17.3 (2014): 342: "In other words, what most Smārta Brahmin practitioners of *bhajana*, and certainly Singer and Raghavan, would see as the ingenuity of Tamil Brahmins as 'preservers' of pan-Indian traditions, I would argue, cannot be disassociated from the historical roles offered to local Smārtas, but also to others, at the Tanjore court as intellectuals, musicians, and performers of drama and dance in a culture of public multilingualism."

[6] John Stratton Hawley, Christian Lee Novetzke, and Swapna Sharma, "Introduction: The Power of Bhakti," in *Bhakti and Power: Debating India's Religion of the Heart*, ed. John Stratton Hawley, Christian Lee Novetzke, and Swapna Sharma (Seattle: University of Washington Press, 2019), 7.

[7] See Hans Bakker, *Ayodhyā*, part 1 (Groningen: Egbert Forsten, 1986), 67–78, 119–124. See also Charlotte Vaudeville, "The Cult of the Divine Name in the Haripāṭh of Dñāndev," *Wiener Zeitschrift für die Kunde Sudasiens* 12–13 (1968–1969): 395–406.

This chapter explores these questions through the intellectual, social, and cultural history of a single book: the *Bhagavannāmakaumudī*, or "The Moonlight of God's Name."[8] Written by the *Bhāgavata* commentator Lakṣmīdhara around the early fourteenth century, probably in Kerala, the *Kaumudī* was a monograph in three chapters that took seriously the theology of the divine name from the *Bhāgavata* and other *purāṇas*. Scholars have briefly discussed the *Kaumudī*'s incipient formulations of the aesthetic theory of *bhaktirasa*,[9] its impact on Gauḍīya Vaiṣṇavism,[10] and its legacy in the Tamil South.[11] Largely ignored, however, is the text's own primary concern: to defend the validity of the *purāṇa*'s claims in the official language of Sanskrit scriptural hermeneutics, or Mīmāṁsā. I argue in this chapter that the *Kaumudī* represents a serious scholastic attempt to accord the genre of *purāṇa*—specifically, the *Bhāgavata Purāṇa*—a superlative place in the hierarchy of Sanskrit scripture. As such, the *Kaumudī* makes an important yet unrecognized intervention in Sanskrit intellectual history. Its social and cultural history is no less significant. At roughly contemporaneous moments in sixteenth-century North India, both Advaita Vēdāntins and Gauḍīya Vaiṣṇavas, generally depicted in hagiographical literature as intractably opposed, laid claim to the *Kaumudī* as a source of theological inspiration. And only a century or so later, the *Kaumudī* made its way back down to South India, where the musical-performative tradition known as the *bhajana sampradāya* began to take shape during the rule of the Thanjavur Marathas. In the latter part of this chapter, I look at the diverse reception history of the *Kaumudī* for what it may reveal about the local character of a text tradition valorized for its universality.

What's in a name? Like most subjects in this book, this chapter is a history of Brahmanical thought. But it insists that such thought is incomplete in its hegemony, that it is speckled with the traces of the subaltern. Conflicts internal to Brahmanical systems of knowledge provincialize the universality

[8] *Śrībhagavannāmakaumudī*, ed. Gosvāmī Dāmodar Śāstrī (Kāśī: Acyutagranthamālā, 1927) (henceforth cited as *Kaumudī*).

[9] Neal Delmonico, "Sacred Rapture: A Study of the Religious Aesthetic of Rupa Gosvamin" (Ph.D. diss., University of Chicago, 1990), 176–183.

[10] Mans Broo, "The Vrindāvan Gosvāmins on Kīrtana," *Journal of Vaishnava Studies* 17.2 (2009): 63–64; Norvin Hein, "Caitanya's Ecstasies and the Theology of the Name," in *Hinduism: New Essays in the History of Religions*, ed. Bardwell L. Smith (Leiden: Brill, 1976), 15–32; Neal Delmonico, "Chaitanya Vaishnavism and the Holy Names," in *Krishna: A Sourcebook*, ed. Edwin F. Bryant (Oxford: Oxford University Press, 2007), 549–575; Barbara Holdrege, "From *Nāma-Avatāra* to *Nāma-Saṁkīrtana*: Gauḍīya Perspectives on the Name," *Journal of Vaishnava Studies* 17.2 (2009): 3–36.

[11] Raghavan, *The Power of the Sacred Name*, 49–55.

that they accord to themselves. All thought, in this view, is local. For the author and the readers of the *Kaumudī* to latch onto the name as a subject of scholastic reflection was a choice only partially inspired by the superposed ideals of a Sanskrit canon. They also called upon a vernacular practice, in the sense of the quotidian, the everyday.[12] Singing the name was one way in which the power of the quotidian could "expand beyond the parameters of its inaugurators or champions."[13] I am interested here not in the cultural politics of vernacularization but in the "bottom-up" effect that everyday practices have had on the world of elite exegesis.[14] For one scholar in medieval Kerala, they would upset the very foundations of thinking about Sanskrit scriptural hierarchy. For his readers, they would affirm that there was more than one way to be a Brahmin in the early modern world.

The *Kaumudī* in Context

In the previous chapter, I identified Lakṣmīdhara as a native of Kerala because most manuscripts of his *Bhāgavata* commentary survive only there. However, I had noted there his connections to the Northeast of India. Lakṣmīdhara's *Kaumudī* was studied and cited by the famous acolytes of Caitanya, Rūpa and Jīva Gōsvāmī, while a commentary on his *Advaitamakaranda* was written by Vāsudēva Sārvabhauma, a famous scholar of Navya Nyāya who was later claimed by Gauḍīya Vaiṣṇava hagiographers as a convert to Caitanya's movement.[15] Moreover, in the second benedictory verse of the *Kaumudī*, Lakṣmīdhara refers to Kr̥ṣṇa as the "beloved of Puṇḍarīka." It is possible that he was referring to Puṇḍalīk, devotee of the Deccan god Viṭṭhal.[16] However, the name "Puṇḍarīka" or "Puṇḍalīka" occurs frequently in general lists of devotees of Viṣṇu in the

[12] Cf. Christian Lee Novetzke, *The Quotidian Revolution: Vernacularization, Religion, and the Premodern Public Sphere in India* (New York: Columbia University Press, 2016), 12–13.

[13] Novetzke, *The Quotidian Revolution*, 15.

[14] Cf. Anand Venkatkrishnan, "Philosophy from the Bottom Up: Eknāth's Vernacular Advaita," *Journal of Indian Philosophy* 48.1 (2020): 9–21.

[15] D. C. Bhattacharya, "Vāsudeva Sārvabhauma," *Indian Historical Quarterly* 16 (1940): 58–69; S. K. De, *Early History of the Vaisnava Faith and Movement in Bengal* (Calcutta: Firma K. L. Mukhopadhyay, 1961), xxiii–xxv, 85–90; Edward Dimock and Tony K. Stewart, *The Caitanya Caritāmr̥ta of Kr̥ṣṇadāsa Kavirāja* (Cambridge: Harvard University Press, 1999), 16; Jonardon Ganeri, *The Lost Age of Reason: Philosophy in Early Modern India 1450–1700 ce* (Oxford: Oxford University Press, 2011), 42–44.

[16] This is how the commentator Anantadēva, a Maharashtrian Brahmin writing away from home, interprets the reference. See *Kaumudī*, 4.

purāṇas.[17] One such Puṇḍarīka shows up in the "Glory of Jagannāth" section of the *Skanda Purāṇa*. Puṇḍarīka and his friend Ambarīṣa lead dissolute lives until they reach Jagannāth at Puri, sing the names of Viṣṇu, and attain liberation there.[18] The all-purifying power of God's name is the central subject of the *Kaumudī*. Finally, although Lakṣmīdhara participated in an alternative commentarial tradition on the *Bhāgavata*, he shared one thing with his contemporary commentator Śrīdhara: a reverence for the god Nṛsiṁha, whose transition into the deity Jagannāth of Puri has been well-documented.[19]

Whether or not Lakṣmīdhara himself traveled back and forth between these regions, the presence of the deity Nṛsiṁha, who is a cross between the fierce Bhairava and the erotic Viṣṇu, returns us to the specter of Śaivism in Lakṣmīdhara's writing. Benedictory stanzas in praise of Śiva are not unusual in Vaiṣṇava works—Śrīdhara has similar ones, for instance—but it is the unity between Śiva and Viṣṇu that returns us to the question of place. As I noted in the previous chapter, the mutuality of Śiva and Viṣṇu in medieval Kerala contrasted with the conflict between the two in many other places. Lakṣmīdhara took great pains in the *Kaumudī* to emphasize the equivalence of the two gods. Like Pūrṇasarasvatī, Lakṣmīdhara described his teacher, Anantānanda Raghunātha, as embodying both Śiva and Viṣṇu:

> Diving into the great ocean of glory
> of the water spraying from his own lotus feet,
> then himself placing it atop his own head:
> he is my guru, my family deity.[20]

The image here is of the River Gaṅgā, which flows from the feet of Viṣṇu onto the head of the waiting Śiva. Only the two are a single entity, the author's

[17] Ramchandra Chintaman Dhere, *Rise of a Folk God: Vitthal of Pandharpur*, trans. Anne Feldhaus (Oxford: Oxford University Press, 2011), 151.

[18] Dhere, *Rise of a Folk God*, 156: "No matter how far someone has fallen . . . still he can be saved just by repeating the name of Viṣṇu: this is the truth that the Māhātmya reveals through this story of the salvation of Puṇḍarīk and Ambarīṣ."

[19] Anncharlott Eschmann, Hermann Kulke, and Gaya Charan Tripathi, "The Formation of the Jagannātha Triad," in *The Cult of Jagannāth and the Regional Tradition of Orissa*, ed. Annecharlott Eschmann, Hermann Kulke, and Gaya Charan Tripathi (New Delhi: Manohar Publications, 1978), 167–196; Sara Adams, "From Narasiṁha to Jagannātha," *Journal of Vaishnava Studies* 17.1 (2008): 5–28.

[20] *Kaumudī*, 135:

> *svapādapaṅkēruhasīkarasya*
> *nimajya māhātmyamahārṇavē yaḥ*
> *dadhau punas taṁ svayam ēva maulau*
> *sa nō gurus tat kuladaivataṁ naḥ.*

family deity (*kuladaivata*), possibly also a reference to his father, named Nṛsiṁha. "The name of that river," he continues, "whether flowing from Viṣṇu's toes or reaching Śiva's thick dreadlocks, washes away all sins. How much more so would the name of that ocean of compassion?"[21] Elsewhere in the *Kaumudī*, Lakṣmīdhara quotes a verse from the *Śivadharmōttara*, an influential Śaiva teaching (*śivaśāsana*), in support of a claim that one must have "faith" (*śraddhā*) in the words of scripture for it to be effective.[22] Faith, in the *Śivadharmōttara*, constitutes the essence of all Śaiva teachings, and it is the only means through which Śiva can truly be attained. These teachings are true because Śiva's speech is infallible. The compassionate Śiva cannot but speak the truth because his utterances are commands (*vidhi*), not mere descriptions of fact (*arthavāda*).[23] His teachings are condensed into the *mantra ōṁ namaḥ śivāya*, repetition of which replaces every treatise and every ritual act.[24] The idea that faith is indispensable is one that Lakṣmīdhara will ultimately dismiss. But the broader issue of whether or not certain textual utterances—in this case, claims in the *purāṇa*s—can be considered commands rather than descriptions of fact structures the *Kaumudī*. While I will reconstruct the Mīmāṁsā context for Lakṣmīdhara's discussion, I suspect that his line of inquiry has its roots in Śaiva discourse.

Echoes of Śaivism reverberate in his engagement with poetry and poetics as well. In a passage that has been considered a precursor to theories of *bhaktirasa*, Lakṣmīdhara suggests that the subjects of a devotee's *rasa*, its foundational (*ālambana-*) and stimulating (*uddīpana-*) factors, could be either Viṣṇu or Śiva in all their descriptive glory, whether heard in the scriptures or witnessed on stage.[25] As in the *Amṛtataraṅgiṇī*, Lakṣmīdhara insists here that the *purāṇa* can be read (and enacted) as *kāvya*. *Bhakti* is a *bhāva*, says Lakṣmīdhara, a religiously cultivated emotion that is transformed into *rasa* by aesthetic factors. Other feelings may come and go, but *bhakti* brooks no

[21] *Kaumudī*, 135:

> *yadaṅghrinakhamaṇḍalād vigalitasya pūrvaṁ punar*
> *yadīyakabarībharārṇavam upēyuṣaḥ pāthasaḥ*
> *aśēṣajagadaṁhasāṁ kimapi nāma nirṇējanaṁ*
> *dayā'mṛtamahāmbudhēḥ kimuta nāma tasyaiva tat.*

[22] *Kaumudī*, 72. On the *Śivadharmōttara*, see Florinda De Simini, *Of Gods and Books: Ritual and Knowledge Transmission in the Manuscript Cultures of Premodern India* (Berlin: De Gruyter, 2016).

[23] *Śivadharmōttara* 1.41, as cited in De Simini, *Of Gods and Books*, 423:

> *vidhivākyam idaṁ śaivaṁ nārthavādaḥ śivātmakaḥ*
> *lōkānugrahakartā yaḥ sa mṛṣārthaṁ kathaṁ vadēt.*

[24] De Simini, *Of Gods and Books*, 66–67.

[25] *Kaumudī*, 80–81. Cf. Delmonico, "Sacred Rapture," 176–183.

interruption in a heart that has been perfumed with the traces of lifetimes of devotion. As a *rasa*, it is enveloped by the experience of one's own inner delight; in fact, *bhakti* can find no better definition than the experience of joy (*ānanda-saṁvid*).[26] Lakṣmīdhara reminds us here of his own comments early in the *Amṛtataraṅgiṇī*, where he used the word "joy," *ānanda*, to describe the fundamental *rasa* of love for God.

Elsewhere he reminds us of Pūrṇasarasvatī, who couldn't resist the occasional sexual wordplay. To conclude his opening benediction, Lakṣmīdhara compares the scripture directing an accomplished sage inward to a courtesan drawing a poor man to her inner chambers:

> He's the king of the egoless,
> *He's the prince of paupers,*
> of all who live by the river of tranquility,
> *of all who hang out on the shores of impotence,*
> and free from the weight of the *guṇas*. And yet,
> *and hasn't got a single good quality. It doesn't matter.*
> Scripture humbly serves him who has no sense of false pride,
> *With false respect she approaches him from afar,*
> and slowly endeavors to lead him within
> *and slowly tries to lead him inside*
> to be enveloped by good fortune.
> *to be surrounded by beautiful women.*[27]

This is not to suggest that all Śaivas were so cavalier, only that medieval Kerala seemed to offer the social conditions of possibility for such writing. Other Śaivas, however, were less inclined to support the kind of interreligious and open-ended approach to *bhakti* prescribed in the *Kaumudī*. Take, for example, the polemic of Gōpīnātha, a Maharashtrian scholar of *dharmaśāstra*

[26] *Kaumudī*, 80: *sa cāyam ādyō bhāvō vṛttyantarair antarā niviśamānair apy anēkajanmavāsan āvāsitē cētasi na vyavacchidyamānō vibhāvādibhī rasarūpatām āpādyamānō nijasukhasaṁvidā nirbharam āliṅgitaḥ svayam ēvānandasaṁvidabhidhānam upacārāsahaṁ dadhānō bhaktir ity abhidhīyatē.*

[27] The italicized lines represent the secondary reading of the verse enabled by the technique of *ślēṣa*, or bitextual poetry. See *Kaumudī*, 2:

> *adhīśaṁ niḥsvānāṁ śamanadataṭīṣu pravasatām*
> *aśēṣāṇām ādyaṁ guṇagarimanirmuktam api yam*
> *mṛṣāmānād dūraṁ śrutir upacarantī savinayaṁ*
> *śanair yatnād antarṇayati subhagānāṁ parivṛḍham.*

from the fifteenth century who had clear affinities for Śaiva theology.[28] In his influential *Jātivivēka*, a discourse on classifying caste communities, Gōpīnātha speaks contemptuously of those who practice precisely the sort of *bhakti* which Lakṣmīdhara advocates:

> Gopīnātha also demonstrated marked hostility to bhakti religion, ascribing menial parentages to "Vaiṣṇavas." . . . Such "Vaiṣṇavas" were lower than Śūdras. . . . They deluded themselves that repeating the name of God was the summit of virtue and a substitute for following their own prescribed place in the social order. Citing the *Viṣṇupurāṇa*, he asserted: "Those who abandon their karma and just recite 'Kṛṣṇa, Kṛṣṇa!' are sinners in the eyes of Hari. The birth of Hari is for the sake of dharma. If you follow your varṇa, āśrama, and the prescribed conduct, you actually worship Viṣṇu, the Highest Man. There is no other way to satiate Him."[29]

Writing as an upholder of normative caste hierarchy, Gōpīnātha associates the everyday practice of singing the name with nonelite castes. Given his social location, he could have been responding to the popularity of Vārkari devotion to Viṭṭhal in the Deccan. He turns the sacred texts of these so-called Vaiṣṇavas against them, although the disapproving remark about people who sing the name of Kṛṣṇa cannot be traced to a particular *purāṇa* and may well have been one of his own inventions.[30] Gōpīnātha's dismissive attitude to such popular practices contrasts with Lakṣmīdhara's. Whatever their relationship may have been, the discrepancy between their attitudes to *bhakti* shows that there was a wide spectrum of Śaivas in the fourteenth and fifteenth centuries, some who rejected and some who accommodated the texts and practices of Vaiṣṇava devotional groups (divided by caste and class) in the name of Vaiṣṇavism itself.

[28] Rosalind O'Hanlon, Gergely Hidas, and Csaba Kiss, "Discourses of Caste over the Longue Durée: Gopīnātha and Social Classification in India, ca. 1400–1900," *South Asian History and Culture* 6.1 (2015): 103. "He was a traditional Smārta Brahman, from a Śaivite scholar family, in which Kashmiri Śaivite influences were strong. In Sanderson's terms, Gopīnātha seems not to have been an initiate into a particular Śaivite sect, but rather to have worshipped Śiva within a broad framework of Vedic ritual and Smārta attachment to the principles of varṇāśramadharma, the orders of castes and life-stages."

[29] O'Hanlon, Hidas, and Kiss, "Discourses of Caste," 111.

[30] O'Hanlon, Hidas, and Kiss, "Discourses of Caste," 120, n. 79 cite *Viṣṇupurāṇa* 3.8.9 and 5.1.151, as well as *Garuḍapurāṇa* 1.229.7 as possible sources. None of these stanzas, however, matches the opening criticism of people reciting the name of Kṛṣṇa.

More interesting than the philosophical or theological impulses "behind" Lakṣmīdhara's work is what he is doing in writing the *Kaumudī*. Most centrally, he places the *Bhāgavata Purāṇa* firmly within the canon of Sanskrit scripture, privileging it more strongly than his predecessors had done. And in the same motion, he opens a space for non-Vedic, non-Sanskrit, popular devotional practices, to puncture the forbidding world of scriptural hermeneutics. He writes approvingly of lyrics (*gāthā*) that are composed in Prakrit and in everyday languages (*prākṛtabhāṣā*)[31] and summarily accepts any sources of praise, whether of "Vedic, Tantric, *paurāṇika*, or human composition," for there is no rule that defines how one should praise God.[32] It is possible that the *Kaumudī*'s location at these multiple intersections—the elite and the everyday, the Śaiva and Vaiṣṇava—contributed to its later impact on a diverse group of scholars. Before attending to its reception, I will focus on the *Kaumudī*'s intervention in the world of Sanskrit scriptural hermeneutics.

A Tale of Two *smṛtis*

The *Kaumudī* is structured in three chapters:

Chapter 1. Statements of the *purāṇas* have intended meanings (*vivakṣitārtha*).
Chapter 2. Singing the name confers a beneficial result on a person (*puruṣārtha*).
Chapter 3. Singing the name on its own is sufficient as the means to a beneficial end.

The concepts of *vivakṣitārtha* and *puruṣārtha* are technical terms in Mīmāṁsā. When Mīmāṁsakas discuss whether the meaning of a word or a sentence is what is intended by it (*vivakṣitārtha*), they are usually trying to figure out whether the word or sentence in question merely conveys meaning or makes a contribution. This maps onto the difference between the semantic

[31] I read this as a *dvandva* compound. Cf. Sheldon Pollock, "Sanskrit Literary Culture from the Inside Out," in *Literary Cultures in History: Reconstructions from South Asia*, ed. Sheldon Pollock (Berkeley: University of California Press, 2003), 63. "The word [*prākṛta*] itself, according to the standard interpretation, refers to the 'common' or 'natural' dialect(s) of which Sanskrit represents the grammatically disciplined variety. But in fact it typically connotes a literary language and only very rarely is used to mean spoken vernaculars (the usual term for these was *bhāṣā*, speech)."
[32] *Kaumudī*, 101 (commenting on *Bhāgavata* 6.3.27), 124.

and pragmatic dimensions of meaning. Andrew Ollett explains: "Let's say Devadatta is going to a party and brings a bottle of wine. When he gets there, he finds that Yajñadatta has already arrived—and that Yajñadatta has brought a bottle of the exact same wine that Devadatta picked up. If their host were a grammarian, he would probably say, 'Great! Now we have two bottles.' If he were a Mīmāṁsaka, he would probably say, 'We already have one of those.'"[33] The example illustrates how Mīmāṁsakas thought about different types of sentence in the Veda which express similar meanings. For the Mīmāṁsaka, it is the Vedic directive (*vidhi*) that has primacy. The *vidhi* is independently meaningful, for it prompts the listener to act and, as such, brings a state of affairs into being. The subjunctive or optative modality trumps the indicative, although indicative sentences can be interpreted to have imperative force. Other sentence categories are meaningful only insofar as they subserve the purpose of carrying out the *vidhi*. The same goes for linguistic elements within a sentence: if they are incidental to the overall purport, the "functional unity" of the sentence, and contribute nothing new, they must be disregarded.[34] At stake in Lakṣmīdhara's intervention, then, is the question of whether sentences in the *purāṇa* can be considered independently meaningful, or whether they are subordinate to some other context, some externally derived injunction. If they are the former, then they can be interpreted as ritual injunctions in and of themselves that provide something beneficial to the human being (*puruṣārtha*).[35] If not, then we cannot take their claims seriously. At best, they support what we already know from the Veda, and at worst, they must be disregarded entirely.

Asserting that the *purāṇa* was in some sense comparable to a Vedic utterance raised questions about the hierarchy of scriptural authority established by Mīmāṁsā. Among all the schools of Brahmanical thought, Mīmāṁsā instituted some of the strictest criteria for scripture to be accepted as normative. This was because the problem of scriptural proliferation—that is, the vast array of Indic text-traditions that presented themselves as sources of valid knowledge about matters beyond the senses—bore directly on the unique authority of the Veda as the source of knowledge and practice. The Mīmāṁsā

[33] Andrew Ollett, "Artha: Semantics versus Pragmatics," *The Indian Philosophy Blog*, April 9, 2016, https://indianphilosophyblog.org/2016/04/09/artha-semantics-versus-pragmatics/.

[34] Lawrence McCrea, "The Hierarchical Organization of Language in Mīmāṁsā Interpretive Theory," *Journal of Indian Philosophy* 28.5 (2000): 448.

[35] On this technical Mīmāṁsā reading of the term *puruṣārtha* instead of the more general "goal of human life," see Patrick Olivelle, "From *trivarga* to *puruṣārtha*: A Chapter in Indian Moral Philosophy," *Journal of the American Oriental Society* 139.2 (2019): 388–390.

argument for a scripture's ultimate validity (*prāmāṇya*) runs briefly as follows: a text cannot have an author, human or divine, for embodied beings lie all the time, and there is no such thing as omniscience or supernatural perception; it cannot refer to historical realities, for that would imply personal authorship; it cannot have a discernible beginning, for that would imply historical contingency. Lawrence McCrea explains: "Eternal texts, the Mīmāṁsakas argue, cannot refer to particular historical persons or events. Those passages in eternal texts which appear to refer to such persons and events must be understood as figuratively praising or otherwise referring to elements of the (eternally recurrent) Vedic sacrifice—what the Mīmāṁsakas call *arthavāda*. Hence, any apparent reference in a purportedly eternal text to the omniscience of a particular scripture-author would either have to be an *arthavāda* passage (and accordingly be interpreted figuratively), or, as a historical reference, would show that the text is not in fact eternal."[36] By this account, only the directly perceived, eternal, unauthored Veda, also known as *śruti*, qualifies as independently authoritative. All other sacred texts can possess only, at best, a derivative authority. Even the genre of *smṛti*, from which most Brahmanical cultural practices were drawn, is usually allocated a place just below *śruti* in the Mīmāṁsā hierarchy of Sanskrit scripture. The genre of *smṛti* was broadly comprised of the epics (*itihāsa*); customs, ethics, and law (*dharmaśāstra*); and ancient myths and legends (*purāṇa*). The Mīmāṁsā tradition constructed a "transcendent legitimacy" around the *smṛti*, considering it almost equivalent to the *śruti*, as "Veda remembered" rather than "Veda recited."[37] Apart from the Brahmanical *smṛti*, however, Mīmāṁsakas disqualified most texts, especially those that belonged to Buddhists, Jains, and Śaiva and Vaiṣṇava sectarian groups, from occupying the same level of normative validity.[38] Lakṣmīdhara's introduction of the genre of *purāṇa*—in particular, the *Bhāgavata Purāṇa*—as a separable category prompted a radical reappraisal of the *śruti-smṛti* continuum. In order to fully appreciate the break effected by the *Kaumudī* here, it is worth reviewing the history of how scriptural interpreters prior to Lakṣmīdhara understood the *purāṇa*.

[36] Lawrence McCrea, "'Just Like Us, Just Like Now': The Tactical Implications of the Mīmāṁsā Rejection of Yogic Perception," in *Yogic Perception, Meditation, and Altered States of Consciousness*, ed. Eli Franco (Wien: Verlag der Österreichischen Akademie der Wissenschaften, 2009), 61, n. 9.

[37] Sheldon Pollock, "The Revelation of Tradition: *śruti, smṛti*, and the Sanskrit Discourse of Power," in *Boundaries, Dynamics and Construction of Traditions in South Asia*, ed. Federico Squarcini (London: Anthem Press, 2011), 41–61.

[38] Andrew Nicholson, *Unifying Hinduism: Philosophy and Identity in Indian Intellectual History* (New York: Columbia University Press, 2010), 170.

The earliest extant Mīmāṁsā writers, Jaimini and Śabara, do not appear particularly interested in the subject. In Jaimini's aphorisms, the *Mīmāṁsā Sūtras* (MS), and Śabara's prose commentary, the primary concern is with delimiting the boundary of *śruti* against *smṛti*. Jaimini and Śabara assert that we may infer the authority of the cultural practices of *smṛti* only insofar as they (a) have the Veda as their root (*śrutimūla*) and (b) are performed by the same agents as those who perform Vedic acts (*kartṛsāmānya*).[39] Neither makes mention of the *purāṇas* at all, perhaps because of their relative unimportance (or indeed absence) at the time that Jaimini and Śabara were writing. For many early Mīmāṁsakas, the epics and *purāṇas* were understood to form a single unit, called *itihāsapurāṇa*. However, the seventh-century Mīmāṁsaka Kumārila Bhaṭṭa expanded the scope and power of *smṛti* so as to virtually eliminate any possible limiting conditions that might hinder its authority. One of these possible conditions, the potentially infinite enlargement of the canon of texts that one could reasonably infer to be authoritative, led Kumārila to reflect on the genre of *itihāsapurāṇa*.[40]

In his *Tantravārttika* commentary on MS 1.3.7, which deals with the question of *smṛti*'s authority, Kumārila engages with an opponent who asks why Buddhist or Jain teachings about compassion, charity, or the practice of meditation, which appear unobjectionable to upper-caste men, should be considered contradictory to Vedic authority. Kumārila responds by defining those texts that have been "accepted by the learned" as the fourteen or eighteen "strongholds of knowledge."[41] These include the *itihāsapurāṇa* but not Buddhist or Jain scriptures. Kumārila explains further that the *itihāsapurāṇa*, although of human authorship, are mentioned in the Veda itself as a source of knowledge. The mention of *itihāsapurāṇa* as the "fifth Veda" in the *Chāndōgya Upaniṣad* (7.1) means only that they serve as

[39] See Pollock, "The Revelation of Tradition," 48: "Insofar as the same people who perform the acts of *dharma* required by the Veda also perform acts of *dharma* 'not based on sacred word,' we must assume that the authority for these other actions is conferred, not by directly perceptible Vedic texts, but by texts inferentially proven to exist."

[40] Kumārila probably did not have any specific *purāṇa* in mind, given that the formula encompasses a whole range of texts, from fictitious prose to royal genealogies to didactic discourses. P. V. Kane notes that Kumārila's remarks across the *Tantravārttika* suggest that some of the extant *purāṇas* existed in his day and "were looked upon by him as authoritative in the province of Dharma equally with the Smrtis of Manu, Gautama and others." See P. V. Kane, "The Tantravārtika and the Dharmaśāstra Literature," *Journal of the Bombay Branch of the Royal Asiatic Society* (N.S.) 1 (1925): 102.

[41] Cf. Cezary Galewicz, "Fourteen Strongholds of Knowledge: On Scholarly Commentaries, Authority, and Power in XIV Century India," in *Texts of Power, The Power of the Text: Readings in Textual Authority across History and Cultures*, ed. Cezary Galewicz (Krakow: Homini, 2006), 141–164.

auxiliary means of arriving at the knowledge of *dharma*. Moreover, this is possible for the *itihāsapurāṇa* only because their authors are the very sages named in the Veda, who are not historical figures but recur eternally with each historical cycle.[42] In other words, the *itihāsapurāṇa* are not independent with respect to *dharma*, but they are accepted as canonical only inasmuch as they support Vedic commands. In these and other passages, Kumārila does not appear to consider the genre to be especially different from *smṛti*. His commentary on MS 1.3.2 suggests that the injunctive and explanatory portions of the *itihāsapurāṇa* work in the same way as those of *dharmaśāstra*. Those messages that have a bearing on *dharma* originate in the Veda; those that do not and, say, serve some worldly purpose, originate in everyday experience.[43] Either way, they are derivative of and subordinate to the Veda.

Kumārila's only other discussion of the purpose of *purāṇas* appears, tellingly, in his commentary on MS 1.2.7. This section deliberates on the difference between linguistic components of the Veda—in particular, between the *vidhi*, the independently authoritative injunction, and the *arthavāda*, a sentence possessing a narrative or descriptive form which is purposeful only in a subordinate position to the overall Vedic ritual context, insofar as it serves to enhance or commend a *vidhi*. Since they are not direct exhortations, *arthavādas* are considered supplementary sources of praise or deprecation of the content of injunctions and prohibitions. They ensure that the listener will be encouraged or prompted to perform or desist from the action specified by the injunction or prohibition. In Śabara's commentary, an opponent argues that a *vidhi* could serve quite well in and of itself to incite the agent to action, making the function of *arthavādas* irrelevant. Śabara agrees, in principle, and essentially responds that we must somehow account for such supplementary passages, since they exist in abundance, after all.[44] If this was a problem for the Veda, which Mīmāṁsakas already held to possess inherent validity, so much more so the *itihāsapurāṇa*, which are comprised almost entirely of narrative passages.

42 *Mīmāṁsādarśana*, vol. 1B, ed. V. G. Apte (Pune: Anandashrama Press, 1929), 202, ll. 21–26.

43 Ganganath Jha, trans., *Tantravārttika* (New Delhi: Sri Satguru Publications, 1983), 119.

44 *Mīmāṁsādarśana*, vol. 1B, 118, ll. 1–4. Kumārila suggests (ll. 14–15), quite sarcastically, that such an objection should have been directed at the purported author of the Veda, who could be grilled on why he made sentences so long, when the purpose could have been accomplished with much less verbiage. In the absence of such an author, there is no scope for such an objection: *yō nāma vēdasya kartā syāt sa ēvaṁ paryanuyujyēta laghunōpāyēna siddhē kiṁ mahāvākyam āśrayasīti. tadabhāvān na paryanuyōgaḥ.*

Kumārila takes this opportunity to apply the same logic of hierarchical organization to their language.[45] Even though he analogizes the work of *vidhi*s in the Veda and in *itihāsapurāṇa*, he views them as the result of very different compositional and intentional processes. The passage is worth quoting in some detail:

> This is the way the statements of the *Mahābhārata*, etc., should be interpreted. They too, falling in line with such injunctions as "One should instruct the four caste-classes," seek to accomplish certain ends beneficial to their human agents.[46] Their result is not contained in the recitation itself, but in the understanding of the means to achieve those aims and to avoid their opposites. Yet even in these works, such as the teachings on charity, kingship, and liberation, there are some direct injunctions, whereas some passages are *arthavāda*s that take the shape of stories about ritual acts done by others and occasions of their performance in ancient times. If we had to derive literal meaning from every single tale, it would obviate the injunction to "instruct the four caste-classes," so we understand some implied praise or condemnation therein. And since their exclusive purpose is either praise or condemnation, one shouldn't spend too much time trying to figure out whether they are true or not. After all, Vālmīki, Vyāsa, and others composed their own works in accordance with their study of the Veda. And since those whom they chose to instruct were of varying intellectual capacities, this makes perfect sense. In one context, some people learn from mere injunctions; others need *arthavāda*s, some shorter and some longer. The authors began their compositions with the desire to attract the minds of anyone and everyone. Now in such works, some injunctions and prohibitions have the Veda as their source, while some are derived from everyday experience and have to do with acquiring wealth and happiness. Similarly, some *arthavāda*s are Vedic in character, some are worldly, and

[45] The thirteenth-century commentator Sōmēśvara Bhaṭṭa perceptively noted that this extension of intra-Vedic interpretive principles into the realm of *itihāsapurāṇa* was closely connected to the discussion of the authority of the *vidyāsthāna*s in MS 1.3. See *Nyāyasudhā*, ed. Pandit Mukunda Shastri (Benares: Vidya Vilasa Press, 1901), 40.

[46] The analogy here, Sōmēśvara points out, is to the Vedic meta-injunction "One should study one's [recension of] the Veda" (*svādhyāyō'dhyētavyaḥ*), which commands other injunctions to command agents. In this way, the so-called *adhyayanavidhi* is the take-off point for the entire process of Vedic ritual. Similarly, the "injunction to instruct" (*śrāvaṇavidhi*) is the meta-injunction for *itihāsapurāṇa* literature, such that its language entirely subserves the purpose of attaining the four aims of human life: piety, pleasure, profit, and liberation. See *Nyāyasudhā*, 40. On the concept of "meta-injunction," see Kei Kataoka, "Scripture, Men and Heaven: Causal Structure in Kumārila's Action-Theory of *bhāvanā*," *Journal of Indian and Buddhist Studies* 49.2 (2001): 12–13.

> some are simply there to make it good poetry. All of them are valid insofar as their role is one of commendation.[47]

Kumārila assigns the *itihāsapurāṇa* literature a meaningful but subordinate role. It is certainly of human origin, though its authors (unlike the Buddha) had based their writings on their study of the Veda. But even within their compositions, there is a hierarchical organization of language. There are some direct injunctions that derive from the Veda. The vast majority of the literature, however, is *arthavāda*. As such, its role is one of either commending or condemning actions that have already been prescribed or proscribed by the Veda. Kumārila finds the whole enterprise mostly uninteresting. The *itihāsapurāṇa* may contain some useful accounts of royal genealogies, pretty hymns to deities, and a certain overall listening pleasure, but one should not give too much credence to their truth-claims. They are, after all, intended for everyone and make concessions to people's diverse intellectual capacities. The scope of the Veda, however, is emphatically restricted. In Kumārila's view, you may dabble in the *itihāsapurāṇa* if you wish, but don't think they will help you in any substantive way.

The twentieth-century Sanskritist Ganganath Jha called Kumārila's view on the authority of *purāṇas* a "liberal" one.[48] When compared to the eleventh-century Mīmāṁsaka Pārthasārathi Miśra, Kumārila does come off as rather broad-minded. In the opening chapter of his *Śāstradīpikā*, Pārthasārathi engages in a fierce polemic against several philosophical schools on issues of epistemology, saving particular rancor for Advaita Vēdānta. In one of these diatribes, he castigates Vēdāntins for their excessive reliance on texts that they have utterly misunderstood and that themselves provoke confusion: "This Advaita doctrine has been promulgated by people who: (a) are deluded by the Upaniṣadic discourses that figuratively discuss the unreality

[47] *Mīmāṁsādarśana*, vol. 1B, 116, ll. 6–16: *ēvaṁ bhāratādivākyāni vyākhyēyāni. tēṣām api hi "śrāvayēc caturō varṇān" ity ēvamādividhyanusārēṇa puruṣārthatvānvēṣaṇād akṣarādi vyatikramya dharmārthakāmamōkṣādharmānarthaduḥkhasaṁsārasādhyasādhanapratipattir upādānaparityāgāṅgabhūtā phalam. tatrāpi tu dānarājamōkṣadharmādiṣu kēcit sākṣād vidhayaḥ kēcit punaḥ parakṛtipurākalparūpēṇārthavādāḥ. sarvōpākhyānēṣu tātparyē sati "śrāvayēd" iti vidhēr ānarthakyāt kathaṁcid gamyamānastutinindāparigrahaḥ. tatparatvāc ca nātīvōpākhyānēṣu tattvābhinivēśaḥ kāryaḥ. vēdaprasthānābhyāsēna hi vālmīkidvaipāyanaprabhṛtibhis tathaiva svavākyāni praṇītāni. pratipādyānāṁ ca vicitrabuddhitvād yuktam ēvaitat. iha kēcid vidhimātrēṇa pratipadyantē. aparē sārthavādēnāparē'lpēnārthavādēnāparē mahatā. sarvēṣāṁ ca cittaṁ grahītavyam ity ēvam ārambhaḥ. tatra tu kēcid vidhipratiṣēdhāḥ śrutimūlāḥ kēcid arthasukhādiṣu lōkamūlās tathārthavādāḥ kēcid vaidikā ēva kēcil laukikā ēva kēcit tu svayam ēva kāvyanyāyēna racitāḥ. sarvē ca stutyarthēna pramāṇam.*

[48] Ganganath Jha, *Pūrva Mīmāṁsā in Its Sources* (Benares: Benares Hindu University, 1942), 215.

of the unstable world and actually praise Brahman and by the *itihāsapurāṇa* that conform to them, (b) do not comprehend the overall meaning of textual statements, and (c) have put zero effort into logical reasoning. Therefore, it is a madman's chatter that should be totally disregarded."[49] The fundamental disagreement here between Pārthasārathi and his Vēdāntin interlocutor is on the value of the Upaniṣads. For Mīmāṁsakas, the Upaniṣads mostly fell under the category of *arthavāda*. Since they do not instruct us in the performance of ritual action, except in certain quasi-ritualistic meditative injunctions, they must be subordinate to the overall ritual context of the Veda. Mīmāṁsakas urged that the Upaniṣads do not actually tell us about really existing things. Their teachings about the self only reinforce the commonsense notion that a sacrificer must have a noncorporeal, permanent self in order to perform his ritual actions and enjoy their fruits in another world. All their talk about the illusory nature of the world is only a figurative way to discuss its inconstancy. As *arthavāda*s, Pārthasārathi says, the Upaniṣads function just like the *itihāsapurāṇa*, whose fictional narratives have no standing of their own and can at best commend the performance of Vedic ritual. Pārthasārathi criticizes Vēdāntic reading practices here more than the texts on which they rely. Nevertheless, he is clear about the role of those texts. The Upaniṣads, lumped together with *itihāsapurāṇa*, must not exceed the scope given to them by Mīmāṁsā interpretive theory.

For Vēdāntins, however, the Upaniṣads were independently meaningful. Not only were they not "merely" *arthavāda*, but they worked as sources of valid knowledge because the ritual portion of the Veda did not exhaust its communicative scope. The Vedas should be understood as offering information and not just injunctions. From this perspective, the Upaniṣads were meaningful precisely because they allowed one to be released from the onerous burdens of ritual activity. A statement is authoritative not because it makes you do something (*cōdanā* or *niyōga*), but because it gets you what you want (*iṣṭasādhana*). It is well known how Vēdāntins overturned the Mīmāṁsā hierarchy of Vedic language in order to support the authority of the Upaniṣads.[50] But early Vēdāntins like Śaṅkara agreed with the Mīmāṁsakas'

[49] *Śāstradīpikā*, ed. Kiśoradāsa Svāmī (Vārāṇasī: Sādhuvelā Saṁskṛta Mahāvidyālaya, 1977), 65: *tasmād brahmaṇaḥ praśaṁsārthair asthāyitvēna prapañcasyāsattvam upacaradbhir aupaniṣadair vādais tadanusāribhiś ca itihāsapurāṇair bhrāntānāṁ vākyatātparyam ajānānāṁ nyāyābhiyōgaśūnyānāṁ pralāpō'yam advaitavāda ity upēkṣaṇīyaḥ.*

[50] Wilhelm Halbfass, "Human Reason and Vedic Revelation in Advaita Vedānta," in *Tradition and Reflection: Explorations in Indian Thought*, ed. Wilhelm Halbfass (Albany: SUNY Press, 1991), 148–151.

desire to limit scriptural proliferation. For Śaṅkara, the Upaniṣads alone, being nothing but the revealed word of the Veda, could effect liberation on the part of its listeners.

Around the turn of the first millennium, however, philosophers who accepted the authority of Śaiva and Vaiṣṇava religious scriptures argued for their validity, sometimes accepting and sometimes rejecting the Mīmāṁsā terms of debate. One such argument was put forward by the ninth-century Śaiva Jayanta Bhaṭṭa in his *Nyāyamañjarī*. Jayanta distinguished types of Āgamas, or non-Vedic scriptures, differentiating between those that did or did not explicitly contradict the Veda. He argued that the Śaiva Āgamas were just as valid as the Veda but not for the reasons that Mīmāṁsakas offered. As a proponent of Nyāya philosophy, Jayanta believed that the authority of scripture rested in its having been composed by a reliable author, namely God. According to Jayanta, both the Śaiva Āgamas and the Veda were composed by God, and as such found mainstream acceptance within a respectable public. In appealing to both divine and human authorities, Jayanta at once extended and limited the scope of authoritative scripture, including the Śaiva Āgamas but excluding Buddhist scriptures that directly contradicted the Veda.

Another serious attempt to expand the canon of Sanskrit scripture was the *Āgamaprāmāṇya* of Yāmuna (eleventh century), considered to be a forerunner of the Śrīvaiṣṇava tradition of Vedānta.[51] In this book, Yāmuna put forth two main arguments for why the Pāñcarātra Āgamas, Vaiṣṇava scriptural texts which technically fell outside the Vedic canon, should be considered valid sources of knowledge. First, he stated that the Āgamas are the direct utterances of the god Viṣṇu and therefore supremely authoritative. Second, he claimed that they achieve Vedic status by being derived from a lost recension of the White Yajurvēda, the Ēkāyana Śākhā. While the former approach strays into broader theistic modes of argument, the latter more closely mirrors the Mīmāṁsā defense of *smṛti* as "Veda remembered." According to Yāmuna's thirteenth-century commentator Vēdānta Dēśika, it was quite possible that, like the *smṛti*, the Āgamas had as their basis Vedic texts that are now lost to us. We may thus infer the authority for practices not validated by extant Vedic texts. In cases of contradiction between *śruti*

[51] Among Śrīvaiṣṇavas, the *Tiruvāymoḷi* of Nammāḻvār was believed to be a "Tamil Veda" that paralleled, not just imitated or derived from, the Sanskrit Veda. See John Carman and Vasudha Narayanan, *The Tamil Veda: Piḷḷān's Interpretation of the Tiruvāymoḷi* (Chicago: University of Chicago Press, 1989).

and *smṛti*, one must differentially situate them according to their relative strength. But if there was contradiction between the Āgama and the Veda, one may choose freely between them, given that differences can be chalked up to particular contexts of time, place, and eligible agents. Vēdānta Dēśika is more circumspect than Yāmuna here in toeing the Mīmāṁsā line.[52] He is content with the argument that the Āgamas have the Veda as their root and gives them an extra edge over *smṛti* with the passing remark that they are also "directly grounded in God's compassion." In both cases, however, authority is derivative. The *smṛti* and the Āgamas occupy the same place on the podium, even if one is stretching its neck a little higher for the photographers.[53]

This state of affairs changed with the advent of the iconoclastic exegete Madhva, who opened the scriptural canon to "all sacred lore."[54] Madhva refashioned the *vēdamūla* doctrine to mean that any text which illuminates the meaning of the Veda, and is therefore "rooted" in it, is independently valid. This included not only Pāñcarātra Āgamas, but the *Mahābhārata*, the *purāṇas*, and all of those "unknown sources" which Madhva was infamous for quoting.[55] In Madhva's account, these authored sources manifested simultaneously with the eternal Veda, since both were transmitted by the god Viṣṇu through a series of hierarchically ordered sages.[56] Thus no one text tradition is given a privileged place; each informs the other in a symbiotic relationship.

The *Bhāgavata Purāṇa*, however, had its own ideas about scriptural hierarchy. Although *purāṇas* were generally classified by Mīmāṁsakas as *smṛti*, they themselves were concerned with appropriating the status of *śruti*, the "fifth Veda." Among *purāṇas*, the *Bhāgavata* was distinctive in

[52] However, see the opening to Vēdānta Deśika's *Pāñcarātrarakṣā* for the unambiguous claim that the Āgamas are valid because they are God's infallible word. *Śrī Pāñcarātrarakṣā of Śrī Vedānta Deśika*, ed. M. Duraiswami Aiyangar and T. Venugopalacharya (Madras: The Adyar Library and Research Centre, 1967), 2.

[53] J. A. B. van Buitenen, *Yāmuna's Āgama Prāmāṇyam* (Madras: Ramanuja Research Society, 1971); M. Narasimhachary, "Introductory Study," in *Āgamaprāmāṇya of Yāmuna*, ed. M. Narasimhachary (Baroda: Oriental Institute, 1976), 11–12. For Dēśika's comment, see *Nyayaparishuddhi by Sri Venkatnath Sri Vedāntāchārya*, ed. Vidyabhūshan Lakshmanāchārya (Benares: Vidya Vilas Press, 1918), 474–475: *sākṣād īśvaradayāmūlatvāt.*

[54] Valerie Stoker, "Conceiving the Canon in Dvaita Vedānta: Madhva's Doctrine of 'All Sacred Lore,'" *Numen* 51.1 (2004): 48–77.

[55] Roque Mesquita, *Madhva's Unknown Literary Sources: Some Observations* (New Delhi: Aditya Prakashan, 2000).

[56] Stoker, "Conceiving the Canon," 60.

its claims to be the quintessential scripture, the fruit and the culmination of the entire Brahmanical canon.[57] This would have posed a significant problem to Mīmāṁsakas had the very genre of *purāṇa* not been so irrelevant to the figures studied so far. But when it emerged from the narrative into the scholastic world, the *Bhāgavata* had a much bigger impact than any previous reworking of Mīmāṁsā. If in the Mīmāṁsā taxonomy, the *Bhāgavata* as *purāṇa* was on a par with *smṛti*, it certainly acted like *śruti*. The *Bhāgavata* believed that its language was just as powerful, just as capable of effecting action and communicating knowledge, as that of the Vedas and the Upaniṣads, and that it was the best and brightest of all the *purāṇas*.[58] This claim bolstered the *Bhāgavata*'s overall strategy to exalt love for God, *bhakti*, above meaningless ritual and dry philosophy. But that strategy remained a rhetorical one, inasmuch as it was confined to the language of scripture and not of scriptural interpretation. It is here that Lakṣmīdhara's intervention in the *Kaumudī* became so crucial. The *Kaumudī* posed a scholastic and not merely rhetorical challenge to the Mīmāṁsā discourse of scriptural orthodoxy by using the language of Mīmāṁsā both to legitimize the authority of the genre of *purāṇa* and to rank it above the genre of *smṛti*. Among the many ritual, ethical, and social norms that the genre of *smṛti* represented, the *Kaumudī* selected for criticism the normative practices of expiation prescribed by *dharmaśāstra*. In these sources of Brahmanical jurisprudence, each transgression had its own corresponding expiation. The intricacies of these practices formed the subject of centuries of Sanskrit scholarship on *dharmaśāstra*. The *Bhāgavata*, however, dispensed with all such practices through narrative and didactic episodes that demonstrated the power of God's name. The *Kaumudī* used the *Bhāgavata*'s criticisms of Brahmanical orthopraxy as a foundation on which to stake a claim for the *purāṇa*'s place in the hierarchy of Sanskrit scripture. Its attempt to expand and, in fact, supplant parts of the Sanskrit scriptural canon reflects one of the first scholastic elaborations of the *Bhāgavata*'s own claims to being a "*purāṇa* that is Veda."[59]

[57] Barbara Holdrege, "From Purāṇa-Veda to Kārṣṇa-Veda: The Bhāgavata Purāṇa as Consummate Śruti and Smṛti Incarnate," *Journal of Vaishnava Studies* 15.1 (2006): 31–70.
[58] Holdrege, "From Purāṇa-Veda to Kārṣṇa-Veda," 52.
[59] Cf. Fred Smith, "Purāṇaveda," in *Authority, Anxiety, and Canon: Essays in Vedic Interpretation*, ed. Laurie L. Patton (Albany: State University of New York Press, 1994), 97–138.

Love Is All You Need

What distinguishes the *Kaumudī*'s treatment of *purāṇa* from earlier discourse on the topic is that the stakes are significantly higher. The *Bhāgavata*'s self-aggrandizing language prompts the *Kaumudī*'s author to reckon with the superiority of its truth-claims and, importantly, its social practices. The *Kaumudī* systematically develops one of these claims: singing God's name removes all sins and provides a beneficial end to its agent. The *Kaumudī* is strewn with quotations from several *purāṇas* that support the power of singing God's name, but it is the *Bhāgavata* that "grabs it by the horns" (*śṛṅg-agrāhikayā*).[60] A single verse from the story of Ajāmila, where we began this chapter, sums up the thesis (*Bhāgavata* 6.2.10):

> For all sinners whosoever,
> this single thing serves as atonement:
> To recite the name of Viṣṇu,
> for one's mind has turned to him.[61]

Such claims about the power of the name are part of the *Bhāgavata*'s narrative strategy of exalting Kṛṣṇa as the ultimate God, but they comprise only a minor section of the text as a whole. Lakṣmīdhara, however, extracts from this story an entire theology of the divine name. The first chapter of the *Kaumudī* seeks to disprove the claim that statements in the *purāṇa* do not have "intended meaning" (*vivakṣitārtha*), in other words, that they do not contribute anything new, because their role is simply to commend. In this chapter, Lakṣmīdhara lambastes the "scaremongering of those who have misunderstood Mīmāṁsā discourse" (*aviditamīmāṁsāvṛttāntānāṁ vibhīṣikā*) who say that the *purāṇa* is merely *arthavāda*[62]—an ironic accusation, to say the least, because virtually every Mīmāṁsaka in history had said precisely that. The specific opponent to whom Lakṣmīdhara was responding is not certain, but given my reconstruction of prior Mīmāṁsā discussions of the *purāṇa*, one can imagine that there was resistance to his efforts. Indeed, the critique that the *purāṇas* were nothing but *arthavāda* was felt closely enough to merit a response in the late

60 *Kaumudī*, 70.
61 *sarvēṣām apy aghavatām idam ēva suniṣkṛtam*
nāmavyāharaṇaṁ viṣṇōr yatas tadviṣayā matiḥ.
62 *Kaumudī*, 16.

Bṛhannāradīya Purāṇa (1.61): "O best of Brahmins, those who proclaim that *purāṇas*, which discuss the entire *dharma*, are *arthavāda*, are going straight to hell."[63] An utterance's being able to contribute something new, and not simply convey meaning, hinged on its ability to effect practical action along the lines of a Vedic command. Lakṣmīdhara's opponent attempts to foreclose that possibility, suggesting that the *purāṇa*'s valorization of singing the name of God simply falls under the category of praise (*stāvakatva*), which is the sole prerogative of the *arthavāda*. This follows closely on Kumārila Bhaṭṭa's note that statements in the *itihāsapurāṇa* are authoritative inasmuch as their role is to commend an injunction previously derived from the Veda. Only Vedic injunctions, in the Mīmāṁsā view, are "self-validating," for instead of describing something that already exists, thereby making a statement potentially falsifiable, they prompt one to bring about a new state of affairs that is not accessible by any other means of knowledge. Lakṣmīdhara responds by appealing to the Vēdāntic view that the validity of a scriptural statement is not limited to its injunctive capacity but includes the ability to instruct us regarding already existent entities. The *purāṇa* is reliable for the same reason: we instinctively understand from it either a course of ritual action or some factual truth.[64] Even its most innocuous claims can and must be interpreted as valid in their own right. All the six Vēdāntic principles that serve as "indicators of purport" (*tātparyaliṅga*)—the unity between opening and closing statements, repetition, novelty, result, plausibility, and commendation—can be applied to stories like Ajāmila's. Moreover, he says, following the classical Vēdāntins Śaṅkara and Maṇḍana Miśra, a *vidhi* is nothing but the unique means to a desired end (*iṣṭasādhana*). Such a statement could be in an injunctive modality or derived from some other discursive context. When the *Bhāgavata* says that all you need is to utter God's name, it fulfills all the criteria of a Vedic command.[65]

In this, at least, Lakṣmīdhara may have found a kindred spirit in his contemporary *Bhāgavata* commentator Śrīdhara. In his commentary on this section of the *Bhāgavata*, Śrīdhara offers some brief remarks that resemble Lakṣmīdhara's more elaborate defense of the *purāṇa*'s injunctive power

[63] R. C. Hazra, *Studies in the Upapurāṇas*, vol. 1 (Calcutta: Sanskrit College, 1958), 312, n. 115: *purāṇēṣu dvijaśrēṣṭāḥ sarvadharmapravaktṛṣu pravadanty arthavādatvaṁ yē tē narakabhājanāḥ*.

[64] *Kaumudī*, 12.

[65] *Kaumudī*, 25. On the invention of the "six indicators of purport" by the tenth-century Advaitin Prakāśātman, see Yigal Bronner and Lawrence McCrea, *First Words, Last Words: New Theories for Reading Old Texts in Sixteenth-Century India* (New York: Oxford University Press, 2021), 41–42.

in the first chapter of the *Kaumudī*. Commenting on *Bhāgavata* 6.2.8, which reaffirms that Ajāmila was released from all his sins by calling out for Nārāyaṇa, Śrīdhara responds to an objection that reciting God's name simply enhances one's everyday ritual activities (*sarvakarmasādguṇya*), and cannot remove sins all by itself:

> Even when God's name is an element of performing ritual actions, it can serve as the ultimate expiation, because of the logic of "distinctness of connection," which suggests that the same thing can be used differently in two cases. It applies here as in the case of *khādira* wood.[66] So we have thousands of cases in the *purāṇa*s where the name functions independently (e.g., *Viṣṇu Purāṇa* 6.8.19): "Even when his name is uttered inadvertently, a person's sins instantly scatter, like so many deer scared off by a lion." One shouldn't think that these are *arthavāda*s, because they are not subordinate to any *vidhi*. Nor should the lack of an explicit injunctive modality make one believe that these sentences must be subordinate to something else. We have indicative sentences in the Veda that serve as *vidhi*s, inasmuch as they communicate something that is not a given, accessible by any other means of knowledge. There are Vedic *mantra*s, too (*Ṛg Veda* 8.11.9; 1.156.3), from which we glean that the name is more powerful than all other acts, including austerity and charity. And as it is, the discourse on the corporeality of gods (*Brahma Sūtra* 1.3) shows that *mantra*s and *arthavāda*s are authoritative with respect to their own subject matter.[67] Therefore, all one's sins can be removed even by the mere semblance of the name of Lord Nārāyaṇa.[68]

[66] *Mīmāṁsā Sūtra* 4.3.5 says that in a case where one and the same thing is both obligatory as well as contingent or optional, there is "distinctness of connection" (*saṁyōgapṛthaktva*), such that the same thing can be used in two cases. In his commentary, Śabara gives the example of two Vedic sentences that enjoin the use of *khādira* wood—one for the purpose of the ritual act (*kratvartha*), and the other for obtaining an end beneficial to the human agent (*puruṣārtha*). Śrīdhara analogizes the work of the *khādira* to that of God's name. In one instance, it supports activities such as austerity and sacrifice, but in another context, it can remove all sins.

[67] See Francis X. Clooney, "*Devatādhikaraṇa*: A Theological Debate in the Mīmāṁsā-Vedānta Tradition," *Journal of Indian Philosophy* 16.3 (1988): 277–298. Cf. Halbfass, "Human Reason and Vedic Revelation in Advaita Vedānta," 150.

[68] *Bhāvārthabōdhinī*, 282: *ayaṁ bhāvaḥ—karmāṅgatvē'pi harināmnaḥ khādiratvādivat saṁyōgapṛthaktvēna sarvaprāyaścittārthatvaṁ yuktam ēva. tathā hi—"avaśēnāpi yannāmni kīrtitē sarvapātakaiḥ pumān vimucyatē sadyaḥ siṁhatrastair mṛgair iva" ityādibhiḥ purāṇair tāvat sahasraśō nāmnaḥ svātantryam avagamyatē. na caitē arthavādā iti śaṅkanīyam, vidhiśēṣatvābhāvāt. na ca vidhyaśravaṇād anyaśēṣatā kalpanīyā yadā "āgnēyō'ṣṭākapālō bhavati" ityādivad aprāptārthatvēna vidhikalpanōpapattēḥ. mantrēṣu ca "martā amartyasya tē bhūri nāma manāmahē. viprāsō jātavēdasaḥ," "āsya jānantō nāma cidviviktana" ityādiṣu nāmnas tapōdānādisarvadharmādhikyam avagamyatē. upapāditaṁ ca mantrārthavādānām api svārthē prāmāṇyaṁ dēvatādhikaraṇē. tasmāc chrīnārāyaṇanāmābhāsamātrēṇaiva sarvāghaniṣkṛtaṁ syād iti.*

The second chapter of the *Kaumudī* is dedicated to refuting the idea that the practice of reciting God's name is effective only as an auxiliary to other ritual acts, particularly expiation.[69] Śrīdhara's argument here looks like Lakṣmīdhara's in a nutshell: There are sentences in the *purāṇa* that tell us that uttering God's name removes all sins. They are not *arthavāda*s because there are no *vidhi*s present to which they could be subordinated. Although they are in the indicative mood, they possess the power of injunction. The same is true of many indicative sentences in the Veda which have been interpreted as injunctions. There are also Vedic *mantra*s that extol the power of God's name, and according to Vēdānta discourse, *mantra*s and *arthavāda*s are just as instructive as *vidhi*s. Therefore, utterances of the *purāṇa* function effectively like Vedic commands. This is an argument admirable for its brevity and self-assurance, but it does not engage thoroughly with Mīmāṁsā's opposition to the *purāṇa*'s independent authority. Nor does it deal with the problem of weighing the language of the *purāṇa* against that of *smṛti*, given that the methods of expiation they prescribe are incommensurate. Even in the few instances where Śrīdhara does bring up this conflict, he softens the *Bhāgavata*'s critique of *smṛti*.[70] Furthermore, at the beginning of his commentary on the *Viṣṇu Purāṇa*, he sticks with the traditional explanation that the *purāṇa*s are authoritative and purposeful because, like *smṛti*, they are the recorded memories of their human authors and they are based on the Veda "like the breath of God" (*īśvaraniśvasitasvarūpatvēna*).[71]

Lakṣmīdhara, however, paints the *dharmaśāstra* tradition, encapsulated here by the term *smṛti*, as inimical to that of the *Bhāgavata*. In the third chapter of the *Kaumudī*, he offers two possibilities when it comes to negotiating the disparity between practices of expiation in the *purāṇa* and the *smṛti*. One is *vyavasthā*, "differential situation," and the other *vikalpa*, or "option theory." These terms were first used in Mīmāṁsā to resolve conflicts between ritual

[69] On the parallels with Śrīdhara's response to the concept of *sarvakarmasādguṇya*, see *Kaumudī*, 33, 48.

[70] *Bhāgavata* 6.3.24, for example, says that "great men" are usually confused by *māyā* and do not know the *dharma* of the *Bhāgavata*. Echoing *Bhagavad Gītā* 2.42, it criticizes them for being dulled by the sweet, flowery language of the Vedas, and for engaging in massive sacrificial rites. Śrīdhara interprets the subject to be great authors of *dharmaśāstra*, who prescribe difficult expiations like doctors prescribe bitter herbs. To say that their minds have been "dulled" by the Vedas really means that they are "absorbed" in them. That is why they engage in super-extensive rituals and not minor ones. For everyday people have faith in great big *mantra*s but not in short ones. Therefore, says Śrīdhara, the *smṛti* writers did not actually mean that there was no scope for accepting the *bhāgavata dharma*. See *Bhāvārthabōdhinī*, 286.

[71] *Viṣṇupurāṇa with Sanskrit Commentary of Sridharacharya*, vol. 1, ed. Thanesh Chandra Upreti (Delhi: Parimal Publications, 1986), 1.

injunctions and were later adopted by authors of *dharmaśāstra*.[72] According to the principle of *vyavasthā*, the alternatives opened up by a conflict between injunctions are restricted to defined groups of people. In the *Kaumudī*, an opponent invokes this principle to say that in the matter of choosing between either singing God's name or performing normative practices of expiation, the people involved must be differentially qualified. Only those who sing with "faith" (*śraddhā*), among other qualities, can achieve its result. Others, however, must undertake expiations prescribed by *smṛti*.[73] Lakṣmīdhara, on the other hand, supports the *vikalpa*, which permits the practitioner an open option between injunctions that are of equal authority. Since the *purāṇa* and the *smṛti* are on equal footing, one may choose freely between them. Lakṣmīdhara sardonically assures his worried opponent that there is still a place for *smṛti* at the end of the day. He analogizes the choice in question to that of choosing between types of medication from a doctor—some are easy to swallow, and others are painful. Some people, he says, are inherently averse to the "easier" medication, so they are given a different one. Since people are generally divorced from God, their hearts engulfed with bad habits that are difficult to resist, they are given other, more complicated methods of expiation.[74]

In the middle of this debate, Lakṣmīdhara offers a fascinating and radically new claim about how one should think about the *purāṇa*. No longer is it sufficient to treat the *purāṇa* and *smṛti* as distinct genres on the same playing field, just to avoid conflict between them:

> We may comfortably say that no scriptural citation conflicts with any other one. It is only in order to settle the minds of eligible agents of middling faith that we have imagined this path of non-contradiction. But there is another, far truer way of thinking, which runs as follows: In matters of contradiction between *smṛti* and *purāṇa*, none of these methods of differentiation really enters into it. For there *does* exist a hierarchy of authority between them. *Smṛtis*, of course, are the utterances of great sages, composed in different

[72] Patrick Olivelle, *The Āśrama System: The History and Hermeneutics of a Religious Institution* (Oxford: Oxford University Press, 1993), 134–136. On the changing nature of the division of scholastic labor between Mīmāṁsakas and *dharmaśāstrīs* from classical to early modern India, see Lawrence McCrea, "Hindu Jurisprudence and Scriptural Hermeneutics," in *Hinduism and Law: An Introduction*, ed. Timothy Lubin, Donald R. Davis Jr., and Jayanth K. Krishnan (Cambridge: Cambridge University Press, 2010), 123–137.

[73] *Kaumudī*, 70–74.

[74] *Kaumudī*, 130.

> words, based on their understanding of the Veda. *But purāṇas are nothing but Vedas.*[75]

In this crucial passage, Lakṣmīdhara goes further than his predecessors in evaluating the place of *purāṇa* in the hierarchy of Sanskrit scripture. Not only does *purāṇa* supplant *smṛti*, but it does so because *purāṇa is Veda.* As we have said before, the *Bhāgavata* accords itself Vedic status in order to represent itself as the revelation of Kṛṣṇa in turn identified with the Vedic revelation.[76] Lakṣmīdhara goes on to provide a defense of this equation on etymological and linguistic terms:

> As it says in the *Mānava Dharmaśāstra* and the *Mahābhārata* (1.12.4ab), "One should corroborate the Veda with *itihāsapurāṇa*." There is also the etymology "X is '*purāṇa*' because it 'fills out' [*pūraṇāt*]." You cannot "fill out" the Veda with something that is other-than-Veda [*avēdēna*]. For instance, you can't complete an unfinished golden bracelet with tin. You may object: "If the word 'Veda' includes both *itihāsa* and *purāṇa*, then we must find something else for '*purāṇa*' (in the verse) to signify. And if it doesn't, then there cannot be complete identification between Veda and *itihāsapurāṇa*." We would reply that insofar as (the *purāṇa* is) a cluster of words of non-personal origin which presents a particular unified meaning, it is no different from Veda. Nevertheless, we indicate their difference on account of interruptions in pitch accent.[77]

According to the opponent, interpreting the *Mahābhārata* verse cited by Lakṣmīdhara involves a possible contradiction. The analogy of filling in gold with gold would imply that the *purāṇa* is not separate from the Veda. But if the *purāṇas* are included in the meaning of the word "Veda," there would be no reason for the text to mention them separately. The verse should

[75] *Kaumudī*, 91, emphasis added: *na kēnacit kiṁcid virudhyata iti sarvaṁ sustham. ēvaṁ madhyamaśraddhānām adhikāriṇāṁ manāṁsi samādhātum utprēkṣatē panthānam avirōdhasya. anya ēva punaḥ panthāḥ pāramārthikaḥ, tathā hi smṛtipurāṇavirōdhē vyavasthādayō naiva niviśante, viṣamaṁ hi prāmāṇyam anayōḥ, vēdād avagatē'rthē padāntarair upanibaddhāni maharṣivākyāni khalu smṛtayaḥ, purāṇāni punar vēdā ēva.*

[76] Holdrege, "From Purāṇa-Veda to Kārṣṇa-Veda," 56.

[77] *Kaumudī*, 91: *śrīmahābhāratē mānavīye ca—"itihāsapurāṇābhyāṁ vēdaṁ samupabṛṁhayēt" iti vacanāt, pūraṇāt purāṇam iti vyutpattēś ca, na ca atra avēdēna vēdasya bṛṁhaṇaṁ saṁbhavati, na hy aparipūrṇasya kanakavalayasya trapuṇā pūraṇaṁ saṁbhavati. nanu yadi vēdaśabdaḥ purāṇam itihāsaṁ ca upādattē tarhi purāṇam anyad ēva anvēṣaṇīyam; yadi tu na, na tarhi itihāsapurāṇayōr abhēdō vēdēna? ucyatē—viśiṣṭaikārthapratipādakasya padakadambakasya apauruṣēyatvād abhēdē'pi svarakramabhēdād bhēdanirdēśō'py upapadyatē.*

simply say, "One should corroborate the Veda with the Veda." Lakṣmīdhara responds that there is a kind of internal differentiation—namely, the lack of fixed sequence of intonation—which accounts for the difference in terminology. The pitch-accented portion of the Veda must be supplemented by the non-tonally regulated *purāṇa*. This is not a historicist claim about the shift from Vedic to classical Sanskrit. *Purāṇa* is nothing but Veda, unauthored and eternal, but it is articulated in slightly different, unaccented words. As such it can be mentioned separately, even if the referent of both Veda and *purāṇa* is the same.[78] The playful connection between *purāṇa*, "ancient lore," and *pūraṇa*, "filling out," allows Lakṣmīdhara to reuse an old concept to describe the function of the genre: corroboration or augmentation (*upabr̥ṁhaṇa*). In the eleventh century, the Śrīvaiṣṇava theologian Rāmānuja used the concept of *upabr̥ṁhaṇa* to bolster the authority of the *Viṣṇu Purāṇa*. Not only did he use the *Viṣṇu Purāṇa* to support his readings of canonical texts of Vedānta; he also read theological concepts from the *purāṇa* into those texts.[79] For Rāmānuja, however, the authority of the *purāṇa*s was predicated on their divine authorship, not their Vedic status. He privileged the *Viṣṇu Purāṇa* because it was composed by the creator-god Brahmā in his most lucid state and because it was accepted most widely by educated people.[80] The *Kaumudī*, however, does away with the gap between Veda and *purāṇa* entirely, saying that one cannot "fill out" or "augment" the Veda with anything that is not Veda. If there is any conflict between Veda and *purāṇa*, says Lakṣmīdhara, the latter loses out only because it happens to come later in the order of recitation, where the content could differ; when it comes to *smr̥ti*, however, the *purāṇa* is always preferable.[81]

Rather shocked by this wholesale overturning of scriptural hierarchy, Lakṣmīdhara's opponent follows the argument to its logical extent. Does Lakṣmīdhara really mean to say that the *purāṇa* completely supersedes

[78] The commentator Anantadēva notes that the mention of "particular but unified meaning" appeals to the principle of "the Brahmin and the mendicants" (*brāhmaṇaparivrājakanyāya*). In a sentence like "The Brahmins should be fed as should the mendicants," the separate mention of the latter, who are really included in the former term, merely emphasizes their position as the special part of the general body. Similarly, the separate mention of *purāṇa* from Veda simply shows that it is a part of the general corpus, differentiated by accent. For an interpretation of this difficult passage as quoted (silently) by Jīva Gōsvāmī, see David Buchta, "Defining Categories in Hindu Literature: The Purāṇas as Śruti in Baladeva Vidyābhūṣaṇa and Jīva Gosvāmi," *Journal of Vaishnava Studies* 15.1 (2006): 92.

[79] Sucharita Adluri, *Textual Authority in Classical Indian Thought: Rāmānuja and the Viṣṇu Purāṇa* (New York: Routledge, 2015).

[80] Sucharita Adluri, "Defining Śruti and Smr̥ti in Rāmānuja's Vedānta," *Journal of Vaishnava Studies* 15.1 (2006): 207–211.

[81] *Kaumudī*, 92.

smṛti? He might as well say that there is no place for the *smṛti* at all.[82] In his response, Lakṣmīdhara doubles down and says, Why stop there? The *purāṇa* has everything you need:

Objection: In that case, wouldn't these statements of the *purāṇa*, having cast off all fetters (i.e., all limits on their textual authority), each communicating their own subject as they desire, render the *smṛtis* empty of meaning entirely, insofar as the latter find themselves stripped of the barest opportunity?

Reply: That's just fine! How could anyone deny the directness of the *purāṇas* and introduce the concept of differential situation? After all, as (Śiva says to Pārvatī) in the *Nāradīya Purāṇa* (2.24.17): "My pretty-faced beloved, I consider the content of the *purāṇas* to be greater than the content of the Vedas! Dear goddess, the Veda is established within the *purāṇa*. There is no doubt on this matter." . . . The *Skanda Purāṇa* (untraced) says something similar: "*Śruti* and *smṛti* are the two eyes, the *purāṇa* is considered the heart. Without *śruti* and *smṛti*, one is blind, and would be one-eyed without one or the other. But it is better to be one-eyed or blind than without one's heart—that is, without the *purāṇa*."[83]

The claim seems tautological: the *purāṇas* are Veda because they tell us that they are (through the voice of Śiva). But it makes sense given the Mīmāṁsā background to the argument. Once again there are traces of Śaiva discourse, buried in the more ecumenical and all-encompassing language of the *purāṇas*. Śaivas were infamous for ranking their Āgamas above the Veda. Perhaps Lakṣmīdhara was channeling that sense of superiority through the *purāṇa*. If *purāṇa* is Veda, then its statements are self-validating, and we can interpret them just like we would Vedic statements. For example, Lakṣmīdhara uses a famous Mīmāṁsā analogy to explicate a verse from the *Viṣṇu Purāṇa* (2.6.40) that supports the overall thesis that singing God's

[82] For comparable readings of *Brahma Sūtra* 2.1.3, which bears on the problem of conflict between *smṛti* and other sources of knowledge, see David Buchta, "Baladēva Vidyābhūṣaṇa and the Vedāntic Refutation of Yoga," *Journal of Vaishnava* 14.1 (2005): 181–208.

[83] *Kaumudī*, 92–93: *ēvaṁ samullaṅghitasakalaśṛṅkhalēṣu yathāsvam ēva svaṁ svam artham abhidadhānēṣu purāṇavacanēṣu manāg api kvacid ēkam avakāśam alabhamānānāṁ smṛtīnāṁ yadi nāma viṣayasarvasvāpahāraḥ prasajyēta. prasajyatāṁ nāma, kathaṁ nu purāṇānām āñjasyam upamṛdya vyavasthāpanaprastāvaḥ. uktaṁ hi nāradīyē—"vedārthād adhikaṁ manyē purāṇārthaṁ varānanē. vēdaḥ pratiṣṭhitō dēvi purāṇē nātra saṁśayaḥ." . . . skāndē ca—"śrutismṛtī hi nētrē dvē purāṇaṁ hṛdayaṁ smṛtam. śrutismṛtibhyāṁ hīnō̃ndhaḥ kāṇaḥ syād ēkayā vinā. purāṇahīnād hṛcchūnyāt kāṇāndhāv api tau varau."*

name is all-purifying: "There is only one form of expiation for the affliction that attaches to a person when he has committed a sin: simply remember God's name."[84] Lakṣmīdhara argues that just like in Vedic injunctions, this statement does not describe the prerequisite for the eligible agent of a ritual action but rather the result of that action:

> For one afflicted by a particular thing, benefit lies in the removal of that thing. In this instance, to say that singing is the means to benefit one afflicted by sin is effectively to say that it is a means to removing sin. The word "simply" is a synonym for "exclusively." The idea is that singing is a self-sufficient means. The word "one" means "once," and the word "remember" restates the initial act prescribed by the injunction, since it brings to mind every iteration of the act of singing God's name. It has as its result an instigation in the form "This all checks out." (In commands like "one desirous of heaven should perform a sacrifice") the term "desirous of heaven" describes not a person, but the particular desired object, heaven, which is first required by the injunction defined by that object. Only in a second-order sense does the term "desirous of heaven" signify the actual eligible ritual participant. This is the conclusion of those who understand the heart of Mīmāṁsā.[85]

In this passage, Lakṣmīdhara argues that the ability to sing God's name to remove sins does not rest on the agent. He does not have to be afflicted, or desire release from that affliction, in order for singing God's name to work. It just so happens that the act of singing does that already. Just as the Vedic injunction to perform a sacrifice to attain heaven does not depend on the agent's desire to attain heaven, the statement in the *purāṇa* that "singing"—here recalled to the mind by the mention of "remembering" God's name—is enough to wipe away one's sins does not depend on any qualification on the part of the singer. The statement he cites here is not an injunction per se, but by offering

[84] *kṛtē pāpē'nutāpō vai yasya puṁsaḥ prajāyatē*
prāyaścittaṁ tu tasyaikaṁ harisaṁsmaraṇaṁ param.

[85] *Kaumudī*, 110: *yō hi yasmād anutaptas tasya tannivṛttir ēva hitaṁ tataś ca pāpād anutaptasya kīrtanaṁ hitasādhanam ityuktē pāpakṣayasādhanam ityuktaṁ bhavati, paraśabdaś ca kēvalaśabdaparyāyaḥ, kīrtanam ēva puṣkalaṁ sādhanam ityarthaḥ. ēkam api sakṛd iti ca harikīrtanasya sarvasyaiva smārakatvāt saṁsmaraṇam ityanuvādaḥ, sa ca prarōcanaphalaḥ; samīcīnaṁ hy ētad iti, svargakāmādipadam api samīhitalakṣaṇasya vidhēḥ prathamāpēkṣit-asamīhitaviśēṣaṇasamarpaṇaparam ēva na puruṣaparam, arthatas tu svargakāmō'dhikārīti mīmāṁsāhṛdayavēdināṁ nirṇayaḥ.*

an "instigation" (*prarōcana*), it functions as an *arthavāda* that recalls previous injunctions in the *purāṇa* itself to sing God's name. The point of this granular analysis is to show that in Lakṣmīdhara's view, every sentence in the *purāṇa* can be treated through the interpretive lens of Mīmāṁsā as if it were the language of the Veda—*because it is.*

The majority of the *Kaumudī* turns on just such increasingly fine points in Mīmāṁsā. For the *purāṇa* as a genre to be officially reckoned among the canon of Sanskrit scripture would have required engaging with the norms of the preeminent discourse on the topic.[86] The *Kaumudī* represents a shift in the way intellectuals trained in Mīmāṁsā perceived the *Bhāgavata Purāṇa*, not merely as a supplementary source, but as an independently authoritative scripture. However, hardly anyone in the Mīmāṁsā camp paid attention to the *Kaumudī*'s arguments. Instead, it was those immersed in the world of Vēdānta who picked up on its ideas. This is not surprising given the author's affinity for Vēdāntic hermeneutical principles and composition of Advaita works. Yet the *Kaumudī*'s Vēdāntic affiliations were not especially straightforward. In order to assess how this text was received by diverse communities in later centuries, we must understand its relationship with the classical tradition of Advaita Vēdānta.

Vēdānta in the Moonlight

Both Lakṣmīdhara in Kerala and Śrīdhara Svāmī in Orissa belonged to a class of Vēdāntins who sought to reenvision their relationship with classical Advaita Vēdānta. Beginning with Ānandagiri and Anubhūtisvarūpācārya in the thirteenth century, Advaita Vēdāntins in Orissa embarked on a project of canonizing Śaṅkara's works while distancing themselves from the competing Advaita of Maṇḍana Miśra. In Kerala, as we saw in the previous chapter, writers like Pūrṇasarasvatī combined Śaiva nondualism and Vaiṣṇava *bhakti* to produce a distinctive local configuration of Advaita that traced itself to

[86] Annabel Brett's comments on the strategies authors must use in order to make intellectual interventions are germane: "Any prospective agent is limited not only in what he or she can conceive, but also in what he or she can legitimate or justify, by the shared horizons of expectation implicit in a particular language. Because of the link between public discourse and public action, an agent proposing an innovative course of action would necessarily also need to engage in one of several possible linguistic strategies (the most common of which is attempting to redescribe the proposed action within the normative terminology of the prevailing discourse)." Annabel Brett, "What Is Intellectual History Now?," in *What Is History Now?*, ed. David Cannadine (London: Palgrave Macmillan, 2002), 119.

the historical Śaṅkara. The links between these two regions and trends may be closer than previously understood. For example, the brand of Advaitic theism that characterized Śrīdhara's *Bhāgavata* commentary may have been transported from South India by one Mādhavēndra Purī, a "Śāṅkarite monk" who was "connected with a whole stream of religious attitudes within *advaita*."[87] Locating the *Bhāgavata Purāṇa* at the center of this stream puts us in a better position to understand this form of Advaita Vēdānta, both connected to its classical heritage and departing from it in identifiable ways.

Despite his own composition of the *Advaitamakaranda* and his thoroughly Advaitic reading of the *Bhāgavata* in the *Amr̥tataraṅgiṇī*, Lakṣmīdhara inhabited the Advaita world at an oblique angle. For example, in the third chapter of the *Kaumudī*, an interlocutor suggests that all the author's talk about "remembering" the name of God actually stands in for something more important: the realization of the nondual Ātman. One should interpret references to a personal god and devotional practice in a language appropriate to Advaita Vēdānta:

> *Objection*: Well who wouldn't say that "remembering Kr̥ṣṇa" can remove all sins, from the most heinous to the miscellaneous? After all, that is nothing but knowledge of Brahman. You see, there are two possible analyses of the word "Kr̥ṣṇa": a) the one who ploughs up [*kr̥ṣati*], that is, tears up or splits apart the forest of *saṁsāra*, or b) the one who drags [*karṣati*], that is, attracts or brings under control the ignorance of Ātman. Kr̥ṣṇa is the supreme Ātman, in other words, existence-and-joy. . . . To remember, or rather, to repeatedly think about that perfect being of joy, who is the Ātman of everyone, is in fact meditation [*nididhyāsana*]. That means either repeated concentration on a similar thought or the removal of heterogeneous thoughts. Meditation serves as an auxiliary to achieving the result of "hearing" the Upaniṣads [*śravaṇa*], which results in the direct understanding of the Ātman. Just like meditation removes the doubt that the Ātman is what the Upaniṣads say it is, it also becomes a means to that understanding by destroying the sins that prevent it.[88]

[87] Hardy, "Mādhavendra Purī," 37.

[88] *Kaumudī*, 62–63: *nanu kō nāma na brūtē kr̥ṣṇānusmaraṇaṁ mahāpātakādiprakīrṇāntasarvāghasaṁharaṇam iti, sā hi brahmavidyā, tathā hi kr̥ṣati vilikhati vidārayati saṁsārāṭavīm iti vā karṣati ākarṣati ātmasātkarōti vā'jñānam iti vā kr̥ṣṇaḥ paramātmā sadānandarūpō vā . . . tasmān niravadyasya sarveṣām ātmabhūtasya sadānandasyānusmaraṇaṁ punaḥ punaś cintanaṁ sajātīyapratyayāvr̥ttilakṣaṇaṁ vijātīyapratyayanirōdhalakṣaṇaṁ vā nididhyāsanam ihōpādīyatē tasya cātmasatattvasākṣātkārakāraṇabhūtaṁ śravaṇaṁ prati phalōpakāryaṅgabhūtasyāsambhāvanānirāsavat tatpratibandhakapātakapradhvaṁsō'pi dvārakāryaṁ bhavaty ēva.*

From the vantage point of classical Advaita, this sort of interpretation would have seemed quite sensible. The opponent invokes the common Vēdāntic triad of *śravaṇa*, *manana*, and *nididhyāsana*, or hearing, reflection, and meditation, a kind of program of scriptural study that culminates in self-knowledge. He provides the specific gloss on that program introduced by Prakāśātman in the tenth century. While hearing the words of the Upaniṣads leads directly to liberation, reflection and meditation serve as auxiliaries to that end by removing doubts about and reentrenching the truth of the Ātman. He offers an Advaitic etymology for the name "Kr̥ṣṇa" so that it refers simply to the Ātman. Given that Lakṣmīdhara introduced this conversation by accusing "some people" (*kēcit*) of wanting to differentially situate the language of *purāṇa* and the authority of *smr̥ti*, we might speculate that this sort of reading of the *Bhāgavata Purāṇa* was prevalent in the milieu into which he made his intervention. His response is quite unambiguous and employs the exuberant language we have become accustomed to from Kerala's religious intellectuals:

> *Reply*: This line of reasoning is unbecoming. First of all, the word "Kr̥ṣṇa" conventionally refers to that Brahman whose skin is dark as the Tamāla tree and who suckled at Yaśōdā's breast. As the maxim goes, the conventional trumps the etymological. Even if it were derivable, the word still refers in every way to that crest-jewel among cowherds, whose infinite joy [*anantānanda*] sparkles through his own uninterrupted greatness, having completely cast aside the fog (of ignorance). He spread the joy of liberation without inhibition: to the infatuated women of the village, who transgressed every (moral) boundary while seized by the influence of the great planet of irresistible passion; to enemies like Pūtanā, whose senses were unrestrained and out of control, possessed by extremely volatile fury; to the birds, animals, snakes, and trees along the Yamunā river, whose minds were oriented mostly outward; and down to the trees, bushes, creepers, and herbs of Vr̥ndāvana, whose senses were wrapped in the dense veils of delusion. All the etymologies you provide refer to him, not Brahman without attributes, since it is the most common referent of the word and the one that most immediately comes to mind.[89]

[89] *Kaumudī*, 64: *idam asundaram, kr̥ṣṇaśabdasya tamālaśyāmalatviṣi yaśōdāstanandhayē brahmaṇi rūḍhatvād, rūḍhir yōgam apaharatīti nyāyāt. yaugikatvē vā durvāramadanamahāgrahagr̥hītatayā samullaṅghitasakalasētūnāṁ gōkulakāminīnām, ativiṣamarōṣāvēśavivaśaviśr̥ṅkhalasakalakaraṇavr̥ttīnāṁ pūtanāprabhr̥tīnām arātīnām, atyantaparācīnacētasāṁ yamunāvanapaśupakṣisarīsr̥pāṇām, atibahalamōhapaṭalīpinaddhasarvēndriyāṇāṁ vr̥ndāvanatarugulmalatāvīrudhām*

According to Lakṣmīdhara, "Kr̥ṣṇa" is not merely a placeholder for the attributeless Brahman. It refers to a visually enchanting, embodied god, responsible for the famous deeds narrated in the *Bhāgavata*. The proper identification is not with the ineffable Brahman but with the immediately present guru; Lakṣmīdhara sneaks in the name of his teacher, Anantānanda, in the description of Kr̥ṣṇa. Unlike the Brahman of classical Advaita, which is exclusively realized through the words of the Upaniṣads, accompanied by Vēdāntic methods of reflection and meditation, Kr̥ṣṇa makes himself available to everyone irrespective of how learned they are. In fact, the crazier the better. Each recipient of liberation in this passage is more and more out of their mind. The women of the village Gōkul cast off every social norm to be in Kr̥ṣṇa's presence; the demons who tried to kill the baby were possessed by rage; birds and snakes only look out for their next meal; and trees and bushes are barely sentient. The nature of liberation is the same as in nondualist realization—that is, pure joy—but it is accessible to a wider, much less intellectually sophisticated range of beings.

That this controversy about liberation takes place within and not outside the realm of Advaita Vēdānta is made apparent later in the third chapter. Here, an opponent challenges Lakṣmīdhara to explain how the act of singing, being an activity, can lead to liberation. As all students of Vēdānta know, it is knowledge, *jñāna*, and not action, *karma*, that leads to liberation:

Objection: Surely singing is an activity, and activities cannot result in liberation. Great teachers have explained through the reasoning of *śruti*, *smr̥ti*, *itihāsapurāṇa*, and *āgama*, that knowledge is the sole means to liberation.

Reply: Only as a means to knowledge is singing a means to liberation. It's the same reason that meditation [*samādhi*] is enjoined in order to produce an effect. Meditation is not a means to liberation but a means to knowledge, and not directly, like "hearing," but by eradicating oppositional thinking. The same goes for singing.[90]

api muktisukham anivāritaṁ vitaratō nityanirastanīhāratayā nirantarasvamahimasamullasadanantānandasya gōpālaśirōmāṇēḥ sarvaprakārō'pi yōgō'syaivēti tasyaivēha grahaṇaṁ na nirguṇasya brahmaṇaḥ prayōgaprācuryāt tatraiva prathamatarapratītēr udayāt.

[90] *Kaumudī*, 120: *nanu kīrtanaṁ kriyā, na ca kriyāsādhanō mōkṣaḥ, tasya śrutismr̥tītihāsapurāṇāgamayuktibhir jñānaikōpāyatvēnācāryair avadhāritatvād jñānasādhanatvam ēva tasya mōkṣasādhanatvam, ata ēva samādhēḥ kāryē vidhānaṁ, na hi samādhir api mōkṣasādhanaṁ, kiṁ tarhi? jñānasādhanam ēva, tad api na sākṣāt śravaṇavad, api tu pratibandhanirāsadvārēṇa, ēvaṁ kīrtanam api.*

In the Vēdāntic triad of *śravaṇa*, *manana*, and *nididhyāsana*, only the first, hearing the words of the Upaniṣads, is supposed to lead directly to liberation. This is because the object of that liberating knowledge, Brahman, is not an object, but is the self, the Ātman. It cannot be achieved or attained by some activity; it is not "out there" for one to get. It can only be known. Hearing the Upaniṣads say that you are Brahman should be enough to make you realize that you are Brahman. Because that patently does not happen, early Advaitins interpreted *manana* and *nididhyāsana* (here called *samādhi*) as auxiliary disciplines that help effect the result of *śravaṇa*. They do so by removing the things that prevent knowledge from arising. For Lakṣmīdhara, singing is like the act of meditation. The obstruction removed by meditation is contradictory thinking, whereas the obstruction removed by singing is one's sins.

Singing, then, is enjoined not as a direct means to liberation but as a means to knowledge, which leads to liberation. Despite his riveting exposition of an intimately personal God and his commitment to everyday devotion, Lakṣmīdhara explains how singing the name of God is an independent but intermediary step in a complex teleology of spiritual practice that he attributes to the *Bhāgavata* itself: singing removes sins and lays the groundwork for one to develop *bhakti* for God, leading to a superabundance of purity and the direct experience of the truth.[91] However, while singing may prepare some people to receive the liberating knowledge of Vēdānta, it makes others receptive to God's grace:

> Now say that one who has heard the teaching of the Upaniṣads, on account of some obstruction, finds that access to knowledge of reality has been closed, as it were. For such a person, *bhakti* for God opens up that knowledge by removing the obstruction in the fashion described above. However, if someone has not heard the doctrine of Vēdānta at all, he may repeat *ad infinitum* the names of Lord Nṛsiṁha, alias the great Viṣṇu, the sole controller of the universe, the great ocean of uninhibited compassion, reclining upon the ocean of ambrosia that is Prahlāda's heart. When he leaves his body, the Lord himself will repeat for him the knowledge of the Ātman that will save him from *saṁsāra*.[92]

[91] *Kaumudī*, 120–121.

[92] *Kaumudī*, 121: *tatra śrutiśiraḥsiddhāntaṁ yasya śrutavatō'pi kutaścit pratibandhāt tattvajñānam utpannam api nimīlitam iva tasya bhagavadbhaktir uktayā rītyā pratibandhaṁ nirudhya tattvajñānam unmīlayati. yaḥ punar aśrutavēdāntasiddhānta ēva jagadēkaniyantur niryantraṇadayā'mṛtamahārṇavasya mahāviṣṇōḥ prahlādahṛdayasudhāsaritpatiparyaṅkaśāyin-*

Lakṣmīdhara does not essentially disagree with the Advaita Vēdānta principle that knowledge of Ātman is the source of liberation, and that liberation is the ultimate goal of human life. For people eligible for such knowledge, that is, members of the three upper castes educated in Vedic recitation, singing the name of God supplements their study. There is, however, an alternative route to liberation apart from the exegetical reading of the Upaniṣads. For people unacquainted with the theoretical apparatus of Vēdānta, singing the name is sufficient to prompt God himself to provide liberating knowledge. Importantly, this happens at the moment of leaving the body and not before. This specifies that the individual experiences *vidēha-mukti*, liberation upon death, perhaps echoing the story of Ajāmila from before. After all, it is still knowledge of Ātman that provides liberation. God simply repeats the preexisting truth of the Veda. And it is not just any god mentioned here, but Nṛsiṁha, the half-man, half-lion incarnation of Viṣṇu. As I mentioned previously, Nṛsiṁha was central to the religious worlds of both Śrīdhara and Lakṣmīdhara. The legend of Prahlāda, repeated in such narratives as the *Bhāgavata* and *Narasiṁha Purāṇa*, engendered devotion to the divine name of Viṣṇu.[93] Prahlāda was an important figure in the *Bhāgavata*. The philosophical teachings that accompanied his story were nondualist yet not identical with the classical Advaita tradition.[94] As such, the figure of Nṛsiṁha leads us to the "greater" Advaita tradition, or Advaita Vēdānta as it falls outside the received canon of Sanskrit philosophical works.[95] For example, Lakṣmīdhara follows by explaining a quote from the late *Nṛsiṁhatāpanīya Upaniṣad*, which could be considered a text of "greater" Vēdānta, as proof of his claim that praise of God ultimately results in the revelation of self-knowledge, for when God is pleased by that praise, he himself bestows knowledge. Lakṣmīdhara follows with an etymologically creative reading of a *mantra* from the *Ṛg Veda* (1.156.3) which prefigures the claim that singing the name of Viṣṇu eventually results in the realization of Brahman.[96]

aḥ śrīnṛsiṁhasya nāmāni nirantaram āvartayati, tasya bhagavān svayam ēva dēhāvasānasamayē saṁsāratārakam ātmajñanam anugṛṇāti.

93 Gerhard Oberhammer, "Review: *Prahlāda: Werden und Wandlungen einer Idealgestalt*," *Oriens* 17 (1964): 269.

94 Friedhelm Hardy, *Viraha-Bhakti: The Early History of Kṛṣṇa Devotion in South India* (Delhi: Oxford University Press, 1983), 538.

95 Michael Allen, "Greater Advaita Vedānta: The Case of Sundardās," *Journal of Indian Philosophy* 48.1 (2020): 49–78.

96 *Kaumudī*, 124. Perhaps not coincidentally, Śrīdhara cites *Ṛg Veda* 1.156.3 in his commentary on *Bhāgavata* 6.2.8, quoted above.

Attempts to find Viṣṇu as the supreme God of the Veda was a common practice in the Śrīvaiṣṇava and Mādhva traditions of Vedānta.[97] However, no previous commentators on this particular *mantra* had read it this way, which suggests that Lakṣmīdhara's interpretations are the product of a unique local intellectual milieu.[98]

Because the introduction of *bhakti* into Vēdānta is most commonly attributed to the non-Advaita traditions, it is important to be clear about the degree of difference between the *Kaumudī* and its predecessors in this regard. Prior to Lakṣmīdhara, theologians of the Śrīvaiṣṇava tradition engaged with texts that promoted *bhakti* for God's name. In the twelfth century, Rāmānuja's younger contemporary Parāśara Bhaṭṭar wrote a Sanskrit commentary on the *Viṣṇusahasranāma*, or the thousand names of Viṣṇu.[99] This text from the *Anuśāsana Parvan* of the *Mahābhārata* became popular in many cultures of recitation across southern India. In his introductory remarks, Parāśara Bhaṭṭar quotes many of the same authorities as Lakṣmīdhara, especially the *Viṣṇudharma* and *Viṣṇu Purāṇas*, in support of the claim that merely uttering the name of God relieves one's sins and leads to liberation. In keeping with Śrīvaiṣṇava tradition, he asserts that this path of *bhakti* is open to members of all castes and stages of life. Calling out to God is like calling out to one's mother; no matter one's situation, their compassion and friendship override all. None of these claims should be considered *arthavāda*, since they express no exaggeration.[100]

So far it seems that Parāśara Bhaṭṭar has anticipated Lakṣmīdhara, but the differences should give us pause. First, although he quotes several *purāṇas* in his commentary, he explicitly ranks the *itihāsa* over the *purāṇa* as a source of authority.[101] Second, he breezes past Mīmāṁsā objections, and even says that although we should not consider them exaggerations, *arthavādas* are sufficient authorities in their own right, so long as they do not conflict with a stronger authority.[102] Third, in contrast to Lakṣmīdhara's relative

[97] Valerie Stoker, "Vedic Language and Vaiṣṇava Theology: Madhva's Use of *Nirukta* in his *Ṛgbhāṣya*," *Journal of Indian Philosophy* 35.2 (2007): 169–199.

[98] For Sāyaṇa's reading, see Max Müller, ed., *Rig-Veda-Sanhita with the Commentary of Sayanacharya*, vol, 2 (London: W. H. Allen & Co., 1854), 200. For Madhva, see *Ṛgbhāṣyam*, ed. K. T. Pandurangi (Bangalore: Dvaita Vedanta Studies and Research Foundation, 1999).

[99] Vasudha Narayanan, "Singing the Glory of the Divine Name: Parāśara Bhaṭṭar's Commentary on the Viṣṇu Sahasranāma," *Journal of Vaishnava Studies* 2.2 (1994): 85–98.

[100] *Sri Visnusahasranama with the Bhashya of Sri Parasara Bhattar*, trans. A. Srinivasa Raghavan (Madras: Sri Visishtadvaita Pracharini Sabha, 1983), 47–59.

[101] *Sri Visnusahasranama*, 4, 8.

[102] *Sri Visnusahasranama*, 58.

ecumenicism, Parāśara Bhaṭṭar is emphatic that Viṣṇu alone, not Brahmā or Śiva, is the god spoken of by every scripture.[103] Finally, though he lists the "cowherd women" (*vallavī*) among the everyday people who were renowned for their devotion to God, he prefers to focus on figures from the *Mahābhārata* and the *Rāmāyaṇa* rather than the *purāṇas*. In fact the *Bhāgavata Purāṇa* hardly features in Śrīvaiṣṇava writing, and when it does, its reputation is often negative. When Vēdānta Ḍēśika wrote his *Rahasyatrayasāra* in the thirteenth century, for example, he placed significant limits on the power of God's name to purify one's sins. This was part of his broader argument that *bhakti* does not fundamentally overturn caste prerogatives. After quoting a series of verses from the *Bhāgavata* (6.2.14, 6.3.24) that praise the liberating power of God's name, Dēśika warns that uttering God's name works only if the person has no hatred for God. Verses like *Bhāgavata* 7.1.32, which say that people can be redeemed whatever their relationship to God, be it lust in the case of the *gōpīs*, fear in the case of Kaṁsa, or hatred in the case of Śiśupāla and others, actually mean that such people had positive associations with God in previous lives.[104]

It is certainly possible that the Śrīvaiṣṇavas, or the broader Pāñcarātra tradition, influenced the concerns of the *Kaumudī*. For example, on occasion Lakṣmīdhara mentions the *aṣṭākṣarabrahmavidyā*,[105] which probably refers to the eight-syllable *mantra ōṁ namō nārāyaṇāya*, revered by Śrīvaiṣṇavas as the *mūlamantra*.[106] He also gives a place of privilege to the Vaiṣṇava Āgamas which prescribe the kinds of activities that make the mind conducive to *bhakti*.[107] In places, Lakṣmīdhara may have even paraphrased the commentary on the *Viṣṇu Purāṇa* by the twelfth-century Śrīvaiṣṇava Viṣṇucitta.[108] But Lakṣmīdhara was also drawing from multiple sources: both Śaiva and

103 *Sri Visnusahasranama*, 75–76.

104 *Srimad Vedanta Desika's Srimad Rahasya Trayasara with Sara Vistara (Commentary) by Uttamur T. Viraraghavacarya* (Madras: Upayavētānta Krantamālai, 1980), 803–805; *Srimad Rahasyatrayasāra of Sri Vedanta Desika*, trans. M. R. Rajagopala Ayyangar (Kumbakonam: Agnihothram Ramanuja Thathachariar, 1956), 340–341; *Śrīmad Rahasyatrayasāram of Śrī Vedānta Deśika*, trans. N. Raghunathan (Madras: The Samskrta Academy, 2018), 623–626.

105 *Kaumudī*, 87, 112.

106 The twenty-seventh chapter of the *Rahasyatrayasāra* deals with the etymology of this *mantra*.

107 *Kaumudī*, 79.

108 Lakṣmīdhara's comments about the "easiness" of singing God's name versus the "difficulty" of *smārta* practices of expiation may have been influenced by Viṣṇucitta's commentary on *Viṣṇu Purāṇa* 2.6.45. Both Viṣṇucitta and Śrīdhara, however, differentially situate the *purāṇa* and *smṛti*, setting aside those more difficult practices for those who do not have faith in God. Lakṣmīdhara, as we saw earlier, rejects the notion of differential qualification. See *Śrīviṣṇupurāṇam śrīviṣṇucittīyākhyayā vyākhyayā sametam*, ed. Aṇṇaṅgarācārya (Kāñcīpuram: Granthamālā Kāryālaya, 1972), 135. Cf. *Viṣṇupurāṇa with Sanskrit Commentary of Sridharacharya*, 220.

Vaiṣṇava *purāṇas* and *āgamas*, late Upaniṣads like the *Nṛsiṁhatāpanīya*, and works of classical Advaita like Surēśvara's *Naiṣkarmyasiddhi*. This pluralism is the hallmark of the greater Advaita tradition and what makes the *Kaumudī* so difficult to pin down in the historiographical categories of Indian philosophy and religion. It may have been the location of the *Kaumudī* at these multiple intersections that influenced its reception by three diverse groups of people in early modern India.

The Sacred Name, North and South

Some of the earliest readers of Lakṣmīdhara's *Kaumudī* were followers of the charismatic preacher Caitanya Mahāprabhu. Based on their origins in the Northeast of India, they came to be known as the Gauḍīya Vaiṣṇavas, although some of the most famous acolytes, the Gōsvāmīs, would move to Brindavan, in north-central India, in the early sixteenth century. Singing the name of God was Caitanya's favorite activity. His followers drew inspiration both from the teacher's example and from the poetry and tales of the *Bhāgavata Purāṇa*, which they made the centerpiece of their theological endeavors. In the process, they sought to distance themselves from the specter of Advaita Vēdānta that followed the *Bhāgavata*. In their view, the theory of nondualism left no room for the personal experience of a visually entrancing God. When Advaitins claimed that there was no essential difference between the individual and God, and that the everyday world was an illusion, they were in fact wrapped up in their own delusions of grandeur. However much it may have unnerved later Gauḍīya hagiographers, the positive presence of Advaita Vēdānta in the tradition is well known, since Caitanya had been formally initiated into the Daśanāmī monastic order of Advaita ascetics.[109] The narrative tradition stresses that Caitanya argued with Advaitins, both at home, as in the purported conversion of Vāsudēva Sārvabhauma, as well as in the Advaita stronghold of Banaras.

Kṛṣṇadāsa Kavirāja's *Caitanyacaritāmṛta* gives us alternately rueful and bullish accounts of Caitanya's activities in that city. In chapter 17 of the *Madhya Līlā*, Caitanya is more or less laughed out of town by the Advaitin Prakāśānanda and his goons, while in chapter 25 the famous

[109] De, *Early History of the Vaisnava Faith and Movement in Bengal*, 15–20.

renunciant is made to recant his ways and acknowledge Caitanya's greatness.[110] Prakāśānanda would have been a prime candidate for anti-Advaita polemic, given the popularity of his defense of the *dṛṣṭisṛṣṭivāda*, a radical form of subjective idealism, in his *Vēdāntasiddhāntamuktāvalī* around the turn of the sixteenth century.[111] The tension between an Advaita that was acceptable to Gauḍīya Vaiṣṇavas, in contrast with its contemporary degeneration and decadence, was present in narrative and philosophy alike. Writing from Brindavan in the sixteenth century, Jīva Gōsvāmī attempted to construct a solid foundation of philosophical argument and understanding for the devotional edifice of Caitanya's Vaiṣṇavism. Jīva worked creatively with the resources available to him from multiple Vēdānta traditions, selecting freely from Rāmānuja, Śrīdhara Svāmī, Madhva, and even Śaṅkara, to carve out a space for his unique philosophical theology.[112] Jīva acknowledged his debt to Śrīdhara in a curious fashion in his *Tattvasandarbha*, the first of six books in which he developed his reading of the *Bhāgavata*: "Our interpretation [of the *Bhāgavata*], however, representing a kind of commentary, will be written in accordance with the views of the great Vaiṣṇava, the revered Śrīdhara Svāmī, only insofar as they conform to pure Vaiṣṇava teaching. His writings were interspersed with the doctrines of Advaita, no doubt in order that he might persuade Advaita ideologues, who nowadays pervade the central regions, to become absorbed in the greatness of the Lord."[113] Jīva's rhetorical distinction between "pure Vaiṣṇava" and "Advaita" doctrines reveals a certain anxiety of influence. While it is impossible to ignore Śrīdhara's Advaitic affinities, they must be reframed to fit the teleology of Gauḍīya Vaiṣṇavism. Even Śaṅkara, Jīva claimed, realized that the *Bhāgavata* was far superior to his own doctrines and taught the philosophy Advaita Vēdānta only because God told him to, in order that his true nature would remain hidden.[114] There is a

[110] Edward C. Dimock, Jr. and Tony K. Stewart, *The Caitanya Caritāmṛta of Kṛṣṇadāsa Kavirāja: A Translation and Commentary*, Harvard Oriental Series 56 (Cambridge: Harvard University Press, 1999), 586–590, 761–763.

[111] See Christopher Minkowski, "Advaita Vedānta in Early Modern History," *South Asian History and Culture* 2.2 (2011): 213. Cf. Sthaneshwar Timalsina, *Seeing and Appearance: History of the Advaita Doctrine of Dṛṣṭisṛṣṭi* (Aachen: Shaker Verlag, 2006).

[112] Ravi Gupta, *The Caitanya Vaiṣṇava Vedānta of Jīva Gosvāmin* (London: Routledge, 2007), 63–91.

[113] Stuart Mark Elkman, *Jiva Gosvamin's Tattvasandarbha: A Study on the Philosophical and Sectarian Development of the Gauḍīya Vaiṣṇava Movement* (Delhi: Motilal Banarsidass, 1986), 118: *bhāṣyarūpā tadvyākhyā tu samprati madhyadēśādau vyāptān advaitavādinō nūnaṁ bhagavanmahimānam avagāhayituṁ tadvādēna karvuritalipīnāṁ paramavaiṣṇavānāṁ śrīdharasvāmicaraṇānāṁ śuddhavaiṣṇavasiddhāntānugatā cēt tarhi yathāvad ēva vilikhyatē.*

[114] Elkman, *Jiva Gosvamin's Tattvasandarbha*, 110.

social context for the distinction too. Jīva's mention of the "central regions" (*madhyadēśa*) in the quote above raises at once a geographical and a historical question. While the classical definition of *madhyadēśa* was simply the country lying between the Himālaya and Vindhya mountains, from the vantage point of sixteenth-century Brindavan, could it have referred to Banaras, where partisans of Advaita Vēdānta so famously rejected Caitanya's brand of "sentimentalist" devotion?[115]

Whatever the case, it is clear that the *Kaumudī* was important to bridging the gap. In the opening to the *Tattvasandarbha*, Jīva laid out his argument for the Vedic status of the *Bhāgavata Purāṇa*.[116] But was it *his* argument? In order to explain that the *purāṇa* was nothing but Veda, Jīva repeated the argument of the *Kaumudī* almost verbatim, without attributing it to Lakṣmīdhara.[117] He would have had no reason to hesitate. As explained in the previous chapter, Lakṣmīdhara's presence in Gauḍīya literature preceded Jīva by a generation. Four of his poetic verses from the *Kaumudī* found their way into the *Padyāvalī*, an anthology of Sanskrit poetry compiled by Jīva's uncle Rūpa Gōsvāmī.[118] And as a perusal of the broader Gauḍīya archive demonstrates, the *Kaumudī* clearly held a favorable place in it.[119]

However, the *Kaumudī*'s Advaitic affinities would not go away. Despite the association of singing God's name with Caitanya's movement, the Gauḍīya Vaiṣṇavas were not the only group to lay claim to the *Kaumudī*. Around the same time in the sixteenth century, not far from where Jīva was writing, a family of Maharashtrian Brahmin migrants to Banaras, the Dēvas, expressed their interest in the *Kaumudī* in a very different way. In the following chapter, I explore the intellectual, social, and cultural history of Banarasi academic life through the corpus of the Dēva family. Here I provide the outlines of their engagement with this text tradition. The patriarch of the family, Anantadēva, wrote a commentary on the *Kaumudī* called the *Prakāśa*. Anantadēva's initial education was in Mīmāṁsā and Advaita Vēdānta under the tutelage of the Banarasi renunciant Rāmatīrtha. He went on to write his own introduction

[115] Gupta, *The Caitanya Vaiṣṇava Vedānta of Jīva Gosvāmin*, 16.

[116] Buchta, "Defining Categories in Hindu Literature," 91–94.

[117] Cf. Elkman, *Jīva Gosvāmin's Tattvasandarbha*, 78.

[118] *Padyāvalī*, ed. S. K. De (Dacca: University of Dacca, 1934), 7 (v. 16), 12 (v. 29), 14 (v. 33), 15 (v. 34).

[119] I am grateful to Rembert Lutjeharms for providing me with a comprehensive list of references to the *Kaumudī* in Gauḍīya Vaiṣṇava literature. To summarize, the texts include Rūpa Gōsvāmī's *Bhaktirasāmṛtasindhu* (3.2.1), Jīva Gōsvāmī's *Tattvasandarbha* (47), *Kṛṣṇasandarbha* (57), *Bhagavatsandarbha* (86, 128, 153, 161, 263, 265), *Prītisandarbha* (110), and his *Sarvasaṁvādinī* commentary on the *Tattvasandarbha* and *Kṛṣṇasandarbha*.

to Vēdānta called the *Siddhāntatattva*. In this textbook, Anantadēva is quite uncompromising about his Advaita affinities. He tells us in the *Prakāśa*, without any sense of ironic distance, that he composed the commentary after writing his Advaita manual.[120] By and large, Anantadēva stays faithful to the text of the *Kaumudī*, departing from the author's intention only once or twice. His was the most popular commentary on the text, others existing only in fragments and one or two manuscripts.[121] Like Rūpa Gōsvāmī before him, Anantadēva also composed devotional dramas on *bhakti*. However, they are very different from Rūpa's use of drama as a mode of religious realization, and they contain none of the technical language of *bhaktirasa*.[122] I show in the next chapter that Anantadēva attempted to portray his life of love for God as distinct from his scholarly ambitions, not constitutive of them. Apart from their shared interest in the *Kaumudī*, there seems to be nothing that connects the Dēvas to the Gōsvāmīs. Unlike Jīva, who tried scrupulously to avoid the ignominy of being classed with the "illusionism" of Advaita Vēdānta, Anantadēva felt no need to apologize for his Advaita heritage. In his *Siddhāntatattva*, he even supported the *dṛṣṭisṛṣṭivāda*, the controversial doctrine of subjective idealism which it is unlikely that the Gōsvāmīs would have ever defended.[123] In the *Prakāśa*, however, he assures the prospective audience that his commentary spreads the illumination of the *Kaumudī* in a manner that "does not contradict the meaning of the entire Vēdānta" (*sarvavēdāntārthāvirōdhataḥ*). "Vēdānta" here probably means "Upaniṣads" more than a particular system, but the fact that Anantadēva had to bring up the problem of the *Kaumudī*'s belonging suggests that this text was moving between communities that had very different philosophical commitments. As I show in the next chapter, nowhere does Anantadēva distance himself from Advaita per se, only other Advaitins and their haughty, self-involved talk about the liberating power of knowledge, divorced from the rhythms of *bhakti*.

One is compelled to ask, then, whether we should see the Dēvas and Gosvāmīs as fraternal twins or as independent agents reenvisioning the legacy of Advaita Vēdānta. Though remarkably similar in nature, their

[120] See *Kaumudī*, 63.
[121] See Siniruddha Dash, ed., *New Catalogus Catalogorum*, vol. 15 (Madras: University of Madras, 2007), 251b.
[122] Cf. Donna Wulff, *Drama as a Mode of Religious Realization: The Vidagdhamādhava of Rupa Gosvāmī* (Chico: Scholars Press, 1984).
[123] *Siddhāntatattva*, ed. Tailanga Rama Sastri (Benares: Government Sanskrit College, 1901), 57–60.

ideas about singing the name of God seem to have moved through different, non-intersecting circles, both during and after their lifetime. The Gauḍīya Vaiṣṇavas exerted their influence across northern India to the courts of Jaipur, where the scholar Baladeva Vidyābhūṣaṇa consolidated their canonical Vēdānta status by connecting Gauḍīya Vaiṣṇavism to Mādhva theology.[124] The works of the Dēvas, however, made their way south, as part of the Maratha conquest of Thanjavur.[125] Not only did manuscripts of their works survive in southern libraries, but their intellectual interest in the divine name was also resuscitated and refashioned by theologians of the Tamil South.

According to V. Raghavan, who proposed the concept of the *Nāmasiddhānta*, a nationwide tradition of singing the name of God, this tradition found clearest shape among the "saints" of the Kaveri delta in the seventeenth and eighteenth centuries: Śrīdhara Vēṅkaṭēśa Ayyāvāḷ, Bhagavannāma ("God's Name") Bōdhēndra, Sadgurusvāmī, Sadāśiva Brahmēndra, Nārāyaṇa Tīrtha, and Tyāgarāja.[126] For Raghavan, these Brahmin figures inherited the long history of singing the name of God, and translated it into the present-day musical-performative tradition of storytelling and devotional singing known as the *bhajana sampradāya*.[127] In response to Raghavan's universalist account, Davesh Soneji has contextualized the origins of the *bhajana sampradāya* within the polyglot literary and musical environment of Maratha-period Thanjavur. The *sampradāya* was the result of "the workings of a highly local, albeit caste- and class-bound culture of public multilingualism" in the courtly milieu of Maratha Thanjavur, and its Brahmin participants, down into the twentieth century, co-opted and universalized the "irreducible pluralism of musical practices" in South

[124] Kiyokazu Okita, *Hindu Theology in Early Modern South Asia: The Rise of Devotionalism and the Politics of Genealogy* (Oxford: Oxford University Press, 2014).

[125] Anand Venkatkrishnan, "Ritual, Reflection, and Religion: The Devas of Banaras," *South Asian History and Culture* 6.1 (2015): 159–161. Several manuscripts of the Dēvas' works are available in the Tanjore Sarasvati Mahal Library. See P. P. S. Sastri, *A Descriptive Catalogue of the Sanskrit Manuscripts in the Tanjore Mahārāja Serfoji's Sarasvatī Mahāl Library*, vol. 13 (Srirangam: Vani Vilas Press, 1931), 5621–5625, 5796–5799. For the full record of the Dēvas' manuscripts, see V. Raghavan, ed., *New Catalogus Catalogorum*, vol. 1, revised ed. (Madras: University of Madras, 1968), 164–167; V. Raghavan, ed., *New Catalogus Catalogorum*, vol. 2 (Madras: University of Madras, 1966), 124.

[126] Raghavan, *The Power of the Sacred Name*, 49–82, 143–152. Cf. R. Krishnamurthy, *The Saints of the Cauvery Delta* (New Delhi: Concept Publishing, 1979).

[127] Milton Singer, "The Rādhā-Krishna *Bhajanas* of Madras City," 90–138, and T. K. Venkateswaran, "Rādhā-Krishna *Bhajanas* of South India," 139–172, both in *Krishna: Myths, Rites, Attitudes*, ed. Milton Singer (Honolulu: East-West Center Press, 1966); Soneji, "The Powers of Polyglossia."

India at this time.[128] Instrumental in preserving these musical practices was the network of Rāmadāsī *maṭhas* that were established in the Thanjavur region between the seventeenth and nineteenth centuries. These institutions helped transport the performance of Marathi *kīrtan* to the Tamil South and possessed their own local performative traditions that were appropriated and largely forgotten by the "classical" music establishment.[129] As I argue in the following chapter, Rāmadāsīs were also likely responsible for the transmission of the Dēvas' works to South India. It is therefore a specific Maharashtrian genealogy that lies behind readings of the *Kaumudī* in the South.

Historical memory, however, locates the text in Orissa. In the story of "God's Name" Bōdhēndra the renunciant travels at the behest of his guru from Kāñcīpuram to Puri to meet the famous Lakṣmīdhara, only to find that he has died. Lakṣmīdhara's son Jagannātha, however, convinces Bōdhēndra of the power of God's name and gives him his father's *Kaumudī* to take back south. Bōdhēndra then devotes himself to writing several works on the power of Rāma's name.[130] Only one of these works has been printed: the *Nāmāmṛtarasāyana*, or "Elixir of the Ambrosia of the Name."[131] A book that reads stylistically like a series of long-winded, repetitive lecture notes, the *Nāmāmṛtarasāyana* is a free-form gloss on a commentary on the *Viṣṇusahasranāma* attributed to Śaṅkara. In this book, Bōdhēndra asserts a claim made popular by the *Kaumudī*: "Because singing the name requires no general rule of observance, it is shown that the act of singing the name, done in whatever way possible, leads to the dissolution of all sins and to liberation, whether performed by a woman, a man, eunuch, or any kind of person whosoever; whether helplessly or out of madness; whether with faith or without faith; whether to ward off the pain induced by thieves or tigers or disease; or whether for the purpose of achieving non-lasting results like *dharma*, *artha*, and *kāma*, or any other purpose."[132] Although this is similar to the

[128] Soneji, "The Powers of Polyglossia," 342. Cf. Indira Viswanathan Peterson, "Multilingual Dramas at the Tanjavur Maratha Court and Literary Cultures in Early Modern South India," *Journal of Medieval History* 14.2 (2011): 285–321.

[129] Soneji, "The Powers of Polyglossia," 344–349. Cf. T. N. Bhima Rao, "Samartha Ramdasi Maths in Tanjore," *The Journal of the Tanjore Maharaja Serfoji's Sarasvati Mahal Library* 17.3 (1964): 1–4.

[130] Krishnamurthy, *The Saints of the Cauvery Delta*, 49–55.

[131] *Nāmāmṛtarasāyanam*, ed. Deva Śaṅkara Śarmā (Tanjore: Poornachandrodayam Press, 1926).

[132] *Nāmāmṛtarasāyanam*, 17–18: *ēvaṁ nāmakīrtanasya niyamasāmānyānapēkṣatvapratipādanāt strīpuṁnapuṁsakānyatamēna yēnakēnacij janēnāvaśēna vōnmādēna vā śraddhayā vā śraddhāṁ vinā vā cōravyāghrarōgādikṛtārtināśāya vā dharmārthakāmānyatamātmakānityaphalāya vānyaprayōjanāya vā yathākathaṁcitkṛtanāmakīrtanēna sakalapāpakṣayō muktiś ca bhavaty ēvēty arthō darśitaḥ.*

view of Śrīvaiṣṇava commentators on the *Viṣṇusahasranāma* discussed earlier, Bōdhēndra explicitly refers to "the *Nāmakaumudī* and Anantadēva's many works" among the inspirations for his own interpretive efforts.[133] He also claims that the argument above had already been made by the famous Advaitin Madhusūdana Sarasvatī, author of the *Advaitasiddhi*, in his commentary on the *Bhagavad Gītā*.[134] In addition to citing classical Advaitins like Nṛsiṁhāśrama, Ānandagiri, and Vidyāraṇya, Bōdhēndra analogized the defense of singing God's name against its naysayers to defending the truth of Advaita Vēdānta against its philosophical opponents, singling out his closest southern rivals, the followers of Rāmānuja and Madhva.[135]

In the writings of Bōdhēndra we also return to the Śaiva presence lurking in the *Kaumudī*. Bōdhēndra is sometimes identified with Bōdhēndra Sarasvatī, understood by tradition to be the fifty-ninth pontiff of the Kāñcī Kāmakōṭi Pīṭha, a famous Advaita monastery that employs the Śrīvidyā ritual tradition of goddess worship. Regardless of his actual monastic affiliation, Bōdhēndra Sarasvatī referred to one of his teachers, Gīrvāṇēndra Sarasvatī, as the head of an *advaitapīṭha*, suggesting an established monastery or institutional center for the propagation of Advaita thought.[136] Gīrvāṇēndra was a highly celebrated and influential figure among scholars of Advaita and Śākta religious intellectuals beyond the monastery. The famous South Indian scholar Nīlakaṇṭha Dīkṣita implicitly claimed to have received a *mantra* from Gīrvāṇēndra through the process of *śaktipāta*, the descent of power or grace at the hand of the initiatory guru.[137] I think it is quite possible that the two Bōdhēndras were the same, due to similarities in benedictory stanzas across works attributed to both and their mutual interest in the nondifference between Śiva and Viṣṇu.[138] Moreover, the distinctive initiatory title borne by nearly all of Gīrvāṇēndra Sarasvatī's gurus and disciples, namely, "-indrasarasvatī," is attested only among the teachers of the Kāmakoṭi Pīṭha and the lineage of Rāmacandrēndra Sarasvatī, better known

[133] *Nāmāmṛtarasāyanam*, 71.
[134] *Nāmāmṛtarasāyanam*, 18.
[135] *Nāmāmṛtarasāyanam*, 45, 47, 48.
[136] Elaine Fisher, *Hindu Pluralism: Religion in the Public Sphere in Early Modern South India* (Berkeley: University of California Press, 2017), 63–64.
[137] Fisher, *Hindu Pluralism*, 65.
[138] In both the *Nāmāmṛtarasāyana* and the *Hariharādvaitabhūṣaṇa*, Bōdhēndra mentions his second guru, Viśvādhikēndra Sarasvatī, invokes the figure of Śaṅkara in very similar fashion, and celebrates Rāma as the embodiment of the unity between Viṣṇu and Śiva. See *Hariharādvaita Bhūṣaṇam by Bodhendrasarasvatī*, ed. T. Chandraeskharan (Madras: Government Oriental Manuscripts Library, 1954), 1. Cf. *Nāmāmṛtarasāyana*, 1–3.

as Upaniṣad Brahmēndra for having commented on 108 Upaniṣads.[139] Whatever the historical or institutional relationship between Bōdhēndra and Brahmēndra, they both wrote works on the concept of God's name. In the *Upēyanāmavivēka*, "Analyzing the Name of the One to Be Attained," Brahmēndra affirms the universally redemptive power of God's name, irrespective of one's caste or social status.[140] In the introduction to his edition of the *Upēyanāmavivēka*, V. Raghavan asserted that it fell in the line of such works as the *Kaumudī*.[141] This is true, but only in part. For the author is not exclusively concerned with literature on *nāmamāhātmya*, the glory of the name. Instead, he quotes profusely from the classical works of Śaṅkara, such as his commentary on Gauḍapāda's *Māṇḍūkyakārikā*, and from late Upaniṣads like the *Rāmatāpanīya*. In doing so, he departs significantly from the *Kaumudī*'s focus on eradicating sins. God's name in the *Upēyanāmavivēka* is not merely the object of devotional singing, but of *bhāvanā*: absorption, immersion, imagination, identification.[142] For Brahmēndra, the name "Rāma" actually does equal Brahman, unlike Lakṣmīdhara's insistence that the name "Kr̥ṣṇa" was singular and could not be subsumed under Brahman in general. Brahmēndra gave special significance to the name of Rāma, treating it as the essence of both the Nārāyaṇa and Śiva *mantras*.[143] Bōdhēndra also centered his devotion to Rāma across his works. And so did Lakṣmīdhara. Although the majority of the *Kaumudī* extols the names and virtues of Kr̥ṣṇa, in his concluding verses Lakṣmīdhara says that it is Rāma's name that, unlike other technical *mantras*, requires "neither initiation, nor gift-giving, nor preparation."[144] However, in the *Upēyanāmavivēka*, one does not invoke the name to save oneself (*hē rāma*); one becomes the name (*rāmō'ham*). Bōdhēndra's

[139] Fisher, *Hindu Pluralism*, 64. Cf. V. Raghavan, "Upanishad Brahma Yogin, His Life and Works," *Journal of the Madras Music Academy* 27 (1956): 113–150. See also Raghavan, *New Catalogus Catalogorum*, vol. 2, 363–367.

[140] Klaus Klostermaier, "Calling God Names: Reflections on Divine Names in Hindu and Buddhist Traditions," *Journal of Vaishnava Studies* 2.2 (1994): 66–68.

[141] *Upeya-Nāma-Viveka (Nāmārthaviveka) of Upaniṣad Brahmayogin*, ed. V. Raghavan (Madras: The Adyar Library and Research Centre, 1967), 3.

[142] Cf. David Shulman, *More Than Real: A History of the Imagination in South India* (Cambridge: Harvard University Press, 2012).

[143] Klostermaier, "Calling God Names," 68.

[144] "It draws you in if your heart is pure and eradicates even the greatest sins. It's easy for anyone, no matter how marginalized; so long as you can utter it, then freedom is yours. You don't need any initiation, no gift-giving or preparation. This *mantra* flowers the moment it touches your tongue: Rāma's name." *Kaumudī*, 133:

> *ākr̥ṣṭiḥ kr̥tacētasāṁ sumahatām uccāṭanaṁ cāṁhasām*
> *ācāṇḍālam amūkalōkasulabhō vaśyaś ca muktiśriyaḥ*
> *nō dīkṣāṁ na ca dakṣiṇāṁ na ca puraścaryāṁ manāg īkṣatē*
> *mantrō'yaṁ rasanāspr̥g ēva phalati śrīrāmanāmātmakaḥ.*

Nāmāmṛtarasāyana similarly argues at length that renunciants who would otherwise be engaged in the standard Advaitic practice of "hearing, reflecting, and meditating" on the words of the Upaniṣads can achieve their aim of unobstructed, immediate self-knowledge much more easily by singing the name of God.[145] The *Kaumudī*, however, saw singing the name of God as an intermediary step leading to liberating knowledge. It emphasized the ability of God's name to remove sins, not its direct contribution to Advaitic realization. Both Bōdhēndra and Brahmēndra move us far afield from the relatively limited concerns of the *Kaumudī*, embedded as they were in a very different southern context.

Echoes of God's Name

The *Kaumudī* was adapted differently by several communities in early modern India: the theologians of Caitanya's charismatic public devotion, the scholarly families of Banaras, and the monastic intellectuals of the multilingual South. Although the *Kaumudī* was primarily dedicated to upholding the independent validity of *purāṇa* as a genre, in response to established discourse on scriptural authority in Mīmāṁsā, its readers applied its theology of the divine name for their own distinct purposes. Modern incarnations of the *Kaumudī* continue to raise questions about its multiple affiliations. Lakṣmīdhara was embedded in the world of Advaita Vēdānta, as were later commentators on the text. But the *Kaumudī* manuscript in the Tanjore Sarasvati Mahal Library is listed under "Caitanya Thought," no doubt due to its popularity among the Gōsvāmīs.[146] In his initial catalogue of the Tanjore manuscripts, A. C. Burnell listed it as a work of Viśiṣṭādvaita.[147] And the editor of the first printed text of the *Kaumudī*, Gōsvāmī Dāmōdar Śāstrī, was explicit about his Mādhva background and the importance of this text to it.[148]

Simply locating the *Kaumudī* at the intersection of philosophical, sectarian, and religious boundaries, however, does little more than refine the historiography of the text. The *Kaumudī* and its readers still shared a fundamental commitment to Sanskrit scholastic discourse. The question I raised

[145] *Nāmāmṛtarasāyana*, 24.
[146] P. P. S. Sastri, *A Descriptive Catalogue of the Sanskrit Manuscripts in the Tanjore Mahārāja Serfoji's Sarasvatī Mahāl Library*, vol. 14 (Srirangam: Vani Vilas Press, 1932), 6383–6385.
[147] A. C. Burnell, *A Classified Index to the Sanskrit Mss. in the Palace at Tanjore* (London: Trübner & Co., 1880), 98.
[148] *Kaumudī*, viii.

at the outset is whether their scholastic interests were provoked by more vernacular, quotidian developments, namely the broader traditions of reciting the name of God. After all, the mere presence of the vernacular does not mean the preservation of local histories. As Davesh Soneji remarks on the upper-caste appropriation of Marathi *kīrtan* in present-day musical performances:

> The performance of Marathi *abhaṅg-kīrtans* as part of "classical" Karnatak music performances is a distinctly twentieth-century phenomenon and has much to do with the urban scripting of the history of Karnatak music as inextricably intertwined with not only the South Indian, but pan-Indian *bhakti* tradition. Marathi *kīrtan* thus becomes integrated, not because of its distinctly local historical connection to the making of this music, but rather because it represents a regional *bhakti* tradition that must be connected, performatively speaking, to Karnatak music's uppercaste, Neo-Advaitic *bhakti* universalism. It is in this process, I would argue, that the local histories of Marathi *kīrtan* in Tanjore become obfuscated.[149]

By subordinating the local Rāmadāsī, Muslim, and courtly histories of performance, Soneji argues, the classical music establishment, exemplified by its scholarly chronicler V. Raghavan, presents a seamless continuity between all traditions of singing the name of God, irrespective of their social location. Ignoring the particular social conditions and historical agents that produced their music and that have privileged one performative tradition over others, upper-caste musicians collapse them into a single *sampradāya*. The regional, for them, is only the individual instantiation of a universal paradigm.

What I have tried to do in tracking the career of the *Kaumudī* is to provincialize this universalism. Singing the name did not mean the same thing even to its Brahmin proponents, who disagreed on key features of philosophy, theology, and everyday practice. In fact, it is precisely the everydayness of the practice that raised the greatest problems in scholastic discourse. In a long aside in his *Prakāśa* commentary on the *Kaumudī*, the sixteenth-century Banarasi scholar Anantadēva elaborates on the consequences of Lakṣmīdhara's summary acceptance of any sources of praise, whether of "Vedic, Tantric, *paurāṇika*, or human composition."[150] For Anantadēva, the problem of indiscriminate language use bore on specific

[149] Soneji, "The Powers of Polyglossia," 365, n. 27.
[150] *Kaumudī*, 122–124.

questions of social location. It is not the case, he argues, that only Sanskrit can be used to praise God. There are plenty of people who don't know Sanskrit, and prescriptions like this must apply to humans in general. In his view, *prākṛta* and *paurāṇika* go hand in hand, not only due to scriptural precedent but also in light of everyday practice:

> In the *Viṣṇupurāṇa* and other books, for example, we learn that Śiśupāla threw insults at God with a disrespectful "Hey you!" and reached him nevertheless. There's no evidence that he only insulted him in Sanskrit. So repeating the glories of God must be done in whatever way possible, or else it would interfere with the storytelling practice of people who recite *purāṇas* in vernacular languages. That's why the *Bhāgavata* (10.47.63cd) says, with respect to the *gōpīs*, that "their singing the stories of God purifies the three worlds." . . . As for those people who criticize each other every day in vernacular tongues, yet insist that one must not praise God in those languages, their real problem is a lack of love for God. Enough said.[151]

Anantadēva's characteristically feisty and sarcastic writing, which we will encounter again in the following chapter, reveals the implicit social context of vernacular language use. The name of God did not have to be uttered in Sanskrit for it was not limited to the world of men. But it echoed in their world, through storytelling, singing, and even scholarship. We cannot say for certain if Lakṣmīdhara's response to Brahmanical orthopraxy, like the *Bhāgavata* itself, drew on vernacular challenges. I have suggested at least that, in the presence of Śaiva discourse and greater Advaita Vēdānta, there is more to it than meets the historical eye. In Anantadēva's commentary, however, the stakes are more recognizable. For him, the problem of singing the name of God was a problem of Brahmin identity. To hurl abuse in everyday language yet uphold the sanctity of Sanskrit was the height of hypocrisy. But why did Anantadēva pick up the *Kaumudī* in the first place? Why did singing the name feature so prominently in his thinking?

[151] *Kaumudī*, 123: *viṣṇupurāṇādau caidyasya bhagavati tvaṁkathādibhir dvēṣaṁ vidadhatō̆pi bhagavatprāptiḥ śrūyatē, na cāsau saṁskṛtavākyair ēva bhagavaddvēṣaṁ vidadha iti pramāṇam asti, tasmād yathākathaṁcid bhagavadguṇānuvādō vihita ēva, anyathā paurāṇikānāṁ prākṛtavākyair arthakathanācārō bādhyēta. ata ēva gōpīr adhikṛtya—"yāsāṁ harikathōdgītaṁ punāti bhuvanatrayam" ityuktaṁ śrībhāgavatē . . . ataś ca prākṛtavākyair aharniśaṁ paranindādi kurvantō yē prākṛtavākyair bhagavadgūnānuvādam akartavyaṁ nirūpayanti tēṣāṁ bhagavadanurāgābhāva ēvāparādhyatītyalam ativistarēṇa.*

In sixteenth-century Banaras, the name of God pulsated all around, from temple sanctums, from minarets, and from pilgrims dancing in the streets. It was one thing to hear the name resounding through the alleys of the city; it was another to get up and join the procession. In the next chapter, I provide an intellectual biography of the Dēva family, Maharashtrian Brahmins who lived in Banaras in the sixteenth and seventeenth centuries. What did it mean for a scholarly family to participate in popular, public devotional settings? Who populated these spaces, and how did they compare to assemblies of Brahmin scholars? How did the personal religious commitments of scholars shape the very lineaments of their research? What does their example tell us about the social and cultural history of intellectual life in early modern India? Following the reverberations of God's name into the center of Brahmin academia will allow us to trace the outlines of everyday life in thicker detail.

3

Family Ties

Introduction

Did your mother ever tell you that book learning would make your head swell up? That you would start reading and stop praying? Maybe you heard it in a story: the arrogant ascetic bested by the humble potter. Or in a poem: you've read thousands of books, but have you studied your own heart? It might have been a passage in scripture: some things are just beyond the mind's reach; truth is revealed to the patient and penitent. Wherever you heard it first, the motif of the contradiction between knowledge and wisdom is as old as it is widespread. Scholarly prowess, in this motif, is inversely proportional to spiritual progress. In early modern Europe, the question of how to integrate learning and piety in a world increasingly beholden to institutions of patronage occupied many Catholic intellectuals. Cautionary tales like *The Life of Pico* exposed the dangers of worldly ambition and scholarly pride. The scholar must "reject the temptations of scholarship" and seek God through love rather than knowledge.[1] In contemporary India, this tension was commonly represented in narratives of *bhakti* poets and saints. The foolish priest, the pompous pandit, the skeptical scholar—all were characters in a divine drama that exalted the lovers of God. But how did things look from the other side, among the Brahmin intellectuals confronted by the critical gaze of *bhakti*?

The opposition between Brahmins and *bhakta*s is a literary trope, of course. *Bhakti* occupied a space between the "high" textual world and that of everyday "popular" performance. On the one hand, Sanskrit texts such as the *Bhagavad Gītā* and the *Bhāgavata Purāṇa* shaped a Hindu ideal of *bhakti* that infused the body of Brahmanical *dharma* with the spirit of dedication to the divine. On the other hand, the vernacular and subaltern religious networks that sprang up across the subcontinent in the second millennium,

[1] Constance Furey, *Erasmus, Contarini, and the Religious Republic of Letters* (New York: Cambridge University Press, 2006), 16.

Love in the Time of Scholarship. Anand Venkatkrishnan, Oxford University Press. © Oxford University Press 2024.
DOI: 10.1093/oso/9780197776636.003.0004

known retrospectively as the "*bhakti* movement," regularly affected distance from highbrow scholarly activity, especially in Sanskrit. This dichotomy between the popular and elite modes of *bhakti*, one with radical egalitarian impulses and the other making concessions to dominant forms of religious authority and political power, persists in scholarship on the subject.[2] To consider elites homogeneous, however, is to take their pretensions to hegemony at face value. Brahmin scholars, even those with otherwise aligned caste interests, disagreed considerably not only on intellectual but also on social issues. This is true for Sanskrit intellectual history on the whole. I am interested here in how everyday religion mediated these disagreements. Were the subversive undercurrents of *bhakti* as a language of social and religious dissent simply overwhelmed by the vast Brahmanical ocean? Or did the incorporation of *bhakti* as an object of systematic theoretical inquiry signal a shift in the way it was possible to conceive of scholarly life, of what it meant to be a Brahmin in the first place? The demotic registers of *bhakti*, I argue, filtered into the forbidding world of Sanskrit intellectuality. Transmuted and translated into the idioms of Brahmanical culture, they nevertheless left a trace in the changing self-presentation of Brahmin elites.

One place to undertake this inquiry is the city of Banaras in present-day Uttar Pradesh. Although Banaras (Skt. Vārāṇasī) was an ancient holy city that had welcomed Hindu pilgrims for centuries, in the sixteenth and seventeenth centuries, under the aegis of Mughal rule, it became an academic haven for Brahmin scholars. Freed from the demands of local patrons and provided with both social stability and ample research funds, Brahmin intellectuals flocked to Banaras from all over the subcontinent. It was hardly an ivory tower; most scholars taught students either in their homes or in the courtyards of wealthy noblemen. The closest to a conference room available was the Muktimaṇḍapa, a celebrated pavilion within the Kāśī Viśvanāth temple on the banks of the River Gaṅgā. From this seat of relative power, Brahmin intellectuals, not unlike their Muslim counterparts down the road,

[2] On the entangled threads of religion, *bhakti*, and equality, see Jon Keune, *Shared Devotion, Shared Food: Equality and the Bhakti-Caste Question in Western India* (New York: Oxford University Press, 2021), 25–65. Cf. John Stratton Hawley, Christian Lee Novetzke, and Swapna Sharma, eds., *Bhakti and Power: Debating India's Religion of the Heart* (Seattle: University of Washington Press, 2019); David Lorenzen, "Bhakti," in *The Hindu World*, ed. Sushil Mittal and Gene Thursby (London: Routledge, 2005), 185–209; Patton Burchett, "Bhakti Rhetoric in the Hagiography of 'Untouchable' Saints: Discerning Bhakti's Ambivalence on Caste and Brahminhood," *International Journal of Hindu Studies* 13.2 (2009): 115–141; Tracy Coleman, "Viraha-Bhakti and Strīdharma: Re-reading the Story of Kṛṣṇa and the Gopīs in the *Harivaṁśa* and the *Bhāgavata Purāṇa*," *Journal of the American Oriental Society* 130.3 (2010): 385–412.

debated the latest philosophical trends, engaged politically with the Mughal administration, and adjudicated public disputes on matters of social hierarchy. Their decisions carried weight as far away as the towns from which they came, evincing a kind of provincialism even among this cosmopolitan crowd. They were, as such, well aware of the world of everyday life, however much they may have disdained its rowdiness. It would have been impossible not to hear the call to prayer from the minarets, the vociferous singing of devotees in procession, and the stinging barbs of street poets.

Not everyone tried to drown out the noise. In this chapter, I amplify the echoes of the streets in the writings of the Dēvas, a family of Maharashtrian Brahmins who established a multigenerational scholarly household in Banaras. The Dēvas built their careers on writing and teaching in the fields of Mīmāṁsā and Advaita Vēdānta, the philosophical preferences of the Banarasi intelligentsia.[3] They also publicly proclaimed their *bhakti* for God, sometimes in support of and sometimes in conflict with their academic ambition. The social history of the "Brahmin ecumene" in early modern Banaras has been the subject of several studies over the past decade and a half.[4] Many scholarly families, particularly from the Maharashtrian regions, moved to this new academic hotspot in the sixteenth and seventeenth centuries. The regional pressures and opportunities for wealth enabled by the rise of the Mughal imperial order "deepened class divides between different Brahman communities, often resulting in fission and . . . new hierarchies of worth amongst Brahmans themselves."[5] The changing social environment in this period "opened in a new way the question of what it meant to be a Brahmin," a question in which Maharashtrians, regarded as "southerners" in this northern city, were constantly involved.[6] It is possible that the Muktimaṇḍapa, the quasi-collegiate study hall of the Kāśī Viśvanāth

[3] Sheldon Pollock, "New Intellectuals in Seventeenth-Century India," *The Indian Economic and Social History Review* 38.1 (2001): 21–22; Christopher Minkowski, "Advaita Vedānta in Early Modern History," *South Asian History and Culture* 2:2 (2011): 217.

[4] Rosalind O'Hanlon and Christopher Minkowski, "What Makes People Who They Are? Pandit Networks and the Problem of Livelihoods in Early Modern Western India," *The Indian Economic and Social History Review* 45.3 (2008): 381–416; Rosalind O'Hanlon, "Letters Home: Banaras Pandits and the Maratha Regions in Early Modern India," *Modern Asian Studies* 44.2 (2010): 201–240; Rosalind O'Hanlon, "The Social Worth of Scribes: Brahmins, Kayasthas, and the Social Order in Early Modern India," *The Indian Economic and Social History Review* 47.4 (2010): 563–595; Rosalind O'Hanlon, "Speaking from Siva's Temple, Banaras Scholar Households and the Brahman 'Ecumene' of Mughal India," *South Asian History and Culture* 2.2 (2011): 253–277.

[5] O'Hanlon, "Speaking from Siva's Temple," 254.

[6] O'Hanlon and Minkowski, "What Makes People Who They Are?," 410.

temple, was important to these southern Brahmins because it was itself located to the south of the central sanctuary.[7]

Maratha Brahmin scholars debated their statuses in public and performed them through the institution of the household, which shaped the education and frequently the career opportunities of Sanskrit intellectuals. The scholarly household offered a way to maximize family intellectual and pedagogical resources and to accumulate the libraries necessary for high-level intellectual work. It was the basis for advantageous marriages between scholar families. The scholarly household forged the two kinds of patriarchal affiliation that mattered most in Sanskrit intellectual culture: between fathers and the sons they educated, and between teachers and their students, who often studied alongside the teacher's sons.[8]

The Dēvas provide us with a case study of such a scholarly household. Like their contemporaries of whom we know a little more, the Bhaṭṭa family, they probably moved to Banaras from Maharashtra in the sixteenth century.[9] Their activity in Banaras can be traced first to Anantadēva (c. 1600 CE), followed by his son Āpadēva (c. 1625 CE), and his grandson Anantadēva II (c. 1650 CE).[10] Anantadēva II was a prominent participant in Banaras's *dharmasabhās*, assemblies of religious experts convened to decide a question of ritual rights. From his *Smṛtikaustubha*, a voluminous compendium of *dharmaśāstra*, we get an intellectual lineage of the family:

> There was once a Brahmin, on the banks of the Gōdāvarī, who kept the Vedic altars and was a devotee of Kṛṣṇa. His name was Ēknāth. His son inherited his qualities and understood the true content of all the sciences. His name was Āpadēva, who obtained from God every heavenly station. He had a son: a prolific Mīmāṁsā scholar, and always eager to serve Kṛṣṇa, his reputation for pedagogy spread far and wide. He was true to his name, Ananta, on account of his "countless" virtues. To the delight of debaters, he wrote the Vēdānta textbook *Siddhāntatattva*. His son was Āpadēva, author

[7] O'Hanlon, "Letters Home," 219.

[8] See Christopher Minkowski, Rosalind O'Hanlon, and Anand Venkatkrishnan, "Social History in the Study of Indian Intellectual Cultures?," *South Asian History and Culture* 6.1 (2015): 3.

[9] Cf. James Benson, "Śaṁkarabhaṭṭa's Family Chronicle," in *The Pandit: Traditional Scholarship in India*, ed. Axel Michaels (Delhi: Manohar, 2001), 105–118.

[10] See P. K. Gode, "Āpadēva, the Author of the Mīmāṁsānyāyaprakāśa and Mahāmahopādhyāya Āpadēva, the Author of the Adhikaraṇacandrikā and Smṛticandrikā—Are They Identical?," in *Studies in Indian Literary History*, vol. 2 (Bombay: Singhi Jain Śāstra Śikshāpīth, 1954), 39–48. Cf. O'Hanlon and Minkowski, "What Makes People Who They Are?," 382; O'Hanlon, "Letters Home," 231–232, 235; Pollock, "New Intellectuals," 18–19.

> of the *Mīmāṁsānyāyaprakāśa*. Learned in the fields of both Mīmāṁsās, he always poured out the infinite ambrosia of his knowledge.[11]

Anantadēva II highlights two features of his scholarly ancestors: they were known for their teaching (*vidyādāna*), and they were committed to the worship of Kr̥ṣṇa. In his view, they inherited this tradition of scholarship and *bhakti* from the first member of the family tree, Ēknāth. Undoubtedly the most striking name to appear on this list, the historical Ēknāth was a Maharashtrian Brahmin saint-poet who lived in the sixteenth century. He spent much of his life in the "notoriously orthodox" town of Paiṭhaṇ, along the Gōdāvarī River in Maharashtra, where he performed poetry in Marathi that often criticized Brahmins for their prejudices, and transgressed caste boundaries by sharing meals with members of nonelite castes.[12] He also wrote sophisticated works of exegesis and epitomized Sanskrit scriptures and epics in the Marathi language. These works, while less well-remembered than his *bhakti* poetry, exhibit a kind of localized, vernacular Vēdānta that is irreducible to the superposed Sanskrit canon of classical Vēdānta.[13]

Scholars disagree as to whether or not the Dēvas were actually descended from Ēknāth.[14] It seems unlikely that a family committed to the social hierarchies of *dharmaśāstra* would have advertised their connections to Ēknāth, when he routinely broke the very laws governing social interaction

[11] *The Smr̥iti Kaustubha of Anant Dēva*, ed. Vasudev Laxman Sastri Pansikar (Bombay: Nirnaya Sagar, 1931), 2–3:

> *āsīd gōdāvarītīrē vēdavēdīsamanvitaḥ*
> *śrīkr̥ṣṇabhaktimān ēka ēkanāthābhidhō dvijaḥ.*
> *tatsutas tadguṇair yuktaḥ sarvaśāstrārthatattvavit*
> *āpadevōʼbhavad dēvāt prāpa yaḥ sakalān manūn.*
> *mīmāṁsānayakōvidō madhuripōḥ sevāsu nityōdyataḥ*
> *vidyādānavibhāvitōttamayaśā āsīt tadīyātmajaḥ.*
> *yasyānantaguṇair ananta iti san nāmārthavattāṁ gataṁ*
> *yēnāvādi ca vādināṁ śrutiśiraḥsiddhāntatattvaṁ mudē.*
> *nyāyaprakāśakartā niravadhividyāmr̥tapradaḥ satatam*
> *mīmāṁsādvayanayavit tanayas tasyāpadēvōʼbhūt.*

[12] Keune, *Shared Devotion, Shared Food*, 129.

[13] Anand Venkatkrishnan, "Philosophy from the Bottom Up: Eknāth's Vernacular Advaita," *Journal of Indian Philosophy* 48.9 (2020): 9–21.

[14] The first time he is mentioned by name is in Anantadēva II's family history. For a positive view, see Pollock, "New Intellectuals," 18, 30; O'Hanlon, "Letters Home," 203; P. V. Kane, *A History of Dharmaśāstra*, vol. 1 (Poona: Bhandarkar Oriental Research Institute, 1930), 450–452. For the negative, see Jon Keune, "Eknāth Remembered and Reformed: Bhakti, Brahmans, and Untouchables in Marathi Historiography" (Ph.D. diss., Columbia University, 2011), 184–188. There is, of course, the third possibility, that Anantadēva was referring to an entirely different Ēknāth altogether. But that would be a little bit like the old classicist joke about how the *Iliad* and the *Odyssey* could not have been written by Homer, but by someone else named Homer.

that the Dēvas so actively promoted. From the perspective of cultural history, however, the association may not be so farfetched. Hagiographies of the saint tell of his stubbornly orthodox son, Haripaṇḍit, who was upset that his father abandoned Sanskrit for Marathi and dared to dine with Dalits. Leaving in a huff for Banaras, Haripaṇḍit returned to Paiṭhaṇ reluctantly at his father's urging, where a miraculous incident changed his mind.[15] Ēknāth didn't need his son to remind him that he was going too far. He had received plenty of hostility the last time he was in Banaras, where he had completed writing the *Ēknāthī Bhāgavat*, a Marathi reading of the eleventh chapter of the *Bhāgavata Purāṇa*. Stories say that his book was met with rumblings of discontent from the city's establishment Brahmins, who were upset that the saint profaned the sacred teaching by transmitting it in the "polluted" vernacular.[16] One can imagine the highly educated Āpadēva as a version of Ēknāth's son, disturbed by his father's freewheeling disregard for caste norms. He moves his family to Banaras, where his children are raised to become proper Sanskrit scholars. But they cannot shake the memory of *bhakti*'s power. A saint is not so easy to forget.

The Dēvas begin to dominate the social and intellectual life of the city. The more they read the *Bhāgavata*, however, the more *bhakti* seeps into their scholarship. They argue forcefully that there is nothing wrong with devotional poems in vernacular languages. They satirize dry, soulless intellectualism. They tell stories and sing songs. They turn their work into praise of God. The Dēvas held out for the possibility that one could love learning and love God at the same time. In this chapter, I explore the influence of *bhakti* on their research, teaching, and scholarly personalities. The Dēvas defended everyday *bhakti* practices from the criticism that they were intellectually shallow and socially disreputable. In doing so, they aired their views on the right way to be a Brahmin—not as radically as Ēknāth, but not deaf to his words either.

How to Be a Vēdāntin

The earliest writing we possess from the Dēva family is by the senior Anantadēva. We met him at the end of the previous chapter when we read

[15] Keune, "Eknāth Remembered and Reformed," 30–31.
[16] Justin Abbott, *The Life of Eknāth* (Delhi: Motilal Banarsidass, 1981), xvii–xxii.

his comments on Lakṣmīdhara's *Bhagavannāmakaumudī*. He began his career by studying Advaita Vēdānta with a renunciant named Rāmatīrtha, who probably lived in Banaras in the sixteenth century.[17] Under Rāmatīrtha's guidance, Anantadēva wrote a primer (*prakriyā*) on Advaita Vēdānta called the *Siddhāntatattva*. Such introductory textbooks increased in popularity over the early modern centuries. They may have begun as a kind of senior thesis or qualifying exam, displaying the student's mastery of a certain subject and familiarity with debates in the field. Anantadēva's book rehearsed in relatively simple language some major doctrines, definitions, and disagreements in the Advaita tradition. He was able to intelligently reconstruct and reconcile the latest philosophical theories, including the *dṛṣṭisṛṣṭivāda*, the controversial concept of subjective idealism which earned many of his contemporaries the pejorative label "crypto-Buddhist."[18] He prided himself on being able to provide the basic views of the system (*siddhāntatattvam*) by navigating the morass of scholarly debates (*gatavāgvivādam*).[19]

Anantadēva's relationship with Advaita Vēdānta was complicated. The serious student of Vēdānta in the *Siddhāntatattva* gives way to a cantankerous critic in the *Bhaktinirṇaya*. Written in a far more polemical style, not unlike the argumentative pamphlets that comprised much intellectual discord in early modern Banaras,[20] the *Bhaktinirṇaya* was an attempt to determine the nature of *bhakti*, who should undertake *bhakti*, what they should do, and how they should read. Anantadēva was not trying to be original. He closely followed the *Bhāgavata Purāṇa* and the commentary by Śrīdhara Svāmī and paraphrased the *Bhagavannāmakaumudī* on the question of singing God's name. His investigation was not idle but exhortatory. The title of the first chapter is "Why You Must Have *bhakti* for God" (*haribhaktikartavyatānirūpaṇam*). The word *kartavyatā* means "a duty," something that literally "must be done." It recalls the entire apparatus of Mīmāṁsā theories of obligatory

[17] See P. V. Sivarama Dikshitar, "Rāmatīrtha," in *Preceptors of Advaita*, ed. T. M. P. Mahadēvan (Secunderabad: Sri Kanchi Kamakoti Shankara Mandir, 1968), 221–225. Cf. Minkowski, "Advaita Vedānta in Early Modern India," 214–215.

[18] *Siddhāntatattvaṁ Nāma Vēdāntaprakaraṇam*, ed. Tailanga Rama Sastri (Benares: Government Sanskrit College, 1901), 57–60 (henceforth cited as *Siddhāntatattva*). Cf. Minkowski, "Advaita Vedānta," 213; Andrew Nicholson, *Unifying Hinduism: Philosophy and Identity in Indian Intellectual History* (New York: Columbia University Press, 2010), 63. On the *dṛṣṭisṛṣṭivāda*, see Sthaneshwar Timalsina, *Seeing and Appearance: History of the Advaita Doctrine of Dṛṣṭisṛṣṭi* (Aachen: Shaker Verlag, 2006).

[19] *Siddhāntatattva*, 60.

[20] See Christopher Minkowski, "I'll Wash Out Your Mouth with My Boot: A Guide to Philological Argument in Mughal-Era Banaras," in *Epic and Argument in Literary History: Essays in Honor of Robert P. Goldman*, ed. Sheldon Pollock (Delhi: Manohar, 2010), 117–141.

ritual action, not to mention the normative prescriptions of *dharmaśāstra*. This is probably what Anantadēva was going for. By giving his work the subtitle *nirṇaya*, meaning "deliberation," "determination," or "the final say," Anantadēva was likely alluding to the very public debates over normative social, ritual, and ethical codes for which the Brahmin pandits of early modern Banaras were known. His grandson Anantadēva II was present among the signatories of several momentous letters of judgment (*nirṇayapatra*) to emerge from the Muktimaṇḍapa of the Kāśī Viśvanāth temple.[21] The *nirṇayapatra* may have been the pandits' response to the Islamic *fatwa* and to the greater public demand for unequivocal, authoritative information in matters of religious dispute. The wider regional audiences of these letters were not only interested in the outcomes of these debates but expected to see paper documents setting them out.[22]

In keeping with the public nature of the *nirṇaya* genre, most of Anantadēva's critiques in the *Bhaktinirṇaya* are not about metaphysics but about social identity and customs. He signals his dissatisfaction with the new intellectual economy of Banaras at the beginning of the book: "Study hard and make all the money you want. Become famous to a bunch of idiots. As for me, I'm going to worship the delightful lotus feet of Gōvinda. I've seen the accumulation of prosperity and pleasure from working life. I'll take *bhakti* for God and relief from suffering instead."[23] The motif of the God-fearing scholar frustrated with his careerist contemporaries recurs in Anantadēva's writing. Over and over again, in the *Bhaktinirṇaya*, Anantadēva castigates his interlocutors for their ethical impropriety, blurring the boundaries between intellectual disagreement and social misconduct. For Anantadēva, *bhakti* was a religion not just of the heart but also of the body and mind. To that end, he questions the intellectualism of Advaita Vēdānta, where radical ideas can be divorced from everyday practice.

[21] O'Hanlon and Minkowski, "What Makes People Who They Are?," 395.

[22] See Rosalind O'Hanlon, "Performance in a World of Paper: Puranic Histories and Social Communication in Early Modern India," *Past and Present* 219 (2013): 87–126.

[23] *Śrīmadanantadēvaviracitaḥ Bhaktinirṇayaḥ*, ed. Ananta Shastri Phadke (Benares: Sanskrit College, 1937), 1 (henceforth cited as *Bhaktinirṇaya*):

abhyasya vidyāṁ dhanam arjayantu
khyātiṁ ca mūrkhān prati sādhayantu
vayaṁ tu gōvindapadāravinda-
dvayaṁ sadānandamayaṁ bhajāmaḥ.
iha khalu karmakṛtānāṁ viṣayasukhānāṁ vipākam ālōkya
bhagavadbhaktiṁ kurmaḥ saṁsṛtiduḥkhāny apākurmaḥ.

Far from the cool and systematic scholarship of the *Siddhāntatattva*, where all Advaita Vēdānta viewpoints are harmonized in summary exposition, the *Bhaktinirṇaya* challenges the conclusions of radical forms of nondualism. For example, the theory of subjective idealism, which Anantadēva had previously defended, is found wanting because it establishes that there is no ultimate reality to the phenomenal world. The world of everyday experience, in this view, is nothing but *māyā*, an illusion projected onto the canvas of the real. All one needs to do to be free of this illusion is to apprehend directly that Brahman, the infinite consciousness that undergirds all existence, is one's true nature. That knowledge, and only that knowledge, will lead to liberation from suffering. Since this is the case, there is little purpose in devotional worship or, for that matter, any activity that involves means and ends. Unmediated awareness of this kind is not dependent on action. In typically belligerent and, at times, shockingly accusatory style, Anantadēva blasts his opponent for the misleading consequences of this claim, and for misreading his own texts:

> There are some introspective types, only skilled at spinning yarns about the knowledge of Brahman [*brahmajñāna*]. They think they have it all figured out just by talking about it. Bereft of love for God, they blabber on as follows: "Why does anyone honor God? The concept of God is nothing but Brahman conditioned by *māyā*, or rather his whimsical incarnation, who controls the illusion. There is nothing to be obtained by it, the agent himself is nothing but Brahman, and so-called agency is illusory anyway. One performs obligatory rituals like bathing and twilight worship only to maintain social propriety, not because there is anything to be gained by it. Prohibited activity is avoided for the same reason, since there's no such thing as hell." Such people should be ignored, for they are deniers in disguise, people who reject the authority of the Vedas [*nāstika*]. "How so," you might wonder, "since they believe that the Upaniṣads are the authority on Brahman?" Well then, how can one deny that the performance of good and bad deeds leads to heaven and hell? Does the Veda not instruct us about that as well? You might argue, "When *brahmajñāna* arises, there is no attaining heaven or hell." Tell me, how can one achieve *brahmajñāna* without developing spiritual prerequisites like disenchantment? If you deny the need for these methods in the first place, then you are denying the validity of such Vedic statements on the topic as "The Brahmin should

become disenchanted" (*Muṇḍaka Upaniṣad* 1.2.12). That makes you as good as a *nāstika*.[24]

In this reading of Advaita, there is no difference between an individual and God, for there is no differentiation in anything. There is little point in having a devotional attitude to a supreme being who is imagined to be separate from oneself. For that matter, there is no reason to keep up Brahmin observances like the daily twilight worship, when the complex of agent, action, and result is just another illusion. On the one hand, the rejection of these everyday customs is part of the ideal of renunciation, which most Advaitins supported. On the other hand, the Advaitin's radical disavowal of ritual obligations and devotional sentiments leads to a total nihilism, the kind that would have been met with accusations of Spinozism in early modern Europe. The Advaitin professes to be interpreting the teachings of the Upaniṣads, but he reads selectively. For the Vedas do insist that one must develop actions and attitudes that prepare one spiritually to receive the teaching of nondualism. Ignoring these relationships of means to ends is to deny that the Vedas know better than we do.

Anantadēva makes a rather dramatic leap here. It is one thing to disagree about the interpretation of a text, but to call someone a *nāstika*, to question their commitment to their own scriptures, was not a very nice thing to do.[25] The exaggerated language highlights the stakes of the conflict. Most often the word was hurled by people against those who belonged to different sects or religions. For many Hindus it meant one who denied the authority of the Vedas, like Buddhists, Jains, and Sāṁkhya philosophers, while others used it to discredit their sectarian opponents. Critics of Advaita Vēdānta, for example, considered the antirealism of the tradition as a fatal flaw: if there is truly no differentiation in the world, there cannot be a teacher or

[24] *Bhaktinirṇaya*, 27: *atra kēcid antarviṣayapravaṇā brahmajñānavārtāmātranirvartananipuṇāḥ tanmātrēṇa ēva kṛtārthaṁmanyā bhagavadbhaktiśūnyāḥ pralapanti māyōpahitē brahmaṇi bhagavati tad līlāvigrahē vā māyini kim ity ādaraḥ kriyatē prāpyābhāvāt svayaṁ kartur ēva brahmarūpatvāt kartṛtvasya mithyātvāt. snānasandhyādikaṁ tu lōkavyavahārārthaṁ kriyatē na tu tēnāpi kiṁcit labdhavyam asti. ēvaṁ niṣiddhavarjanam api narakābhāvāt lōkavyavahārārtham ēva. ta ētē nāmāntarēṇa nāstikā ity upēkṣyāḥ. kathaṁ nāstikāḥ vedāntānāṁ brahmaṇi prāmāṇyābhyupagamād iti cēt. hanta tarhi (kathaṁ) svarganarakādyabhāvaḥ puṇyapāpānuṣṭhānē. vēdēna ēva brahmapratipādanavat puṇyapāpānuṣṭhātṝṇāṁ svarganarakādipratipādanāt. jātē brahmajñānē nāsti svarganarakaprāptir iti cēt. kathaṁ vairāgyādisādhanābhāvē brahmajñānāvāptir bhavatām. vairāgyādisādhanam ēva na bhavati iti cēt tatpratipādakasya "brāhmaṇō nirvēdam āyād" ityādivēdavacanasya aprāmāṇyābhyupagamēna nāstikatvāt.*

[25] On affirmers (*āstika*) and deniers (*nāstika*) in Indian history, see Nicholson, *Unifying Hinduism*, 166–184.

a student either, vitiating the authority of the very scriptures of Vēdānta.[26] Anantadēva, however, was an insider to the tradition and wanted to ward off the implications of such criticisms. It is not simply that the Vēdāntin does not take *bhakti* seriously. It is that he twists the teaching about nondualism in the Upaniṣads for his own irreverent purposes. Anantadēva's problem is not with nondualism but with nondualists.

To be specific, his problem is with Brahmin philosophers who reject their social responsibilities, who feel that they can get away with "knowledge" (*jñāna)* at the expense of *bhakti*. Against these upstarts, Anantadēva holds up the Brahmin practitioner of Vedic rites as the ideal candidate for *bhakti*. Not only is taking delight in God's stories "especially" (*viśēṣatō*) true of Brahmins; *bhakti* itself emerges from the same Brahmanical practices as the desire to study Vēdānta. In fact, such practices are indispensable. Without the attitudes generated by them, neither *bhakti* nor Vēdānta culminates in liberation.[27] Responding to the critique that the path of *bhakti* he proposes is unsupported by the majority of philosophers, Anantadēva doubles down and appeals to an "everyday" experience that paraphrases the language of "delight" (*praharṣa*) and "love" (*anurāga*) from the *Bhagavad Gītā* (11.36):

> So what if it is in the minority? Not everyone is going to discuss everything. Anyway it's just common sense. It is a matter of universal experience that when you start hearing or singing the glories of God, you begin to feel a sense of delight. This is all the more the case for those who have developed faith by performing sacrifices and other Brahmanical activities. When someone is delighted with something, they form a love for that thing, just like the *cakōra* bird's love for the moon. When you fall in love, that object starts to pulsate in your heart, and any attachment to other things simply slips away, as it does for a young woman obsessed with her lover.[28]

[26] In the eleventh-century drama *Prabōdhacandrōdaya*, one philosopher tries to convince the character "Upaniṣad" that she herself, the very symbol of Vedic orthodoxy, is a *nāstika*. The idea may be that the Vēdāntic view of liberation is not so different from the materialist view that death is the end of suffering. See Michael Allen, "Dueling Dramas, Dueling Doxographies: The *Prabodhacandrodaya* and *Saṁkalpasūryodaya*," *Journal of Hindu Studies* 9.3 (2016): 279, 294, n. 17.

[27] *Bhaktinirṇaya*, 34: *yajñādyanuṣṭhānasādhyavividiṣāvirahē vēdāntavicārō'pi yathā na mōkṣaphalaparyavasāyī tathā yajñādyanuṣṭhānasādhyaśraddhāvirahē saṁkīrttanādibhaktir api na mōkṣaphalaparyavasāyinī.*

[28] *Bhaktinirṇaya*, 34–35: *kim ētāvatā. na hi sarvē sarvaṁ nirūpayanti. yuktā cēyaṁ praṇālikā. tathā hi. bhagavataḥ śravaṇakīrttanādyanuṣṭhānē praharṣaḥ sakalajanānām anubhavasiddhaḥ. viśēṣatō yajñādyanuṣṭhānajanyaśraddhāviśēṣavatām. yadanubandhēna ca praharṣō yasya yasya tatrānurāgaḥ sampadyatē. cakōrādēr iva candrādau. anurāgē ca sampadyamānē tatsphuraṇaṁ tadanyaviṣayēṣu cittānubandhaśaithilyaṁ ca. navataruṇyā iva vallabhaviṣayē.*

We all know, says Anantadēva, that hearing the stories of God gives you happiness and fulfillment. It's true, there are people who find no joy in singing the glories of God, let alone have love for him. But that's their problem. If your experience doesn't match what the texts say, it means you're doing something wrong. Just because a sick man doesn't enjoy drinking milk, that doesn't mean milk is not in itself delicious.[29] This example is classic Anantadēva. He uses it repeatedly to defend his writing against jealous scholars. As he says in the opening lines of his commentary on the *Bhagavannāmakaumudī*, "So what if some stupid critics disrespect this well-written work out of envy in their heart? Just because sick people do not have a taste for it, sweet whole milk is not at fault."[30] Anantadēva sees his critics as missing two kinds of love: love for God and love for his own work. If only they had that love, they would see that there is a right way to be a Brahmin, a Vēdāntin. But who can save scholars from themselves?

A Portrait of the Scholar as an Old Man

Anantadēva felt ill at ease among his prolific yet profligate colleagues. Like the *anti-philosophes* of eighteenth-century France, Anantadēva was worried by "the privileges and the perils of knowledge seeking and creative endeavor."[31] If the primary tension for the *gens de lettres* of Enlightenment France was between the social graces of public life and the intellectual liberty of solitary research, for the Brahmins of Anantadēva's Banaras it was between personal gain and pious sentiment.[32] While encomia to eminent scholarly figures were not uncommon in the Banaras of his day,[33] Anantadēva questioned the

[29] *Bhaktinirṇaya*, 35: *nanu kēṣāñcit bhagavacchravaṇakīrttanādināpi na praharṣō dṛśyatē, natarāṁ bhagavaty anurāgaḥ. satyam. naitāvatā kācit kṣatir vacanānubhavayōḥ. na hi jvaritānāṁ dugdhapānē harṣō na dṛśyata iti tan na harṣahētuḥ.*

[30] *Bhagavannāmakaumudī*, ed. Govinda Damodar Sastri (Kāśī: Acyutagranthamālā, 1927), 1:

samyaṅnirūpitam idaṁ yadi nādriyantē
duṣṭā nikṛṣṭamatayō hṛdi matsarēṇa
kiṁ tāvatā jvaravatām arucēr na jātu
dugdhasya śuddhamadhurasya vidūṣaṇaṁ syāt.

Variations on this stanza are found in Anantadēva's *Kṛṣṇabhakticandrikā*, discussed in this chapter, and in the *Sampradāyanirūpaṇa*, an unpublished autocommentary on his *Siddhāntatattva*. See P. Peterson, *A Sixth Report in Search of Sanscrit Mss. in the Bombay Circle* (Bombay: Government Central Press, 1899), 23–24.

[31] Anne Vila, *Suffering Scholars: Pathologies of the Intellectual in Enlightenment France* (Philadelphia: University of Pennsylvania Press, 2018), 4.

[32] See Vila, *Suffering Scholars*, 69.

[33] Consider the festschrift for Kavīndrācārya Sarasvatī, a seventeenth-century *sannyāsī* who was recognized by the Mughal political order and maintained an impressive library of Sanskrit

scholar's tendency toward overweening ambition and self-aggrandizement. He commented on the relationship between the scholar and the social world in essays like the *Bhaktinirṇaya* and through the medium of the theater.[34] We do not know whether either of Anantadēva's dramas (*nāṭaka*), the *Kṛṣṇabhakticandrikā* and the *Manōnurañjana*, was ever performed live.[35] At the very least they circulated among different Brahmin communities in Banaras.[36] The *Manōnurañjana* is a theatrical rendering of stories about Kṛṣṇa from the *Bhāgavata Purāṇa*. The *Kṛṣṇabhakticandrikā*, on the other hand, is a one-act college play about conflicts between students of religion and philosophy. In some respects, it resembles the famous eleventh-century allegorical drama *Prabōdhacandrōdaya* by Kṛṣṇa Miśra. The *Prabōdhacandrōdaya* presents Vēdānta as the superlative tradition of Brahmanical philosophy, "a triumph achieved through a strategic alliance of the various philosophical schools and devotional sects."[37] The *Kṛṣṇabhakticandrikā* has a similarly doxographical outline. Characters of different philosophical and sectarian persuasions are conquered in debate by two separate protagonists of *bhakti*, a "great Vaiṣṇava" (*mahāvaiṣṇava*) and a "devotee of Kṛṣṇa" (*kṛṣṇabhakta*).[38] The first is dispatched to deal with a partisan Śaiva and Vaiṣṇava by convincing them that Śiva and Viṣṇu are just manifestations of one God, while the other argues with pedantic grammarians, prideful logicians, materialist Mīmāṁsakas, and haughty Vēdāntins. Unlike the strategic inclusivist of the *Prabōdhacandrōdaya*, however, their task is not to enlist these debaters in a greater goal but to show them that they have gone astray. Another possible

manuscripts. See *Kavīndracandrodaya*, ed. Har Dutt Sharma and M. M. Patkar (Poona: Oriental Book Agency, 1939). Cf. *Kavindracharya List*, ed. R. Ananta Krishna Sastry (Baroda: Central Library, 1921).

[34] On the use of theater as a key medium for commenting on the *philosophe* as a social figure, see Vila, *Suffering Scholars*, 70–76.

[35] See "*Śrīkṛṣṇabhakticandrikānāṭakam*," in *Kāvyētihāsasasaṅgraha* (Pune: Mahādeva Ballaḷa Nāmajōśī, 1881), 1–28, and *The Manonurañjana Nāṭaka*, ed. Mangal Dēva Shastri (Allahabad: The Superintendent Printing and Stationery, 1938) (henceforth cited as *Kṛṣṇabhakticandrikā* and *Manōnurañjana*).

[36] A late seventeenth-century copy of the *Kṛṣṇabhakticandrikā* in the Bodleian Library, Oxford (Ms. Sansk. d. 88), was written in the Śāradā script. That means the text was probably being read by Kashmiri Brahmins in Banaras, not just Maharashtrians like the Dēvas. I owe this suggestion to Alexis Sanderson. See Moriz Winternitz and A. B. Keith, *Catalogue of Sanskrit Manuscripts in the Bodleian Library*, vol. 2 (Oxford: Clarendon Press, 1905), 174–176.

[37] Allen, "Dueling Dramas, Dueling Doxographies," 275. While religious divides are bridged by the nonsectarian tradition of Vēdānta, the philosophical schools are embraced provisionally as allies against *nāstikas*, but not on the path to liberation (279).

[38] Baldev Upadhyaya, "A Devotional Drama in Sanskrit," *Indian Historical Quarterly* 12 (1936): 721–729.

model for Anantadēva was the *Āgamaḍambara* by Jayanta Bhaṭṭa, an academic drama from ninth-century Kashmir about debates between religious scholars vying for political patronage. But unlike the protagonists of this play, who provide sophisticated refutations of each other's philosophical positions, the debaters of the *Kṛṣṇabhakticandrikā* mostly resort to *ad hominem* invective, insisting that the other's theories depend on the truth of their own.

The *kṛṣṇabhakta*, hero of the *Kṛṣṇabhakticandrikā*, was once a scholar, accustomed to the ego-driven arena of academia. In this he resembles the playwright himself. In the autobiographical sketch provided in the *Manōnurañjana*, Anantadēva tells us that he was "given over to the study of the 'prior' and 'latter' Mīmāṁsās, and generally spent his days instructing others in those disciplines."[39] He studied with his father, Āpadēva, the Brahmin savant Nārāyaṇa Bhaṭṭa,[40] and the renowned renunciant Rāmatīrtha, whom he credits with the "amazing" ability (*āścaryam*) to be absorbed simultaneously in "the study of philosophy" (*darśanābhyāsa*) and "the name of God" (*paramēśvaranāma*). For a moment, at least, it seems possible to celebrate love in the time of scholarship:

> True scripture is the entire milky ocean,
> its daily study is Mount Mandara,
> and analytical reflection is the churning.
> But that pure ambrosia, the blessed name of God,
> even among devotees who exhaust their efforts,
> only reaches the lips of a select few,
> through the grace of Śrī's beloved.[41]

Although he established a household which produced at least three generations of scholars, Anantadēva was uncomfortable with academic success. He concludes the *Manōnurañjana* with a rueful, searching reflection: "Through

[39] *Manōnurañjana*, 3:

> *yaḥ pūrvōttaramīmāṁsāpariśīlanaśīlavān*
> *tadīyādhyāpanēnaiva samayaṁ khalu nītavān.*

[40] On the Bhaṭṭa family, see Benson, "Śaṁkarabhaṭṭa's Family Chronicle"; Haraprasad Shastri, "Dakshini Pandits at Benares," *The Indian Antiquary* 41 (1912): 7–13.

[41] *Manōnurañjana*, 4:

> *sacchāstraṁ nikhilaṁ payōmbudhir ayaṁ tasyātha dainaṁdinā-*
> *bhyāsō mandaraparvatō nayacayair ālōcanaṁ manthanam*
> *tatra śrīharināma śuddham amṛtaṁ śrāntēṣv ananyēṣv api*
> *śrīkāntasya kṛpāvaśēna tu mukhē kēṣāṁcid ēvāñcati.*

studying scriptures, teaching students, and writing books for fame and renown, my mind became proud of its accomplishments. But now, through my merit alone, in each word that praises Kṛṣṇa and his virtues, it finds delight in the billows of the milky ocean of joy."[42] In the *Kṛṣṇabhakticandrikā*, the character of the *kṛṣṇabhakta* is an exemplar of this new life of love for God. Eager to share the good news that there is peace beyond academic politics, the *kṛṣṇabhakta* finds himself grating against the self-serving scholarship of his immodest colleagues. As the stage manager's sidekick comments in the prologue of the play, "Most people try to study the sciences, earn money, and gain prestige before their peers." He finds it remarkable, then, that "the poet Anantadēva repeatedly turns his heart to *bhakti*." Echoing the beginning of the *Bhaktinirṇaya*, the stage manager replies, "He's got the right idea. For such people will never find true happiness until they grasp onto God's lotus feet, no matter how much they learn, how much money they make, or what scholarly distinction they achieve. It is hard to acquire those things, let alone maintain them. And yet, people strive for prestige."[43] In the *Kṛṣṇabhakticandrikā*, status is not the solution but the problem. Words for "prestige" (*pratiṣṭhā*, *rūḍhi*) are repeated no fewer than six times in the play. For it is all that anyone truly wants: "Study the sciences with your teacher and teach as many students as you can. What does a scholar want from this, at the end of the day? To become famous among fools and to amass a fortune."[44]

[42] *Manōnurañjana*, 102:

śāstrāṇāṁ pariśīlanair bhṛśam ahō śiṣyēṣu cādhyāpanaiḥ
khyātyuddēśakṛtair babhūva tu mahākṛtyābhimānaṁ manaḥ
puṇyair ēva tu samprati pratipadaṁ gōvindatattadguṇa-
ślāghyaṁ saukhyapayōdhivīcinicayēṣv ānandam āvindati.

[43] *Kṛṣṇabhakticandrikā*, 2:

***naṭaḥ*—**
śīlanē sarvavidyānāṁ dhanānām api cārjanē
sarvalōkapratiṣṭhāyāṁ yatantē bahavō janāḥ.
tad ētad āścaryam. yad ayaṁ kaviḥ svahṛdayaṁ punaḥ punaḥ śrīkṛṣṇabhaktipravaṇ-
aṁ kurutē.
sūtradhāraḥ—*ucitam ēva kurutē. yataḥ*—
anēna khalu jantunā sakalaśāstram abhyasyatāṁ
dhanaṁ vipulam āpyatāṁ sakalasabhyatā labhyatām
na tāvad ayam aśnutē hṛdayasaukhyam ātyantikaṁ
na yāvad avalambatē yadupatēḥ padāmbhōruham.
pratyuta vidyāditrayasya—
arjanē bahavaḥ klēśāḥ arjitasya ca rakṣaṇē
sarvalōkapratiṣṭhāyāṁ yatantē bahavō janāḥ.

[44] *Kṛṣṇabhakticandrikā*, 15:

adhītya śāstrāṇi gurōḥ sakāśād adhyāpya śiṣyān api bhūrivāraṁ
dvāvēva sādhyau viduṣā pumarthau mūḍhēṣu rūḍhiś ca ghanaṁ dhanaṁ ca.

Scholarly sophistication, in this view, is sophistry in disguise, a competitive power grab where victory means both prestige and patronage. When a Śaiva supremacist and his student are insulted by an approaching Vaiṣṇava, the student wants to run away. His teacher responds angrily to the student's cowardice, laying bare his mercenary attitude to scholarly debate: "What the hell are you talking about? What's this about leaving without besting this wicked man? Do you take me for a fool? Listen, knowledge is only useful if you can make someone else look silly. Cleverness only lives up to its name if you get someone else's money with it. Therefore, you must study everything you can, conquer others in debate, gain prestige, and build a great portfolio."[45]

The trope of the cynical, status-obsessed scholar was not unique to Anantadēva's drama, though perhaps the reappearance of this motif had something to do with the new opportunities for intellectuals in early modern India. Consider the following satirical comment by Nīlakaṇṭha Dīkṣita, writing from the South of the subcontinent around the same time: "A humble seeker of truth must study for a long time. But if you want to win in debate, shamelessly raise a big commotion. You get tenure [*pratiṣṭhā*] by teaching and writing books. Who knows? Maybe you'll gain true erudition by the time you die!"[46] Or this frustrated comment by the famous Banarasi Advaitin, Madhusūdana Sarasvatī, explaining why he has decided to write about the *Bhāgavata Purāṇa*: "Day after day, this life is frittered away pointlessly, in the perpetual company of no-good people, and with one trouble after another. But when it is sprinkled with the ambrosia of God's stories, even a moment might be worth living. That's why I have made this effort."[47] Certainly there

[45] *Kṛṣṇabhakticandrikā*, 7:

> *śaivaḥ (sakrōdham)—kiṁ brūṣē. durjanam anirjityaivāpasarpaṇavārtā. tat kiṁ mūrkhaṁ mām abhijānāsi. paśya—*
> *nāsau vidyā bhavati prabhavati na yayā parābhavō'nyasya*
> *bhavati ca na nipuṇatā sā na yayā paradhanam upānayati.*
> *tasmāt—*
> *adhyetavyākhilā vidyā nirjetavyāś ca vādinaḥ*
> *ānetavyā pratiṣṭhā ca saṁcetavyāś ca sampadaḥ.*

[46] *The Minor Poems of Nilakantha Dikshita* (Srirangam: Vani Vilas Press, 1911), 3–4:

> *abhyāsyaṁ lajjamānēna tattvaṁ jijñāsunā ciraṁ*
> *jigīṣuṇā hriyaṁ tyaktvā kāryaḥ kōlāhalō mahān*
> *pāṭhanair granthanirmāṇaiḥ pratiṣṭhā tāvad āpyatē*
> *ēvaṁ ca tathyavyutpattir āyuṣō'ntē bhavēn na vā.*

[47] *The Harilīlāmṛtam by Śrī Bopadeva with a Commentary by Śrī Madhusūdana Saraswatī and Śrīmad Bhāgavata (First Śloka) with the Paramahaṁsapriyā Commentary by the Same Commentator*, ed. Parajuli Pandit Devi Datta Upadhyaya (Benares: Chowkhamba Sanskrit Series, 1933), 58:

are local concerns that animate the *Kṛṣṇabhakticandrikā*. Take this disgruntled complaint from a grammarian about an irreverent philosopher of the "new logic" (*navya nyāya*), a fashionable theoretical language that was becoming increasingly popular in Banaras:[48] "They study the new logic, attend academic conferences puffed with conceit, treat even the senior professors with contempt, and take their seats at the head of the table. If anyone starts to talk theory, they give each other meaningful glances, roll their eyes sarcastically, and criticize that person to no end."[49] This is what the *kṛṣṇabhakta* finds as he enters the scene: squabbling scholars trying to outdo one another for position among pandits. He sighs to himself, "Why did they study so hard if their hearts were just going to turn to hatred? Lord above, it's like the withering of a tree that could give you anything you want." He sees potential in these pointy-headed intellectuals, but they are wasting it in misguided pursuits. "Guys, listen," he continues aloud, "you're well-educated, you've taught many students, and have become great pandits. And this is the end game? To go to conferences, advertise your fancy credentials, argue loudly about something or the other, and defeat your opponent by any means necessary?"[50] An adjacent Mīmāṁsaka (M), who is treated with more respect in the text than are the grammarian and logician, quickly cedes to the *kṛṣṇabhakta*. He renounces his pursuit of wealth and status and instead seeks to learn about the true goal of human life, *bhakti*. At this juncture, a scholar of

> *anudinam idam āyuḥ sarvadāsatprasaṅgair*
> *bahuvidhaparitāpaiḥ kṣīyatē vyartham ēva*
> *haricaritasudhābhiḥ sicyamānaṁ tad ētat*
> *kṣaṇam api saphalaṁ syād ity ayaṁ mē śramō'tra.*

[48] On the prominence of Navya Nyāya in early modern India, see Jonardon Ganeri, *The Lost Age of Reason: Philosophy in Early Modern India 1450–1700* (Oxford: Oxford University Press, 2011); Samuel Wright, *A Time of Novelty: Logic, Emotion, and Intellectual Life in Early Modern India, 1500–1700 c.e.* (New York: Oxford University Press, 2021).

[49] *Kṛṣṇabhakticandrikā*, 13:

> *navyaṁ nyāyam adhītya saṁsadam upāgatya smayāvēśataḥ*
> *śiṣṭān apy avamatya dhṛṣṭamatayaḥ prauḍhāsanēṣv āsatē*
> *śāstraṁ vakti yadaiva kaścana tadā tē'nyōnyam udvīkṣitair*
> *bhrūkṣēpair hasitais tathōpahasitair ēnaṁ tiraskurvatē.*

[50] *Kṛṣṇabhakticandrikā*, 15:

> *kvaiṣāṁ śāstraśravaṇaṁ dvēṣapravaṇaṁ manaḥ kva cāmīṣām*
> *hara hara kalpatarūṇāṁ dāridryōpadravō bhavati. . . . arē paṇḍitāḥ—*
> *vidyām adhyayanair avāpya viśadām adhyāpya śiṣyān bahūn*
> *pāṇḍityaṁ samupārjitaṁ yad amalaṁ tasyēdam antyaṁ phalam*
> *yad gatvā sadasi prakarṣam adhikaṁ saṁsūcayann uccakair*
> *yatkiṁcit pralapēt paraṁ paribhavēt kair apy upāyair bhṛśam.*

Vēdānta (V) enters, the final character to hold out against the *kr̥ṣṇabhakta*. He immediately goes on the offensive:

V: Hey, why are you trying to convert people who have no grounding in proper study of the Upaniṣads? What does the name "Kr̥ṣṇa" or love for him have anything to do with liberation? When it comes to the ultimate reality, Brahman, everything is ultimately a construct, not real.

M: Hey yourself! You prattle on about how things are "constructed," and won't let it go in the least. Some scholarship *that* is: you only *de*construct the ideas of others.

V: I am Brahman, as described by the Upaniṣads, no doubt about it! Understand that everything you see is like a mirage. For that reason, you can only attain the Ātman when there is no such thing as right or wrong, heaven or hell. There can't possibly be *bhakti* to Kr̥ṣṇa at that point.

M: Enough! This is blasphemous drivel![51]

The harangue goes on a little longer until the *kr̥ṣṇabhakta* gets fed up with the debaters. He is triggered by the echo of his own past and dismisses their pointless palaver:

You can go ahead and argue all day about the meaning of scripture, since you continue to think that that's the source of your ever-increasing fortune. *I used to do the same, but not anymore.* For now I have the joy of uninterrupted service to Lord Kr̥ṣṇa.[52]

[51] *Kr̥ṣṇabhakticandrikā*, 17:

***vēdāntī** (śrīkr̥ṣṇabhaktaṁ prati)—katham arē upaniṣatpariśīlanaśūnyān pratārayasi.*
kvēyaṁ kr̥ṣṇasamākhyā kva ca tadbhaktiḥ kva vā pumarthō̆sau
kalpitam ēva samastaṁ brahmaṇi nāsty ēva vāstavaṁ kiṁcit.
***mīmāṁsakaḥ**—*
rē kalpitam iti khalu jalpasi jahāsi naivālpam apy ētat
buddhiṁ parasya bhēttuṁ kēvalam ētad hi pāṇḍityam.
***vedāntī**—*
āgamaśirōnirūpyaṁ brahmaivāhaṁ na saṁśayas tatra
yān api paśyasi viṣayān mr̥gajalam iva tān avaihi tvam.
ataś ca—
yatra na dharmādharmau svargō narakaś ca dūratō̆pāstau
tatrātmānaṁ labhatāṁ kutra śrīkr̥ṣṇagōcarā bhaktiḥ.
***mīmāṁsakaḥ**—alam alam. ētan nāstikapralapanam.*

[52] *Kr̥ṣṇabhakticandrikā*, 17:

***śrīkr̥ṣṇabhaktaḥ**—*
yuṣmābhiḥ pariśīlyatāṁ pratidinaṁ śāstrārthakōlāhalas

I have italicized this confessional statement not only because it reminds us of Anantadēva's conclusion to the *Manōnurañjana*, but because it is representative of the ideal of scholarship that he attempted to fashion. The apparent contrast between the careerist aspirations of scholarly elites and the simple piety of religious devotion is not quite thoroughgoing. Anantadēva seems to disown pointless scholarly debate in favor of spontaneous spiritual fervor, but this belies the firmly intellectual context of his entire work, to which he refers frequently, and not always with a sense of remorse. The point is not to *not* be a scholar, but to be "well-rounded," in modern terms. The literary historian Baldev Upadhyaya once read the *Kr̥ṣṇabhakticandrikā* as "a noble embodiment of the firm conviction of the author in the supremacy of the *Bhakti-mārga* (Way of *Bhakti*)."[53] No doubt, there is an almost evangelical, starry-eyed quality to the rhetoric of the reformed characters, complete with stage directions in which they speak "out of love, stripped of the desire to cause rifts" (*śithilīkr̥tabhēdābhinivēśaḥ svānurāgēṇa*). More interesting, however, is Anantadēva's representation of the scholarly space. When the stage manager of the *Kr̥ṣṇabhakticandrikā* walks out onto the set, he is directed to stand before an "audience of scholars" (*paṇḍitamaṇḍalīm*), which the author compares to "the halls of Indra, lined with thousands of glittering eyes" (*ākhaṇḍalasabhām iva vilōkanacaṭulasahasranayanāvalīm*). Anantadēva's ethical unease with these settings suggests that *bhakti* was not simply a public expression of personal devotion but a means to counteract the corrupting effects of the new intellectual economy. There is a deep ambivalence in his writing toward the intellectual marketplace of early modern Banaras. The very networks and systems of patronage that made Brahmin immigrants like himself so successful are the ones he criticizes for their materialistic excess. In this semifictional world, then, Anantadēva's *bhaktimārga* comes to be less a path to salvation from the torment of worldly life than a way to come to terms with it. Scholarship is still important, and you can still make money, but only in the service of God.

tatraivāniśavardhamānaśubhatādhyāsānuvr̥ttēr vaśāt
prāg aṅgīkr̥ta ēva sō'yam adhunā nāsmābhir ādrīyatē
śrīgōpālapatēs trikālabhajanānandānubandhād iha.

[53] Upadhyaya, "A Devotional Drama in Sanskrit," 728.

The Making of a Mīmāṁsaka

Anantadēva mentioned that he was a scholar of "both" Mīmāṁsas. We have seen his criticism of the "latter" Mīmāṁsā, through the caricature of a nihilist Vēdāntin, but what about the "prior" Mīmāṁsā? We noted in the previous chapter that Anantadēva had written a commentary on Lakṣmīdhara's *Bhagavannāmakaumudī*. The *Kaumudī* posed a challenge to the Mīmāṁsā discourse of scriptural orthodoxy by arguing that claims in the *purāṇa*s should be accorded the same authority as Vedic utterances. The most significant claim that Lakṣmīdhara wanted to defend was that singing the name of God (*saṁkīrtana*) removes all sins. Anantadēva translated these largely conceptual concerns into the social context of early modern Banaras. For him, *saṁkīrtana* was not just a textual prescription from the *Bhāgavata* and other *purāṇa*s but an everyday practice of public devotion, a practice he encouraged Brahmins to take up. When an interlocutor in the *Bhaktinirṇaya* finds no place or precedent for this form of religiosity, Anantadēva takes umbrage and responds in characteristically pugnacious fashion: "On this point, we find some people who fancy themselves Mīmāṁsakas, who are devoid of God's worship, who can't stand singing the name of God, and are only gearing up to fall into the pit of hell, prattling on as follows: 'There is no such *dharma* as "singing" available to us in the *śruti* or *smṛti*. Especially Brahmins, who are eligible to perform rituals like the *agnihōtra*, cannot possibly engage in singing. Verses you have cited to that effect are simply *arthavāda*.'"[54]

We are familiar from the previous chapter with the debate about whether or not the language of the *purāṇa* is *arthavāda*, a statement that merely confirms or commends the content of a previously existing injunction. What is new about Anantadēva's version of this debate is its sociology: *bhakti* on one side, Brahmins on the other. The question is no longer whether *saṁkīrtana* is or is not textually sanctioned. The question is who should do it and why. The politics of performing *bhakti* in early modern India involved questions of authority, belonging, competition, dissemination, and ethical formation. The poetry of *bhakti*, both in Sanskrit and in regional languages, circulated through musical performance, improvised storytelling,

[54] *Bhaktinirṇaya*, 6: *atra kēcid bhagavadbhajanaśūnyā mīmāṁsakaṁmanyāḥ paramēśvarasaṁkīrtanāsahiṣṇavaḥ kevalaṁ narakē patiṣṇavaḥ pralapanti. saṁkīrtanaṁ nāma na kaścid dharmaḥ śrutiṣu smṛtiṣu vā prasiddhaḥ. viśēṣatō brāhmaṇānām agnihōtrādyadhikāriṇāṁ saṁkīrtanaṁ na saṁbhavati. "dhyāyaṇ kṛtē" ityādivākyaṁ tv arthavādamātram iti.*

and public memory.[55] In the sixteenth and seventeenth centuries, tales from the *Bhāgavata Purāṇa*, and more broadly the stories of Kṛṣṇa, were claimed and performed by different publics, including non-Brahmin, tribal, Muslim, and other polyglot groups. John Stratton Hawley comments on this vibrant period:

> Guru Nanak knows about enacted Krishna stories like this, and he does not like them one bit:
>
> How many Krishna-tales there are, how many opinions on the Vedas!
> How many beggars dance and, twisting and falling,
> beat time with their hands!
> The mercenary fellows go into the market-place and draw out
> the market crowd.
>
> Then there are the Ahirs whose performances of the Krishna story fascinated Malik Muhammad Jayasi, as he tells us in his *Kanhāvat* of 1540; he is eager to elevate such performances to a level where they have a chance of capturing the attention of more refined audiences. A decade before Jayasi, Lalachdas "Halvai" had been active in a place he called Hastigram, near Rae Bareilly, creating his own Avadhi shortening of the tenth book of the *Bhāgavata*. Before the end of the century (1595), there appeared a vernacular commentary on the eleventh book by Chaturdas, and let us remember that when Eknath produced his famous Marathi treatment of the eleventh book in the sixteenth century, he was sitting in Banaras.[56]

Perhaps it was this proliferation of forms and communities laying claim to the *Bhāgavata* that led to the composition of the *Bhāgavata Māhātmya*, a preface appended to the text in the early eighteenth century. In the *Bhāgavata Māhātmya*, Brahmin redactors tried to impose a stringent set of qualifications on performers and audiences of the text, circumscribed by caste, gender, educational attainment, and moral purity.[57] But in Anantadēva's time, the market was open, and he wanted Brahmins to get in on the ground floor. To

[55] Cf. Christian Novetzke, *Religion and Public Memory: A Cultural History of Saint Namdev in India* (New York: Columbia University Press, 2008).
[56] John Stratton Hawley, "Did Surdas Perform the *Bhāgavata-purāṇa*?," in *Tellings and Texts: Music, Literature, and Performance in North India*, ed. Francesca Orsini and Katherine Butler Schofield (Cambridge: Open Book Publishers, 2015), 211–212.
[57] John Stratton Hawley, "The *Bhāgavata Māhātmya* in Context," in *Patronage and Popularisation, Pilgrimage and Procession: Channels of Transcultural Translation and Transmission in Early Modern South Asia*, ed. Heidi R. M. Pauwels (Wiesbaden: Harrassowitz, 2009), 81–100.

hear him tell it, some of his colleagues saw it as beneath them. At any rate, Mīmāṁsakas were classical atheists. As the twelfth-century poet Śrīharṣa quipped in his *Naiṣadhīyacarita* (11.64cd), "She refused to give her assent to the king, like Mīmāṁsā denying the lord with the moon as his crown."[58] Early Mīmāṁsakas had a healthy skepticism for the enthusiasm of devotional religion, which they associated with those ineligible for Vedic rites. Why should they sully themselves by doing something that everyday people do, when they don't even believe in God? Anantadēva's opponent singles out *saṁkīrtana* as a caste-specific practice inappropriate for Brahmins:

> On this point, there are some self-styled scholars who say that *saṁkīrtana* is the prerogative of those who do not belong to the three upper castes. For the latter are constantly engaged in obligatory rituals from dawn to dusk, and have no time for singing. Moreover, from the verse: "The Ṛg, Yajur, Sāma, and Atharva Veda are all effectively studied by the one who utters the two-syllable word, Hari," we are given to understand that since an uneducated person becomes learned by singing the name of God, it is the uneducated "lower" castes who are entitled to that activity. Consider also the following: "Women, Śūdras, and Brahmins-in-name-only are not qualified to study the Vedas. So the sage Vyāsa, out of compassion, composed the story of the *Mahābhārata*" (*Bhāgavata Purāṇa* 1.4.25). The *Mahābhārata*, here a synecdoche for the *purāṇas*, was composed for the sake of women, lower castes, and the like. Since *saṁkīrtana* is a *purāṇic* practice, it must only apply to those people. For nowhere in the Vedas is there the injunction: "One must sing about God." Perhaps Kṣatriyas, Vaiśyas, and Śūdras can engage in singing because they do not have to teach. But Brahmins, who are occupied by their teaching and other responsibilities, cannot find the time for singing, so it must be the prerogative of those other than Brahmins.[59]

[58] *Srīharsha's Naishadhīyacharita*, ed. Pandit Śivadatta (Bombay: Nirnaya Sagar, 1912), 251: *mīmāṁsayēva bhagavaty amṛtāṁśumaulau tasmin mahībhuji tayānumatir na bhējē*. The commentator Nārāyaṇa hastened to clarify that Mīmāṁsā did not deny the existence of God, only that he was the author of the Vedas.

[59] *Bhaktinirṇaya*, 8–9: *tatra kēcit paṇḍitaṁmanyā manyantē. atraivarṇādhikāram iti. traivarṇikānāṁ brāhmamuhūrtōpakramapradōṣaparisamāpanīyanityakarmavyagrāṇāṁ saṁkīrtanē kālābhāvāt. kiṁ ca—"ṛgvēdō'tha yajurvēdaḥ sāmavēdō hy atharvaṇaḥ adhītās tēna yēnōktaṁ harir ity akṣaradvayam" ity anadhītasya nāmasaṁkīrtanēna adhītasaṁpattiśravaṇād anadhītaśūdrādhikāratvaṁ nirṇīyatē. api ca—"strīśūdradvijabandhūnāṁ trayī na śrutigōcarā iti bhāratam ākhyānaṁ kṛpayā muninā kṛtam" iti strīśūdrādīnām arthē bhāratanirmāṇād bhāratasya ca purāṇamātrōpalakṣaṇatvāt saṁkīrtanasya ca paurāṇatvāt strīśūdrādhikāratvaṁ nirṇīyatē. na hi kēśavasaṁkīrtanaṁ kuryād iti kvacid vēdē śrūyatē. athavā kṣatriyādīnām adhyāpanādivyāpārābhāvāt syāt kathaṁcit saṁkīrtanādhikāraḥ. brāhmaṇānāṁ tv*

According to the opponent, the public act of devotional singing may be accorded scriptural sanction, but only for those who do not belong to the three self-appointed "upper" castes. Not only is it a low-caste practice, but it detracts from the Brahmin's pedagogical responsibilities. *Bhakti*, in the opponent's eyes, is not suited to the serious, scholarly lifestyle of the Brahmin. Anantadēva defends his own position by pointing out: (a) that if Brahmins have time to perform frivolous, self-interested *sōma* sacrifices, then they can surely find the time for some devotional singing,[60] (b) that just because *purāṇas* are accessible to "lower" castes does not mean that they are not also Brahmin texts, and (c) that among the six *karmas* associated with full Brahmin status, three of them, including teaching, serve merely as the source of one's livelihood and are therefore not absolutely required. The topic of the six *karmas*, which refers to a quote in *The Laws of Manu* (10.76), became a particular point of contention in determining Brahmin status in early modern India.[61] A so-called full Brahmin was known as a *ṣaṭkarmī*, one entitled to perform six *karmas*: *adhyayana* and *adhyāpana* (studying the Vedas for oneself and teaching them to others), *yajana* and *yājana* (conducting a sacrifice and procuring sacrifice through another), and *dāna* and *pratigraha* (giving gifts and accepting gifts). The lesser *trikarmī* Brahmin was entitled only to *adhyayana*, *yājana*, and *pratigraha*. However, Anantadēva says that *adhyāpana*, "teaching," is not so important in the larger scheme of things. This suggests that he conceived of teaching in a broader sense than intended by Manu. It included the array of pedagogical responsibilities for Brahmin scholars in early modern Banaras. If his teacher Rāmatīrtha could simultaneously study philosophy and meditate on God, then there was no excuse for other scholars. Singing the name of God not only could but should become a marker of Brahmin identity.

The problem was that God's name could be sung in any language, in any place. We have seen in the stories of Ēknāth that the Brahmins of Banaras were protective of the Sanskrit language. The same motif recurs in many *bhakti* narratives: renegade poets and philosophers are punished for daring to use the everyday, quotidian language of the people to communicate

adhyāpanādivyāpṛtānāṁ na kathaṁcit saṁkīrtanakālō labhyata iti brāhmaṇētarādhikāraṁ saṁkīrtanam iti.

[60] The implication here is that Vedic ceremonies like the *jyōtiṣṭōma* are not obligatory (*nitya*) but prompted by a desire for personal gain (*kāmya*), hence susceptible to the accusation of frivolity.

[61] O'Hanlon, "Letters Home," 224, n. 94.

religious truths. Anantadēva's Banarasi contemporary, Madhusūdana Sarasvatī, placed qualifiers on *bhakti*'s universal appeal. After showing that the *Bhāgavata* was superlative among scriptures because of its accessibility to everyday people, Madhusūdana hastened to add that it was not its potential vernacularity but its antiquity that made it a source of authority: "One may wonder that if this were the case, then the *Bhāgavata* could be considered just the same as those works by modern-day poets which talk about Brahman, since women, Śūdras, and the like, are able to listen to them. In response, *Bhāgavata* 1.1.2 clarifies that the text was 'composed by the great sage.'"[62] The reader is compelled to wonder who these "newfangled poets" (*abhinavakavi*) might be, if anything more than the generic straw men that pepper Sanskrit intellectual writing. If their compositions were available to "women and Śūdras," the classic formula for those outside the pale of Brahmanical discourse, it is unlikely that they would have been in Sanskrit, according to the language ideology that underpins the use of the term.[63] Madhusūdana's reinforcement of the *Bhāgavata*'s antiquity suggests an upper-caste anxiety about the proliferation of subaltern song and a more general resistance to vernacular versions of the *Bhāgavata*. As Hawley concludes in his excursus on vernacular *Bhāgavatas*:

> I can well imagine how this remarkable profusion of *Bhāgavatas* by the late seventeenth century in north India—and the performative mêlée that it implies—might have produced a certain anxiety in groups of Brahmins who understood the *Bhāgavata Purāṇa* to be their own special domain. And then there is the social component. Bhūpati was not a Brahmin but a Kāyasth, and in this he was not alone. A Gujarati named Keśav Kāyasth had composed a *Kṛṣṇakrīḍākāvya* in the late fifteenth century, and you may remember that Lālac was a *halvāī*: he or someone in his family sold sweets. . . . Against this polyglot, poly-caste backdrop, did certain Brahmins want to

[62] *Śrīmadbhāgavatādyaślokatrayasya ṭīkā Śrīmanmadhusūdanasarasvatīkṛtā*, ed. Śrīyuktakṛṣṇagōpālabhakta (Kālikātā: Śrīyuktaramāramaṇabhakta, 1893), 17: *nanv ēvaṁ saty abhinavakavikāvyasyāpi brahmapratipādakasya strīśūdrādiśravaṇayōgyatvēna ētattulyatā syād ity āsaṅkya āha mahāmunikṛtē iti*. I am grateful to Joel Bordeaux for directing me to the appropriate page number in this edition, published in Bengali script.

[63] On the use of the compound *strīśūdrādika* to mark a vernacular turn of authors' attention toward nonelite, quotidian life, see Christian Lee Novetzke, *The Quotidian Revolution: Vernacularization, Religion, and the Premodern Public Sphere in India* (New York: Columbia University Press, 2016), 15. Cf. Keune, *Shared Food, Shared Devotion*, 93–94.

reassert their own particular capacities and training—and thereby reassert the power of the original text?[64]

The language of religion, in the case of *bhakti*, bears on the problem of caste and gender. Whether or not religion is the historical key to vernacularization is a question we will not litigate here.[65] In Anantadēva's writing, at least, there is evidence of tension regarding the propriety of using Sanskrit versus using vernacular languages for religious purposes. In this seemingly innocuous passage from the *Bhaktinirṇaya* about the grammaticality of speech, Anantadēva engages with a long tradition of arguments about the ethical implications of language use in Sanskrit intellectual history:[66]

> One should not object by saying that the prohibitions "(A Brahmin) is not to barbarize" and "This 'barbarian' is none other than incorrect speech" mean that one should not reiterate the glories of God in the vernacular [*bhāṣā*]. For since such utterances are enjoined, those prohibitions do not apply. It is also incorrect to suggest that the prohibitions place a restriction on the injunction that one must sing the names and glories of God, such that one may only sing in grammatical language [*sādhuśabda*]. For those prohibitions can be understood to refer to activities (such as everyday speech) that generally arise from the desire of the people who perform them (rather than to activities such as singing the names of God, that arise directly from injunctions that tell us to perform them). It is not as though we directly hear the injunction "One must sing the names and glories of God exclusively in grammatical language."[67]

[64] Hawley, *A Storm of Songs*, 71–72.

[65] See Sheldon Pollock, *The Language of the Gods in the World of Men: Sanskrit, Culture, and Power in Premodern India* (Berkeley: University of California Press, 2006), 423–436; Cf. Novetzke, *The Quotidian Revolution*, 5–19.

[66] An early discussion of this controversy, which is discussed repeatedly in Mīmāṁsā, can be found in the *Mahābhāṣya* of the grammarian Patañjali, who famously links linguistic and moral propriety: "Therefore, a Brahmin is not to barbarize. . . . [I]n fact, this barbarian is none other than that incorrect speech" (*tasmād brāhmaṇēna na mlēcchitavai. . . . mlēcchō ha vā ēṣa yad apaśabdaḥ*). See S. D. Joshi and J. A. F. Roodbergen, eds., *Patañjali's Vyākaraṇa-Mahābhāṣya: Paspaśāhnika* (Pune: University of Poona, 1986), 37–38. Cf. Pollock, *The Language of the Gods in the World of Men*, 66, n. 53.

[67] *Bhaktinirṇaya*, 26: *na ca "na mlēcchitavai" "mlēccho vā yad apaśabdaḥ" iti niṣiddhatvād bhāṣayā bhagavadguṇānuvādō'py akartavya iti vācyam. tasya vihitatvēna niṣēdhāpravṛttēḥ. na ca bhagavadguṇanāmakīrtanakartavyatāvidhēr uktaniṣēdhānurōdhēna saṁkōcō yuktaḥ sādhuśabdēna ēva bhagavadguṇanāmakīrtanaṁ iti vācyam. niṣēdhasya rāgaprāptaviṣayakatvēnāpy upapattēḥ. na ca ēvaṁ sākṣāt śrūyatē sādhuśabdēna ēva bhagavadguṇanāmakīrtanaṁ kartavyam iti.*

Anantadēva argues, in the technical vocabulary of Mīmāṁsā, that general prohibitions against speaking vernacular languages do not override specific injunctions that require one to sing God's names. Prohibitions against ungrammaticality, that is, non-Sanskrit speech, have to do with limiting an activity generally taken for granted, like speaking in any way one likes, rather than with restricting the force of a particular injunction. There is no rule that one must sing the names of God *only in Sanskrit*. The issue of whether grammaticality was a general moral principle or one restricted to the ritual domain formed a significant point of contention between early modern Mīmāṁsakas.[68] In his *Mīmāṁsākaustubha*, the mid-seventeenth-century scholar Khaṇḍadēva, who may have been a relative of the Dēva family,[69] criticized his colleague Dinakara Bhaṭṭa for indiscriminately prohibiting ungrammatical speech. Khaṇḍadēva ultimately agreed with Dinakara's xenophobic idea that people should guard against learning foreign languages, but he distinguished carefully between barbarian languages (*barbarādibhāṣā*) and the vernaculars (*bhāṣāśabda*) used by "all vernacular intellectuals in their everyday activities *as well as in chanting the name and virtues of Hari*."[70] Khaṇḍadēva appears to speak of such vernacular religious activity as commonly accepted, but in Anantadēva we find the matter still unresolved.

By the late seventeenth century, it seems to have become commonplace to assert a defense of Mīmāṁsā theism as something eternally present in the system.[71] Sheldon Pollock remarks on this "very sustained and highly unusual" line of argument in the *Mīmāṁsākutūhala* by Kamalākara Bhaṭṭa. Like Anantadēva, Kamalākara wanted to distinguish himself from those "other" Mīmāṁsakas who refused the seductions of God's love. He responded to the clever jab from the poet Śrīharṣa, cited above, with utter seriousness: "Some reproach the Mīmāṁsaka with being an atheist and so having no business talking about the 'Way of Faith' (*bhaktimārga*). This slur may apply to some, but as for me, I believe in God."[72] Khaṇḍadēva, too, felt uncomfortable with the uncompromising atheism of classical Mīmāṁsā, especially the position that the deities invoked in the Vedas were no more than linguistic

[68] Sheldon Pollock, *The Ends of Man at the End of Premodernity* (Amsterdam: Royal Netherlands Academy of Arts and Sciences, 2005), 54–57.
[69] Pollock, "New Intellectuals," 18.
[70] Pollock, *The Ends of Man*, 55, 56, n. 92, italics mine.
[71] Pollock, "New Intellectuals," 13–14.
[72] *Mīmāṁsākutūhala*, ed. P. N. Paṭṭābhirāma Śāstrī (Varanasi: Sampurnanand Sanskrit University, 1987), 44: *nanu nirīśvaravādinas tē kōyaṁ bhaktimārgapravēśaḥ? patatv ayaṁ pravādāśanir ēkadēśiṣu asmākan tv asty ēva īśvaraḥ*. Translated in Pollock, *The Ends of Man*, 62.

constructs.[73] After reconstructing this view of the early Mīmāṁsakas, Khaṇḍadēva immediately recoils: "This is the essence of Jaimini's point of view. But even in the act of explaining it as such, my lips feel unclean. My only recourse is to remember God!"[74] Khaṇḍadēva's student Śambhu Bhaṭṭa comments here that his teacher was responding to the possible criticism that if one were to deny the materiality of gods altogether, it would be tantamount to admitting unbelief (*nāstikatva*).[75] This is a dramatic shift from the classical tradition. In the Sanskrit introduction to his edition of Kamalākara's *Mīmāṁsākutūhala*, P. N. Paṭṭābhirāma Śāstrī offered up a distinction between practical (*yājñika*) and philosophical (*dārśanika*) Mīmāṁsakas, mapping onto their respective attitudes toward God. The former invoke him at the beginning and end of rites and worship an embodied deity (*saguṇa*), while the latter find no purchase in such invocations, but do acknowledge a formless God (*nirguṇa*). At the tail end of those who inherited Mīmāṁsā as a living discipline, Śāstrī may have been onto something about what was motivating his early modern ancestors.

Pollock, however, sees this as an anomaly, a blip in the general tendency of early modern Mīmāṁsakas to reentrench old ways of thinking. Since the idea of a theistic Mīmāṁsā "produced no systemwide change," Pollock asserts that "the social and political upheavals . . . of the era left no mark whatever on the moral vision of *mīmāṁsakas* (the question of language use aside)."[76] But why did God-talk find its way into these early modern writings in the first place, when it was so alien to earlier writing in the discipline? How did it make its way into a thought-world that was purportedly confident of its conservatism? Were these isolated instances or symptoms of a shift in the way the discipline constituted itself? Even if not, why is "systemwide change" the measure by which to evaluate the impact of social changes on intellectual history? Surely there is analytical value in exploring apparent anomalies outside the matrix of success or failure. The writings of subsequent generations

[73] See Francis X. Clooney, "What's a God? The Quest for the Right Understanding of *dēvatā* in Brāhmaṇical Ritual Theory (*mīmāṁsā*)," *International Journal of Hindu Studies* 1.2 (1997): 337–385.

[74] *The Bhattadipika of Khaṇḍadēva with Prabhavali Commentary of Sambhu Bhatta*, vol. 4, ed. S. Subrahmanya Sastri (Delhi: Sri Satguru Publications, 1987), 202: *iti jaiminimataniṣkarṣaḥ. mama tv ēvaṁ vadatō'pi vāṇī duṣyatīti harismaraṇam ēva śaraṇam.* Commenting on this surprising twist, Francis Clooney perceptively notes that "The discourse on *īśvara*—the one truly effective and real *dēvatā*—and the discourse on the myriad *dēvatās* are not entirely distinct; they have permeable boundaries, even in the minds of Mīmāṁsakas, who think about both." Clooney, "What's a God?," 354.

[75] Clooney, "What's a God?," 381, n. 17.

[76] Pollock, *The Ends of Man*, 62.

of the Dēva family show us that Anantadēva's concerns about *bhakti* and Brahmanism did not die with him.

Fathers and Sons

Anantadēva's son Āpadēva became famous for writing a primer on Mīmāṁsā, the *Mīmāṁsānyāyaprakāśa*. It is still used as an introductory textbook for students of Mīmāṁsā to this day. Most of the book is about the hermeneutical principles of Mīmāṁsā, all of which try to determine the nature of *dharma* and the Vedic injunctions that characterize it. The most basic definition of *dharma* in Mīmāṁsā is the *yajña*, the Vedic sacrifice. Performing this *dharma* leads to beneficial ends for the *yajña*'s patron. They may not be immediate but can instead show up as rewards after one dies. At the end of the book, however, Āpadēva makes a significant revision to this notion of *dharma*: "When performed with reference to the particular thing for which it has been enjoined, this *dharma* becomes the cause of that thing. But when it is performed with the attitude of offering [*arpaṇa*] to Lord Gōvinda, it becomes the cause of the highest good. And there is no dearth of authoritative statements to support such performance with the attitude of surrender. As stated in the *smṛti* (*Bhagavad Gītā* 9.17): 'Whatever you do, eat, sacrifice, donate, or perform as penance, son of Kunti—do that as an offering to me.' "[77]

The account provided here closely follows the Vēdāntic inflection given to the teaching of *karmayōga*—which one might call "the practice of everyday life"—by the Advaita philosopher Śaṅkara in the introduction to his commentary on the *Bhagavad Gītā*. There, Śaṅkara says, "The *dharma* of worldly life, meant for worldly prosperity, has been enjoined with respect to people of different castes and stages of life, and leads to the obtaining of various heavenly stations. Nevertheless, if it is performed with the attitude of offering to God, without a desire for its results, then it contributes to purity of mind. A pure mind, by being eligible for the discipline of knowledge, brings about knowledge, and as such becomes the cause of the highest good."[78]

[77] *Mīmāṁsā-Nyāyā-Prakāśa by Āpadēva*, ed. Vasudev Shastri Abhyankar (Poona: Bhandarkar Oriental Research Institute, 1972), 277–278: *sō'yaṁ dharmō yaduddēśēna vihitas taduddēśēna kriyamāṇas taddhētuḥ śrīgōvindārpaṇabuddhyā kriyamāṇas tu niḥśrēyasahētuḥ. na ca tadarpaṇabuddhyānuṣṭhānē pramāṇābhāvaḥ. "yat karōṣi yad aśnāsi yaj juhōṣi dadāsi yat yat tapasyasi kauntēya tat kuruṣva madarpaṇam" iti smṛtēḥ.*

[78] *Śrīmadbhagavadgītā Ānandagiriviracitaṭīkāsaṁvalitaśāṅkarabhāṣyasamētā*, ed. Kāśīnātha Śāstrī Āgāśē (Pune: Anandashrama Press, 1896), 7: *abhyudayārthō'pi yaḥ pravṛttilakṣaṇō dharmaḥ varṇāśramāṁś cōddiśya vihitaḥ sa dēvādisthānaprāptihētur api sann īśvarārpaṇab-*

While the introduction of Vēdānta into a Mīmāṁsā textbook is interesting in its own right, there is more to Āpadēva's conclusion than a mere reiteration of Śaṅkara's thinking. For in a stanza that immediately follows his claim about the attitude of "offering to God" (*arpaṇa*) he stresses that it is *bhakti* for God that infuses the whole scholarly enterprise:

> Where am I, of dull mind,
> and where this textbook that
> conforms to Bhāṭṭa Mīmāṁsā?
> As such, this is but a play of *bhakti*
> to the feet of Gōvinda and my guru.[79]

This talk of *bhakti*, let alone playfulness, appears incongruous in a work of Mīmāṁsā. However, Āpadēva had precedents for his expression of devotional piety. We find here echoes of a stanza from Śrīdhara Svāmī's commentary on the *Bhāgavata Purāṇa*:

> Where am I, of dull mind,
> and where this churning of the milky ocean?
> What place has a tiny atom
> where Mount Mandara itself sinks?[80]

Āpadēva may have wanted to link the *Gītā*'s concept of *arpaṇa* to the *Bhāgavata Purāṇa* precisely because Śrīdhara himself had done so earlier in his commentary on *Bhāgavata* 11.2.36, a virtual restatement of *Bhagavad Gītā* 9.17.[81] Like his father, Āpadēva was a thoroughgoing *kr̥ṣṇabhakta*. According to his son Anantadēva II, not only was Āpadēva learned in all scholarly disciplines, but he was born "solely for the purpose of showing the

uddhyā'nuṣṭhīyamānaḥ sattvaśuddhayē bhavati phalābhisandhivarjitaḥ. śuddhasattvasya ca jñānaniṣṭhāyōgyatāprāptidvārēṇa jñānōtpattihētutvēna ca niḥśrēyasahētutvam api pratipadyatē.

[79] *Mīmāṁsā-Nyāya-Prakāśa*, 278:

> *kvāhaṁ mandamatiḥ kvēyaṁ prakriyā bhāṭṭasammatā*
> *iti bhaktēr vilāsō'yaṁ gōvindagurupādayōḥ.*

[80] *Bhāvārthabōdhinī*, 13:

> *kvāhaṁ mandamatiḥ kvēdaṁ manthanaṁ kṣīravāridhēḥ*
> *kiṁ tatra paramāṇur vai yatra majjati mandaraḥ.*

The motif of self-deprecating comparison, of course, is an old one in Sanskrit literature. See, for example, the second stanza of Kālidāsa's *Raghuvaṁśa*.

[81] *Bhāvārthabōdhinī*, 627.

true Vaiṣṇava path."[82] We would likely see more evidence of this zealousness in Āpadēva's unpublished *Bhaktikalpataru*, where "there is ample description of the modes and regulations of God's worship, including the festival of swinging baby Kṛṣṇa's cradle."[83] It should not be a surprise, then, that his religious commitments filtered into his scholarly writing. Although Āpadēva's navigation of the terrain between *bhakti* and Mīmāṁsā seems inchoate, it was by no means an isolated phenomenon. His nephew Bābādēva picked up on his uncle's citation of *Bhagavad Gītā* 9.17 in a work called the *Arpaṇamīmāṁsā*.[84] As its title portends, the *Arpaṇamīmāṁsā* used the language of Mīmāṁsā to explicate the concept of *arpaṇa*, offering one's actions to God. It attempts to understand the nature of the injunction "Do this as an offering to me." In his opening remarks, Bābādēva explains the purpose of this stanza for Mīmāṁsā:

> As we all know, in this twelve-chapter Pūrva Mīmāṁsā system, the great sage Jaimini analyzed several principles connected with the performance of every *dharma*, including: the different means of valid knowledge, the application of subordinate rites, the sequence of performance, eligibility for ritual activity, analogical extension, and the relevant adjustments and restrictions on the elements to be extended. But even after having carefully studied and performed these *dharma*s, people experience significant suffering, such as having to return to the mortal world after enjoying the pleasures of heaven. Seeing this state of affairs and unable to tolerate it, God, the very embodiment of compassion, under the pretext of teaching Arjuna, explained the means to liberation in the following stanza: "Whatever you do, eat, sacrifice, donate, or perform as penance, son of Kunti—do that as an offering to me."[85]

[82] *Mathurāsētu*, MS SAN 2638, British Library, f. 46v: *sakalaśāstrārthatattvavidvaiṣṇavasanmārgapratipādanaikaprayōjanagṛhītāvatāra.*

[83] *Mathurāsētu*, f. 45r: *bhagavatpūjāvidhiḥ . . . dōlōtsavādinā vidhaparicaryāvidhisahitaḥ sapramāṇaḥ vistarō'smattātacaraṇasaṁkalpōtthitē bhaktikalpatarāv ēva nirūpitō'sti.*

[84] In the colophons to both his works, Bābādēva says that he is the son of Bāladēva, son of Anantadēva (sometimes written Ānandadēva). Two verses cited by Bābādēva in the *Arpaṇamīmāṁsā* as being his grandfather's correspond to verses in Anantadēva's *Manōnurañjananāṭaka*. See V. Krishnamacharya, "Adhikaraṇādarśa of Bābādēva," *Adyar Library Bulletin* 14.1 (1950): 49–55. The editor of the *Manōnurañjana* notes that one of the manuscripts used for the printed edition appears to have stayed in the family, as it belonged to Bābādēva's son Jagannāthadēva. See *The Manonurañjana Nāṭaka* (Sanskrit introduction), 3.

[85] *Arpaṇamīmāṁsā*, MS 40 C.5, Adyar Library, Chennai, ff. 3–4: *iha khalu jaiminimaharṣiṇā athātō dharmajijñāsētyādi prabhutvādāv ijyaṁ sarvavarṇānāṁ syād ityantādhikaraṇair dvādaśalakṣaṇapūrvamīmāṁsāyāṁ sarvadharmēṣu pramāṇabhēdaśēṣaprayuktikramādhikārātidēśōhabādhatantraprasaṅgā vicāritāḥ. tatraivaṁvidhavicāritair api dharmair anuṣṭhitair janasya svargādibhōgōttarakālikamartyalōkapravēśādirūpaduḥkhātiśayadarśanāt tadasahiṣṇur bhagavān*

Bābādēva proceeds to go into exhaustive detail about the grammatical composition of the words in the sentence, in order to understand how exactly the injunction in the verse works, as he would with any other Vedic injunction. This is fundamentally a work of Mīmāṁsā, replete with arguments that draw upon properly Mīmāṁsā discursive topics. If Āpadēva's citation of the *Gītā* was ancillary to the primary focus of his textbook, the *Arpaṇamīmāṁsā* sought to make the *Gītā* an essential part of Mīmāṁsā intellectual production. It was an elaboration of Āpadēva's citation into a full-fledged theistic hermeneutics. We might understand Āpadēva's textbook as a guide for students, *How to Do Mīmāṁsā (and Get Rich Trying)*, and Bābādēva's essay as a supplement, *How to Do Mīmāṁsā (and Feel Good about It)*.

The influence of Vēdānta upon Āpadēva's and Bābādēva's writing is not incidental to their interest in *bhakti*. In the previous chapter we saw that early Mīmāṁsakas relegated the content of the Upaniṣads to marginally helpful notions about a permanent self that allowed a ritual agent to understand that he may enjoy the fruits of his action in the future. While Vēdāntins selectively applied Mīmāṁsā principles to their study of the Upaniṣads, Mīmāṁsakas took little interest in their self-proclaimed hermeneutical successors. The two remained at cross-purposes when it came to the means to liberation, the concept of God, the value of epic and *purāṇic* literature, and whether or not ritual action could materially effect soteriological ends.[86] The situation appears to have changed considerably in the early modern period. Several works on Mīmāṁsā at this time were written by people who had clear commitments to Vedāntic exposition and vice versa. This was true not only of the Dēvas, who wrote on both Mīmāṁsā and Advaita Vēdānta, but also of other families in early modern Banaras, like the Bhaṭṭas. The Bhaṭṭa family made a concerted effort to reconcile the two historically adversarial intellectual traditions. Kamalākara Bhaṭṭa's cousin Nīlakaṇṭha Bhaṭṭa remembered his father, Śaṅkara Bhaṭṭa, as the fusion of two historical individuals, Śaṅkara and Kumārila Bhaṭṭa. While the two had demonstrated

karuṇāmūrtir arjunōpadēśakaitavēna muktyupāyaṁ kathayāmāsa—"yatkarōṣi yadaśnāsi yajjuhōṣi dadāsi yat yattapasyasi kauntēya tatkuruṣva madarpaṇam" iti.

86 See Chakravarthi Ram-Prasad, "Knowledge and Action I: Means to the Human End in Bhāṭṭa Mīmāṁsā and Advaita Vedānta," *Journal of Indian Philosophy* 28.1 (2000): 1–24; Chakravarthi Ram-Prasad, "Knowledge and Action II: Attaining Liberation in Bhāṭṭa Mīmāṁsā and Advaita Vedānta," *Journal of Indian Philosophy* 28.1 (2000): 25–41; Aleksandar Uskokov, "Deciphering the Hidden Meaning: Scripture and the Hermeneutics of Liberation in Early Advaita Vedānta" (Ph.D. diss., University of Chicago, 2018), 367–372.

contradictory paths to liberation, in his father they took on a single form, and through him adopted "non-duality between the Mīmāṁsakas."[87]

Kamalākara's own essay collection, the *Mīmāṁsākutūhala*, contained a lengthy essay on the issue of whether or not liberation can be achieved through a combination of knowledge and action (*jñānakarmasamuccaya*).[88] In this essay, Kamalākara reconstructs the intellectual history of this debate in Mīmāṁsā and Advaita Vēdānta. Kamalākara argues, quite against the grain, that the Mīmāṁsā view of liberation is not different from that of Vēdānta. He deploys fragments from Kumārila Bhaṭṭa's lost writings to argue that he was sympathetic to Vēdānta, but in a qualified sense, in order to make room for the continued performance of ritual actions after the arising of knowledge. That he reframes the debate in this way already indicates a creative act, one that prefigured modern scholarship on the subject of Kumārila's affiliations.[89] He goes on to add a dimension to the topic that none of its previous participants would have entertained, and it is here that Mīmāṁsā, Vēdānta, and *bhakti* come together. Kamalākara asks his Vēdāntin interlocutor why he believes that actions, *karma*, can only be a precursor to knowledge, *jñāna*, and not independently capable of leading to liberation. For there are thousands of statements from a range of scriptures about actions that do lead directly to liberation, such as dying in Kāśī, bathing in its holy waters, giving gifts in Gayā, and, most pertinently, *bhakti* for God. Even if the Vēdāntin thinks that Vedic ritual is meaningless, he would not say the same

[87] *The Vyavahāramayūkha of Bhaṭṭa Nīlakaṇṭha*, ed. P. V. Kane (Poona: Bhandarkar Oriental Research Institute, 1926), 1:

virōdhimārgadvayadarśanārthaṁ
dvēdhā babhūvātra paraḥ pumān yaḥ
śrīśaṅkarō bhaṭṭa ihaikarūpō
mīmāṁsakādvaitam urīcakāra.

[88] For a comparable discussion in Anantadēva II's *Bhāṭṭālaṅkāra*, a commentary on his father's Mīmāṁsā primer, see *Mimansā Nyāya Prakāsa by Apadeva with a Commentary Called Bhattalankar by Pandit Ananta Deva*, ed. M. M. Sri Lakshmana Sastri (Benares: Vidya Vilas Press, 1921), 489–497. Perhaps in response to Kamalākara, however, Anantadēva II reiterates the views of the twelfth-century Mīmāṁsaka Pārthasārathi Miśra against Sōmēśvara Bhaṭṭa, particularly on the subject of whether or not liberation involves the experience of joy. On the "scholastic turn" in late Mīmāṁsā, where works are structured around doctrinal splits between Pārthasārathi and Sōmēśvara, see Lawrence McCrea, "Playing with the System: Fragmentation and Individualization in Late Pre-colonial Mīmāṁsā," *Journal of Indian Philosophy* 36.5 (2008): 577–578. Āpadeva is generally held to support Pārthasārathi's position when it gets down to brass tacks. See Franklin Edgerton, *The Mīmāṅsā Nyāya Prakāśa or Āpadevī* (Delhi: Sri Satguru Publications, 1986), 7.

[89] See John Taber, "Kumārila the Vedāntin?," 159–184 and Kiyotaka Yoshimizu, "Kumārila's Reevaluation of the Sacrifice and the Veda from a Vedānta Perspective," 201–253, both in *Mīmāṁsā and Vedānta: Interaction and Continuity*, ed. Johannes Bronkhorst (Delhi: Motilal Banarsidass, 2007). Cf. Roque Mesquita, "Die Idee der Erlösung bei Kumārila Bhaṭṭa," *Wiener Zeitschrift für die Kunde Südasiens* 38 (1994): 451–484.

about devotional activity. For both you and I, he says to his opponent, are equally dedicated to sacred texts like the *Bhagavad Gītā* (11.53–54) and the *Bhāgavata Purāṇa* (11.20.29–30). These texts say that *bhakti* supersedes all other means to liberation. The Vēdāntin has little ground to privilege some scriptural statements over others on this topic.[90]

This is the discussion that comprises Kamalākara's "sustained and highly unusual" defense of Mīmāṁsā theism, in Pollock's words, culminating in his refutation of the well-worn charge that Mīmāṁsakas are atheists.[91] It would be highly unusual only if we did not have evidence for exactly this sort of incorporation of *bhakti* in the wider world of early modern scholarship. Perhaps the point is to search not for "systemwide change" (*pace* Pollock) but for change we can believe in. I have noted the gradual yet unmistakable shifts in the discursive registers of an intellectual tradition. These shifts do not take place at the level of doctrine but are present in new hermeneutical concerns. In the case of the Dēvas and Bhaṭṭas, the majority of their pedagogical activity was conducted in the realm of Mīmāṁsā and Vēdānta, but their personal religious commitments had an equally significant effect on their scholarly careers. The question that remains is if their "formal and technical concerns can be mapped onto the social changes of the early modern world."[92]

Scholarship, Society, and Social History

Bhakti, it was once said, was a movement, a wave.[93] While the scholars in this chapter sought to demonstrate the compatibility of their intellectual traditions with everyday religious practices, some philosophers found themselves "swimming against the tide" of this intellectual culture.[94] Recall Anantadēva's portrayal of the "new" logicians, openly disdaining their elders and sneering at their colleagues. Perhaps this was more than literary flair. The

[90] *Mīmāṁsākutūhala*, 40–43.

[91] A more thorough understanding of Kamalākara's views on Mīmāṁsā and Vēdānta would be possible if one were to study his unpublished *Vēdāntakautūhala*, a book that he mentions at the end of his *Śāntiratna*. See K. Madhava Krishna Sarma, "The Vēdāntakautūhala of Kamalākarabhaṭṭa," *Poona Orientalist* 9.1–2 (1944): 70–72.

[92] O'Hanlon and Minkowski, "What Makes People Who They Are?," 410.

[93] John Stratton Hawley, *A Storm of Songs: India and the Idea of the Bhakti Movement* (Cambridge: Harvard University Press, 2015), 52–55.

[94] Andrew Nicholson, "Review of *The Lost Age of Reason: Philosophy in Early Modern India 1450–1700*, by Jonardon Ganeri," *Journal of the American Oriental Society* 133.1 (2013): 160.

conflict between scholars of Mīmāṁsā and Navya Nyāya in early modern India often mapped onto regional animosity, Banaras being the stronghold of the former and Mithilā and Bengal the site of the latter.[95] Early modern Bengal was also home to large-scale Vaiṣṇava *bhakti*, represented not only by poets and scholars of the Gauḍīya Vaiṣṇava community inspired by Caitanya Mahāprabhu, but also by a boom in temple construction sponsored by the rulers of the Malla polity.[96] For poets and politicians in this period, as Samuel Wright shows, the concept of joy (*prīti*) as the human being's love for God—and not, importantly, God's own happiness—both enabled devotees to form individual relationships with God and justified the construction of temples where kings and commoners alike could take pleasure in God.[97] In the seventeenth century, Bengali scholars of Navya Nyāya like Gadādhara Bhaṭṭācārya responded to this pervasion of *bhakti* in literary and political culture, this joyous linking of the human with the divine, by writing essays about how God cannot be a locus of *prīti*. In doing so, according to Wright, they were actually arguing that "joy cannot be used to build political and social space in Western Bengal."[98] Instead, *prīti* was profoundly human for the Nyāya intellectuals, exemplified in the way that they gave meaning to the social space of Bengal, which they associated with "Sanskrit logic of the highest caliber."[99] Rather than being the land of love for God, then, Bengal for these scholars was an object of "logical pathos," a sense of belonging to "an integrated philosophical community" particular to this region above all others.[100] Whether or not Gadādhara had specific people in mind when he criticized the facile equation of joy and divine love,[101] Wright's argument that his intellectual intervention had a bearing on very local developments in Bengali politics and society is persuasive.

The Dēvas' vigorous defense and propagation of an intellectually savvy *bhakti* tradition, however much it drew on canonical Sanskrit texts, similarly

95 Consider the story of the Banarasi scholar Nārāyaṇa Bhaṭṭa besting his colleagues from Mithilā and Bengal in a debate held at the home of a high-ranking Mughal officer, about whether or not Brahmins were entitled to be fed at *śrāddha* ceremonies. See Shastri, "Dakshini Pandits at Benares," 9–10. For regional conflicts between Nyāya scholars of Mithilā and Bengal, see Wright, *A Time of Novelty*, 118–119.

96 Wright, *A Time of Novelty*, 97–125.

97 Wright, *A Time of Novelty*, 105–116.

98 Wright, *A Time of Novelty*, 99.

99 Wright, *A Time of Novelty*, 118.

100 Wright, *A Time of Novelty*, 123.

101 Wright understands the *dēvatācaitanyavādi* in Gadādhara's essay to be a direct reference to "Lord Caitanya," but I think it is more likely that it means "one who believes that God is consciousness." See Wright, *A Time of Novelty*, 104.

reflects their attention to regional social affairs. While this was true more generally of the Brahmin assemblies of Banaras, who adjudicated matters of social and religious dispute from the provincial towns of their origin, the Dēvas had specific religious communities in mind. Anantadēva II, for example, composed a Vaiṣṇava ritual manual called the *Mathurāsētu* that aimed to explain the greatness of the city of Mathurā "by generating satisfaction for those of you living there itself, as you sing the glories of and take as your sole refuge the God who goes by the names Hari, Kēśava, and Gōvinda."[102] Probably modeled on the *Tristhalīsētu* of Nārāyaṇa Bhaṭṭa, a Brahmin pilgrim's guide to the city of Banaras, the *Mathurāsētu* describes the glory of various holy sites in Mathurā and the appropriate rites to observe.[103] Anantadēva II quotes both his father's *Bhaktikalpataru*, mentioned earlier, and his grandfather's *Bhaktinirṇaya* and *Bhaktiśata*, an unpublished set of one hundred stanzas in praise of Kṛṣṇa.[104] Part 2 of the *Mathurāsētu* describes the methods of proper Vaiṣṇava initiation and practice for those inhabitants of Mathurā who wish to develop "joy towards Lord Kṛṣṇa" (*śrīkṛṣṇaprīti*), not unlike those Bengali Vaiṣṇavas who, under the Mughal aegis, had begun to reconstruct the city of Brindavan both in its actual physical location and in their own polities.[105] Other apparent similarities with the Gauḍīyas include the discourse of *bhaktirasa*, "which takes the form of loving devotion, having delight as its stable emotion, enveloped in an incomparable ecstasy that manifests through the aid of all the aesthetic factors."[106]

But the similarities go only so far. The *Mathurāsētu* also draws upon an early sixteenth-century Tantric manual of Rāma worship, the *Rāmārcanacandrikā*, even reproducing in the manuscript a diagram of syllables to be used for esoteric recitation by Vaiṣṇava initiates.[107] Rāma

[102] *Mathurāsētu*, f. 1v: *mathurāmaṇḍalamahimānaṁ tatraiva satāṁ harikēśavagōvindanāmānam ananyaśaraṇatayā bhajatāṁ tatrabhavatāṁ santōṣajananēna* [lacuna] *pradarśayāmaḥ*.

[103] See Richard Salomon, ed. and trans., *The Bridge to the Three Holy Cities: The Sāmānya-praghaṭṭaka of Nārāyaṇa Bhaṭṭa's Tristhalīsetu* (Delhi: Motilal Banarsidass, 1985).

[104] See *Mathurāsētu*, f. 42r–43v. For a brief description of the *Bhaktiśata* manuscript in the British Library, which was lost at sea on a transatlantic journey, see *Catalogue of the Sanskrit Manuscripts of the Library of the India Office*, part 4, ed. Ernst Windisch and Julius Eggeling (London: Secretary of State for India in Council, 1894), 829–830. I thank Pasquale Manzo for delivering this sad news to me with great sympathy.

[105] *Mathurāsētu*, f. 30r: *mathurāvāsināṁ nṝṇāṁ śrīkṛṣṇaprītim icchatāṁ tatkāraṇāni vakṣyāmi sapramāṇāni samprati*. On the Bengali Vaiṣṇavas and Brindavan, see Wright, *A Time of Novelty*, 115 and Hawley, *A Storm of Songs*, 150–179.

[106] *Mathurāsētu*, f. 43v: *ata ēva imam ēva prēmabhaktirūpaṁ ratyākhyasthāyibhāvaṁ vibhāvādis-ahakārēṇābhivyaktaniratiśayānandapariṣvaktaṁ bhaktirasam āhuḥ*.

[107] For the diagram, see *Mathurāsētu*, f. 30v, in the lower right corner. It appears immediately after Anantadēva's discussion of the appropriate times and customs of initiation (*dīkṣākāla*). On the *Rāmārcanacandrikā*, see Hans Bakker, "Reflections on the Evolution of Rāma Devotion in the Light

devotion in northern India especially flourished from the eleventh and twelfth centuries onward. Sanskrit texts such as the *Agastyasaṁhitā* and *Rāmapūrvatāpanīya Upaniṣad* describe Rāma both as a being beyond all attributes (*nirguṇa*) and as an object of personal worship (*saguṇa*).[108] The combination of Advaita Vēdānta with *bhakti* was well-established in the Rāma-*bhakti* tradition. Subsequent texts like the *Adhyātma Rāmāyaṇa* would go on to influence the Rāmānandī order of ascetics and the Avadhi-language *Rāmcaritmānas* by Tulsīdās in the sixteenth century.[109] Ānandavana, author of the *Rāmārcanacandrikā*, claimed a direct lineage to Advaita authors from Gauḍapāda to Śaṅkara and Surēśvara.[110] These Rāma texts, like the *Bhagavannāmakaumudī* on which Anantadēva wrote a commentary, also proclaimed the salvific power of reciting the *mantra* of Rāma's name.[111] It is possible that Anantadēva's guru, Rāmatīrtha, owed his "amazing" ability to combine philosophical inquiry and religious practice to this North Indian milieu of Rāma-*bhakti*.

What, then, of the Dēvas' Maharashtrian sensibilities, especially given their purported connection to the Brahmin *bhakta* Ēknāth? How did the Dēvas' regional identities contribute to those percolating debates on what it meant to be a Brahmin in the sixteenth century and beyond? For more concrete evidence of the Dēvas' local connections, instead of turning to Ēknāth, we might consider another Maharashtrian saint figure from the seventeenth century: Rāmdās. Although Anantadēva II spent his life in Banaras and his absentee patron lived in Almora, Uttarakhand, he taught students from all over the subcontinent. One of his students was Raghunātha Navahasta, a protégé of Queen Dīpābāi of Thanjavur.[112] Raghunātha made sure to let

of Textual and Archeological Evidence," *Wiener Zeitschrift für die Kunde Südasiens* 31 (1987): 24 and n. 77.

108 Hans Bakker, *Ayodhyā*, part 1 (Groningen: Egbert Forsten, 1986), 67–181. Cf. Hans Bakker, "An Old Text of the Rāma Devotion: The *Agastyasaṁhitā*," in *Navonmeṣaḥ: Mahamahopadhyaya Gopinath Kaviraj Commemoration Volume* (Varanasi: M. M. Gopinah Kaviraj Centenary Celebration Committee, 1987), 300–306; Bakker, "Reflections on the Evolution of Rāma Devotion," 9–42.

109 Bakker, *Ayodhyā*, 122–124. Cf. Michael Allen, "Sītā's Shadow: Vedāntic Symbolism in the *Adhyātma-Rāmāyaṇa*," *Journal of Vaishnava Studies* 20.1 (2011): 81–102.

110 Bakker, *Ayodhyā*, 123, n. 10.

111 Bakker, *Ayodhyā*, 119–124; Bakker, "An Old Text of the Rāma Devotion," 302–303. Cf. Hans Bakker, "Rāma Devotion in a Śaiva Holy Place," in *Patronage and Popularisation, Pilgrimage and Procession: Channels of Transcultural Translation and Transmission in Early Modern South Asia*, ed. Heidi Rika Maria Pauwels (Wiesbaden: Harrassowitz Verlag, 2009), 67–79.

112 P. K. Gode, "The Identification of Raghunātha, the Protégé of Queen Dīpābāi of Tanjore and His Contact with Saint Rāmadāsa—Between A.D. 1648 and 1682," in *Studies in Indian Literary History*, vol. 2 (Bombay: Singhi Jain Śāstra Śikshāpīth, 1954), 404–415.

his readers know that he was close with his teacher, frequently referring to himself in colophons as "Anantadēva's own" (*anantadēvīya*) and "blessed by Anantadēva" (*anantadēvānugṛhīta*). After leaving Banaras, Raghunātha became the personal instructor of the itinerant Marathi Brahmin preacher Samartha Rāmdās. As a specialist in ancient lore (*purāṇik*), Raghunātha was appointed priest at the Rāma temple of Chāphaḷ, in Satara district, where Rāmdās set up a large seminary. Halfway between Pune and Kolhapur, the Chāphaḷ Maṭh was the center of Rāmdās's activities. Raghunātha occupied this position until 1683 CE, when political turmoil prompted him to settle in Maratha Thanjavur under the patronage of Queen Dīpābāī. Here he turned to writing works of epic poetry and popular science, including recipe books and consumer catalogues, in both Sanskrit and Marathi for a courtly audience. Raghunātha appears to have moved easily between the world of "high" Brahmanical learning in Banaras, the very local responsibilities of a temple priest affiliated with a celebrated saint, and the consumerist appetites of a newly transplanted Marathi elite in South India.[113] As a *purāṇik*, a scholar versed in the *purāṇa* tradition, Raghunātha would have been able to mediate between elite and popular worlds as part of his very profession.[114] Raghunātha's *Janārdana-Mahōdaya*, a Sanskrit manual of Vaiṣṇava ritual, may have owed its sections on Rāma and Hanumān worship to the influence of the saint's popular activities, and vice versa.[115] Raghunātha was, in this sense, the Dēvas' true protégé, not by reproducing and building upon their intellectual expertise but as a scholar constantly reinventing himself: for pious flocks of devotees, for midlevel military officials, and for elite men and women of the Thanjavur court. It is likely through the network of Rāmdāsī institutions, and perhaps through Raghunātha himself, that the Dēvas' writings reached the South.

Rāmdās, for his part, represents the Dēvas' inverse: a charismatic preacher first, and a scriptural exegete second. While he did know some

[113] See Anand Venkatkrishnan, "Leaving Kashi: Sanskrit Knowledge and Cultures of Consumption in Eighteenth-Century South India," *The Indian Economic and Social History Review* 57.4 (2020): 567–581.

[114] Cf. V. Narayana Rao, "Purāṇa," in *The Hindu World*, ed. Sushil Mittal and Gene Thursby (New York: Routledge, 2004), 114: "A typical *paurāṇika* . . . chooses a section of a Purāṇa for a discourse, reads out a portion of the text in Sanskrit or the regional language, and comments on it, incorporating material from other similar texts and expanding on their relevance to that specific place and point in time."

[115] P. K. Gode, "A Rare Manuscript of Janārdana Mahodaya by Raghunātha Gaṇeśa Navahasta, Friend of Saint Rāmadāsa—Between A.D. 1640 and 1682," in *Studies in Indian Literary History*, vol. 2 (Bombay: Singhi Jain Śāstra Śikshāpīth, 1954), 416–424.

Sanskrit, everything that he wrote was in Marathi.[116] His most famous Marathi composition, the *Dāsbōdh*, mirrors many of the texts of Rāma-*bhakti* described previously. The *Dāsbōdh* espouses a broadly Advaita Vēdānta philosophy while foregrounding popular practices of *bhakti*, in particular the practice of *kīrtan*, devotional singing, which in some instances was to be followed by Vēdāntic exposition.[117] The *Dāsbōdh* also provides a fascinating description of the social space of the Rāmdāsī community. At the beginning of the eighth chapter, "A Description of the Audience" (*sabhāvarṇana*), Rāmdās cites a famous Sanskrit stanza where the god Viṣṇu says that he dwells wherever his *bhakta*s gather to sing. Rāmdās translates the stanza into Marathi and proceeds to explain what makes this assembly (*sabhā*) so special: "Here there is the love-filled singing of *bhaktas*, God's sacred utterances, songs about God, exegesis of the Vedas, stories from the *purāṇa*s. God's glories are recounted, there are dialogues on all sorts of interpretive problems, the science of the inner self (is studied), and debates rage over difference and non-difference. Conversation results in satisfactory conclusions, removes doubts, and sets minds to meditation."[118] Not only is there a prominent place here for *bhakti*, but scholarly inquiry also finds a welcome home, just as the Dēvas would have wanted. The chapter goes on to list the motley crew that comprises the *sabhā*, ranging from "staff-wielders, dreadlocked ascetics, and Nāth *yogis* wearing earrings" (*daṇḍadhārī jaṭādhārī nāthpanthī mudrādhārī*) to "tricksy logicians and great poets" (*dhūrta tārkika kavīśvara*) and "scholars and storytellers, virtuosos and Vedicists" (*paṇḍit āṇi purāṇik vidvāṁs āṇi vaidik*).[119] If we juxtapose this vignette from the *Dāsbōdh* alongside the "assemblies" we have seen so far, the *dharmasabhā* and *paṇḍitasabhā*, we find yet another noncourtly public space for intellectual, literary, and religious activity. The *Dāsbōdh*'s *sabhā* claims to be a space for different participants with different interests and capabilities. At first blush its description may appear hyperreal, a literary exaggeration. Yet it could very well resemble the Dēvas' own multipurpose milieu of early modern Banaras. Far from being restricted to the self-professedly elite assembly

116 Wilbur S. Deming, *Rāmdās and the Rāmdāsīs* (New Delhi: Vintage Books, 1990 [1928]), 31–32.

117 Deming, *Rāmdās and the Rāmdāsīs*, 90–100, 120.

118 *Śrīdāsabodha* (Pune: Bhaṭ āṇi Maṇḍalī, 1915), 13 (1.8.4–6): *prēmaḷa bhaktāṁcī gāyaṇē | bhagavadvākyēṁ harikīrtanēṁ | vedavyākhyāna purāṇaśravaṇa | jēthēṁ nirantara || paramēśvarācē guṇānuvāda | nānā nirūpaṇāṁcē saṁvāda | adhyātmavidyā bhēdābhēda- | mathana jēthē || nānā samādhānēṁ tṛptī | nānā āśaṁkānivṛttī | cittīṁ baisē dhyānamūrtī | vāgvilāsēṁ ||*

119 *Śrīdāsabōdha*, 14 (1.8.10–16).

of the Muktimaṇḍapa, the Dēvas' *sabhā* covered much more ground than that of top-down Brahmanical jurisprudence. It encompassed different linguistic registers, intellectual disciplines, and religious worldviews.

At the same time, all of these *sabhā*s were fundamentally Brahmin-dominated spaces. When I referred to the "demotic" character of *bhakti* in the introduction to this chapter, I deliberately did not mean "democratic."[120] In this sense, the connection between Rāmdās and the Dēvas is quite easy to understand. Rāmdās is primarily remembered for his disputed role in the regime of the Maratha king Shivaji, a relationship that has been interpreted variously at different historical junctures by those with different political sensibilities.[121] In terms of his basic social views, however, even sympathetic commentators acknowledge that "Rāmdās . . . was not a social reformer. He accepted the Hindu social system as he found it. . . . While the Svāmī was friendly with low castes, he did not make a definite place for them in the movement; and the low-caste element has never held the place of honour among Rāmdāsīs that it has at Paṇḍharpūr."[122] For some, Rāmdās remained the exemplary case of *bhakti*'s inability to maintain a critical edge in early modernity, stamping out the possibility of reformation.[123] As Anna Schultz notes in her work on Marathi devotional performance and Hindu nationalism, Rāmdās broke from the egalitarian *vārkarī* tradition, upheld Brahmanical hierarchies, encouraged involvement in politics, and laid "the musical and political foundations for *rāṣṭrīya* (nationalist) *kīrtan* in the seventeenth century."[124] If the Dēvas had given up their scholarly careers to become full-time musical performers, they would have found kindred spirits among the followers of Rāmdās.

What should we make, then, of Anantadēva II's self-proclaimed connection to Ēknāth, a much more troublesome social figure, albeit no less Brahmin? It may be that, in some cases, "Brahmin actors felt the *bhakti*

[120] On the question of *bhakti* and the "democratic spirit," see Keune, *Shared Food, Shared Devotion*, 60–65.

[121] Prachi Deshpande, *Creative Pasts: Historical Memory and Identity in Western India, 1700–1960* (New York: Columbia University Press, 2007), 131–132, 183–188.

[122] Deming, *Rāmdās and the Rāmdāsīs*, 212.

[123] See Veena Naregal, "Language and Power in Precolonial Western India: Textual Hierarchies, Literate Audiences, and Colonial Philology," *The Indian Economic and Social History Review* 37.3 (2000): 264: "[Rāmdās's] prolific compositions reveal that by the late seventeenth century vernacular devotional expression was patently less anti-hierarchical and more inclined to uphold the benefits of institutional structures in the religious and political spheres."

[124] Anna Schultz, *Singing a Hindu Nation: Marathi Devotional Performance and Nationalism* (Oxford: Oxford University Press, 2013), 26.

impulse deeply enough to train its mirror willingly on the regressive habits associated with the class to which they themselves belonged."[125] Christian Novetzke suggests instead that we attend to the "literary-performative" field of *bhakti* in which poets and saints articulated a public critique of caste.[126] When Brahmin performers of Marathi *kīrtan* presented a caricature of the greedy, foolish, orthodox Brahmin, they discursively separated "bad Brahmins" from "Brahmanism" in general. According to Novetzke, Ēknāth was one such "Brahmin double," both a critic of caste and an upholder of the status quo, simultaneously transgressing the social norms of Brahmin *dharma* and maintaining the institution.[127] The Dēvas, too, spent quite a bit of time criticizing Brahmin scholars for their haughtiness. Of course, that critique belonged to a very different social context: the very city where Ēknāth purportedly had to face the wrath of the Brahmin establishment for his Marathi commentary on the *Bhāgavata*. But if, in the cultural memory of Marathi *bhakti*, Banaras was painted as the stronghold of oppressive Brahmanical orthodoxy, what were the Dēvas trying to accomplish with their version of *bhakti*? Why did they argue that it was perfectly acceptable to use vernacular languages to sing God's name when they did not write a word of Marathi?[128] Why did they write vast compendia of Mīmāṁsā, Vēdānta, and *dharmaśāstra*, only to insist that loving God was the greatest thing to which a person could aspire? One could say that, like the members of the "religious republic of letters" in early modern Europe, scholarly life for the Dēvas was "synonymous with the quest for transcendence, the desire for salvation, and the longing for God."[129] But there is more than personal religiosity at play here. The Dēvas were deeply invested in the social consequences of *bhakti*. This did not mean that they transgressed caste boundaries; quite to the contrary, they reinforced them on the very ground of *bhakti*. Their critique of caste was a critique of the scholarly caste and its casual disregard for the rhythms of divine love. Perhaps the Dēvas were trying to refract the notion of

[125] Hawley, *A Storm of Songs*, 7.

[126] Christian Novetzke, "The Brahmin Double: The Brahminical Construction of Anti-Brahminism and Anti-caste Sentiment in the Religious Cultures of Precolonial Maharashtra," *South Asian History and Culture* 2.2 (2011): 232–252.

[127] Novetzke, "The Brahmin Double," 243.

[128] Although none of the Dēvas wrote a word of Marathi, the space for vernacular communication among scholarly families was probably wider than the extant written record may reveal. Consider the example of the *Gīrvāṇavāṅmañjarī* by Dhuṇḍirāja, a Sanskrit primer that translated Marathi idioms into Sanskrit for everyday use in Banaras. See Madhav Deshpande, "On Vernacular Sanskrit," in *Sanskrit and Prakrit: Sociolinguistic Issues*, ed. Madhav Deshpande (Delhi: Motilal Banarsidass, 1993), 33–51.

[129] Furey, *Erasmus, Contarini, and the Religious Republic of Letters*, 13.

the "Brahmin double" in a social world where upper-caste identity was being constantly threatened, renegotiated, and—that perennial Brahmin anxiety—corrupted. They did not just engage in theoretical reflection on how to define "being Brahmin."[130] They worked it out in debate, in deliberation, and in drama. To be a "good" Brahmin, it was not enough to master a scholarly discipline. One had to show the appropriate comportments of humility and worship and offer up (*arpaṇa*) one's accomplishments to God. Perhaps invoking Ēknāth was the Dēvas' way of reminding themselves of this.[131]

The question that drives this chapter is how we should study the influence of popular religious movements on intellectual life. By "popular" I mean the multilingual traditions of poetry, performance, and pilgrimage that constituted the *bhakti* networks of early modern India. I have argued that, in the case of the Dēvas, their intellectual interests were sparked by texts and traditions from a wider range than generally comprised the *śāstric* scope of the Brahmin elite of Banaras. The Dēvas experienced the city as a competitive, hypercritical, and very worldly arena in which scholarly pride and the lure of passing celebrity drove out the very possibility of artless religious sentiment. In both scholarly and polemical writings, they argued that the everyday practices of *bhakti*—specifically, the public acts of singing, storytelling, and sermonizing—were appropriate not just for women and lower castes but for Brahmins like themselves as well. In the eyes of the Dēvas' opponents, these practices were ones Brahmins should avoid because they interfered with their academic careers. The Dēvas, on the other hand, believed that their scholarship was enhanced by *bhakti*. They wanted to be remembered not only as excellent scholars but also as faithful devotees. It was important to them to be the right kind of Brahmin, one who wielded both spiritual and social power and remained uncorrupted by the temptations of the new intellectual economy. *Bhakti* reminded the Dēvas of where they came from, a provinciality that reared its head even in the universalist language of Sanskrit scholarship. Their personal religious

[130] Cf. Samuel Wright, "History in the Abstract: 'Brahman-ness' and the Discipline of Nyāya in Seventeenth-Century Vārāṇasī," *Journal of Indian Philosophy* 44.5 (2016): 1041–1069.

[131] Cf. Adheesh Sathaye, *Crossing the Lines of Caste: Viśvāmitra and the Construction of Brahmin Power in Hindu Mythology* (New York: Oxford University Press, 2015), 143–144: "As Kunal Chakrabarti explains, purāṇic literature served as a 'cultural resource which enabled little communities to transform themselves into a regional community which could be culturally identified and territorially demarcated.' . . . Brahmin *paurāṇikas* engaged in similar modes of identification, albeit in the elite register of Sanskrit, but nevertheless based on regionalized evaluations of the binary opposition between being Brahmin and becoming the Other kind of Brahmin."

commitments prompted them to change the very frameworks and aims of Mīmāṁsā and Vēdānta, those systems of Sanskrit knowledge which were so often impervious to the world around them. For *bhakti* was on the move in early modern India, and it moved scholars to think in new ways about their intellectual inheritances.

4
Threads of *bhakti*

Introduction

In the previous chapter, I asked how popular religious traditions shaped the Sanskrit intellectual sphere when *bhakti* became an object of systematic theoretical inquiry. There, I approached the question obliquely by reading the works of several generations of Brahmin scholars, the Dēvas. In monographs like the *Arpaṇamīmāṁsā*, in polemical pamphlets like the *Bhaktinirṇaya*, in stage-plays and ritual handbooks and paratextual comments, the Dēvas performed their scholarly *habitus* as Brahmin intellectuals engaged with the wider world of *bhakti*. The concept of a "system" in Sanskrit learning, the *śāstra*, had a specific form. The major systems of knowledge traced their origin to aphorisms, or *sūtras* (lit. "threads"), brief investigations that required an interpretive apparatus in scholastic prose. The *sūtra*s generated commentaries upon commentaries that refined and expanded on their ideas. Early modern philosophers devoted renewed commentarial attention to these foundational texts of their traditions.[1] Into this frenzy entered the *Bhakti Sūtras*. In seeking to theorize *bhakti* as a system, the *Bhakti Sūtra*s modeled themselves on the aphorisms of Mīmāṁsā and Vēdānta. They drew inspiration from the *Bhāgavata Purāṇa* and confronted the theories of Advaita Vēdānta. In this chapter, I follow the uncertain paths charted between *bhakti* and Advaita Vēdānta beginning with the intellectual history of *Bhakti Sūtras*. In order to understand better the relationship of the *Bhakti Sūtra*s to the disciplines they recover and resist, I reconstruct their historical context and revise their chronology. Although they have featured prominently in the modern historiography of *bhakti*, the *Bhakti Sūtra*s were rather unimportant in their time, and largely ignored by the Vaiṣṇava communities of northern India. To provide specificity to their intellectual intervention, in the bulk of

[1] Sheldon Pollock, "New Intellectuals in Seventeenth-Century India," *The Indian Economic and Social History Review* 38.1 (2001): 10; Christopher Minkowski, "Advaita Vedānta in Early Modern History," *South Asian History and Culture* 2.2 (2011): 211.

Love in the Time of Scholarship. Anand Venkatkrishnan, Oxford University Press. © Oxford University Press 2024.
DOI: 10.1093/oso/9780197776636.003.0005

this chapter I focus on the writings of Nārāyaṇa Tīrtha, a lesser-known figure in Advaita history and author of works on Nyāya, Vēdānta, and *yōga*. In his *Bhakticandrikā*, a commentary on the *Bhakti Sūtras*, Nārāyaṇa went farther than anyone in Advaita intellectual history in arguing that *jñāna* is subordinate to *bhakti*. While this radical departure from classical Advaita Vēdānta doctrine has been noticed previously,[2] I address the mechanics of the shift. I discuss the logic of Nārāyaṇa's exegesis and the ways in which it complicates a straightforward account of the compatibility or incompatibility of *bhakti* with Advaita Vēdānta. I show how Nārāyaṇa extended the theory of *bhakti* provided by the *Bhakti Sūtras* beyond their confines and into his commentary on Patañjali's *Yōga Sūtras*. I conclude the genealogy of the *Bhakti Sūtras* by exploring their surprising cameo in the writings of Bhāskararāya, a practitioner of Śākta Tantra living in South India. For Bhāskararāya, *bhakti* was a key step in a pedagogical program for the Tantric aspirant. As they have throughout this book, the threads of *bhakti* weave in between Śaivism and Vaiṣṇavism, Advaita and non-Advaita Vēdānta, Sanskrit universalism and regional specificity.

Accounts of the relationship between *bhakti* and Advaita Vēdānta have tended to fall along two major lines. In one view, a theology of religious devotion to an embodied god cannot be squared with a monist philosophy that does away with distinctions between the individual and God. *Bhakti* and the realist ontology it requires can hold only a subordinate place in such a system, as a preparatory stage for nondual knowledge. Theologies of *bhakti*, primarily Vaiṣṇava in character, are viewed as responses or challenges to the forbidding fortress of Advaita Vēdānta in the history of Indian philosophy.[3] Another line of interpretation prefers to see no essential break between the two. *Bhakti* either exists primordially in Advaita Vēdānta, or it is successfully reconciled in the work of certain major figures of the tradition.[4] In some versions, vernacular-language *nirguṇi* poetry is considered coreferential with Advaita Vēdānta philosophy.[5] For many modern commentators,

[2] Adya Prasad Mishra, *The Development and Place of Bhakti in Śāṅkara Vedānta* (Allahabad: University of Allahabad, 1967), 235–254.

[3] See, e.g., Surendranath Dasgupta, *A History of Indian Philosophy*, vol. 4: *Indian Pluralism* (Cambridge: Cambridge University Press, 1961).

[4] See Sanjukta Gupta, *Advaita Vedānta and Vaiṣṇavism: The Philosophy of Madhusūdana Sarasvatī* (London: Routledge, 2006); Shoun Hino, "The Beginnings of *Bhakti's* Influence on Advaita Doctrine in the Teachings of Madhusūdana Sarasvatī," in *Indian Philosophy and Text Science*, ed. Toshihiro Wada (Delhi: Motilal Banarsidass, 2010), 101–114.

[5] See Krishna Sharma, *Bhakti and the Bhakti Movement: A New Perspective* (New Delhi: Munshiram Manoharlal, 1987).

discerning the proper relationship between *bhakti* and Advaita Vēdānta involves questions of philosophical and political ethics.[6] Let us look at some representatives of these views.

In 1967, seventeen years after successfully submitting his doctoral thesis at Allahabad University, Adya Prasad Mishra published a revised version of his dissertation as the book *The Development and Place of Bhakti in Śāṅkara Vedānta.* In this book, Mishra traced each discussion of the term *bhakti* in Advaita Vēdānta intellectual history, as well as its incipient formulations in the Vedic corpus. While devoting significant attention to Śaṅkara's own writings, Mishra assigned a distinct place in postclassical Vēdānta to the sixteenth- and seventeenth-century thinkers Madhusūdana Sarasvatī and Nārāyaṇa Tīrtha. According to Mishra, these two alone represented the final stage of "Neo-Bhakti," for they accorded *bhakti* a space alongside *jñāna* as an independent path to liberation.[7] "[T]he monistic ideal of Śāṅkara Vedānta," Mishra concluded, "is not only not against Bhakti, but, on the contrary, it preaches it in positive and assertive terms."[8] Adya Prasad Mishra's dissertation advisor in the Sanskrit Department at Allahabad was the prolific scholar Umesh Mishra. His magnum opus was the monumental and learned *History of Indian Philosophy*, of which he published two volumes, leaving the third in manuscript form.[9] In the first volume of the set, Umesh Mishra made it clear that *bhakti* was incompatible with "the Highest Aim of philosophy, that is, Absolute Monism which alone aims at Perfect Unity amid diversity." *Bhakti* could make one fit only for *jñāna*, for it required a degree of individuality in one's relationship with God. Therefore, he said, "Dualism cannot be removed and Absolute Monism is never possible with Bhakti as the direct means of realizing the Ultimate Reality."[10] In writing a

[6] See Paul Hacker, "Schopenhauer and Hindu Ethics," in *Philology and Confrontation: Paul Hacker on Traditional and Modern Vedanta*, ed. Wilhelm Halbfass (Albany: State University of New York Press, 1995), 273–318; Andrew J. Nicholson, "Vivekananda's Non Dual Ethics in the History of Vedanta," in *Swami Vivekananda: His Life, Legacy, and Liberative Ethics*, ed. Rita D. Sherma (Lanham: Lexington Books, 2021), 51–72.

[7] The term "Neo-Bhakti" was perhaps first used by Kshitimohan Sen to refer to the "cult" or "movement" connecting the Tamil *ālvārs*, the Śrīvaiṣṇavas, and the Caitanyaites. See Kshitimohan Sen, *Medieval Mysticism of India* (London: Luzac & Co., 1936), 46, 48, 50. Hawley suggests that the popularity of the term owed to R. G. Bhandarkar's *Vaiṣṇavism, Śaivism, and Minor Religious Systems* (Strassburg: Trübner, 1913) but the book does not use the word. Sen only cites Bhandarkar's work in a general sense. See John Stratton Hawley, *A Storm of Songs: India and the Idea of the Bhakti Movement* (Cambridge: Harvard University Press, 2015), 248.

[8] Mishra, *The Development and Place*, ii.

[9] See Govinda Jha, *Umesh Mishra*, trans. Jayakanta Mishra (New Delhi: Sahitya Akademi, 1995).

[10] Umesh Mishra, *History of Indian Philosophy*, vol. 1 (Allahabad: Tirabhukti Publications, 1957), 31–33.

thesis that directly contradicted such statements, Adya Prasad Mishra must have clashed with his advisor. Indeed, in his otherwise encouraging foreword to *The Development and Place*, Umesh Mishra remarked, "The subject sounded to many apparently contradictory." Nevertheless, he signed off on the thesis with the caveat "*Bhakti* is really for the lower stage."[11] Others have picked up on Umesh Mishra's skepticism. In his studies of the famous Advaitin Madhusūdana Sarasvatī, Lance Nelson found an irresolvable tension between Madhusūdana's orthodox nondualism and devotional spirituality.[12] For Madhusūdana to say, in his *Bhaktirasāyana*, that *bhakti* could be the highest goal of human life left a number of unresolved theoretical difficulties.[13] The metaphysical paradox of being a lover of God and of nondual knowledge made such a claim simply not "justifiable in terms of Śaṁkara's Advaita."[14] In rereading Adya Prasad Mishra's work, Nelson was rather less sanguine about Mishra's belief that one could seamlessly reconcile the two.[15]

Each of these views, however, is susceptible to what Quentin Skinner has called the "mythology of doctrines" and the "mythology of coherence."[16] The mythology of doctrines assumes that each classic writer in a particular system—in this case, of Advaita Vēdānta philosophy—must articulate some doctrine constitutive of that system. "Besides the crude possibility of crediting a writer with a meaning they could not have intended to convey," writes Skinner, "there is the more insidious danger of too readily finding expected doctrines in classic texts."[17] For all his impressive textual breadth, Adya Prasad Mishra fell prey to precisely this fallacy. Once he held *bhakti* to be constitutive of Advaita Vēdānta discourse, it was a small step to hold that

[11] Mishra, *The Development and Place*, "Forward [*sic*]."

[12] Lance Nelson, "Bhakti in Advaita Vedānta: A Translation and Study of Madhusūdana Sarasvatī's Bhaktirasāyana" (Ph.D. diss., McMaster University, 1986); Lance Nelson, "Madhusūdana Sarasvatī on the 'Hidden Meaning' of the *Bhagavadgītā*: Bhakti for the Advaitin Renunciate," *Journal of South Asian Literature* 23.2 (1988): 73–89; Lance Nelson, "Bhakti Rasa for the Advaitin Renunciate: Madhusūdana Sarasvatī's Theory of Devotional Sentiment," *Religious Traditions* 12.1 (1989): 1–16; Lance Nelson, "Bhakti Preempted: Madhusūdana Sarasvatī on Devotion for the Advaitin Renouncer," *Journal of Vaishnava Studies* 7.2 (1998): 53–74; Lance Nelson, "The Ontology of *Bhakti*: Devotion as *Paramapuruṣārtha* in Gauḍīya Vaiṣṇavism and Madhusūdana Sarasvatī," *Journal of Indian Philosophy* 32.4 (2004): 345–392; Lance Nelson, "Theological Politics and Paradoxical Spirituality in the Life of Madhusūdana Sarasvatī," *Journal of Vaishnava Studies* 15.2 (2007): 19–34.

[13] Nelson, "The Ontology of *Bhakti*," 363.

[14] Nelson, "Bhakti in Advaita Vedānta," 308. Cf. Nelson, "The Ontology of *Bhakti*," 386.

[15] Nelson, "Bhakti in Advaita Vedānta," 323–355.

[16] Quentin Skinner, *Visions of Politics*, vol. 1: *On Method* (Cambridge: Cambridge University Press, 2002), 59–72.

[17] Skinner, *Visions of Politics*, 61.

the classic texts of the discipline proleptically gestured toward its full elaboration later within the tradition. Nelson's study was also informed by a search for consistency, albeit negatively defined. In showing that Madhusūdana was unable to account philosophically for his multiple affiliations, Nelson provided an example of the "mythology of coherence," a line of thinking in the history of ideas in which "writers are first classified according to a model to which they are then expected to aspire."[18] In this view, there is some inner coherence to an author's writing that it is the duty of the interpreter to reveal, despite the presence of contradictions and ambivalences. An author's failure in the matter of resolving antinomies requires the interpreter to do so on his behalf.[19] Since *bhakti* and Advaita Vēdānta are at metaphysical odds, Madhusūdana must be a bad Advaitin, a bad *bhakta*, or a conflicted soul in search of philosophical clarity. Nelson's own view, to be sure, was more nuanced than this. He demurred from making final judgments about Madhusūdana's project, preferring to show that in Madhusūdana's writing, *bhakti* became a subject of theoretical inquiry in ways it had not previously in Advaita.[20]

As such, these are not so much methodological "errors" as they are incomplete approaches to a historical question. "[T]he history of thought," as Skinner wrote, summarizing the view of R. G. Collingwood, "should be viewed not as a series of attempts to answer a canonical set of questions, but as a sequence of episodes in which the questions as well as the answers have frequently changed."[21] Neither Mishra nor Nelson was entirely off-base. The history of *bhakti* in Advaita Vēdānta does take a turn with Madhusūdana, if slightly anticipated by Śrīdhara Svāmī, and he does present many philosophical problems that can be evaluated on their success or failure. But what if, instead of searching for philosophical consistency, we attempted to understand what Advaitic *bhakta*s were doing in writing as they did? What if the context for their sometimes radical shifts in the history of ideas lay outside the "classic" texts of the genre, for instance, in minor commentaries or performed poetry? What if they called into question the very coherence of

[18] Skinner, *Visions of Politics*, 69.

[19] Skinner, *Visions of Politics*, 71.

[20] See Nelson, "The Ontology of *Bhakti*," 390: "[I]t is difficult to decide whether or not he was successful, even in his own terms. I would not presume to have worked out a final estimate in so short a compass; much depends on one's guess as to what exactly Madhusūdana was trying to accomplish in the [*Bhaktirasāyana*]. But I think I have at least demonstrated how even one considered among the greatest of Advaitin polemicists was caught up in this movement."

[21] Quentin Skinner, "A Reply to My Critics," in *Meaning and Context: Quentin Skinner and His Critics*, ed. James Tully (Cambridge: Polity, 1983), 234.

the philosophical tradition in which they operated? What if we did not assume the coherence of that tradition to begin with? I have already had occasion in this book to ask why Śaṅkara's Advaita is the yardstick against which innovations in Advaita intellectual history should be measured. Decades of scholarship on Sanskrit poetry and philosophy have criticized the obsession with classical texts across genres.[22] Moreover, Advaita was a multipronged tradition, ranging from Upaniṣadic exegesis to Śaiva and Śākta Tantra. The paradox of nondualist *bhakti* was as much a Śaiva as a Vaiṣṇava preoccupation.[23] Madhusūdana Sarasvatī was only its most famous and recognizable representative. But the "great man" version of Indian intellectual history often obscures more than it reveals.[24] To see Madhusūdana as the best and last Advaitic devotee is to prioritize hagiography over historical understanding. For that understanding, we must turn not to the canonical works of major figures but to those on the margins of the classical. Intellectual historians have found it salutary to focus on "minor" figures in the history of ideas, emphasizing "discontinuity, unintended consequences, tragic failures and lost traditions of political argument."[25] Minor figures illuminate paths not taken as well as neglected elements in the thought of canonical scholars. The figures in this chapter, Nārāyaṇa Tīrtha and Bhāskararāya, are not exactly minor in the sense of ignored or inconsequential. However, their ideas about *bhakti* offer a different perspective on the historiography of the term.

Premodern Threads, Modern Tapestries

The idea of the *bhakti* movement, and the importance of the *Bhakti Sūtras* to it, was influenced by the British scholar-administrator G. A. Grierson. Grierson argued that Christianity was the origin of Hindu *bhakti*.[26] In a famous turn of phrase, Grierson called *bhakti* the "flash of lightning" that came

[22] See, e.g., Yigal Bronner, *Extreme Poetry: The South Asian Movement of Simultaneous Narration* (New York: Columbia University Press, 2010), 11.

[23] Hamsa Stainton, *Poetry as Prayer in the Sanskrit Hymns of Kashmir* (New York: Oxford University Press, 2019), 97–158.

[24] On "the poverty of the great man version of Islamic intellectual history," see Justin Stearns, *Revealed Sciences: The Natural Sciences in Islam in Seventeenth-Century Morocco* (Cambridge: Cambridge University Press, 2021), 68–72.

[25] See Richard Whatmore, *What Is Intellectual History?* (Cambridge: Polity, 2015), 40, with reference to J. G. A. Pocock, Caroline Robbins, John Burrow, and Bernard Bailyn.

[26] G. A. Grierson, "Modern Hinduism and Its Debt to the Nestorians," *Journal of the Royal Asiatic Society* 39.2 (1907): 311–335.

upon the darkness of Indian religion, a passage that would be translated into Hindi by Hazariprasad Dvivedi as the "movement" or "wave" of *bhakti*.[27] He believed that the *Bhakti Sūtras* by Śāṇḍilya were important enough to this argument to merit an appendix with a summary of their contents. Grierson called this "official textbook" of *bhakti* a "modern Sanskrit treatise." What he meant by "modern" was anything that exhibited what he believed to be "decisively Christian" influences, such as the writings of Rāmānuja and Viṣṇusvāmī, which belonged to "the more modern phases of the doctrine."[28] In fact, the modern historical moment at which the *Bhakti Sūtras* were canonized was the colonial period. Their status was clinched as a result of the interaction between Orientalist scholars, Christian missionaries, and Hindu apologists in British India. Grierson relied on the edition of the *sūtras* produced by James Ballantyne (1861) and its subsequent translation by E. B. Cowell (1878). Ballantyne's edition of the text was prompted by an earlier series of essays on Christianity contrasted with Hindu philosophy, in the preface to which he remarked:

> There are some Sanskrit works, yet untranslated, which the writer must study before deciding upon his theological terminology for India. Among these works is the *Aphorisms of Sāndilya*. Sāndilya rejects the Hindū (gnostic) theory that *knowledge* is the one thing needful, and contends that knowledge is only the handmaiden of *faith*. Hence, however defective his views may be in other respects, his work seems to provide *phraseology* of which a Christian missionary may advantageously avail himself. This remark might form the text for an extended dissertation on the Christian's right to the theological language and the theological conceptions of his opponents.[29]

Interest in the *Bhakti Sūtras*, then, had a clear polemical purpose for their British readers. Current debates about them are in many ways conditioned by this specific history. Understanding their full impact on Indian intellectual history, however, requires attention to their precolonial life. How

[27] See Hawley, *A Storm of Songs*, 51–52.

[28] Grierson, "Modern Hinduism and Its Debt to the Nestorians," 314–317.

[29] See James Ballantyne, *Christianity Contrasted with Hindu Philosophy* (London: James Madden, 1858), iii–iv. On Ballantyne's pedagogical attempts to employ Sanskrit-based education as a tool for the propagation of Christianity among the learned Hindu elite, see Michael Dodson, "Re-presented for the Pandits: James Ballantyne, 'Useful Knowledge,' and Sanskrit Scholarship in Benares College during the Mid-Nineteenth Century," *Modern Asian Studies* 36.2 (2002): 257–298.

popular were the *Bhakti Sūtras* among Sanskrit exegetes? Who were these exegetes? In what context were the aphorisms composed, and what was their relationship with the *sūtra* traditions they invoked? And how old were the *Bhakti Sūtras*, really? Historians of Indian philosophy, whether writing in English, Hindi, or Sanskrit, have tended to place them around the turn of the first millennium CE.[30] This claim is largely based on three correlations: (a) the *sūtras*' conceptual proximity to the *Bhāgavata Purāṇa*; (b) the name of the author, Śāṇḍilya, as a recognized authority on devotional worship from the early Upaniṣads; and (c) a rumored commentary on the aphorisms by the eleventh-century Śrīvaiṣṇava theologian Rāmānuja.[31] Let us consider them one by one.

The first is the easiest to substantiate; the *sūtras* do indeed exhibit significant inspiration from the *Bhāgavata*, but this does not make them coeval.[32] Śāṇḍilya, for his part, lived what Steven Lindquist calls a "literary life," devotional worship (*upāsanā*) being his leitmotif across different contexts.[33] Leaving aside the fact that Vedic *upāsanā* looks very different from the *Bhāgavata*'s *bhakti*, attributing authorship of the *Bhakti Sūtras* to Śāṇḍilya probably fulfilled a narrative agenda. Marshaling a figure known to be associated with devotional worship invested the *Bhakti Sūtras* with both antiquity and authority, a common practice of historical memory in premodern South Asia. As for Rāmānuja, the only evidence for his purported commentary comes courtesy of an indirect citation from a seventeenth-century commentary on the text. I will discuss the relevant passage further on, but simply note here that it is not at all clear that an actual text is being cited, nor can the absence of the *Bhakti Sūtras* within Śrīvaiṣṇava circles be attributed to sheer negligence.

[30] See, e.g., Suvīrā Rainā, *Nāradīya ēvaṁ Śāṇḍilya-bhaktisūtrōṁ kā tulanātmaka adhyayana: bhakti kē ādyapravartaka ācāryōṁ kē bhakti-sūtrōṁ tathā unasē prabhāvita bhakti sampradāyōṁ kā prāmāṇika vivēcana* (Delhi: Eastern Book Linkers, 1989); *Śāṇḍilya Bhakti-Sūtra with Bhakticandrikā by Nārāyaṇa Tīrtha*, ed. Baldev Upadhyaya (Varanasi: Varanaseya Sanskrit Vishvavidyalaya, 1967), 1–23.

[31] In his impressive précis of Indian religious literature, J. N. Farquhar suggested that the *Bhakti Sūtras* may be of Nimbārki origin, but provided hardly any evidence to back this up. See J. N. Farquhar, *An Outline of the Religious Literature of India* (London: Oxford University Press, 1920), 233–234, 240.

[32] See Gupta, *Advaita Vedānta and Vaiṣṇavism*, 121: "There are two famous *Bhakti-sūtras*—the *Śāṇḍilya-bhakti-sūtra* (*ŚBhS*) and the *Nārada-bhakti-sūtra* (*NBhS*). . . . I take up these two *Bhakti-sūtras*, not because of their antiquity, (they are obviously late and certainly later than [the *Bhāgavata*]), but because they have made an attempt to introduce *bhakti* as a *Śāstra* in the model of the six *Darśana*."

[33] Steven Lindquist, "Literary Lives and a Literal Death: Yājñavalkya, Śākalya, and an Upaniṣadic Death Sentence," *Journal of the American Academy of Religion* 79.1 (2011): 33–57.

In fact, one is hard-pressed to find *any knowledge at all* of the aphorisms for much of Sanskrit intellectual history. Even the Gauḍīya Vaiṣṇavas, together with the Vallabha Sampradāya the most significant proponents of *bhakti* as a sphere of independent theological inquiry, seem to have made no mention of the *sūtras* in any of their works.[34] The most well-known commentator on the *Bhakti Sūtras*, the seventeenth-century scholar Svapnēśvara, may have had a faint, if oblique, connection to the Gauḍīya Vaiṣṇavas. He claimed to be the grandson of Vāsudēva Sārvabhauma, a famous scholar whom Gauḍīya hagiographers claimed as a convert to Caitanya's movement. But Vāsudēva Sārvabhauma's writings are limited to the subjects of Navya Nyāya and Advaita Vedānta, and Svapnēśvara's commentary betrays no affinity to Caitanya's theology whatsoever.[35] It is more probable that he belonged to an Advaita Vēdānta milieu, though he departs significantly from Advaita doctrines in the course of his commentary. For example, Svapnēśvara begins his commentary by saying that liberation is achieved when individuals attain Brahman, from whom they are totally nondifferent. The everyday experience of *saṁsāra*, therefore, is not natural (*sāhajika*) but constructed by contingent elements (*upādhi*), just like a crystal is seen as red when a red flower is placed next to it. So far, the account sounds nondualist, to the point of referring to a simile used famously by the tenth-century Advaitin Vācaspati Miśra. However, Svapnēśvara follows with some rather un-Advaitin claims. Since *saṁsāra* is conditional, he says, it cannot be removed by *ātmajñāna* but only by either removing the conditioning itself, the object of conditioning, or the relationship between them. That requires something else, something called *bhakti* for God. After all, *saṁsāra* is quite real and cannot be wished away.[36] This is a far cry from the Advaita view that both worldly life and liberation from it are constructs. Like Nārāyaṇa Tīrtha, our main subject in this chapter, Svapnēśvara toes the line between theistic and nontheistic Advaita Vēdānta.

As far as I can tell, the first public appearance of the *Bhakti Sūtras* coincides with their first extant commentaries in the seventeenth century, perhaps when the *sūtras* themselves were composed. Much like the *Bhāgavata* itself,

[34] See S. K. De, *Early History of the Vaisnava Faith and Movement in Bengal* (Calcutta: Firma K. L. Mukhopadhyay, 1961), 111–165 (on the six Gosvāmīs of Brindavan), 201–203 (on the works cited in Rūpa Gōsvāmī's *Bhaktirasāmṛtasindhu*), 220–221 (works cited in Rūpa's *Ujjvalanīlamaṇi*), and 413–421 (works cited in Jīva Gōsvāmī's *Ṣaṭsandarbha*).

[35] De, *Early History of the Vaisnava Faith*, 89, n. 1.

[36] See *The Aphorisms of Śāṇḍilya with the Commentary of Swapneśwara*, ed. J. R. Ballantyne (Calcutta: Baptist Mission Press, 1861), 1–3.

the *Bhakti Sūtras* seem to have been most prevalent in Advaitic circles. In previous chapters, I demonstrated the increasing influence of the *Bhāgavata* on writing in Mīmāṁsā and Advaita Vēdānta between the fifteenth and seventeenth centuries. From Mīmāṁsā arguments that the genre of *purāṇa* possessed Vedic scriptural authority to internecine polemic between Advaitins, scholars in this period debated the appropriate scope of the *Bhāgavata* in the realm of hermeneutics and philosophical theology. They also made use of other theistic scriptures that accorded to themselves the authority and the sobriquet of Upaniṣad: the *Gōpāla-*, *Rāma-*, and *Nṛsiṁha-Tāpanīya Upaniṣad*, and the *Bṛhannāradīya Purāṇa.* Taken together, these trends eventuated in the *Bhakti Sūtras*: a new set of ancient aphorisms to rival the old guard, intrusive entrants into a scholastic field that bristled at the thought of *bhakti* occupying a theoretical space alongside *jñāna* and *karma.* The *Bhakti Sūtras* do more than simply find *bhakti* a seat at the table; they herald its supremacy. After defining *bhakti* as "supreme love for God," *Bhakti Sūtras* 1.1.3–5 claim that one who is absorbed in love for God finds immortality. Absorption, they say, is not equivalent to *jñāna*, since one can know God's glory and still hate him. At the end of the day, *jñāna* pales before *bhakti.* The *sūtras* do not even allow that *jñāna* and *bhakti* could be independent paths to liberation undertaken by differentially qualified people. According to *Bhakti Sūtra* 1.2.7, there is simply no contest, no open option (*vikalpa*) between the two. Svapnēśvara comments, "Because it has been determined that *jñāna* is a subordinate element [*aṅga*], there is no scope for the position that there is an option between *jñāna* and *bhakti.* After all, there is no equal choice between two elements in hierarchical relation. The word 'also' indicates that a synthesis, too, [is refuted]."[37] What seemed straightforward to Svapnēśvara was not nearly so clear-cut to his rough contemporary, Nārāyaṇa Tīrtha. In this commentary on this *sūtra,* he reconstructed a salient objection, supported by several textual sources, that two routes (*mārgadvaya*) should be open to two different kinds of aspirants. He found it troubling that the author of the *sūtras* could dismiss the entirety of Vēdānta study: "Even if it makes good sense to propose an option, the author of the *sūtras* doesn't see it that way.... He will demonstrate everywhere that *jñāna* is totally unnecessary."[38] He distances

[37] *The Aphorisms of Śāṇdilya with the Commentary of Swapneśwara*, 17: *ētēna jñānasyāṅgatvanirṇayēna jñānabhaktyōr atra vikalpapakṣō'pi pratyuktaḥ, nirākṛta iti mantavyam. na hy aṅgāṅginōr ēkatra vikalpō bhavatīti. apiśabdāt samuccayō'pīti.*
[38] *Śāṇḍilya Bhakti-Sūtra with Bhakticandrikā by Nārāyaṇa Tīrtha*, 84: *yadyapi vikalpa ucitas tathā'pi sūtrakṛtā nādṛtaḥ... sarvatra jñānānāvaśyakatāṁ vakṣyati sūtrakāraḥ* (henceforth cited as *Bhakticandrikā*).

himself from the author again in his commentary on *Bhakti Sūtra* 2.2.29, where he reiterates his support for the "two paths" to liberation but concedes that "in the view of the author of the *sūtras*, *bhakti* is the sole path to liberation, while *jñāna* is merely a means, not another path."[39] Here and elsewhere, Nārāyaṇa Tīrtha brings his own unique concerns into his commentary on the *Bhakti Sūtras*, which sometimes depart from the text and sometimes refashion the very hermeneutical traditions in which he worked. In the following section, I explore what happens when a self-proclaimed Advaita Vēdāntin reads the *Bhakti Sūtras*, and what it may reveal about the complex, shifting terrain of Advaita in early modern India.

Nārāyaṇa Tīrtha and the Moonlight of Bhakti

There are a number of Nārāyaṇa Tīrthas who lived in the seventeenth century.[40] The first Nārāyāṇa Tīrtha, pupil of Vāsudēva Tīrtha and Rāmagōvinda Tīrtha and author of the *Bhakticandrikā* commentary on the *Bhakti Sūtras*, boasts an impressive scholastic résumé and variety of disciplinary expertise. Many of his commentaries include the same epithet, *-candrikā*, or "moonlight": the *Yōgasiddhāntacandrikā* on the *Yōga Sūtras*, the *Nyāyacandrikā* on Viśvanātha Nyāyapañcānana's *Bhāṣāparicchēda*, and the *Sāṁkhyacandrikā* on Īśvara Kr̥ṣṇa's *Sāṁkhyakārikā*. At least three of his works focus on *bhakti*: the *Bhakticandrikā*; the *Vēdastutivyākhyā*, a commentary on a section of the *Bhāgavata Purāṇa* (10.87); and the *Bhaktyadhikaraṇamālā*, a representation of the *Bhakti Sūtras* by discursive topic. The other Nārāyaṇa Tīrtha, pupil of Śivarāmatīrtha, composed the famous *Kr̥ṣṇalīlātaraṅgiṇī*, a Sanskrit dance-drama popular in South India.[41] The two were different people, but there are some overlaps. First, both composed Sanskrit works on *bhakti* in different genres. Second, both were Advaita Vēdāntins

[39] *Bhakticandrikā*, 234–235: *tasmāt siddhaṁ mōkṣē mārgadvayam ēvēty asmākīnaḥ panthāḥ . . . . sūtrakr̥nmatē tu bhaktiyōga ēvaikō mōkṣamārgaḥ, jñānaṁ tu mōkṣasādhanam ēva, na mārgāntaram.*

[40] Ko Endo, "The Works and Flourishing Period of Nārāyaṇa Tīrtha, the Author of the *Yōgasiddhāntacandrikā*." *Sambhāṣā* 14 (1993): 41–60.

[41] See V. Raghavan, *The Power of the Sacred Name* (Bloomington: World Wisdom Press, 2011), 75–82; B. Natarajan, *Sri Krishna Leela Tarangini by Narayana Tirtha*, vol. 1 (Madras: Mudgala Trust, 1988), 56–169. It is also likely that he was the composer of a Telugu drama called the *Pārijātaharaṇa Nāṭaka*, since the *Kr̥ṣṇalīlātaraṅgiṇī* was especially popular among performance traditions centered around *pārijāta* narratives. See Davesh Soneji, "Performing Satyabhāmā: Text, Context, Memory and Mimesis in Telugu-Speaking South India" (Ph.D. diss., McGill University, 2004), 54–55.

with Śaiva ties.[42] And third, both can be connected with the Sanskrit intellectual life of the Banaras region. Nārāyaṇa Tīrtha, pupil of Śivarāmatīrtha, wrote a primer on Mīmāṁsā, the *Bhāṭṭabhāṣāprakāśikā*, and was supposed to have been the Mīmāṁsā teacher of Nīlakaṇṭha Caturdhara, the Banaras-based commentator on the *Mahābhārata*.[43] Moreover, manuscripts of the *Kṛṣṇalīlātaraṅgiṇī*, with Sanskrit commentaries in Grantha script, have also been found in Banaras.[44] Nārāyaṇa Tīrtha, pupil of Rāmagōvinda Tīrtha, had a close relationship with Madhusūdana Sarasvatī. He quoted liberally from Madhusūdana's *Bhaktirasāyana* in his *Bhakticandrikā*, referring to him fondly as "the old man" (*vṛddha*) and "the teacher" (*ācārya*). He also wrote a commentary (*Laghuvyākhyā*) on Madhusūdana's Advaita work *Siddhāntabindu*, which was expanded upon by his student Gauḍa Brahmānanda, who also commented on Madhusūdana's *Advaitasiddhi*, suggesting a kind of teaching lineage. None of this means that either Nārāyaṇa Tīrtha was based in Banaras. We know of the *Kṛṣṇalīlātaraṅgiṇī*'s southern provenance, for instance. The author of the *Bhakticandrikā* was at least in the vicinity of Banaras. He composed his *Vēdastutivyākhyā* while living in Prayāga (*srītīrtharājakē*).[45] He was also very interested in responding to the challenge of Śrīvaiṣṇavism, though whether this was a particularly southern or northern problem is a debate I open up later.[46]

42 Nārāyaṇa Tīrtha, pupil of Śivarāmatīrtha, is said to have composed some Advaita works: the *Pañcīkaraṇavārtikavivaraṇa*, with the autocommentary *Dīpikā*, and the *Subōdhinī* subcommentary on the beginning of Śaṅkara's *Brahmasūtrabhāṣya*. According to Guruswamy Sastrigal's Tamil commentary on the *Kṛṣṇalīlātaraṅgiṇī*, Nārāyaṇa Tīrtha was referring to his preceptor Śivarāmatīrtha in the *Subōdhinī* by each word in his name: "Śiva" signifying nonduality (*advaitaṁ śivam*), the negation of difference; "Rāma" being the consciousness-self in which the liberated revel (*ramantē*); and "Tīrtha" being the holy place/person to which others belonging to the monastic community attend (*tīrthāgraṇīsēvitam*). See Natarajan, *Sri Krishna Leela Tarangini*, 105.

43 P. K. Gode, "Exact Date of the Advaitasudhā of Lakṣmaṇa Paṇḍita (A.D. 1663) and His Possible Identity with Lakṣmaṇārya, the Vedānta Teacher of Nīlakaṇṭha Caturdhara, the Commentator of the Mahābhārata," in *Studies in Indian Literary History*, vol. 3 (Poona: Prof. P. K. Gode Collected Works Publication Committee, 1956), 53.

44 See Raghavan, *The Power of the Sacred Name*, 81.

45 *Vedastuti Vyākhyā*, MS 3631, Shri Raghunath Temple MSS., Jammu, f. 16r (henceforth referred to as *Vēdastuti Vyākhyā*).

46 When it came to interreligious debate, challenges flew back and forth up and down the subcontinent. Madhusūdana Sarasvatī's *Advaitasiddhi* was written in response to the southern Mādhva Vyāsatīrtha's *Nyāyāmṛta*, which in turn sparked a series of public debates, ripostes, and conferences between Advaita and Dvaita partisans. See Madhav Deshpande, "Will the Winner Please Stand Up: Conflicting Narratives of a Seventeenth-Century Philosophical Debate from Karnataka," in *Knowing India: Colonial and Modern Constructions of the Past: Essays in Honor of Thomas R. Trautmann*, ed. Thomas Trautmann and Cynthia Talbot (New Delhi: Yoda Press, 2011), 366–380. That there was a rapid circulation of manuscripts and communication between Sanskrit intellectuals north and south by this time is evident from the fact that the Banarasi Mīmāṁsaka Ananta Bhaṭṭa personally sent a copy of his Mīmāṁsā work, the *Śāstramālāvyākhyāna*, to Nīlakaṇṭha Dīkṣita in Madurai for peer review. See Elaine Fisher, *Hindu Pluralism: Religion and the Public Sphere in Early Modern South India* (Oakland: University of California Press, 2017), 52.

I am interested in the relationship of this Nārāyaṇa Tīrtha with Madhusūdana Sarasvatī, the more famous exponent of what Adya Prasad Mishra called "Neo-Bhakti" in Advaita Vēdānta. At first blush, it may seem that Nārāyaṇa Tīrtha simply recapitulates his predecessor's thinking on the subject, but the differences warrant investigation. In his *Bhakticandrikā* commentary on *Bhakti Sūtra* 1.1.2, Nārāyaṇa Tīrtha raises an objection to the idea that *bhakti* is possible for Advaitins at all. If God is no different from the individual, says this opponent, it makes no sense for him to have *bhakti* toward himself. This is a common enough problem, but Nārāyaṇa Tīrtha's response veers into uncharted territory:

Reply: You are confused. *Bhakti* is a particular kind of love. Non-dualist *jñāna* offers no obstruction to it.

Objection: But isn't knowledge of God's grandeur [*māhātmya*] the cause of *bhakti*? If we cannot differentiate God, who always achieves his aims, from the individual, who consistently misses the mark and possesses innumerable flaws, then to deny God's grandeur is to vitiate the possibility of *bhakti*, which requires that one understand it.

Reply: You've completely missed the point. "Grandeur" means a preponderance of good qualities, which in turn means truth, knowledge and joy, as we understand from *Brahma Sūtra* 3.3.12. Advaita does not simply constitute the plenitude that is one's own nature. Therefore, non-dualist *jñāna*, by way of the knowledge of grandeur, is itself the cause of utterly satisfactory love for that undifferentiated object. So how can it obstruct *bhakti*? Let us say that qualities like achieving one's aim without obstruction are part of the everyday empirical world, since they are based on the constituent element of creation known as *sattva*. As such, they would only conditionally belong to God, who must be defined as different from the individual human being. Nevertheless, knowledge of God's grandeur is still not annulled for Advaitins. Rather, that love which, assisted by the unseen traces of previous lives, begins with desolation [*hāni*] and culminates in dissolution [*galita*],[47] causes one to forget everything in the everyday world. The only qualitative difference between pure awakening and *bhakti* is

[47] Nārāyaṇa Tīrtha refers here to his previous breakdown of *prēma*, or "love," into fifteen stages: *upta, patta, lalita, milita, kalita, chalita, calita, krānta, vikrānta, saṁkrānta, vihṛta*, [*saṁhṛta*, which he inexplicably fails to discuss], *galita*, and *saṁtṛpta*. As far as I can tell, this typology bears no resemblance to any other. Future scholars may be able to identify its precedents.

that in the former, distractions like hunger remain, while in the latter, they too disappear.[48]

Until this point in his commentary, Nārāyaṇa Tīrtha has been reconstructing almost verbatim a passage from Madhusūdana's *Bhaktirasāyana* (1.7). Here, however, he appears to import a completely different discussion, absent from Madhusūdana's treatise, about the knowledge of God's grandeur (*māhātmya*), a definition of *bhakti* found in Madhva's *Bhāratatātparyanirṇaya* (1.85) and referred to later by Vallabhācārya and the Gōsvāmīs.[49] The fact that Nārāyaṇa Tīrtha quoted this definition at all exemplifies his departure from Madhusūdana, who eschewed discussion of God's *māhātmya* entirely.[50] Most striking, he rereads nondualist *jñāna* as being totally subordinate to *bhakti*. Even Madhusūdana does not go this far. He accords analogous, non-intersecting spaces to *jñāna* and *bhakti*. In his view, there are those who prefer (and are capable of) attaining liberation through knowledge, while others prefer absorption in divine love. In this respect Madhusūdana is unorthodox, no doubt, but not as radical as some

[48] *Bhakticandrikā*, 27: *nanv asmin matē katham paramātmani bhaktiḥ sambhavati? jīvābhinnē tasmin svasminn ēva bhaktyayōgāt. na hi svasminn ēva bhaktir upapadyata iti cēt. bhrāntō'si; snēhaviśēṣarūpāyāṁ bhaktāv advaitajñānasyāpratibandhakatvāt. nanu māhātmyajñānaṁ bhaktau kāraṇam asatyasaṅkalpādyanēkadōṣāśrayajīvābhēdē ca paramātmanas tatprasaktyā satyasaṅkalpatvādimāhātmyasya bādhēna tadbhānapūrvā bhaktiḥ pratibadhyēta ēva iti cēt. abhiprāyam ajñātavān asi. yatō māhātmyaṁ guṇagarimā guṇāś ca "ānandādayaḥ pradhānasya" iti nyāyēna satyajñānānandāḥ, na tu pūrṇatvādayaḥ svarūpātmakā ēvādvaitaghaṭitā ity advaitajñānaṁ māhātmyajñānavidhayā'khaṇḍārthē santṛptaprēmṇi kāraṇam ēva iti tat kathaṁ bhaktau pratibandhaṁ syāt. satyasaṅkalpādayas tu guṇāḥ sāttvikaprakṛtimūlatayā vyāvahārikā apy upādhinā jīvād bhinna ēva īśē abhimatā iti, tatrāpi māhātmyasya bādhō na sambhavaty advaitinām. api tu hānipūrvikā galitāntā prītiḥ saṁskārādṛṣṭasacivā yā punaḥ prapañcajātam ēva vismārayati. iyāṁs tu viśēṣaḥ kēvalabōdhē'śanādivikṣēpō na nivartatē, bhaktau sō'pi nivartata iti.*

[49] Madhva defines *bhakti* as "a firm love beyond everything else, predicated on knowing God's grandeur. That's what leads to liberation and nothing else." See *Sarvamūlagranthāḥ*, vol. 4, ed. K. T. Pandurangi and Vidwan Krishnacharya Upadhyaya (Bangalore: Dvaita Vedanta Studies and Research Foundation, 2011), 11:

> *māhātmyajñānapūrvas tu sudṛḍhaḥ sarvatō'dhikaḥ*
> *snēhō bhaktir iti prōktaḥ tayā muktir na cānyathā.*

Vallabha cites this verse in his *Tattvārthadīpa*. See Dasgupta, *A History of Indian Philosophy*, vol. 4, 347, n. 1. Rūpa and Jīva Gōsvāmī cite it with variations in the *Bhaktirasāmṛtasindhu* and *Prītisandarbha*, respectively.

[50] See Nelson, "The Ontology of *Bhakti*," 382: "He must of course specify what he means here by 'knowledge of the Lord.' Is it reverent awareness of God's greatness (*māhātmya-jñāna*), as in Vallabha's definition of *bhakti*? Although such an understanding of knowledge might be expected in a devotional treatise, it is not what Madhusūdana has in mind." Gianni Pellegrino claims that, based on his commentary on the *Saṁkṣēpaśārīraka* of Sarvajñātman (2.51, 1.62, and 1.220), Madhusūdana knew of Vallabha's works. See Gianni Pellegrino, "'Old Is Gold!' Madhusūdana's Way of Referring to Earlier Textual Tradition," *Journal of Indian Philosophy* 43.2–3 (2015): 283, n. 15. However, a brief perusal of the verses in question yields no evidence to support this claim.

previous commentators have suggested. There are some instances where Madhusūdana appears to valorize *bhakti* over *jñāna*.[51] The first instance is in his commentary on *Bhaktirasāyana* 1.32–34, where Madhusūdana claims that *bhakti* is "predicated on knowledge *qua* disenchantment" (*jñānavairāgyapūrvikā*). Lance Nelson believes that this definition of *jñāna* is "clearly the Advaitins' direct realization of Brahman." He adduces further proof from Madhusūdana's typology of the eleven "grounds" (*bhūmikā*) of *bhakti*, of which the "understanding of one's true nature" (*svarūpādhigati*) forms only the sixth. Finally, he asserts that Madhusūdana's definition of the "knowledge of the Lord" (*prabōdha*) that precedes the highest levels of *bhakti* "retains all the characteristics of the Advaitins' realization of the Supreme."[52]

However, it is not clear that what Madhusūdana means by "knowledge" in these contexts (either *jñāna*, *adhigati*, or *prabōdha*) is the immediate realization of the nondual Ātman that results in liberation. In the first instance, his descriptions suggest that *jñāna* is an intellectual or existential understanding of the transient illusoriness of the phenomenal world and the truth of God's nondual reality. This is nothing but disenchantment, which gives rise to *bhakti*. This would accord with Śaṅkara's description of the stage to liberation called the "arising of knowledge" (*jñānōtpatti*). This is the second stop on the path, preceded by purity of being, achieved by performing the *āśrama* practices and followed by their renunciation. "Clearly," comments Aleksandar Uskokov, "*jñānotpatti* does not stand for knowing oneself as Brahman, but is intimately related to the status of ritual and *āśrama* duties."[53] Instead, knowledge of this sort is equivalent to disenchantment, as the definition of *bhakti* would have it. Second, on the eleven stages of *bhakti*, the mention of "understanding one's own nature" as the sixth need not be "practically the same as the *Brahma-vidyā* of the Advaita school."[54] Madhusūdana does use the word *sākṣātkāra*, the "direct apprehension" of the Ātman, in referring to this stage, but the term is qualified with the clause "as being distinct from the gross and subtle bodies" (*sthūlasūkṣmadēhadvayātiriktatvēna*). This could very well be a propaedeutic technique, preparing the groundwork for, but not actually culminating in, nondual knowledge. His language is ambiguous enough to allow for a similar distinction between the

[51] *Śrībhagavadbhaktirasāyanam*, ed. Gosvami Damodar Shastri (Kāśī: Acyutagranthamālā, 1927), 41–60.

[52] Nelson, "Bhakti in Advaita Vedānta," 190–198; Nelson, "The Ontology of *Bhakti*," 383.

[53] Aleksandar Uskokov, "Deciphering the Hidden Meaning: Scripture and the Hermeneutics of Liberation in Early Advaita Vedānta" (Ph.D. diss., University of Chicago, 2018), 360.

[54] Gupta, *Advaita Vedānta and Vaiṣṇavism*, 132.

existential understanding and phenomenological experience of nondual knowledge. Finally, Madhusūdana defines "knowledge of the Lord" as follows: "Everything other than Bhagavān, because it is transient, is false [*māyika*] like a dream. It is devoid of true significance, painful, and to be shunned. Bhagavān alone is real; He is the supreme Bliss, self-luminous, eternal, the one to be sought after. This is the kind of knowledge spoken of."[55] Nothing in this definition necessitates that such "knowledge" is anything more than an intellectual awareness that allows the devotee to attain true *bhakti*. This is not to say that it cannot be interpreted as experiential, but Madhusūdana seems to describe it as a propositional truth.

All this is to say that Nārāyaṇa Tīrtha is much more unambiguous, and he knows it. He directs his response at "the rash judgments of *certain Advaitins* who say that *bhakti* is incompatible with Advaita and only the prerogative of dualists."[56] According to Nārāyaṇa Tīrtha, the challenge of *bhakti* was not external but internal to the Advaita interpretive community. Notwithstanding the development of Advaita Vēdānta as a "large-tent" system of philosophical theology in early modern India, the example of Nārāyaṇa Tīrtha questions how coherent that community might have been.[57] He continues to challenge orthodoxies further on. In his commentary on *Bhakti Sūtra* 1.1.5, which asserts that *jñāna* is subordinate to *bhakti*, Nārāyaṇa Tīrtha redefines the very nature of liberation:

> In truth [*vastutas tu*],[58] even though ignorance is only destroyed by means of knowledge, that is not liberation, for insofar as it is a state other than joy and the absence of sorrow, it is not in and of itself a goal of human life. Rather, only love for God is, for it takes the form of joy, in being enveloped in the experience of one's own self-luminous inner joy. . . . In fact, attaining Brahman, too, is not beneficial for the human being if defined as the destruction of ignorance, but rather only when characterized by a distinctive love.[59]

[55] Translated in Nelson, "The Ontology of *Bhakti*," 383.

[56] *Bhakticandrikā*, 28: *tasmād advaitē bhaktir na sambhavatīti dvaitinām abhiprayōjanēti cādvaitināṁ kēṣāṁcid vacanam sāhasamātram*, italics mine.

[57] Cf. Minkowski, "Advaita Vedānta in Early Modern India," 223.

[58] See Yigal Bronner and Gary Tubb, "*Vastutas Tu*: Methodology and the New School of Sanskrit Poetics," *Journal of Indian Philosophy* 36.5 (2008): 619–632.

[59] *Bhakticandrikā*, 57: *vastutas tu jñānād ēvājñānanāśō yadyapi bhavati, tathāpi na sa mōkṣaḥ, sukhaduḥkhābhāvānyatvēna svatō'puruṣārthatvāt, kintu bhagavatprītir ēva tasyāḥ svaprakāśanijasukhasaṁvidāliṅgitatvēna sukharūpatvābhyupagamād . . . vastutō brahmāvāptir api nā'jñānanāśōpalakṣitā pumarthaḥ, kintu vijātīyaprēmōpalakṣitaiva.*

Nārāyaṇa Tīrtha says that only love for God is the goal of human life. He follows Madhusūdana in this respect. While early Nyāya philosophers defined liberation as the absence of suffering, later Naiyāyikas held that joy had a place in liberation. Madhusūdana Sarasvatī attacked this view in the *Bhaktirasāyana*, saying that it was much simpler to hold that joy on its own—and therefore *bhakti*—could be the aim of life.[60] However, in saying that love is the only thing that makes knowledge of nondual truth meaningful, Nārāyaṇa Tīrtha goes beyond his predecessor. Madhusūdana was ready to argue that *bhakti* is the highest goal of human life, independent from the Advaitic search for liberation. However, though they may be equivalent, they are not the same thing, and they do not intersect. *Bhakti* is not simply "*brahmavidyā* by any other name," says Madhusūdana. They are totally different with respect to the form they take, their respective means, their results, and their eligible agents. The result of *bhakti* is total love for God, whereas the result of *brahmavidyā* is the total removal of ignorance, the root of all evil. This does not mean, however, that the former *supersedes* the latter, as Nārāyaṇa Tīrtha seems to suggest.[61] Moreover, equivalence does not mean hierarchy, which is what Nārāyaṇa Tīrtha and the *Bhakti Sūtra*s urge. He sums up his argument with a worldly comparison:

> So it is proven that love alone—enveloped in God who is the experience of joy and achieved by knowing the truth—is the goal of human life, since it does not disappear even at the time of liberation. For it even surpasses knowledge. Consider a lover in the pangs of separation. Even when he experiences the thrill of his beloved's touch, that joy becomes beneficial only to him because he has desired it. Joy does not become beneficial to humans simply by being "known." That is why God became everything to the *gōpī*s, but not to wicked people like Duryōdhana.[62]

[60] Nelson, "Bhakti in Advaita Vedānta," 467, n. 56.

[61] See *Śrībhagavadbhaktirasāyanam*, 10–11. Cf. Nelson, "The Ontology of *Bhakti*," 379: "What Madhusūdana seems to be suggesting here is a homology, but not an identity, between the mental states associated with *bhakti* and *brahma-vidyā*. In orthodox Advaita, we have the *akhaṇḍākāracittavṛtti*, the 'mental mode taking on the form of the Undivided,' that leads to realization of Brahman and destruction of ignorance (and of itself). There is, Madhusūdana wants us to understand, a parallel structure in *bhakti*. . . . [B]oth *brahma-vidyā* and *bhakti* are evoked by scripture, Brahman-knowledge arising through the wellknown practice of the *śravana* ('hearing') of the great sayings of the Upaniṣads, *bhakti* through the 'hearing of the glories of the Blessed Lord' (*bhagavad-guṇa-śravaṇa*) from the scriptures of *bhakti*, preeminently the *BhP*."

[62] *Bhakticandrikā*, 59: *tasmāt siddham—muktikālē'py abādhāt tattvajñānasādhyaḥ sukhasaṁvidbhagavadāliṅgitaḥ prēmaiva pumartha iti. jñānād apy adhikatvāt. kāmukasya iva viraktasya api kāminīsaṁsparśajasukhānubhavē'pi iṣyamāṇatayā tatsukhasya kāmukaṁ praty ēva*

Joy, another word for God, is not meaningful because it is known but because it is cherished. Knowledge as such is incomplete. Even accomplished *jñānīs* are out of luck without *bhakti*. He elaborates on this idea in his *Vēdastutivyākhyā*, a commentary on selected stanzas from *Bhāgavata Purāṇa* 10.87: "Even those who have attained *jñāna* through the Vēdāntic method of hearing, reflecting, and meditating on the Upaniṣads do not achieve liberation without *bhakti* for God. This is because without God's favor, their mind is not prepared for liberation. With *bhakti*, however, they achieve liberation. No one disputes any of this."[63]

The expression "no one disagrees" (*na kasyāpi vivādaḥ*) was a kind of signature for Nārāyaṇa Tīrtha. It may have been his way to reconcile multiple conflicting interpretations both within and outside the Advaita camp. For someone who explicitly wanted to defend the relationship of *bhakti* with Advaita, Nārāyaṇa Tīrtha was quite willing to import other Vēdānta traditions into his commentary. In his commentary on *Bhakti Sūtra* 2.1.7, for example, Nārāyaṇa Tīrtha introduces an interpretation that he attributes to *śrīmadrāmānujācāryāḥ*, referring to the Śrīvaiṣṇava philosopher Rāmānuja with both the customary honorific plural and an honorable appellation. I believe this is the first historical mention of Rāmānuja in connection with the *Bhakti Sūtras*. This passage concerns the Viśiṣṭādvaita Vēdānta tradition's belief in the plurality of individual souls (*jīvas*) and the singularity of God (*īśvara*). Nārāyaṇa Tīrtha reconstructs the doctrine in dialectical fashion and concludes his own Advaita response with an interesting conciliatory note:

> The truth is [*vastutaḥ*], the Paramātman is the controller of all beings. He is, in other words, the Lord, defined by such terms as eternal knowledge. He is forever singular, abundantly furnished with characteristics such as compassion for his devotees, and referred to by names like Brahma, Viṣṇu, Śiva, Rāma, and Kṛṣṇa. The individual soul, for his part, who is part of God like a son is part of his father, is bound by the fetters of beginningless ignorance. Somehow, due to the merits he has accrued by performing all sorts of good deeds in past lives, and out of the desire to know the truth, he takes refuge in a true teacher. By worshipping the teacher as God himself, through his

puruṣārthatvāt. jñāyamānatvamātrēṇa sukhasya puruṣārthatvānabhyupagamāt. ata ēva bhagavān api gōpīnāṁ pumartha āsīt, na duṣṭaduryōdhanādīnām.

[63] *Vēdastuti Vyākhyā*, f. 10v: *śravaṇādipraṇāḍyā prāptajñānā api bhagavadbhaktiṁ vinā bhagavatprasādābhāvēna muktyupadhāyakadhiyō'saṁbhavān na mōkṣaṁ labhantē bhagavadbhaktau tu labhanta ēva tatprasādēna tādṛśadhiyā mōkṣa ityatra na kasyāpi vivādaḥ.*

> grace he directly apprehends his self. Once the bonds of ignorance have been loosened, he attains unity with God. In that state, there is not even a trace of phenomenal existence.
>
> Nobody disputes any of this. All of these debates over the imbrication of difference and non-difference, and the relative reality of the phenomenal world, are simply a nominal controversy. All thoughtful people should at least acknowledge that according to every school of thought, the world is not eternal, since it does not exist for one who is liberated.[64]

Nārāyaṇa Tīrtha's summary raises several questions beyond the immediate problem of whether the opponent in question is really Rāmānuja, an unlikely interlocutor given the virtual absence of engagement with the *Bhakti Sūtra*s among his followers. Why does Nārāyaṇa Tīrtha spend so much time on this issue? Why would he make an appeal to the *mukta*, the one who is liberated, in trying to reconcile Advaita with Viśiṣṭādvaita, when the very experience of liberation was a contested concept between the two schools?[65]

Nārāyaṇa Tīrtha also replies to the Śrīvaiṣṇavas in his commentary on Patañjali's *Yōga Sūtra* 1.24, which says, "God is a particular kind of person, untouched by suffering, actions, their results, and intentions." In a brief aside, Nārāyaṇa Tīrtha brings up the Viśiṣṭādvaita opposition to the Advaita theory that the difference between the individual and God is only conditional, not essential. "But some followers of Rāmānuja," he says, "misunderstand the author's intention as I have described it, simply latching on to the most obvious sense of words like 'particular' and giving it a completely different spin."[66] Did the new prominence of Śrīvaiṣṇavas in the *bhakti* traditions of northern India compel Nārāyaṇa Tīrtha to respond with his form of Advaitic theism?[67] Whoever his interlocutors were, Nārāyaṇa Tīrtha

[64] *Bhakticandrikā*, 119: *vastutaḥ paramātmā nityajñānādilakṣaṇō bhagavān sadaikarūpō bhaktavātsalyādyanēkaguṇōlbaṇaḥ brahmaviṣṇuśivanārāyaṇarāmakṛṣnādiśabdaiś ca vyapadēśyaḥ sarvajīvaniyantā, jīvas tu pituḥ putra iva tadaṁśō'nādyajñānapāśanibaddhaḥ kathañcit prāktanā'nēkaśubhādṛṣṭaphalād vividiṣayā sadgurvāśrayaṇēnēśabuddhyā tadbhajanēna tatkṛpayā svasya sākṣātkārād ajñānapāśanivṛttyā tatsāyujyam āpnōti, na tatra prapañcagandhō'pīty atra na kasyāpi vivāda iti bhēdābhēdānyatarāvalambanavādaḥ prapañcasatyatvamithyātvavādaś ca saṁjñākalahamātram. sarvamatē'pi prapañcasyānityatā muktasya prapañcābhāvād iti sudhībhir vibhāvanīyam.*

[65] See Christopher Framarin, "The Problem with Pretending: Rāmānuja's Arguments against *Jīvanmukti*," *Journal of Indian Philosophy* 37.4 (2009): 399–414.

[66] *Yōgasiddhāntacandrikā of Srinarayanatirtha*, ed. Vimala Karnatak (Varanasi: Chowkhamba Sanskrit Series, 2000), 32: *kēcit tu rāmānujānusāriṇa ittham abhiprāyam ajānantō viśēṣaśabdādisvārasyamātrēṇānyathābhāvam upavarṇayanti* (henceforth cited as *Yōgasiddhāntacandrikā*).

[67] See Hawley, *A Storm of Songs*, 99–147, 224–225.

was clearly aware of the other Vēdānta options around him. Although he derived most of his rhetoric on *bhaktirasa* from Madhusūdana Sarasvatī,[68] he elaborated on the Gauḍīya Vaiṣṇava distinction between types of *bhakti* and even quoted passages from Rūpa Gosvāmī's *Bhaktirasāmṛtasindhu*, referring to him as yet another older authority (*vṛddha*).[69] Like the Dēvas and Gōsvāmīs, Nārāyaṇa Tīrtha was drawing from a similar set of sources. He certainly knew of Lakṣmīdhara's *Bhagavannāmakaumudī*, as borne out by a long section in his commentary on *Bhakti Sūtra* 2.2.20 that recaps many of the arguments therein.[70] In an apparent rejection of classical Advaita teaching, couched in his commentary on *Bhakti Sūtra* 2.1.4, he argues that it is possible to have *bhakti* toward a God without attributes "because it is taught in Vēdānta that even in non-difference, there can be the relationship of attributes and the possessor of attributes, just like a snake and its coils. And this perspective of God having attributes comes to rest in his being without attributes, so the Advaita doctrine is not vitiated. Anyway, enough of that."[71] The herpetological simile refers to *Brahma Sūtra* 3.2.27: "But since both difference and non-difference are mentioned, the relationship is like that between the snake and its coil." In Śaṅkara's reading, this was a way to make sense of those times when the Upaniṣads referred to Brahman and the individual as different and nondifferent. When the Upaniṣads used the language of nondifference, it was like referring to a snake as a whole, whereas the language of difference was like referring to its different parts: a coil, a hood, length, and so forth. Nārāyaṇa Tīrtha, however, reads the *sūtra* as saying that even in nondifference, one can speak of the relation of attributes and their possessor. This reading steers close to that of Madhva, founder of the Dvaita tradition, who was the only one of all prior Vēdānta commentators who took this *sūtra* to refer to Brahman as both the qualities and possessor of qualities.[72] For an ostensible Advaitin, this is simply not cricket. One can sense a

[68] See his long extracts from the *Bhaktirasāyana* in *Bhakticandrikā*, 30–52, and his account of the aesthetic elements of *bhaktirasa* paired with his own illustrative verses on 63–68.

[69] *Bhakticandrikā*, 235–240. Cf. *The Bhaktirasāmṛtasindhu of Rūpa Gosvāmin*, trans. David L. Haberman (New Delhi: Indira Gandhi National Centre for the Arts and Motilal Banarsidass Publishers, 2003), 34–45 (1.2.74–118). These stanzas detail the *aṅgas*, or elements, of *bhakti*. Not all of them match between the two texts, but most interesting are the places where Nārāyaṇa Tīrtha replaces the word *kṛṣṇa* in the *Bhaktirasāmṛtasindhu* with the more neutral word *īśa*, e.g., *Bhaktirasāmṛtasindhu* 1.2.82ab: "Inability to bear hatred or slander of Kṛṣṇa/Īśa or his devotees."

[70] See *Bhakticandrikā*, 180–189.

[71] *Bhakticandrikā*, 78–79: *abhēdē'py ahikuṇḍalādivad guṇaguṇibhāvasya vēdāntē vyutpādanāt. sa cāyaṁ saguṇavādō nirguṇatvē viśrāmyatīti nādvaitasiddhāntabhaṅgōpīty āstāṁ vistaraḥ.*

[72] See Kiyokazu Okita, *Hindu Theology in Early Modern South Asia: The Rise of Devotionalism and the Politics of Genealogy* (Oxford: Oxford University Press, 2014), 234–236.

degree of nervousness in his insistence that this reading does not contradict Advaita doctrine.[73]

Nārāyaṇa Tīrtha saves his most drastic departure from Advaita tradition for the moment when he comments on *Bhakti Sūtra* 3.1.7 (itself a reference to *Brahma Sūtra* 3.2.37): "The results [of action] come from God, according to Bādarāyaṇa, because they are visible." To summarize this debate, an opponent argues that only *karma* gives people the results of their action; adding God to the equation is unnecessary. A third party interjects, saying that it is actually *karma* from a previous birth that gives people their present results. Consider the disparity between Yudhiṣṭhira's and Duryōdhana's experiences in the *Mahābhārata*. Bad things happen to good people and vice versa. Nārāyaṇa Tīrtha rejects each of these objections and asserts that God, independently, of his own volition, gives rise to all things. In an extraordinary departure from virtually all classical Vēdānta, he follows by saying that one need not even avoid the traditional accusation that God may be regarded as partial or cruel. He is referring to *Brahma Sūtra* 2.1.34, which serves as a kind of Vēdāntic theodicy. God, in this model, does not decide the fate of human beings, he simply dispenses the positive or negative consequences of each individual's action. However, for Nārāyaṇa Tīrtha, imputing partiality to God is a desirable consequence of this debate because difference is the natural state of affairs. After all, individuals are not the same; some are independent and others are not. A king who is partial does not stop being a king, unlike us, who presumably lose something of ourselves in the process. Nor does this mean that *karma* is meaningless, because (a) it operates within particular limits and (b) it prompts God to be either angry or pleased. Nārāyaṇa Tīrtha concludes his argument for God's partiality by citing Draupadī's famous speech to Yudhiṣṭhira in the *Mahābhārata* when they have been exiled from the kingdom to the forest. Frustrated by Yudhiṣṭhira's lack of accountability and his insistence that everything happens for a reason, Draupadī lashes out: "The arranger does not act towards beings like a mother or father. He is prompted as if by anger, just like everyone else."[74] Draupadī's withering, almost heretical critique of an absurd, fickle god is firmly shut down in

[73] Nārāyaṇa Tīrtha summarizes the means-end relationship between *saguṇa-* and *nirguṇa-bhakti* near the end of his commentary on the *Vēdastuti*, referring readers to the *Bhakticandrikā* for greater detail. See *Vēdastuti Vyākhyā*, f. 16v: *yathā cānayōḥ sādhyasādhanabhāvas tat(h)ōktaṁ śāṇḍilyasūtraṭīkāyāṁ bhakticandrikāyām asmābhir itīha saṁkṣēpaḥ.*

[74] *Mahābhārata* 3.31.37:

na mātṛpitṛvad rājan dhātā bhūtēṣu vartatē
rōṣād iva pravṛttō'yaṁ yathā'yam itarō janaḥ.

the epic, even if it leaves unsettling questions.[75] But here, it actually provides scriptural sanction for Nārāyaṇa Tīrtha's radical reenvisioning of Advaita Vēdānta.[76]

For Nārāyaṇa Tīrtha, the *Mahābhārata* was contested territory in more ways than one. *Bhakti Sūtra* 2.2.23 brings up the question of the extent to which subaltern castes are eligible to participate in *bhakti*: "All qualify including the despised, on account of it being passed down, just like universal [*dharma*]." In Nārāyaṇa Tīrtha's commentary, this raises questions regarding the very definition of caste, a topic regularly discussed by Naiyāyikas at the time.[77] An opponent argues that the very notion of *brāhmaṇatva*, Brahminness, cannot be determined based on birth (*jāti*), but rather is defined by one's qualities (*guṇa*). In support of this definition, he cites a dialogue between Yudhiṣṭhira and Nahuṣa in the same "forest" chapter of the *Mahābhārata*. In this dialogue, Yudhiṣṭhira tells Nahuṣa that caste is very difficult to figure out, given the total intermixture of castes (*varṇasaṁkara*). One had to foreground character (*śīla*) rather than birth. Nārāyaṇa Tīrtha rejects this "empty claim" (*riktaṁ vacanam*), quoting several normative Brahmanical texts to reassert that Brahmin-ness is based on birth alone.[78] The opponent's claim, of course, was not quite anti-essentialist. The *Mahābhārata* was obsessed with the problem of *varṇasaṁkara* and with delimiting the boundaries of an ideal social order. But in the seventeenth century, when Nārāyaṇa Tīrtha was writing, *varṇasaṁkara* seems to have provoked a different kind of anxiety. As I discussed in the previous chapter, the question "Who is a Brahmin?" was to be contextualized within the rise of subaltern castes in political orders under the Mughal aegis, their visibility in certain urban publics (such as Banaras), and the new social mobility afforded to heterogeneous scholarly and scribal communities that claimed upper-caste status. It is no surprise, then, that the same concerns should arise when it came to universality of *bhakti*, in spite of the fact that such an idea was articulated not in regional-language poetry but in the Sanskrit scholastic domain.

Other than this retrenchment of caste determinism, what are we to make of Nārāyaṇa Tīrtha's repeated departures from the norm? One possibility is that

[75] See Angelika Malinar, "Arguments of a Queen: Draupadī's Views on Kingship," in *Gender and Narrative in the* Mahābhārata, ed. Simon Brodbeck and Brian Black (London: Routledge, 2007), 86–88.

[76] This paragraph is a paraphrase of *Bhakticandrikā*, 252–255.

[77] See Samuel Wright, "History in the Abstract: 'Brahman-ness' and the Discipline of Nyāya in Seventeenth-Century Vārāṇasī," *Journal of Indian Philosophy* 44.5 (2016): 1041–1069.

[78] *Bhakticandrikā*, 196–198.

he was taking his predecessor Madhusūdana to a logical extreme, opening the floodgates to submerge nondual philosophy in religious devotion. But beyond the writings of his student Gauḍa Brahmānanda, we find little more extant work by Advaitins in this vein. Such an interpretation also focuses exclusively on the philosophical issues at stake instead of their historical context. A more likely explanation is that Nārāyaṇa belonged to a spectrum of early modern Vēdāntins who claimed a history of scholastic engagement with the *Bhāgavata Purāṇa* and other scriptures. This spectrum ranged between the Gauḍīya Vaiṣṇavas, the Vallabha Sampradāya, and, of course, Madhusūdana and his associates. Nārāyaṇa Tīrtha was at once indebted to and distinct from the broader Advaita world. He was one of a number of early modern Advaitins who adopted creative exegetical tactics to read *bhakti* practices from the *Bhāgavata Purāṇa* back into canonical texts like the Vedas.[79] Like Anantadēva, he took on Mīmāṁsā orthodoxy, dismissing a famous passage from Kumārila Bhaṭṭa's *Ślōkavārttika* that denied the existence of God.[80] And in his commentary on *Bhakti Sūtra* 2.2.25, he even paraphrased Anantadēva's *Bhaktinirṇaya* and used the Mīmāṁsā language of option theory to argue that either study of Vēdānta or *bhakti* for God could bring about liberation.[81] Nārāyaṇa Tīrtha was fully a participant in the *bhakti*-infused Mīmāṁsā and Advaita Vēdānta of his day, and added his unique, sometimes dissonant voice to the chorus.

Bhakti, *Yōga*, and the Beautiful Goddess

A significant feature of early modern Sanskrit intellectual history was the blurring of disciplinary boundaries. While Sanskrit intellectuals had always written widely across *śāstras*, seemingly without preference for one over another, it was the very reinscription of disciplinary boundaries in early

[79] See *Bhakticandrikā*, 86–91, where Nārāyaṇa Tīrtha finds precedents in the *Ṛg Vēda* for each of the nine forms of *bhakti* in the *Bhāgavata*. On the creative etymological approach adopted by the scholar Nīlakaṇṭha Caturdhara to elucidate the "hidden meaning" of Vedic mantras in the epics and *purāṇas*, see Christopher Minkowski, "Nīlakaṇṭha Caturdhara's *Mantrakāśīkhaṇḍa*," *Journal of the American Oriental Society* 122.2 (2002): 329–344, and Christopher Minkowski, "Nīlakaṇṭha Caturdhara and the Genre of Mantrarahasyaprakāśikā," in *Proceedings of the Second International Vedic Workshop*, ed. Y. Ikari (Kyoto, forthcoming). Nīlakaṇṭha owed his readings of the *Vēdastuti* to prior commentaries by Madhusūdana and Nārāyaṇa Tīrtha. See Christopher Minkowski, "The Vedastuti and Vedic Studies: Nīlakaṇṭha on Bhāgavata Purāṇa X.87," in *The Vedas: Texts, Langauge, Ritual*, ed. Arlo Griffiths and Jan E. M. Houben (Groningen: Egbert Forsten, 2004), 125–142.

[80] *Bhakticandrikā*, 139–140.

[81] *Bhakticandrikā*, 215–217. Cf. *Bhaktinirṇaya*, 38–46.

modern doxographical writing that made their mutual imbrication distinctive.[82] The seventeenth-century scholar Bhaṭṭōji Dīkṣita, for example, found his penchant for Advaita Vēdānta filtering into his works on grammar, and vice versa.[83] Kamalākara Bhaṭṭa wrote a series of essays on Mīmāṁsā that engaged with topics specific to Vēdānta. The sixteenth-century Vēdāntin Vijñānabhikṣu urged that Sāṁkhya, *yōga*, and Vēdānta constituted a single teaching.[84] This context helps make sense of Nārāyaṇa Tīrtha's incorporation of the theory of *bhakti* from the *Bhakti Sūtra*s into his commentary on Patañjali's *Yōga Sūtra*s, called the *Yōgasiddhāntacandrikā*. Nārāyaṇa Tīrtha's main project in the *Yōgasiddhāntacandrikā* was to reread the discipline of Patañjali's *yōga* as both indispensable and subordinate to Advaita Vēdānta. Drawing on a long history of the intersection of Advaita and *yōga*, Nārāyaṇa Tīrtha identified *samādhi*, or absorption, with the Advaitic practice of *nididhyāsana*, repeated meditation on one's unity with Brahman. He offered a set of fourteen *yōga*s that sequentially enabled one to come to know the Ātman. These *yōga*s began with Śaiva practices of ritual homologization and culminated in a Vaiṣṇava theology of loving devotion (*prēmabhaktiyōga*).[85] The *Yōgasiddhāntacandrikā* shows that Nārāyaṇa Tīrtha was attuned to a broader *yōga* world that ranged from Śākta Tantric practitioners to the Nāth tradition.[86] What concerns me here is how Nārāyaṇa Tīrtha incorporated the theology of the *Bhakticandrikā* into the *Yōga Sūtra*s, since it means that his attention to *bhakti* was not restricted to the genre of texts in which one may expect its appearance.

In *Yōgasiddhāntacandrikā* 1.23–32, Nārāyaṇa Tīrtha provides several indications that *bhakti* shaped his understanding of the *Yōga Sūtra*s. Across these *sūtra*s there are mentions of God and meditation on a single entity.

[82] See Nicholson, *Unifying Hinduism*, 144–164.

[83] See Jonathan Peterson, "The Language of Legitimacy and Decline: Grammar and the Recovery of Vedānta in Bhaṭṭoji Dīkṣita's *Tattvakaustubha*," *Journal of Indian Philosophy* 48.1 (2020): 23–47.

[84] See Nicholson, *Unifying Hinduism*, 108–123.

[85] See *Yōgasiddhāntacandrikā*, 2. The full list is *kriyāyōga*, *caryāyōga*, *karmayōga*, *haṭhayōga*, *mantrayōga*, *jñānayōga*, *advaitayōga*, *lakṣyayōga*, *brahmayōga*, *śivayōga*, *siddhiyōga*, *vāsanāyōga*, *layayōga*, *dhyānayōga*, and *prēmabhaktiyōga*. The manuscript from Mysore used for the edition contains glosses, perhaps added by a later copyist, that clarify what some of these *yōga*s entail: *advaitayōga* is understanding the purport of Vēdāntic statements about the nondual Supreme Self; *brahmayōga* is attention to the *nāda*, Brahman as sound; *śivayōga* is the general feeling of oneness with God; *siddhiyōga* is purifying one's veinal channels; *vāsanāyōga* is the desire for liberation, to know the truth of the Ātman; *layayōga* is the *samprajñāta samādhi* described in *Yōga Sūtra* 1.17–18; *dhyanayōga* is reflecting on the embodied form of Śiva, Viṣṇu, and other gods; and *prēmabhaktiyōga* is the uninterrupted flow of love, an exclusive consciousness of God's lotus feet.

[86] Jason Schwartz, "Parabrahman among the Yogins," *International Journal of Hindu Studies* 21.3 (2017): 379–382.

They turn out to be fertile ground for Nārāyaṇa Tīrtha to plant the seeds of *bhakti*. For example, *Yōga Sūtra* 1.23 prescribes "surrender to God" (*īśvarapraṇidhāna*). Nārāyaṇa Tīrtha explains, "Surrender is the means by which the heart is made to focus exclusively on someone; in other words, love, over and over again. The idea is that *samādhi* is available most effortlessly through *bhaktiyōga*, to be described further on, which involves understanding that what leads to love are things like worship through mantras and recitation."[87] A long excursus in his commentary on *Yōga Sūtra* 1.26, which says God was the teacher of the ancients (*pūrvēṣām api guruḥ*), defends the concept of *avatāras*, God's manifestations on earth, mirroring a discussion in his *Bhakticandrikā* on *Bhakti Sūtra* 2.2.29.[88] With liberal use of late sectarian scriptures like the *Rāma-*, *Gōpāla-*, *and Nṛsiṁha-Tāpinīya Upaniṣad*, Nārāyaṇa Tīrtha argues at length that figures like Rāma and Kṛṣṇa are not simply exalted individuals but the playful incarnations of the one supreme God. Interestingly, and perhaps pointing to his association with charismatic gurus, Nārāyaṇa Tīrtha also says that "great souls of the present day should also be regarded as such."[89] He goes on to taxonomize the *avatāras* according to the Pāñcarātra Āgamas, but unlike other Vaiṣṇavas who adopt the same system, he does not commit to the supremacy of Viṣṇu, and instead emphasizes that Śiva and Viṣṇu are on the same footing. In this he joined other early modern Advaitins like Anantadēva, who expressed the sentiment that "[t]hose who zealously put down either Śiva or Viṣṇu by elevating the other should not be considered devotees at all."[90] Nārāyaṇa Tīrtha's crucial discussion of *bhaktiyōga*, of *bhakti* as *yōga*, comes in his preface to *Yōga Sūtra* 1.32, which reads, "To prevent distractions, practice [concentrating on] a single truth." For Nārāyaṇa Tīrtha, "practice" is nothing but *bhakti*, and the "truth" to which it is directed is God:

[87] *Yōgasiddhāntacandrikā*, 26: *praṇidhīyatē tadēkamātraniṣṭhaṁ manaḥ kriyatē'nēnēti punaḥpunārūpaṁ prēma tatsādhanamantrajapārādhyatvajñānādirūpād vakṣyamāṇād bhaktiyōgād anāyāsēna āsannatamaḥ samādhilābhō bhavatītyarthaḥ*.

[88] See *Yōgasiddhāntacandrikā*, 35–40. Cf. *Bhakticandrikā*, 143–151.

[89] *Yōgasiddhāntacandrikā*, 38: *ēvam . . . ādhunikā api mahānubhāvā mantavyāḥ*.

[90] See *Bhaktinirṇaya*, 46: *yē tu viṣṇōr utkarṣēṇa śivāpakarṣābhinivēśinaḥ, yē ca śivōtkarṣēṇa viṣṇōr apakarṣābhinivēśinas tē ubhayē'pi na bhaktā iti mantavyam*. Also see Christopher Minkowski, "Nīlakaṇṭha's Mahābhārata," *Seminar* 608 (2010): 32–38, on Nīlakaṇṭha Caturdhara's assertion of why "partisan quarreling about the hierarchy of particular forms of the deity was misguided and harmful." And as we saw in Chapter 2, the one-time head of the Śaṅkara *maṭha* at Kāñcīpuram, Bōdhēndra Sarasvatī, wrote a tract that sought to abolish the hierarchy between Śiva and Viṣṇu, the *Hariharādvaitabhūṣaṇa*. He built on previous work by people like Appayya Dīkṣita, who composed hymns on multiple deities at the behest of religiously diverse patrons. See Yigal Bronner, "Singing to God, Educating the People: Appayya Dīkṣita and the Function of *Stotras*," *Journal of the American Oriental Society* 127.2 (2007): 113–130.

> It is only devotion to God [*bhajana*] that provides the greatest result, for "even a little bit of this *dharma* releases one from great fear" (*Bhagavad Gītā* 2.40). Just as a spark of fire, however tiny, becomes a blaze when fed by a clump of grass, and accomplishes every requisite effect, so too are the acts of devotion [*praṇidhāna*], even such minor ones as inadvertently uttering the name of God, capable of obliterating a host of sins, as they did for Ajāmila. And magnified by that very act of destruction, they become capable of accomplishing the heart's desire, when rounded out by faith and a longing for the object of devotion. Therefore, *praṇidhāna* alone is indispensable.[91]

Whereas previous commentators on the *Yōga Sūtra*s had identified the word *praṇidhāna* with *bhakti*, they usually restricted it to basic forms of worship or offering one's actions to God.[92] Nārāyaṇa Tīrtha, however, breaks down *praṇidhāna* into four types: preeminent (*paramamukhya*), principal (*mukhya*), subordinate (*mukhyajātīya*), and aspirational (*mukhyakalpa*). The first of these is nothing but love (*prēma*), the greatest exemplars of which are the *gōpī*s of the *Bhāgavata*. By hearing and singing God's glories, their hearts melted like a porous copper pot, transforming into an intense stream that flowed only to him, in fact conforming to his shape. This describes *prēmabhaktiyōga*, which Nārāyaṇa Tīrtha defines as "the uninterrupted flow of extreme, exclusive love for God's lotus feet." For those unable to achieve that, there are three progressively less intensive practices: *nididhyāsana* or meditation, acts of piety and fasting, and relinquishing the results of action and offering them to God. It is an open question how integral God was to the early *yōga* tradition. *Yōga Sūtra*s 1.23–26 suggest that God could be worshiped, embodied, and perhaps even capable of bestowing grace, having an active role in the world even if he was not its creator. For Nārāyaṇa Tīrtha, there is no doubt whatsoever. His primary sources of *bhakti* are the *Bhāgavata Purāṇa*, the *Bhagavad Gītā*, and several late theistic Upaniṣads.

[91] *Yōgasiddhāntacandrikā*, 49–50: *bhagavadbhajanasyaivāgnivādapūrṇasyāpy asya "svalpam apy asya dharmasya trāyatē mahatō bhayāt" iti vadatā bhagavatā mahāphalapratipādanāt. yathā'gnikōṇō'tisvalpō'pi tṛṇarāśiṁ jvālayaṁs tenaiva varddhitaḥ pūrṇaḥ sarvāṇi sūcitāni kāryāṇi janayati. tathā bhagavatō yathākathañcinnāmōccāraṇādirūpam api praṇidhānam ajāmilādēr iva pāparāśiṁ nāśayat tēna nāśēnaivādhikaṁ sampādyamānaṁ śraddhādinā pūrṇaṁ bhajanīya icchāsahakṛtaṁ sarvābhilaṣitaṁ sādhayati. tasmāt praṇidhānam ēvāvaśyakam.*

[92] Cf. Bhōja's *Rājamārtaṇḍa* commentary on *Yōga Sūtra* 1.23. *Yogasūtram by Maharṣipatañjali with Six Commentaries*, ed. Paṇḍit Ḍhuṇḍhirāj Śāstrī (Varanasi: Chaukhambha Sanskrit Sansthan, 1982), 28. See Christopher Chapple, "*Īśvarapraṇidhāna* and Bhakti," *Journal of Vaishnava Studies* 14.1 (2005): 29–42.

By invoking the "melted hearts" of the *gōpīs*, Nārāyaṇa Tīrtha was also probably referring to Madhusūdana's *Bhaktirasāyana*, which defines *bhakti* as the "transformation of a heart melted by devotion into a constant stream that flows toward the Lord of all."[93] But instead of according it a separate conceptual or generic space, he places it at the center of *yōga* practice, making *bhakti* constitutive of an entirely different system of knowledge.

If Nārāyaṇa Tīrtha's religious sensibilities complicate the binary between Śaivas and Vaiṣṇavas, we could attribute it to his inclination to play down sectarian conflict, like many other contemporary Advaitins. However, the *Bhakti Sūtras*' theory of *bhakti* was not confined to the Vaiṣṇava world at all. One of the handful of precolonial scholars to refer to the *Bhakti Sūtras* was Bhāskararāya (c. 1700–1775 CE), a Śākta theologian from Maharashtra who spent much of his life in the Tamil South. Bhāskararāya is famous for his writings on the Śrīvidyā Tantric tradition of goddess worship. His main works include the *Saubhāgyabhāskara* commentary on the *Lalitāsahasranāmastōtra*, the *Sētubandha* commentary on the *Nityāṣōḍaśikārṇava Tantra*, the *Guptavatī* commentary on the *Dēvī Māhātmya*, and the *Varivasyā Rahasya*, an important Śrīvidyā ritual manual. In a biography of his teacher, Bhāskararayā's student Umānandanātha describes how he began his career in Gujarat, vanquishing adherents of the Vallabha and Mādhva communities, before moving to the banks of the Kaveri River.[94] It is possible that this story was motivated by sectarian discontent. Puruṣōttama Pītāmbara, a follower of Vallabha from Surat, had written a tract denouncing the Śaiva ideology of Appayya Dīkṣita's *Śivatattvavivēka*. Whether or not Bhāskararāya actually participated in such debates, he was most certainly in the Śaiva-Śākta camp. Bhāskararāya mentions the *Bhakti Sūtras* a handful of times in the *Saubhāgyabhāskara* and the *Sētubandha*.[95] Although many of these references are perfunctory, a few stand out. In the *Lalitāsahasranāma* the "beautiful goddess" Lalitā is called a "lover of *bhakti*, attainable by *bhakti*,

[93] *Śrībhagavadbhaktirasāyanam*, 13:

> *drutasya bhagavaddharmād dharāvāhikatāṁ gatā*
> *sarvēśē manasō vṛttir bhaktir ity abhidhīyatē.*

[94] See *Varivasyārahasya by Śrī Bhāskararāya Makhin*, ed. S. Subrahmaṇya Śāstrī (Madras: Adyar Library and Research Centre, 1968 [1934]), xxv–xxvii.

[95] See *Śrīlalitāsahasranāmastotram with 'Saubhāgyabhāskara' by Bhāskararāya*, ed. Batukanathashastri Khiste and Shitala Prasada Upadhyaya (Varanasi: Sampurnanand Sanskrit University, 2003), 10, 88–89, 96, 181, 332 (henceforth cited as *Saubhāgyabhāskara*). Cf. *Nityāṣoḍaśikārṇavaḥ with the Commentary "Setubandha" by Bhāskararāya*, ed. Shitala Pradasa Upadhyaya (Varanasi: Sampurnanand Sanskrit University, 2005), 3, 61, 271, 308 (henceforth cited as *Sētubandha*).

and won over by *bhakti*." Commenting on these names, Bhāskararāya says, "*Bhakti* is of two kinds: primary and secondary. Primary *bhakti* is a particular transformation of the heart called 'love.' It has God as its object. As the *Bhaktisūtra* (1.1.2) says: 'That is supreme love for God.' The definite article 'that' signifies *bhakti*, as we understand from the first *sūtra*: 'Now, therefore, an inquiry into *bhakti*.' The word 'supreme' is an adjective for *bhakti*. 'Love' is being predicated on that specific type of supreme or rather primary *bhakti*. It is for that very reason, say earlier commentators, that 'the word "supreme" excludes secondary *bhakti*.'"[96]

Bhāskararāya is familiar not only with the *Bhakti Sūtras*, which he alternately calls the *Śāṇḍilya Sūtra* and the *Bhakti Mīmāṁsā*, but also with the broader discourse of Vaiṣṇava *bhakti*. He describes the everyday practices of secondary *bhakti* according to the "eightfold" typology of *Āditya* and *Garuḍa Purāṇas*, adding that the "ninefold" and "tenfold" typologies of the *Bhāgavata* and *Bṛhannāradīya Purāṇas* are not categorically distinct but are partial supplements (*avayutyānuvāda*). He also refers to a commentarial tradition on the *Bhakti Sūtras*, although it does not seem to be that of either Svapnēśvara or Nārāyaṇa Tīrtha.[97] It is possible that he was responding to some of his own Śaiva contemporaries. Nīlakaṇṭha Dīkṣita, for instance, defined *bhakti* as a synonym for *upāsanā*, the esoteric worship of a particular deity, that must be accompanied by the ritual techniques of the Śaiva Āgamas.[98] Bhāskararāya criticizes this definition, using the *Bhakti Sūtras* to bolster his argument: "Some say that worship [*upāsanā*] is simply love [*anurāga*] whose object is the deity. That is incorrect. Otherwise, the act of distinguishing *bhakti* from *upāsanā* in such injunctions as 'One infused with *bhakti* should perform worship' would make no sense. The word *bhakti* refers to nothing but *anurāga*. As it is said in *Bhakti Sūtra* 1.1.1–2: 'Now, therefore,

[96] See *Saubhāgyabhāskara*, 88: *bhaktir dvividhā mukhyā gauṇī cēti. tatrēśvaraviṣayakō'nurāgākhyaś cittavṛttiviśēṣō mukhyabhaktiḥ. tathā ca bhaktimīmāṁsāsūtram "sā parānuraktir īśvarē" iti. "athātō bhaktijijñāsā" iti sūtrōpāttā bhaktis tatpadārthaḥ. tasyāḥ parēti viśēṣaṇam. parāṁ mukhyāṁ bhaktiviśēṣam uddiśyānuraktir lakṣaṇatvēna vidhīyata iti tadarthaḥ. ata ēva parēti gauṇīṁ vyāvartayatīti bhāṣyam.*

[97] See, e.g., *Saubhāgyabhāskara*, 332. Bhāskararāya comments on the hemistich, "How can someone who does not sing this hymn become a devotee?" He interprets the different ways in which "singing" (*kīrtana*) works for different kinds of devotees, according to the taxonomy provided in *Bhagavad Gītā* 7.16. He attributes this interpretation to the "commentarial section beginning with *Bhakti Sūtra* 2.2.27," which says that "great sinners (qualify for *bhakti*) when in great pain." I do not find this mode of explication, or even a contextual reference to *Bhagavad Gītā* 7.16, in either Svapnēśvara's or Nārāyaṇa Tīrtha's commentary.

[98] Fisher, *Hindu Pluralism*, 74.

an inquiry into *bhakti*. That is supreme love for the Lord.' Therefore, *upāsanā* must be defined as an activity other than *anurāga*."[99]

In basic terms, these citations show that Bhāskararāya considered the *Bhakti Sūtras* relevant to his Śākta commentary. Like the Śaivas from Kerala we encountered in the first chapter, he treated Vaiṣṇava works as canonical sources. This was not so unusual for the time; his contemporary Kāśīnātha Bhaṭṭa reached for the *Bhakti Sūtras* to define *bhakti* for Śiva at the very beginning of his *Śivabhaktirasāyana*.[100] However, Bhāskararāya's most striking recognition of *bhakti* as a full-fledged system comes in the introduction to the *Sētubandha*. In this passage, Bhāskararāya provides an account of upper-caste education. To paraphrase: Bhāskararāya begins with a taxonomy of the *vidyās*, or knowledge systems, that God transmitted to people for the purpose of accomplishing the goals of human life. Each of these *vidyās* was intended for people with different intellectual and social abilities. They were also hierarchically structured. In brief, this educational sequence is as follows: Once a (male, twice-born) child is past the age of play, he should learn to read and recite the Sanskrit language (*akṣarābhyāsa*). In order to learn grammar (*chandas*), he is taught *belles lettres* (*kāvya*). Then comes the science of logic and epistemology (*nyāya*), which teaches him that the self is distinct from the body, mind, and so forth. In order to understand what constitutes his ritual and moral duty, *dharma*, he then studies the tradition of Vedic hermeneutics (*pūrvamīmāṁsā*). So far this educational scheme—literature, grammar, logic, and hermeneutics—matches what some called *vyutpatti*.[101] However, Bhāskararāya calls these systems "grounded in non-knowing" (*ajñānabhūmikā*). True knowledge, in good Vēdāntic terms, is the realization of Brahman and thereupon liberation. For this purpose, it helps to study the Upaniṣads and the *Brahma Sūtras* (*uttaramīmāṁsā*). According to the *Yōga Vāsiṣṭha*, these latter systems of true knowledge are divided

[99] See *Sētubandha*, 61: *dēvatāviṣayakō'nurāga ēvōpāsanēti kēcit. tan na. bhaktimān upāsītētyādividhau bhaktēr upāsanātō bhēdēna nirdēśānupapattēḥ. anurāgasyaiva bhaktipadavācyatvāt. "athātō bhaktijijñāsā" "sā parānuraktir īśvarē" iti śāṇḍilyasūtrāt. tasmāt anurāgavyāvṛttā kriyaivōpāsanā.* I am grateful to Eric Steinschneider for drawing my attention to this passage.

[100] *A Descriptive Catalogue of the Sanskrit Manuscripts in the Government Collection under the Care of the Royal Asiatic Society of Bengal*, vol. 8, ed. Chintaharan Chakravarti (Calcutta: Asiatic Society of Bengal, 1940), 617. Kāśīnātha also argued that the *Dēvībhāgavata* was the true *Bhāgavata Purāṇa*. See Christopher Minkowski, "I'll Wash Out Your Mouth with My Boot: A Guide to Philological Argument in Mughal-Era Banaras," in *Epic and Argument: Essays in Honor of Robert P. Goldman*, ed. Sheldon Pollock (Delhi: Manohar, 2010), 117–141.

[101] Sheldon Pollock, "The Social Aesthetic and Sanskrit Literary Theory," *Journal of Indian Philosophy* 29.1 (2001): 197–229.

into seven: the desire to know (*vividiṣā*), rumination (*vicāraṇā*), subtlety (*tanumānasā*), clarity (*sattvāpatti*), detachment (*asaṁsakti*), experiencing the object (*padārthabhāvinī*), and the sublime (*turyag*). Between the second and third stage and lasting until the fifth stage appears an important intermediary stage called *bhakti*. At this time, one studies the *Bhakti Sūtras* (*bhaktimīmāṁsā*). Only upon achieving *bhakti* does one directly experience Brahman (*aparōkṣānubhava*), and attain liberation after leaving the body (*vidēhakaivalya*). Progressive access to each of these states, however, is gained only after several lifetimes.[102] Bhāskararāya pauses to analyze the system he calls *bhakti*:

> Thus after serious effort put in over innumerable births, one is well-suited to gradually climb up to the stage of understanding the verbal truth of the Supreme Brahman. At this point, one develops a distinct degree of mental purity, such that one is neither excessively attached to nor utterly disdainful of *saṁsāra*. Such a person is eligible for the path of *bhakti*, as adumbrated in *Bhāgavata Purāṇa* 11.20.8: "Neither disgusted nor extremely attached, he achieves perfection through *bhaktiyōga*." That *bhakti* is of two kinds: secondary and primary. Secondary *bhakti* includes meditation, worship, recitation, and singing the names of the embodied Brahman [*saguṇa*], practices that can be combined wherever possible. Primary *bhakti*, however, is a particular kind of love that arises from that. Secondary *bhakti* also has several intermediate stages. . . . After progressing through each of these stages over several lifetimes, one develops secondary *bhakti* for the Beautiful Goddess of Triple City [*tripurasundarī*], and when well-established therein, one finally attains supreme *bhakti* for her.[103]

We find here another clear elaboration of the *bhaktimārga* so treasured by the *Bhāgavata* and its interpreters, repurposed to fit a particular Śākta intellectual and soteriological project. This rather uncontroversial, almost universalized discussion of *bhakti* immediately leads into Bhāskararāya's

[102] The preceding is a paraphrase of *Sētubandha*, 2–3.

[103] *Sētubandha*, 3–4: *tad ēvam aparimitair janmabhir mahatā prayatnēna parabrahmaṇaḥ śābdattvaniścayabhūmikāparyantaṁ kramēṇa samyagārūḍhasya saṁsārē nātyantam āsaktir nāpi dṛḍhō nirvēda ityākārikā vilakṣaṇā cittaśuddhiḥ sampadyatē. sō'yaṁ bhaktimārgē'dhikārī. "na nirviṇṇō na cā"saktō bhaktiyōgō'sya siddhidaḥ" iti vacanāt. sā ca bhaktir dvividhā—gauṇī parā cēti. tatrādyā saguṇasya brahmaṇō dhyānārcanajapanāmakīrtanādirūpā sambhavatsamuccayikā. parabhaktis tv ētajjanyānurāgaviśēṣarūpā. ādyāyā api bahavō'vāntarabhūmikāḥ . . . anēna kramēṇaitā bhūmikā anantair janmabhir ārūḍhasya paścāt tripurasundaryāṁ gauṇabhaktyudayas tatra samyaṅnirūḍhasya tasyāṁ parabhaktyudayā iti sthitiḥ.*

defense of the validity and efficacy of more specifically Śrīvidyā scriptural traditions and ritual practices. He goes on to specify the methods of worshiping the goddess (*sundaryupāsti*) in both internal and external formats (*antar-* and *bahiryāga*), which is the subject matter of the *Nityāṣōḍaśikārṇava*. Bhāskararāya also saw an intellectual continuity between his works; he refers often to the *Saubhāgyabhāskara* in his *Sētubandha* and divides *bhakti* into primary and secondary modes in both.

If not the culmination of all religious activity, *bhakti* was nevertheless integral to Bhāskararāya's Tantric worldview. Far away from the northern obsession with the beauty of Kr̥ṣṇa, Bhāskararāya was captivated by a different dazzling deity, the beautiful goddess of the South, Lalitā Tripurasundarī. So did *bhakti* find its way back south. Like A. K. Ramanujan's famous story about Aristotle's knife, it had changed hands and points a few times, but stayed more or less the same.[104]

Tying the Threads

I have shown in this chapter that the intersections between *bhakti* and Advaita Vēdānta in early modern India, at least in the Sanskrit scholastic world, were much more complex than mainstream histories of Indian philosophy and religion suggest. I focused on a text only recently made canonical, the *Bhakti Sūtra*s of Śāṇḍilya. Their hostility to the nondualist emphasis on knowledge notwithstanding, the *Bhakti Sūtras* became the object of study primarily among Advaitins themselves. I follow the career of one such commentator, Nārāyaṇa Tīrtha, and situate his occasionally radical claims about the primacy of *bhakti* in the context of the broader Advaita world and in his own diverse body of work. Nārāyaṇa Tīrtha shows affinity in turns for Advaita Vēdānta, Gauḍīya Vaiṣṇavism, and Śaiva Yōga. Perhaps these labels themselves have led us astray.[105] I demonstrate that these very

[104] See A. K. Ramanujan, "Three Hundred *Rāmāyaṇas*: Five Examples and Three Thoughts on Translation," in *The Collected Essays of A. K. Ramanujan*, ed. Vinay Dharwadker (New Delhi: Oxford University Press, 1999), 156.

[105] Cf. Lawrence McCrea, "Playing with the System: Fragmentation and Individualization in Late Pre-colonial Mīmāṁsā," *Journal of Indian Philosophy* 36.5 (2008): 576–577: "[T]he nature of the disciplinary and doctrinal commitments entailed by the choice to write within a particular 'system,' the range of variation in these commitments, and the way they changed over time, need to be seriously explored. It is really not at all clear, for our period or any other, what it means . . . to 'be' a Naiyāyika or a Mīmāṁsaka—what it implies about one's beliefs, one's writing and reading practices, and one's social, religious, and intellectual affiliations."

same discourses on *bhakti* became central to the South Indian Śrīvidyā practitioner Bhāskararāya. Here was yet another Advaita, embedded and embodied in the Śākta intellectual and ritual world of the Tamil South. Bhāskararāya presents another genealogy of Advaita and *bhakti* that has escaped historiographical attention.

There were many Advaitas, many Advaitins, and many *bhaktas* within the Sanskrit scholastic sphere in the seventeenth century and beyond. How their deliberations may have impacted or even been influenced by vernacular cultural and intellectual production is a question that deserves further investigation. Although it is difficult to substantiate hagiographical narratives about the relationship between Madhusūdana Sarasvatī and Tulsīdās, author of the Avadhi *Rāmcaritmānas*, it seems that at least a prominent member of the Rām Rasik vernacular devotional community, Mahant Rāmcaraṇdās (1760–1831 CE), was well-acquainted with these Sanskrit discussions about *bhakti*. With the help of the *paṇḍits* of Ayōdhyā, this early nineteenth-century exegete offered a theology of *bhakti* in his *Ānand Laharī*, a Hindi commentary on the *Rāmcaritmānas*, that bears close resemblance to the concerns of Madhusūdana and Nārāyaṇa Tīrtha.[106] He recapitulates a distinction we find in their works between the *Bhāgavata*'s "ninefold" *bhakti* and the more specialized *bhakti* of supreme love (*prēma*). Like his Sanskrit predecessors, he distinguishes this latter *bhakti* from those that are "mixed with action" (*karmamiśra*) and "mixed with knowledge and action" (*karmajñānamiśra*).[107] And although he uses the familiar pejorative "illusionist" (*māyāvādī*) to refer to certain Advaita factions, he cites many Sanskrit Advaita texts and may have even considered Advaita to be a Vaiṣṇava school of philosophy.[108] Similarly, the *Bhaktamāl* of Nābhādās (1600 CE), a text which, by the late nineteenth century, "had become a key ingredient in the nationalist-tinged Hindu devotionalism that would come to define modern Hinduism," pays obeisance not only to vernacular *bhakti* poets but also to famous exegetes of the Advaita Vēdānta tradition: Śaṅkara, Citsukha, Nṛsiṁhāraṇya, and Madhusūdana Sarasvatī, among others.[109] Writing on the cusp of a time

[106] See Vasudha Paramasivan, "Between Text and Sect: Early Nineteenth Century Shifts in the Theology of Ram" (Ph.D. diss., University of California Berkeley, 2010), 93–125.

[107] Paramasivan, "Between Text and Sect," 119. Cf. *Bhakticandrikā*, 162–163. This typology is first articulated in the *Bhāgavatamuktāphala* by Vōpadēva in the thirteenth century.

[108] Paramasivan, "Between Text and Sect," 116.

[109] See James Hare, "Contested Communities and the Re-imagination of Nābhādās' *Bhaktamāl*," in *Time, History and the Religious Imaginary in South Asia*, ed. Anne Murphy (London: Routledge: 2011), 162. Cf. Mishra, *The Development and Place of Bhakti in Śāṅkara Vedānta*, 6–7.

when other Vaiṣṇava intellectuals tried to exclude Advaita from among the representatives of a big-tent Hinduism by pointing to *bhakti* as "the only real religion of the Hindus," Rāmcaraṇdās occupies an unusual place in the history of ideas.[110]

This brief exploration of intellectual history on the margins of the classical returns us to our initial questions about historical method itself. My reading, like that of my predecessors, focuses on the content of these intellectuals' unique and often unprecedented arguments. However, my aim is not to account for either their consistency or inconsistency but to understand their writing in context. That context proves to be more complex and wide-ranging than the frame of philosophical "schools" allows us to comprehend. Perhaps a more genealogical approach to the history of Advaita would require us to revisit the very systematicity of the system. Instead of assuming the coherence of Advaita Vēdānta as a school of philosophy and singling out individual authors for their deviations from a norm, we might consider the tradition itself fragmented and fractured. Whether this means paying closer attention to premodern schisms between Smārta and Bhāgavata Advaitins, understanding the relationship between Vaiṣṇava and Śaiva Advaitins north and south, or offering our own analytical distinctions between classical and greater Advaita, we should become more expansive with the kinds of texts we are reading and the ways in which we read them.

[110] See Vasudha Dalmia, *The Nationalization of Hindu Traditions: Bhāratendu Hariśchandra and Nineteenth-Century Banaras* (New Delhi: Oxford University Press, 1997), 338–429. Consider also the "four-*sampradāy*" rubric, a genealogical narrative in which the sectarian traditions of Rāmānand, Keśav Bhaṭṭ Kāśmīrī, Caitanya, and Vallabhācārya found their ancestry in four Vaiṣṇava (i.e., non-Advaita) Vēdānta counterparts in the South. See Hawley, *A Storm of Songs*, 99–147.

Conclusion

Introduction

Each chapter in this book resolves an argument about the *Bhāgavata Purāṇa* in Indian intellectual history. In Chapter 1, I showed that there was a Śaiva reception of the *Bhāgavata* in medieval Kerala that has gone virtually unrecognized. I contextualized these Śaiva writers in the complex social order of their time and place. And I demonstrated that despite the uniqueness of their commentarial writings, they were connected to the later history of the *Bhāgavata*. I pursued one of these connections in Chapter 2 by studying the intellectual, social, and cultural history of the *Bhagavannāmakaumudī*, a book by one of the scholars from Kerala that cemented the *Bhāgavata*'s status as Veda by overturning centuries of hermeneutical precedent. I traced the *Kaumudī*'s journey up and down the subcontinent as it influenced the very different concerns of different religious communities. What these communities shared was the belief that repeating the divine name would remove all sins and prepare one for liberation. In Chapter 3, I explored how this *bhakti* trope shaped reflections about Brahmin identity in the writings of a single scholarly family, the Dēvas of Banaras. Originally from Maharashtra, the Dēvas incorporated *bhakti* into their writings across Sanskrit disciplines and in venues of public debate and performance. They were scholars and storytellers who, like the *Bhāgavata* itself, circulated in a wide social sphere. In Chapter 4, I argued that the *Bhāgavata* was enshrined as *śāstra*, a theoretical system, in the *Bhakti Sūtras*, likely written in the same circles. I showed that readers of the *Bhakti Sūtras* had complicated relationships with the disciplines in which they worked. I supported scholarly calls to revisit the concept of the system in Indian intellectual history and suggested that the tendency to evaluate authors as either faithful to or deviating from the doctrines of a school is more harmful than helpful in understanding their thought.

Another thread through the book's chapters was my search for scholarly life. I was interested in eliciting ways of being from the abstract genre of

Love in the Time of Scholarship. Anand Venkatkrishnan, Oxford University Press. © Oxford University Press 2024.
DOI: 10.1093/oso/9780197776636.003.0006

Sanskrit *śāstra* in order to understand the formation of Brahmin intellectuals beyond the self-contained system of elite education. Toward this end, I appealed to the concept of subtext in scholarly prose: signature expressions, playfulness, irascibility, winks and nudges. On occasion, I used this concept to find traces of nonelite, everyday religion in the cosmopolitan language of Sanskrit *śāstra*. In Chapter 1, I argued that both "high" and "low" forms of goddess worship in northern Kerala shaped a distinctive commentarial tradition. In Chapter 2, I suggested that the quotidian practice of singing the name of God urged a reappraisal of Sanskrit theories of scripture. In Chapter 3, I followed the social commentary of Marathi *bhakti* into the intellectual lives of the Brahmin elite of Banaras. In Chapter 4, I zeroed in on how *bhakti* as theory prompted some scholars to reimagine their relationship to *yōga*, Tantra, and Advaita Vēdānta. Whether or not I have been successful in my attempt to provincialize the history of Brahmin scholarship will depend on how this approach is taken up in the future.

When I first came to this project many years ago, the questions that I asked were mostly historiographical in nature, befitting my newfound identity as an intellectual historian. I was interested in problems in the study of Sanskrit knowledge. Studies of *śāstra* in late precolonial India had ignored religion; this was a problem. Histories of Indian philosophy had obsessed over doctrinal changes rather than hermeneutical innovations; this was a problem. Tales told about the *Bhāgavata Purāṇa* had sidelined Śaivism; this was a problem. This was a problem, that was a problem, from problems came other problems, until, to rephrase a Vedic *mantra*, only problems remained. I no longer think in terms of problems. Instead, I listen to the voices I hear in the scholastic record. They whisper possibilities. They speak of feelings not faded. They cast dissonant spells, fashioning a world beyond and within their words. They warn me: we are not so different, you and I. For this is now a study of scholarly life, which is to look into a mirror darkly.[1] The Dēvas, for example, seem awfully familiar. Like privately religious scholars, they struggled with the tension between material success and personal piety. Like members of any academic family, they wanted both to honor their heritage and to stake out their own positions. Like

[1] Cf. Constanze Güthenke, "Shop Talk: Reception Studies and Recent Work in the History of Scholarship," *Classical Receptions Journal* 1.1 (2009): 113: "A way of doing the history of scholarship that critically takes into account notions of authorship and of what image of the scholar and of scholarship we assume in the first place then ought to act as a necessary corrective to a kind of nostalgia for the scholar in communion with his or her object of study."

immigrants in search of new economic opportunities, they tried to maintain a sense of continuity with the culture of their origin. And like public intellectuals in the modern academy, they participated in a wide discursive sphere, while keeping in place the specialized language of scholarship and the social hierarchies of caste, class, and gender. My desire for contemporaneity, or rather anachronism, is reflected in my choices of translation, which are methodological choices. I have spoken of prestige, portfolios, and precarity; fun, freedom, and *philosophes*; textbooks, theory, and tenure. These are ways not only to overcome the soporific nature of Sanskrit *śāstra* but also to resist its self-appointed otherworldliness. There are, of course, more material ways to bring it to life: reading texts philologically alongside inscriptional records; understanding the circulation of texts within reading communities; researching manuscript economy; studying scribal practice; perusing family libraries, personal collections, and institutional memories.[2] I have brought the insights of social history to bear on this book. But I am interested in reading out from the text rather than back into it.

How we come to know something shapes what we say about it. I have wondered, more than argued, about how the scholars in this book came to know what they wrote about. My guide has been attention to prose style, to subtext and paratext, and to social spaces like monasteries, temple grounds, theaters, and city streets. Yet in the writing of this book, I have conformed to the very scholarly conventions I find so frustrating in *śāstra* by withdrawing myself from the text. Textual scholars have few opportunities to show their work, to pull back the illusory curtain of solitary, objective research and display everything that goes into what they write. But this is exactly what I want to know of the scholars in this book. If they are not so different from us, or we from them, then reflecting on the present is a reflection on the past. The following vignettes turn the lens back on myself and how I came to write this book. They concern each of the topics above—style, subtext, and space—with reference to my work. These stories begin, as with all my thinking, with the everyday life of the life of the mind.

[2] See Whitney Cox, *Modes of Philology in Medieval South India* (Leiden: Brill, 2017); Samuel Wright, *A Time of Novelty: Logic, Emotion, and Intellectual Life in Early Modern India* (New York: Oxford University Press, 2021); Jahnabi Barooah, "History from the Margins: Literary Culture and Manuscript Production in Western India in the Vernacular Millennium," *Manuscript Studies: A Journal of the Schoenberg Institute for Manuscript Studies* 6.2 (2022): 197–222; Dominik Wujastyk, "Rāmasubrahmaṇya's Manuscripts: Intellectual Networks in the Kaveri Delta, 1693–1922," in *Aspects of Manuscript Culture in South India*, ed. Saraju Rath (Leiden: Brill, 2012), 235–252.

The Elements of Style

Virginia Woolf once lamented that "Elizabethan prose, for all its beauty and bounty, was a very imperfect medium. It was almost incapable of fulfilling one of the offices of prose which is to make people talk, simply and naturally, about ordinary things."[3] Even if we recognize the exhortatory nature of Woolf's comment—that this is what prose *should* do—and her modernist desire to find the sublime in the ordinary, she could easily have been talking about Sanskrit prose. Sanskrit prose is of two types, literary and scholastic. Although there are few examples of the former, it has received more attention than the latter. Like most academic writing, Sanskrit scholarly prose often feels stolid and withdrawn. It was never theorized, only practiced. Yet its conventions did not emerge out of nowhere, nor did they stay the same. While I will not build toward a theory here, I do want to provide an example from my own life of what happens when one pays attention to prose style. The example comes from a paper I coauthored with the great Sanskritist Andrew Ollett on a literary commentary by Nārāyaṇa, who lived in Kerala in the seventeenth century.[4] Nārāyaṇa's commentary provides a rare glimpse of the life of Sanskrit scholarship and of what historians of science call "the importance of character both for historical research and as a key hermeneutical tool for historical analysis."[5]

My interest in Nārāyaṇa's character, however, cannot be separated from my own character. Coming to his writing was an accident of circumstance. When I was teaching Sanskrit at Harvard University, I agreed to read the *Bhagavadajjukam* with a graduate student interested in Pallava-period art. The *Bhagavadajjukam* was a satirical drama from the seventh century that poked fun at the allure of religion and sex. At the time I was going through the papers of Charles Lanman, professor of Sanskrit at Harvard from 1880 to 1926. Many of the Sanskrit books in Harvard's library were from Lanman's personal collection, including the 1925 edition of the *Bhagavadajjukam* with the commentary by Nārāyaṇa, presented to Lanman with the handwritten compliments of the editor, P. Anujan Achan. These material traces

[3] Virginia Woolf, "The Strange Elizabethans," in *The Second Common Reader*, ed. Andrew McNeillie (London: Harcourt, 1986 [1932]), 9. I am grateful to Max Bean for mentioning this passage to me.

[4] Andrew Ollett and Anand Venkatkrishnan, "Plumbing the Depths: Reading Bhavabhūti in Seventeenth-Century Kerala," *Asiatische Studien/Études Asiatiques* 76.3 (2022): 583–622.

[5] Projit Bihari Mukharji, "Truth as Materio-Moral Practice: *The Calling of History* for Histories of Science," *Comparative Studies of South Asia, Africa and the Middle East* 36.2 (2016): 356.

of gift-giving and scholarly fellowship were probably what made me reach out to Andrew in the first place. I needed his help to understand Nārāyaṇa's thinking, which became immediately more interesting than the play itself. Nārāyaṇa had an unusual take on the satire. Instead of reading it as a bawdy critique of religious hypocrites, Nārāyaṇa understood a deeper message hidden in the comedy. There was Vēdānta all over it, he said; you just had to read it the right way. What interested and confused me was how Nārāyaṇa tried to distinguish mainstream theories of secondary meaning from what he called "true meaning" or "inner meaning." This was more than just a redeployment of the fantastical etymologies that Vēdāntins liked to use to make the Vedas mean whatever they wanted them to mean. It was a thoughtful, if frustratingly brief, engagement with Sanskrit theories of literary meaning. It was also an irreducibly local reading, by which I mean an example of the regional quality of Sanskrit thought. In the context of literary commentary, Andrew and I have called this "the Kerala treatment." Obsessing over inner and deeper meanings was a hallmark of the Kerala treatment. Nārāyaṇa was not alone in finding new ways to read old texts. But he was unique in how he went about it. I read his commentary on the *Bhagavadajjukam* as an example of "deep reading" that drew from and contributed to concepts of inner meaning in contemporary traditions of Kerala stage performance. Figuring he had to have said more in his other surviving work, a commentary on Bhavabhūti's *Uttararāmacarita* (eighth century CE), I enlisted Andrew's help to read and appreciate Nārāyaṇa's sensitive reading. What we found over the next two years of reading together was more complicated and expansive.

Far from making Bhavabhūti a mouthpiece for Vēdānta, which would have been understandable, given the poet's playful use of philosophical language, Nārāyaṇa took an interest in the inner thoughts of the play's characters. He expounded on the emotional weight behind the smallest utterances: an interjection, a sigh, a lamentation. He thematized the intensity of characters' emotions, as they "plunged over and over again" (*nimajjanōnmajjana*) into their past experiences. He paused frequently at pregnant moments—sometimes literally, as in the first act when a pregnant Sītā sleeps on Rāma's chest—to tell us what was going on in a character's head. It was as if he were reliving the play, a play that is itself about reliving the past, as he was writing about it. To me, Nārāyaṇa's setups evoked the long *nirvahaṇam* or "flashback" on the occasion of a character's entrance in Kūṭiyāṭṭam performances of Sanskrit theater in Kerala. David Shulman speaks of the creation in Kūṭiyāṭṭam of "an entire world of visions, memories, wishes, fantasies, perceptions . . . obsessive projections, lost chunks of stories—everything, in short, that must have existed in the awareness of each of its characters and that can be conjured up by the actor as he shapes or kneads the empty space around him."[6] I was convinced that Nārāyaṇa was going to the theater every day, repeatedly plunging in and out of the dramatic space. The play was as heart-melting for Nārāyaṇa as it was for the characters. Nārāyaṇa was, simply, *in his feelings* about Bhavabhūti. The way he wrote gave it away. An entire world of visions and memories, everything that must have existed in his awareness, floated before me.

How do we assess scholarly life in Sanskrit culture? These are usually matters of social and cultural history. However, given the frequent absence of firm contextual evidence, I would like to encourage the study of style in scholastic prose. In the same way that poets have what Nārāyaṇa, alluding to Bhavabhūti's own words in *Mālatīmādhava* 1.10, called "signature expressions" (*vacanaprauḍhi*), scholars had style. Sometimes there is more in the subtext than context. Subtext is the place where the personal becomes public. Nārāyaṇa read subtext everywhere. He believed that to be a sensitive reader meant getting at the deeper meaning behind what an author was saying, a meaning that was simultaneously right before us. Is it possible for us to do the same?

Maybe it is if we start with ourselves. If I am in my feelings about returning life to scholarly prose, it is because I think that theory is actually feelings. In his memoir *Stay True*, for example, writer Hua Hsu takes a moment to tell a story about the writing of *The Gift* by the French sociologist Marcel Mauss. *The Gift* was originally published as an essay in a special issue of the journal *L'Année Sociologique* in 1923. The issue began with a long "In Memoriam" section that paid tribute to a generation of scholars who were lost in World War I. Mauss "projects into a future that never arrived," writes Hsu, "imagining 'what this would have become, if there had been no war' and his colleagues had continued living and working together. . . . [He] compels us to know them as thinkers as well as friends—to hold on to the possibilities of what could have been."[7] This counterfactual world of scholarly collaboration and the melancholy that accompanies it, Hsu continues, permeates the writing of *The Gift*:

[6] David Shulman, "Creating and Destroying the Universe in Twenty-Nine Nights," *New York Review of Books*, November 24, 2012, https://www.nybooks.com/daily/2012/11/24/creating-and-destroying-universe-twenty-nine-night/.

[7] Hua Hsu, *Stay True: A Memoir* (New York: Doubleday, 2022), 104.

> In this context, Mauss's idea of the gift takes on a new resonance. He's not just speculating about alternatives to market-driven systems of exchange; he dreams of an entirely different way of living. He is salvaging a lost world, trying to see through on a set of impossible potentialities. When Mauss turns his discussion of gifts to gestures of "generosity" or speaks of sitting together "around the common wealth," he is trying to remind us that there are other ways of being than of "economic man." That remnants of "another law, another economy and another mentality" survive alongside the ones we perceive to be inevitable and final.[8]

When I read *The Gift* as a graduate student, I never knew that Mauss was dreaming of a lost world and the one yet to come. I thought he was trying to punish me a hundred years later. But the meaning behind what he was saying was right before me. It isn't just that I didn't have the full context; I didn't have the eyes to see or the ears to listen. Nārāyaṇa showed me the way.

Subtext, Paratext, Intertext

Often the only things we know about a scholar are buried in the paratext. In the Sanskrit manuscript, there are no copyright pages, tables of contents, acknowledgments, footnotes, or indices. Instead, there are stanzas written at the beginning and end of the text, followed by a colophon, that provide some autobiographical or spatiotemporal information about the text's composition. Sometimes there are post-colophons written by the scribe that detail the circumstances of writing. These are valuable sources for the social history of intellectual life. Some have called them "depositories of emotion" that assign intellectual value to a manuscript within a reading community and generate affective relationships to the subject and the practice.[9] I have invoked a few paratexts in this book to illustrate different sensibilities: Anantadēva's memory of Maharashtra, Āpadēva's Vaiṣṇava zealousness, Raghunātha's repeated reference to his doctoral advisor, and so on. But subtext is about showing without telling. I have found evidence of life not only in the paratext but also in the intertext. Among the habits of scholarly prose left untheorized by Sanskrit scholars was intertextuality. There is a treasure for intellectual

[8] Hsu, *Stay True*, 104–105.
[9] Wright, *A Time of Novelty*, 189–190.

historians in the many allusions, adaptive reuses, and unattributed citations that permeate Sanskrit scholarship.[10] Although a concept does not need to be theorized to be recognized and applied, one wonders if the practice was so common as to be unremarkable. When the poet Murāri speaks of King Daśaratha's old age "that whitens the vicinity of his ears" in the *Anargharāghava* (1.15), he is referring to Kālidāsa's *Raghuvaṁśa* (12.2), yet none of the commentators picks up on it. When I read this passage with the scholar Vidwan H. V. Nagaraja Rao, however, he recognized the allusion instantly, brushing it off as if it were dust settling from the winter air in Mysore. It was a similar intertextual moment that led me to discover the alternative commentarial tradition on the *Bhāgavata* in Kerala. But the discovery was not mine alone. It was a family affair.

My parents do not really understand what I do, but they believe that my work has its own value, simply because I am the one doing it. I am by training a philologist, by accident an intellectual historian, and by temperament a peacemaker. The first identifies the materiality of a text, amassing physical evidence to reconstruct words and their meanings so that we become the best-informed readers possible. The second attends to changes in the history of ideas and approaches writers in the past with generosity in order to understand what they were doing in writing as they did. The third believes in pluralism, in intellectual and in social life, and works to build bridges between communities otherwise separated by belief and practice. At the university, this is called interdisciplinarity. At home they call it love. When I began a luxurious but lonely postdoctoral fellowship in Oxford, I wondered how I would keep these parts of myself together. Without the community of my colleagues in graduate school, I returned to what sustained my research in the first place: the encouragement of my family. Instead of engaging in our usual polite inquiries, I asked my mother if she would consider working with me on a new research project. A friend had photographed a Sanskrit manuscript for me from a library in southern India. It was the *Amṛtataraṅgiṇī*, Lakṣmīdhara's commentary on the *Bhāgavata*, which I discussed in Chapter 1. The manuscript was written in Grantha, a South Indian script once used widely by speakers of Tamil and Malayalam to write Sanskrit. I speak a very dialectal version of Malayalam-inflected Tamil but never learned to read or write either. My mother knows both but does not have

[10] See Elisa Freschi and Philipp A. Maas, eds., *Adaptive Reuse: Aspects of Creativity in South Asian Cultural History* (Wiesbaden: Harrassowitz, 2017).

the requisite level of expertise in Sanskrit. With our powers combined, and the help of a Grantha primer, we were able to move through the text much faster than I could have on my own. Because my mother lives in India, we had to conduct these sessions virtually. We met nearly every morning over the course of two months, perhaps the first people to read this text in the decades since it was catalogued.

We began by slowly analyzing the bare text: identifying the copyist's unique ligatures, applying punctuation for organizational purposes, differentiating the commentary on one verse from the next, and producing a working transcript. Along the way, we made notes on the content, comparing its style and substance with those of other major interpreters. It quickly became clear that the *Amṛtataraṅgiṇī* had a distinct interpretive take on the *Bhāgavata.* At the time I had been reading Rāghavānanda's commentary on the *Bhāgavata.* Suddenly, I began to find passages from the *Amṛtataraṅgiṇī* oddly familiar. They had been repeated verbatim by Rāghavānanda. His reuse of the commentary was more extensive and not always in agreement, but proved its regional importance. I formulated a case for the alternativeness of this commentarial tradition, and worked to answer the question that if it was a tradition, why it was overshadowed, and why it survived. The resulting chapter performed the basic task of revising the assumptions of current historiography. But it has been pared down to its argumentative core, stripped of serendipity and joy, my mother excised from the text. As an intellectual historian, I am often more concerned with the history of ideas than the ideas themselves. Why should my own case be any different? Why should I not be fully forthcoming about the conditions of my research, rather than leave its illocutionary effects for a future graduate student to reveal?

After all, my mother was no silent subaltern or native informant. She is a devotee of the same god celebrated by the *Bhāgavata,* knowledgeable in both the philosophical wisdom he teaches and the inscrutable tricks he plays. Though ours was a scholarly, not a spiritual exercise, she would bring out her tattered copy of the *Bhāgavata* to check against the commentary, supplying notes she had made over decades of attending religious lectures and remarking with surprise when Lakṣmīdhara failed to find certain verses of interest. These discussions oriented me to the many histories of the text's reception and to the interventions that Lakṣmīdhara thought it meaningful to make. Sometimes we discussed the finer points of methodology. When I obsessed over a corrupt reading, I heard a more insistent voice from the computer window, saying, "I am a pragmatist. Is it useful for you? Then okay.

Otherwise let's move on; I have tea on the stove." If I have not convinced her to take credit for coauthorship, it is because her distrust of publicity exceeds her desire for recognition. But she will not fail to remind you, and rightly, that she has literally fed my success. If you read my book subtextually, you will find love in the time of scholarship.

Location, Location, Location

Can I tell you a secret? I've never been to the Rājarājēśvaran temple in Taḷipparamba. The scene with which I began Chapter 1 was reconstructed from Kerala tourism videos and government survey publications. I can imagine being there; I've been to many places like it, from mainstream Śiva temples in the center of the state to popular goddess shrines on the coast to sacred groves in the northern forests. It was too important not to open with. As I read the works of Pūrṇasarasvatī and Rāghavānanda, I grew convinced that the intellectual hodgepodge demonstrated in their work, between Śaivism, Vaiṣṇavism, Advaita Vēdānta, literary theory, and goddess worship, was reflected in the social spaces they inhabited. The text, in other words, was an artifact of place. This should have been blindingly obvious. But I never would have come to this realization had I not been living in a place that obsessively memorialized the past.

In Oxford, you are literally walking on the dead. Bus routes curve around graveyards, chapels are littered with tombstones, and portraits and statues loom over you, looking as though they must fall, before they are squirreled away underground. Frustrated by my stagnating work, I turned to reading outside my field. At my partner's recommendation, I began *The Friend* by Alan Bray. Author of a celebrated book on homosexuality in Renaissance England, Bray turned his attention to the social and cultural history of friendship, and how religion may have facilitated rather than inhibited homosocial intimacy. As with many books in the Bodleian Library, I could read it only in situ. One afternoon, on the second floor of the rotunda of the Radcliffe Camera, I came across an image in *The Friend* of two monks buried together. The caption beneath the image of the memorial brass read, "In the chapel of Merton College, Oxford." I looked up from the book and out the window across from me, where I could see the towers of Merton College Chapel. I reshelved the book, walked outside, and within a few minutes was standing over the very tomb that Bray had described. It was a magical moment enabled, rather than constrained, by the weight of the past. Once I finished the book, I made a pilgrimage to the chapel of Christ's College, Cambridge, where *The Friend* begins as Bray's long-delayed attempt to make sense of a monument commemorating the joint burial of two men.

To see these images from the book in everyday life attuned me to the way a text is suffused with its surroundings. The cacophony of a Banaras street, the songs streaming from a Thanjavur stage, the shuffling of palm leaves in a Kerala monastery, all echo in the texts I have studied in this book. Social spaces are central to Sanskrit scholarship, as they are to mine: the thrilling possibility of a New York apartment, the loneliness of an Oxford college flat, the strange comfort of a Somerville attic, and the warmth of a Chicago sun room. The world is hidden in words.

Read Softly

One of my teachers once told me to "read hard." He wanted me to develop mastery, thoroughness, rigor, and other male-coded virtues, in the Sanskrit language. But my attitude to knowledge, like religion, is to wear it lightly. To take either of them too seriously is to deny oneself the scope for error, for frivolity, for furtive pleasures. The same goes for Sanskrit scholarship. To be dazzled by its virtuosity is to miss the darkness at the edges. In this book I have tried to peer into that darkness, the unknown and perhaps unknowable, to retrieve fragments of life, of lives that hover just beyond reach. I am not advocating for a return to a hermeneutics of suspicion at the expense of charity or respect. I mean something more like a hermeneutics of surprise: to allow oneself to be caught unaware by the multiple voices in the text.[11] Sometimes they lead you astray. Listen anyway. You might save a life.

[11] Cf. Eve Kosofsky Sedgwick, "Paranoid Reading and Reparative Reading: Or, You're So Paranoid, You Probably Think This Essay Is about You," in *Touching Feeling: Affect, Pedgaogy, Performativity*, ed. Eve Kosofsky Sedgwick (Durham: Duke University Press, 2003), 146: "[T]o a reparatively positioned reader, it can seem realistic and necessary to experience surprise. Because there can be terrible surprises, however, there can also be good ones."

Bibliography

Primary Sources

Advaitamakaranda. Edited by R. Krishnaswami Sastri. Srirangam: Vani Vilas Press, 1926.

Āgamaprāmāṇya. Edited by M. Narasimhachary. Baroda: Oriental Institute, 1976.

The Aphorisms of Śāṇḍilya with the Commentary of Swapneśwara. Edited by J. R. Ballantyne. Calcutta: Baptist Mission Press, 1861.

Arpaṇamīmāṁsā. MS 40 C.5, Adyar Library, Chennai.

Bhagavannāmakaumudī. Edited by Gosvami Damodar Sastri. Kāśī: Acyutagranthamālā, 1927.

Bhāgavata Purāṇa of Kṛṣṇa Dvaipāyana Vyāsa with Sanskrit Commentary Bhāvārthabodhinī of Śrīdhara Svāmin. Edited by J. L. Shastri. Delhi: Motilal Banarsidass, 1983.

Bhāgavata Vyākhyā (Amṛtataraṅgiṇī). MS. R. No. 2795, Government Oriental Manuscripts Library, Chennai.

Bhagavatsandarbha. Edited by Haridāsa Śāstrī. Vrindavan: Gadadhar Gaurahari Press, 1983.

The Bhaktirasāmṛtasindhu of Rūpa Gosvāmin. Edited and translated by David L. Haberman. New Delhi: Indira Gandhi National Centre for the Arts and Motilal Banarsidass Publishers, 2003.

Bhaktisandarbha. Edited by Haridāsa Śāstrī. Vrindavan: Gadadhar Gaurahari Press, 1985.

The Bhattadipika of Khandadeva with Prabhavali Commentary of Sambhu Bhatta. Vol. 1. Edited by N. S. Ananta Krishna Sastri. Bombay: Nirnaya Sagar, 1922.

The Bhattadipika of Khandadeva with Prabhavali Commentary of Sambhu Bhatta. Vol. 4. Edited by S. Subrahmanya Sastri. Delhi: Sri Satguru Publications, 1987 [Madras, 1952].

Bhāvaprakāśana of Śāradātanaya. Edited by Yadugiri Yatiraja Swami and K. S. Ramaswami Sastri. Baroda: Oriental Institute, 1968.

The Brahmasūtra-Shānkarbhāshyam with the Commentaries Bhāshya-Ratnaprabhā, Bhāmatī and Nyāyanirṇaya. Edited by Mahādeva Śāstrī Bakre. Revised edition. Wāsudev Laxmaṇ Śāstrī Paṇśīkar. Bombay: Nirnaya Sagar, 1934.

The Daśarūpaka of Dhanaṁjaya. Edited by T. Venkatacharya. Madras: The Adyar Library and Research Centre, 1969.

Dṛgdṛśyavivēkaḥ. Edited by K. Achyuta Poduval. Sri Ravi Varma Samskrita Grandhavali Vol. 6. Tripunithura: The Sanskrit College Committee, 1958.

Ēknāthī Bhāgavat. Edited by Vāsudev Lakṣmaṇśāstrī Paṇśīkar. Bombay: Nirnaya Sagar, 1925.

The Haṁsasandeśa. Edited by K. Sāmbaśiva Śāstrī. Trivandrum Sanskrit Series, No. 129. Trivandrum: Superintendent, Government Press, 1937.

Hariharādvaitabhūṣaṇam by Bodhendrasarasvatī. Edited by T. Chandrasekharan. Madras: Superintendent, Government Press, 1954.

The Harilīlāmṛtam by Śrī Bopadeva with a Commentary by Śrī Madhusūdana Saraswatī and Śrīmad Bhāgavata (First Śloka) with the Paramahaṁsapriyā Commentary by the Same Commentator. Edited by Parajuli Pandit Devi Datta Upadhyaya. Benares: Chowkhamba Sanskrit Series, 1933.

Kamalinīrājahaṁsa of Pūrṇasarasvatī. Trivandrum: The Superintendent, Government Press, 1947.

Kavīndracandrodaya. Edited by Har Dutt Sharma and M. M. Patkar. Poona: Oriental Book Agency, 1939.

Kavindracharya List. Edited by R. Ananta Krishna Sastry. Gaekwad's Oriental Series No. 17. Baroda: Central Library, 1921.
Kāvyētihāsasasaṅgraha. Pune: Mahādeva Ballaḷa Nāmajōśī, 1881.
Kṛṣṇasandarbha. Edited by Haridāsa Śāstrī. Vrindavan: Gadadhar Gaurahari Press, 1983.
Kulārṇava Tantra. Edited by Tārānātha Vidyāratna. Delhi: Motilal Banarsidass, 1965.
The Laghustuti of Srī Laghu Bhaṭṭāraka with the Commentary of Srī Rāghavānanda. Edited by T. Gaṇapati Sāstrī. Trivandrum: Superintendent, Government Press, 1917.
Mālatīmādhava of Bhavabhūti with the Rasamañjarī of Pūrṇasarasvatī. Edited by K. S. Mahādēva Śāstrī. Trivandrum Sanskrit Series No. 170. Trivandrum: Government Central Press, 1953.
The Manonurañjana Nāṭaka. Edited by Mangal Deva Shastri. Allahabad: The Superintendent Printing and Stationery, 1938.
Mathurāsētu. MS SAN 2638, British Library, London.
Mīmāṁsādarśana. Vol. 1B. Edited by V. G. Apte. Pune: Anandashrama Press, 1929.
Mīmāṁsākoṣaḥ. Part 4. Edited by Kevalānanda Saraswatī. Wai: Prajña Pāṭhashālā Maṇḍala Grantha Mālā, 1956.
Mīmāṁsākutūhala. Edited by P. N. Paṭṭābhirāma Śāstrī. Varanasi: Sampurnanand Sanskrit University, 1987.
Mīmāṁsā-Nyāya-Prakāśa by Āpadeva. Edited by Mahamahopadhyaya Vasudev Shastri Abhyankar. Pune: Bhandarkar Oriental Research Institute, 1972.
Mimansā Nyāya Prakāsa by Apadeva with a Commentary Called Bhattalankar by Pandit Ananta Deva. Edited by M. M. Sri Lakshmana Sastri. Benares: Vidya Vilas Press, 1921.
The Minor Poems of Nilakantha Dikshita. Srirangam: Vani Vilas Press, 1911.
Muktāphala of Vopadeva with Kaivalyadīpikā of Hemādri. Edited by Durgamohan Bhattacarya. Calcutta: Calcutta Oriental Press, 1944.
Nāmāmṛtarasāyanam. Edited by Deva Śaṅkara Śarmā. Tanjore: Poornachandrodayam Press, 1926.
Nāṭyaśāstra of Bharatamuni with the Commentary Abhinavabhāratī by Abhinavaguptācārya. Vol. 1, Revised. Edited by K. Krishnamoorthy. Vadodara: Oriental Institute, 1992.
Nityāṣoḍaśikārṇavaḥ with the Commentary "Setubandha" by Bhāskararāya. Edited by Shitala Prasada Upadhyaya. Varanasi: Sampurnanand Sanskrit University, 2005.
Nyāyamañjarī of Jayanta Bhaṭṭa. Edited by K. S. Varadacharya. Mysore: Oriental Research Institute, 1969.
Nyayaparishuddhi by Sri Venkatnath Sri Vedāntāchārya. Edited by Vidyabhūshan Lakshmanāchārya. Benares: Vidya Vilas Press, 1918.
Nyāyaratnadīpāvaliḥ by Ānandānubhava. Edited by V. Jagadisvara Sastrigal and V. R. Kalyanasundara Sastrigal. Madras: Government Oriental Manuscripts Library, 1961.
Nyāyasudhā. Edited by Pandit Mukunda Shastri. Benares: Vidya Vilasa Press, 1901.
Padyāvalī. Edited by S. K. De. Dacca: University of Dacca, 1934.
The Paramārthasāra of Bhagavad Ādisesha with the commentary of Rāghavānanda. Edited by T. Gaṇapati Sāstrī. Trivandrum: Travancore Government Press, 1911.
Pratyabhijñāhṛdaya of Kṣemarāja. Edited by J. C. Chatterji. KSTS No. 3. Srinagar: Kashmir Pratap Steam Press, 1911.
Prītisandarbha. Edited by Haridāsa Śāstrī. Vrindavan: Gadadhar Gaurahari Press, 1986.
Ṛgbhāṣyam. Edited by K. T. Pandurangi. Bangalore: Dvaita Vedanta Studies and Research Foundation, 1999.
Saṁkṣepaśārīrakam. Vol. 2. Edited by Hari Narayan Apte. Pune: Ānandāśrama Press, 1918.
Śāṇḍilya Bhakti Sūtra with Bhakticandrikā by Nārāyaṇa Tīrtha. Edited by Baladeva Upādhyāya. Varanasi: Varanaseya Sanskrit Vishvavidyalaya, 1967.
The Saraswatī Kaṇṭhābharaṇa by Dhāreshvara Bhojadeva. Edited by Paṇḍit Kedārnāth Śarmā and Wāsudev Laxmaṇ Śāstrī Paṇśīkar. Bombay: Nirnaya Sagar, 1934.
Sarvamūlagranthāḥ. Vol. 4. Edited by K. T. Pandurangi and Vidwan Krishnacharya Upadhyaya. Bangalore: Dvaita Vedanta Studies and Research Foundation, 2011.

Śāstradīpikā. Edited by Kiśoradāsa Svāmī. Vārāṇasī: Sādhuvelā Saṁskṛta Mahāvidyālaya, 1977.

Siddhāntatattvaṁ Nāma Vēdāntaprakaraṇam. Edited by Tailanga Rama Sastri. Benares: Government Sanskrit College, 1901.

The Sivastotravali of Utpaladevāchārya with the Sanskrit Commentary of Kṣemarāja. Edited by Rājānaka Lakṣmaṇa. Varanasi: The Chowkhamba Sanskrit Series Office, 1964.

The Smṛiti Kaustubha of Anant Deva. Edited by Vasudev Laxman Sastri Pansikar. Bombay: Nirnaya Sagar Press, 1931.

Sreemad Bhagavatam 10th Skandha Part 1, with the Commentary of Raghavananda Muni. Edited by M. B. Sankaranarayana Sastri. Trichur: The Mangalodayam Press, 1949.

Śrībhagavadbhaktirasāyanam Śrīmanmadhusūdanasarasvatīyativaraviracitam. Edited by Gosvami Damodar Shastri. Kāśī: Acyutagranthamālā, 1927.

Śrīdāsabōdha. Pune: Bhaṭ āṇi Maṇḍalī, 1915.

Srīharsha's Naishadhīyacharita. Edited by Pandit Śivadatta. Bombay: Nirnaya Sagar, 1912.

Śrīlalitāsahasranāmastotram with 'Saubhāgyabhāskara' by Bhāskararāya. Edited by Batukanathashastri Khiste and Shitala Prasada Upadhyaya. Varanasi: Sampurnanand Sanskrit University, 2003.

Śrīmadanantadēvaviracitaḥ Bhaktinirṇayaḥ. Edited by Ananta Shastri Phadke. Benares: Sanskrit College, 1937.

Śrīmadbhagavadgītā Ānandagiriviracitaṭīkāsaṁvalitaśāṅkarabhāṣyasamētā. Edited by Kāśīnātha Śāstrī Āgāśē. Pune: Anandashrama Press, 1896.

Śrīmadbhāgavatādyaślokatrayasya ṭīkā Śrīmanmadhusūdanasarasvatīkṛtā. Edited by Śrīyuktakṛṣṇagōpālabhakta. Kālikātā: Śrīyuktaramāramaṇabhakta, 1893.

Śrīmadbhāgavatam anēkavyākhyāsamalaṅkṛtam. Edited by Krishna Shankar Shastri. Ahmedabad: Śrībhāgavatavidyāpīṭha, 1965.

Śrīmad Bhāgavata Mahāpurāṇam. Edited by P. Radhakrishna Sarma. Tirupati: Tirumala Tirupati Devasthanam, 1989.

Śrīmadbhāgavatamahāpurāṇam: Mūlamātram. Gorakhpur: Gita Press, 1953.

Śrīmad Bhāgavataṁ Kṛṣṇapadīsamētam. Edited by Achyuta Poduval and C. Raman Nambiar. Sri Ravi Varma Samskrita Grandhavali No. 11. Tripunithura: Sanskrit College Committee, 1963.

Srimad Rahasyatrayasāra of Sri Vedanta Desika. Translated by M. R. Rajagopala Ayyangar. Kumbakonam: Agnihothram Ramanuja Thathachariar, 1956.

Śrīmad Rahasyatrayasāram of Śrī Vedānta Deśika. Translated by N. Raghunathan. Madras: The Samskrta Academy, 2018.

Srimad Vedanta Desika's Srimad Rahasya Trayasara with Sara Vistara (Commentary) by Uttamur T. Viraraghavacarya. Madras: Upayavētānta Krantamālai, 1980.

Śrīmukundamālā with Tātparyadīpikā of Rāghavānanda. Edited by K. Rama Pisharoti. Annamalainagar: Annamalai University, 1933.

Śrī Pāñcarātrarakṣā of Śrī Vedānta Deśika. Edited by M. Duraiswami Aiyangar and T. Venugopalacharya. Madras: The Adyar Library and Research Centre, 1967.

Śrīviṣṇupurāṇam śrīviṣṇucittīyākhyayā vyākhyayā sametam. Edited by Aṇṇaṅgarācārya. Kāñcīpuram: Granthamālā Kāryālaya, 1972.

Sri Visnusahasranama with the Bhashya of Sri Parasara Bhattar. Translated by A. Srinivasa Raghavan. Madras: Sri Visishtadvaita Pracharini Sabha, 1983.

Tantraratna. Vol. 3. Edited by T. V. Ramachandra Dikshita. Varanasi: Vārāṇaseya Saṁskṛta Viśvavidyālaya, 1963.

Tattvasandarbha. Edited by Haridāsa Śāstrī. Vrindavan: Gadadhar Gaurahari Press, 1982.

Upeya-Nāma-Viveka (Nāmārthaviveka) of Upaniṣad Brahmayogin. Edited by V. Raghavan. Madras: The Adyar Library and Research Centre, 1967.

The Uttararāmacharita of Bhavabhūti with the Commentary of Vīrarāghava. Edited by T. R. Ratnam Aiyar and Kāśīnātha Pāṇḍurang Parab. Bombay: Nirnaya Sagar, 1903.

Vedāntasāra of Sadānanda with the Commentary "Bālabodhinī" of Āpadeva. Srirangam: Vani Vilas Press, 1911.

The Vedāntasāra of Sadānanda, Together with the Commentaries of Nṛsiṁhasarasvatī and Rāmatīrtha. 5th edition. Edited by G. A. Jacob. Bombay: Nirnaya Sagar, 1934.
Vēdastuti Vyākhyā. MS 3631, Shri Raghunath Temple MSS., Jammu.
Viṣṇubhujaṅgaprayātastōtram. Edited by C. K. Raman Nambiar. Sri Ravi Varma Saṁskṛita Granthavali Vol. 1, No. 3. Tripunithura: The Sanskrit College Committee, 1953.
Viṣṇupurāṇa with Sanskrit Commentary of Sridharacharya. Vol. 1. Edited by Thanesh Chandra Upreti. Delhi: Parimal Publications, 1986.
The Vyavahāramayūkha of Bhaṭṭa Nīlakaṇṭha. Edited by P. V. Kane. Poona: Bhandarkar Oriental Research Institute, 1926.
Yogasiddhāntacandrikā of Srinarayanatirtha. Edited by Vimala Karnatak. Varanasi: Chowkhamba Sanskrit Series, 2000.
Yogasūtram by Maharṣipatañjali with Six Commentaries. Edited by Paṇḍit Ḍhuṇḍhirāj Śāstrī. Varanasi: Chaukhambha Sanskrit Sansthan, 1982.

Secondary Sources

Abbott, Justin E. *The Life of Eknāth*. Delhi: Motilal Banarsidass, 1981.
Adams, Sara M. "From Narasimha to Jagannātha: The Long Journey from Forest to Temple." *Journal of Vaishnava Studies* 17.1 (2008): 5–28.
Adluri, Sucharita. "Defining Śruti and Smṛti in Rāmānuja's Vedānta." *Journal of Vaishnava Studies* 15.1 (2006): 193–219.
Adluri, Sucharita. *Textual Authority in Classical Indian Thought: Rāmānuja and the Viṣṇu Purāṇa*. New York: Routledge, 2015.
Algazi, Gadi. "Scholars in Households: Refiguring the Learned Habitus, 1480–1550." *Science in Context* 16.1–2 (2003): 9–42.
Allen, Michael. "Dueling Dramas, Dueling Doxographies: The *Prabodhacandrodaya* and *Saṁkalpasūryodaya*." *Journal of Hindu Studies* 9.3 (2016): 273–297.
Allen, Michael. "Greater Advaita Vedānta: The Case of Sundardās." *Journal of Indian Philosophy* 48.1 (2020): 49–78.
Allen, Michael. *The Ocean of Inquiry: Niścaldās and the Premodern Origins of Modern Hinduism*. New York: Oxford University Press, 2022.
Allen, Michael. "Sītā's Shadow: Vedāntic Symbolism in the *Adhyātma-Rāmāyaṇa*." *Journal of Vaishnava Studies* 20.1 (2011): 81–102.
Ariav, Talia, and Naresh Keerthi. "Churning Selves: Intersecting Biographies in the *Nīlakaṇṭhavijaya*." *Cracow Indological Studies* 24.1 (2022): 29–60.
Arondekar, Anjali. *For the Record: On Sexuality and the Colonial Archive in India*. Durham: Duke University Press, 2009.
Ayrookuzhiel, Abraham. "Chinna Pulayan: The Dalit Teacher of Sankaracharya." In *The Emerging Dalit Identity: The Re-assertion of the Subalterns*, edited by Walter Fernandes, 63–80. New Delhi: Indian Social Institute, 1996.
Bakker, Hans. *Ayodhyā*. Part 1. Groningen: Egbert Forsten, 1986.
Bakker, Hans. "An Old Text of the Rāma Devotion: The *Agastyasaṁhitā*." In *Navonmeṣaḥ: Mahamahopadhyaya Gopinath Kaviraj Commemoration Volume*, edited by Gopinath Kaviraj, 300–306. Varanasi: M. M. Gopinah Kaviraj Centenary Celebration Committee, 1987.
Bakker, Hans. "Rāma Devotion in a Śaiva Holy Place." In *Patronage and Popularisation, Pilgrimage and Procession: Channels of Transcultural Translation and Transmission in Early Modern South* Asia, edited by Heidi Rika Maria Pauwels, 67–79. Wiesbaden: Harrassowitz Verlag, 2009.
Bakker, Hans. "Reflections on the Evolution of Rāma Devotion in the Light of Textual and Archeological Evidence." *Wiener Zeitschrift für die Kunde Südasiens* 31 (1987): 9–42.
Balasubramanian, R., ed. *Theistic Vedānta*. New Delhi: Centre for Studies in Civilizations, 2003.
Ballantyne, James. *Christianity Contrasted with Hindu Philosophy*. London: James Madden, 1858.

Bansat-Boudon, Lyne, and Kamalesha Datta Tripathi. *An Introduction to Tantric Philosophy: The Paramārthasāra of Abhinavagupta with the Commentary of Yogarāja*. London: Routledge, 2011.

Barooah, Jahnabi. "History from the Margins: Literary Culture and Manuscript Production in Western India in the Vernacular Millennium." *Manuscript Studies: A Journal of the Schoenberg Institute for Manuscript Studies* 6.2 (2022): 197–222.

Benson, James. "Śaṁkarabhaṭṭa's Family Chronicle: The Gādhivaṁśavarṇana." In *The Pandit: Traditional Scholarship in India*, edited by Axel Michaels, 105–118. New Delhi: Manohar, 2001.

Berkey, Jonathan. *The Transmission of Knowledge in Medieval Cairo: A Social History of Islamic Education*. Princeton: Princeton University Press, 1992.

Bhandarkar, R. G. *Vaiṣṇavism, Śaivism and Minor Religious Systems*. Strassburg: Trübner, 1913.

Bhattacharya, Dinesh Chandra. "Vāsudeva Sārvabhauma." *Indian Historical Quarterly* 16 (1940): 58–69.

Brett, Annabel. "What Is Intellectual History Now?" In *What Is History Now?*, edited by David Cannadine, 113–131. London: Palgrave Macmillan, 2002.

Brodbeck, Simon. *Krishna's Lineage: The Harivamsha of Vyāsa's Mahābhārata*. New York: Oxford University Press, 2019.

Bronkhorst, Johannes. *How the Brahmins Won: From Alexander to the Guptas*. Leiden: Brill, 2016.

Bronkhorst, Johannes, ed. *Mīmāṁsā and Vedānta: Interaction and Continuity*. Delhi: Motilal Banarsidass, 2007.

Bronkhorst, Johannes. "Vedānta as Mīmāṁsā." In *Mīmāṁsā and Vedānta: Interaction and Continuity*, edited by Johannes Bronkhorst, 1–91. Delhi: Motilal Banarsidass, 2007.

Bronner, Yigal. *Extreme Poetry: The South Asian Movement of Simultaneous Narration*. New York: Columbia University Press, 2010.

Bronner, Yigal. "Singing to God, Educating the People: Appayya Dīkṣita and the Function of *Stotras*." *Journal of the American Oriental Society* 127.2 (2007): 113–130.

Bronner, Yigal. "A Text with a Thesis: The *Rāmāyaṇa* from Appayya Dīkṣita's Receptive End." In *South Asian Texts in History: Critical Engagements with Sheldon Pollock*, edited by Yigal Bronner, Whitney Cox, and Lawrence McCrea, 45–63. Ann Arbor: Association for Asian Studies, 2011.

Bronner, Yigal, and Lawrence McCrea. *First Words, Last Words: New Theories for Reading Old Texts in Sixteenth-Century India*. New York: Oxford University Press, 2021.

Bronner, Yigal, and Gary Tubb. "*Vastutas tu*: Methodology and the New School of Sanskrit Poetics." *Journal of Indian Philosophy* 36.5 (2008): 619–632.

Broo, Mans. "The Vrindāvan Gosvāmins on Kīrtana." *Journal of Vaishnava Studies* 17.2 (2009): 57–71.

Brooks, Douglas Renfrew. *Auspicious Wisdom: The Texts and Traditions of Śrīvidyā Śākta Tantrism in South India*. Albany: State University of New York Press, 1992.

Bryant, Edwin F. "The Date and Provenance of the *Bhāgavata Purāṇa* and the Vaikuntha Perumal Temple." *Journal of Vaishnava Studies* 11.1 (2002): 51–80.

Buchta, David. "Baladeva Vidyābhūṣaṇa and the Vedāntic Refutation of Yoga." *Journal of Vaishnava Studies* 14.1 (2005): 181–208.

Buchta, David. "Defining Categories in Hindu Literature: The Purāṇas as Śruti in Baladeva Vidyābhūṣaṇa and Jīva Gosvāmi." *Journal of Vaishnava Studies* 15.1 (2006): 87–107.

Buchta, David. "Dependent Agency and Hierarchical Determinism in the Theology of Madhva." In *Free Will, Agency, and Selfhood in Indian Philosophy*, edited by Matthew R. Dasti and Edwin F. Bryant, 255–278. Oxford: Oxford University Press, 2014.

Burchett, Patton. "Bhakti Rhetoric in the Hagiography of 'Untouchable' Saints: Discerning Bhakti's Ambivalence on Caste and Brahminhood." *International Journal of Hindu Studies* 13.2 (2009): 115–141.

Burchett, Patton. *A Genealogy of Devotion:* Bhakti, *Tantra, Yoga, and Sufism in North India.* New York: Columbia University Press, 2019.

Burnell, A. C. *A Classified Index to the Sanskrit Mss. in the Palace at Tanjore.* London: Trübner & Co., 1880.

Carman, John, and Vasudha Narayanan. *The Tamil Veda: Piḷḷān's Interpretation of the Tiruvāymoḻi.* Chicago: University of Chicago Press, 1989.

Chakrabarty, Kunal. *Religious Process: The Puranas and the Making of a Regional Tradition.* New Delhi: Oxford University Press, 2001.

Chakravarti, Chintaharan, ed. *A Descriptive Catalogue of the Sanskrit Manuscripts in the Government Collection under the Care of the Royal Asiatic Society of Bengal.* Vol. 8. Calcutta: Asiatic Society of Bengal, 1940.

Chapple, Christopher. "*Īśvarapraṇidhāna* and Bhakti." *Journal of Vaishnava Studies* 14.1 (2005): 29–42.

Chartier, Roger. "Intellectual History or Sociocultural History? The French Trajectories." In *Modern European Intellectual History: Reappraisals and New Perspectives,* edited by Dominick LaCapra, 13–46. Ithaca: Cornell University Press, 1982.

Chatterjee, Nandini. *Negotiating Mughal Law: A Family of Landlords across Three Indian Empires.* Cambridge: Cambridge University Press, 2020.

Chettiarthodi, Rajendran. "A Scholar Poet from the Neighbouring Land: Uddaṇḍa Śāstrin's Perceptions of Kerala," *Cracow Indological Studies* 22.1 (2020): 73–94.

Clark, Matthew. *The Daśanāmī-Saṁnyāsīs: The Integration of Ascetic Lineages into an Order.* Leiden: Brill, 2006.

Clooney, Francis X. "*Devatādhikaraṇa*: A Theological Debate in the Mīmāṁsā-Vedānta Tradition." *Journal of Indian Philosophy* 16.3 (1988): 277–298.

Clooney, Francis X. "What's a God? The Quest for the Right Understanding of *devatā* in Brāhmaṇical Ritual Theory (*mīmāṁsā*)." *International Journal of Hindu Studies* 1.2 (1997): 337–385.

Clooney, Francis X. "Why the Veda Has No Author: Language as Ritual in Early Mīmāṁsā and Post-modern Theology." *Journal of the American Academy of Religion* 55.4 (1987): 659–684.

Coffey, John, and Alister Chapman. "Introduction: Intellectual History and the Return of Religion." In *Seeing Things Their Way: Intellectual History and the Return of Religion,* edited by Alister Chapman, John Coffey, and Brad S. Gregory, 1–23. Notre Dame: University of Notre Dame Press, 2009.

Colas, Gérard. "History of Vaiṣṇava Traditions: An Esquisse." In *The Blackwell Companion to Hinduism,* edited by Gavin Flood, 229–270. Oxford: Blackwell Publishing, 2003.

Coleman, Tracy. "Dharma, Yoga, and Viraha-Bhakti." In *The Archaeology of Bhakti I: Mathurā and Maturai, Back and Forth,* edited by Emmanuel Francis and Charlotte Schmid, 31–62. Pondicherry: Institut Français de Pondichéry; Paris: École Française d'Extrême-Orient, 2014.

Coleman, Tracy. "Viraha-Bhakti and Strīdharma: Re-reading the Story of Kṛṣṇa and the Gopīs in the *Harivaṁśa* and the *Bhāgavata Purāṇa*." *Journal of the American Oriental Society* 130.3 (2010): 385–412.

Collins, Randall. *The Sociology of Philosophies: A Global Theory of Intellectual Change.* Cambridge: Harvard University Press, 1999.

Cort, John. "Bhakti in the Early Jain Tradition: Understanding Devotional Religion in South Asia." *History of Religions* 42.1 (2002): 59–86.

Cox, Whitney. "Making a Tantra in Medieval South India: The Mahārthamañjarī and the Textual Culture of Cōla Cidambaram." Ph.D. diss, University of Chicago, 2006.

Cox, Whitney. *Modes of Philology in Medieval South India.* Leiden: Brill, 2017.

Cox, Whitney. "Purāṇic Transformations in Cola Cidambaram: The Cidambaramāhātmya and the Sūtasaṁhitā." In *Puṣpikā: Tracing Ancient India through Texts and Traditions,* vol. 1, edited by Nina Mirnig, Péter-Dániel Szánto, and Michael Williams, 25–48. Oxford: Oxbow Books, 2013.

Cox, Whitney. "Reading Jalhaṇa Reading Bilhaṇa: Literary Criticism in a Sanskrit Anthology." *Journal of the American Oriental Society* 141.4 (2021): 867–894.

Cox, Whitney. "A South Indian Śākta Cosmogony: An Annotated Translation of Selections from Maheśvarānanda's *Mahārthamañjarīparimala*, gāthās 19 and 20." *Journal of Indian Philosophy* 40.2 (2012): 199–218.

Dalmia, Vasudha. *The Nationalization of Hindu Traditions: Bhāratendu Hariśchandra and Nineteenth-Century Banaras*. Delhi: Oxford University Press, 1997.

Dasgupta, Surendranath. *History of Indian Philosophy*. Vol. 4. Cambridge: Cambridge University Press, 1961.

Dash, Siniruddha, ed. *New Catalogus Catalogorum*. Vol. 15. Madras: University of Madras, 2007.

De, Sushil Kumar. *Early History of the Vaisnava Faith and Movement in Bengal*. Calcutta: Firma K. L. Mukhopadhyay, 1961.

Delmonico, Neal. "Chaitanya Vaishnavism and the Holy Names." In *Krishna: A Sourcebook*, edited by Edwin F. Bryant, 549–575. Oxford: Oxford University Press, 2007.

Delmonico, Neal. "Sacred Rapture: A Study of the Religious Aesthetic of Rupa Gosvamin." Ph.D. diss., University of Chicago, 1990.

Deming, Wilbur S. *Rāmdās and the Rāmdāsīs*. New Delhi: Vintage Books, 1990 [1928].

Deshpande, Madhav. "Will the Winner Please Stand Up: Conflicting Narratives of a Seventeenth-Century Philosophical Debate from Karnataka." In *Knowing India: Colonial and Modern Constructions of the Past: Essays in Honor of Thomas Trautmann*, edited by Cynthia Talbot, 366–380. New Delhi: Yoda Press, 2011.

Deshpande, Prachi. *Creative Pasts: Historical Memory and Identity in Western India, 1700–1960*. New York: Columbia University Press, 2007.

De Simini, Florinda. *Of Gods and Books: Ritual and Knowledge Transmission in the Manuscript Cultures of Premodern India*. Berlin: De Gruyter, 2016.

Dhere, Ramchandra Chintaman. *Rise of a Folk God: Vitthal of Pandharpur*. Translated by Anne Feldhaus. Oxford: Oxford University Press, 2011.

Dikshitar, P. V. Sivarama. "Rāmatīrtha." In *Preceptors of Advaita*, edited by T. M. P. Mahadevan, 221–225. Secunderabad: Sri Kanchi Kamakoti Shankara Mandir, 1968.

Dimock, Edward, and Tony K. Stewart. *The Caitanya Caritāmṛta of Kṛṣṇadāsa Kavirāja: A Translation and Commentary*. Harvard Oriental Series 56. Cambridge: Harvard University Press, 1999.

Dodson, Michael. "Re-presented for the Pandits: James Ballantyne, 'Useful Knowledge,' and Sanskrit Scholarship in Benares College during the Mid-Nineteenth Century." *Modern Asian Studies* 36.2 (2002): 257–298.

Edgerton, Franklin. *The Mīmāṅsā Nyāya Prakāśa or Āpadevī*. Delhi: Sri Satguru Publications, 1986 [1929].

Eggeling, Julius. *Catalogue of the Sanskrit Manuscripts in the Library of the India Office*. London: Secretary of State of India in Council, 1887.

Elayavoor, Vanidas. *Lore and Legends of North Malabar: Selections from the Vadakkan Aitihyamala*. Translated by Ashvin Kumar. Kottayam: DC Books, 2016.

Eḷayāvūr, Vāṇidās. *Vaṭakkan Aitihyamāla*. Kottayam: Current Books, 1996.

Elkman, Stuart Mark. *Jiva Gosvamin's Tattvasandarbha: A Study on the Philosophical and Sectarian Development of the Gauḍīya Vaiṣṇava Movement*. Delhi: Motilal Banarsidass, 1986.

Endo, Ko. "The Works and Flourishing Period of Nārāyaṇa Tīrtha, the Author of the *Yogasiddhāntacandrikā*." *Sambhāṣā* 14 (1993): 41–60.

Eschmann, Anncharlott, Hermann Kulke, and Gaya Charan Tripathi. "The Formation of the Jagannātha Triad." In *The Cult of Jagannāth and the Regional Tradition of Orissa*, edited by Anncharlott Eschmann, Hermann Kulke, and Gaya Charan Tripathi, 167–196. New Delhi: Manohar Publications, 1978.

Farquhar, J. N. *An Outline of the Religious Literature of India*. London: Oxford University Press, 1920.

Fisher, Elaine. *Hindu Pluralism: Religion and the Public Sphere in Early Modern South India.* Oakland: University of California Press, 2017.

Fisher, Elaine. "Public Philology: Text Criticism and the Sectarianization of Hinduism in Early Modern South India." *South Asian History and Culture* 6.1 (2015): 50–69.

Flood, Gavin. "Śaiva and Tantric Religion." In *An Introduction to Hinduism*, edited by Gavin Flood, 148–173. Cambridge: Cambridge University Press, 1996.

Framarin, Chrisopher. "The Problem with Pretending: Rāmānuja's Arguments against *Jīvanmukti*." *Journal of Indian Philosophy* 37.4 (2009): 399–414.

Freeman, Rich. "Genre and Society: The Literary Culture of Premodern Kerala." In *Literary Cultures in History: Reconstructions from South Asia*, edited by Sheldon Pollock, 437– 502. Berkeley: University of California Press, 2003.

Freeman, Rich. "The Literature of Hinduism in Malayalam." In *The Blackwell Companion to Hinduism*, edited by Gavin Flood, 159–181. Oxford: Blackwell Publishing, 2003.

Freeman, Rich. "Śāktism, Polity and Society in Medieval Malabar." In *Goddess Traditions in Tantric Hinduism*, edited by Bjarne Wernicke Olesen, 141–173. London: Routledge, 2016.

Freeman, Rich. "Untouchable Bodies of Knowledge in the Spirit Possession of Malabar." In *Images of the Body in India*, edited by Axel Michaels and Christoph Wulf, 125–155. New Delhi: Routledge, 2011.

Freschi, Elisa, and Phillip A. Maas, eds. *Adaptive Reuse: Aspects of Creativity in South Asian Cultural History*. Wiesbaden: Harrassowitz Verlag, 2017. This refers to footnote 10 in the Conclusion.

Fuller, C. J. *The Camphor Flame: Popular Hinduism and Society in India.* Princeton: Princeton University Press, 1992.

Furey, Constance. *Erasmus, Contarini, and the Religious Republic of Letters.* New York: Cambridge University Press, 2006.

Gail, Adalbert. *Bhakti im Bhāgavatapurāṇa: Religionsgeschichtliche Studie zur Idee des Gottesliebe in Kult und Mystik des Viṣṇuismus.* Wiesbaden: Otto Harrassowitz, 1969.

Galewicz, Cezary. "Fourteen Strongholds of Knowledge: On Scholarly Commentaries, Authority, and Power in XIV Century India." In *Texts of Power, the Power of the Text: Readings in Textual Authority across History and Cultures*, edited by Cezary Galewicz, 141–164. Krakow: Homini, 2006.

Ganeri, Jonardon. "Contextualism in the Study of Indian Intellectual Cultures." *Journal of Indian Philosophy* 36.5 (2008): 551–562.

Ganeri, Jonardon. *The Lost Age of Reason: Philosophy in Early Modern India 1450–1700.* Oxford: Oxford University Press, 2011.

Gode, P. K. "Āpadeva, the Author of the Mīmāṁsānyāyaprakāśa and Mahāmahopādhyāya, Āpadeva, the Author of the Adhikaraṇacandrikā and Smṛticandrikā—Are They Identical?" In *Studies in Indian Literary History*, edited by P.K. Gode, vol. 2, 39–48. Bombay: Bhāratīya Vidyā Bhavan, 1954.

Gode, P. K. "Date of Śrīdharasvāmin, Author of the Commentaries on the Bhāgavata Purāṇa and Other Works—Between c. A.D. 1350 and 1450." In *Studies in Indian Literary History*, edited by P.K. Gode, vol. 2, 169–175. Bombay: Bhāratīya Vidyā Bhavan, 1954.

Gode, P. K. "Exact Date of the Advaitasudhā of Lakṣmaṇa Paṇḍita (A.D. 1663) and His Possible Identity with Lakṣmaṇārya, the Vedānta Teacher of Nīlakaṇṭha Caturdhara, the Commentator of the Mahābhārata." In *Studies in Indian Literary History*, edited by P.K. Gode, edited by P.K. Gode, vol. 3, 48–54. Poona: Prof. P. K. Gode Collected Works Publication Committee, 1956.

Gode, P. K. "The Identification of Raghunātha, the Protégé of Queen Dīpābāi of Tanjore and His Contact with Saint Rāmadāsa—Between A.D. 1648 and 1682." In *Studies in Indian Literary History*, vol. 2, 404–415. Bombay: Bhāratīya Vidyā Bhavan, 1954.

Gode, P. K. "Raghunātha, a Protégé of Queen Dīpābāi of Tanjore, and His Works—Between A.D. 1675–1712." In *Studies in Indian Literary History*, edited by P.K. Gode, vol. 2, 391–403. Bombay: Bhāratīya Vidyā Bhavan, 1954.

Gode, P. K. "A Rare Manuscript of Janārdana-Mahodaya by Raghunātha Gaṇeśa Navahasta, Friend of Saint Rāmadāsa—Between A.D. 1640 & 1682." In *Studies in Indian Literary History*, edited by P.K. Gode, vol. 2, 416–424. Bombay: Bhāratīya Vidyā Bhavan, 1954.

Golovkova, Anya. "The Forgotten Consort: The Goddess and Kāmadeva in the Early Worship of Tripurasundarī." *International Journal of Hindu Studies* 24.1 (2020): 87–106.

Gomez, Kashi. "Sanskrit and the Labour of Gender in Early Modern South India." *Modern Asian Studies* 57.1 (2023): 167–194.

Goodding, Robert Alan. "The Treatise on Liberation-in-Life: Critical Edition and Annotated Translation of the *Jīvanmuktiviveka* of Vidyāraṇya." Ph.D. diss., University of Texas, Austin, 2002.

Gordon, Peter E. "Contextualism and Criticism in the History of Ideas." In *Rethinking Modern European Intellectual History*, edited by Daniel M. McMahon and Samuel Moyn, 32–55. Oxford: Oxford University Press, 2014.

Grafton, Anthony. "A Sketch Map of a Lost Continent: The Republic of Letters." *Republics of Letters: A Journal for the Study of Knowledge, Politics, and the Arts* 1.1 (2009): 1–18.

Grierson, George A. "Modern Hinduism and Its Debt to the Nestorians." *Journal of the Royal Asiatic Society* 39.2 (1907): 311–335.

Guha, Ranajit. "Chandra's Death." In *A Subaltern Studies Reader: 1986–1995*, edited by Ranajit Guha, 34–62. Minneapolis: University of Minnesota Press, 1997.

Gupta, Ravi M. *The Caitanya Vaiṣṇava Vedānta of Jīva Gosvāmī*. London: Routledge, 2007.

Gupta, Ravi M. "Why Śrīdhara Svāmī? The Makings of a Successful Sanskrit Commentary." *Religions* 11.9 (2020): 1–14.

Gupta, Ravi M., and Kenneth Valpey. *The Bhāgavata Purāṇa: Selected Readings*. New York: Columbia University Press, 2017.

Gupta, Sanjukta. *Advaita Vedānta and Vaiṣṇavism: The Philosophy of Madhusūdana Sarasvatī*. London: Routledge, 2006.

Gurevitch, Eric. "Everyday Sciences in Southwest India." Ph.D. diss., University of Chicago, 2022.

Güthenke, Constanze. "Shop Talk: Reception Studies and Recent Work in the History of Scholarship." *Classical Receptions Journal* 1.1 (2009): 104–115.

Hacker, Paul. "Distinctive Features of the Doctrine and Terminology of Śaṅkara: Avidyā, Nāmarūpa, Māyā, Īśvara." In *Philology and Confrontation: Paul Hacker on Traditional and Modern Vedanta*, edited by Wilhelm Halbfass, 57–100. Albany: State University of New York Press, 1995.

Hacker, Paul. "Relations of Early Advaitins to Vaiṣṇavism." In *Philology and Confrontation: Paul Hacker on Traditional and Modern Vedanta*, edited by Wilhelm Halbfass, 33–40. Albany: State University of New York Press, 1995.

Hacker, Paul. "Schopenhauer and Hindu Ethics." In *Philology and Confrontation: Paul Hacker on Traditional and Modern Vedanta*, edited by Wilhelm Halbfass, 273–318. Albany: State University of New York Press, 1995.

Halbfass, Wilhelm. "Human Reason and Vedic Revelation in Advaita Vedānta." In *Tradition and Reflection: Explorations in Indian Thought*, edited by Wilhelm Halbfass, 131–204. Albany: State University of New York Press, 1991.

Hardy, Friedhelm. "Mādhavendra Purī: A Link between Bengal Vaiṣṇavism and South Indian *Bhakti*." *Journal of the Royal Asiatic Society of Great Britain and Ireland* 1 (1974): 23–41.

Hardy, Friedhelm. *Viraha-Bhakti: The Early History of Kṛṣṇa Devotion in South India*. Delhi: Oxford University Press, 1983.

Hare, James. "Contested Communities and the Re-imagination of Nābhādās' Bhaktamāl." In *Time, History and the Religious Imaginary in South Asia*, edited by Anne Murphy, 150–166. London: Routledge: 2011.

Hatcher, Brian A. *Bourgeois Hinduism, or the Faith of the Modern Vedantists: Rare Discourses from Early Colonial Bengal*. Oxford: Oxford University Press, 2008.

Hatcher, Brian A. *Hinduism before Reform*. Cambridge: Harvard University Press, 2020.

Hawley, John Stratton. "The *Bhāgavata-Māhātmya* in Context." In *Patronage and Popularisation, Pilgrimage and Procession*, edited by Heidi Pauwels, 81–100. Wiesbaden: Otto Harrassowitz, 2009.

Hawley, John Stratton. "Did Surdas Perform the *Bhāgavata-purāṇa?*" In *Tellings and Texts: Music, Literature, and Performance in North India*, edited by Francesca Orsini and Katherine Butler Schofield, 209–230. Cambridge: Open Book Publishers, 2015.

Hawley, John Stratton. "The Four *Sampradāys*: Ordering the Religious Past in Mughal North India." *South Asian History and Culture* 2.2 (2011): 160–183.

Hawley, John Stratton. *A Storm of Songs: India and the Idea of the Bhakti Movement.* Cambridge: Harvard University Press, 2015.

Hawley, John Stratton, Christian Novetzke, and Swapna Sharma, eds. *Bhakti and Power: Debating India's Religion of the Heart.* Seattle: University of Washington Press, 2019.

Hawley, John Stratton, Christian Lee Novetzke, and Swapna Sharma. "Introduction: The Power of Bhakti." In *Bhakti and Power: Debating India's Religion of the Heart*, edited by John Stratton Hawley, Christian Lee Novetzke, and Swapna Sharma, 3–22. Seattle: University of Washington Press, 2019.

Hazra, R. C. "The Bhāgavata-Purāṇa." *New Indian Antiquary* 1 (1938): 522–528.

Hazra, R. C. "The Śiva-dharmottara." *Purāṇa* 27.1 (1985): 181–210.

Hazra, R. C. *Studies in the Upapurāṇas.* Vol. 1. Calcutta: Sanskrit College, 1958.

Hein, Norvin. "Caitanya's Ecstasies and the Theology of the Name." In *Hinduism: New Essays in the History of Religions*, edited by Bardwell L. Smith, 15–32. Leiden: Brill, 1976.

Hiltebeitel, Alf, ed. *Criminal Gods and Demon Devotees: Essays on the Guardians of Popular Hinduism.* Albany: State University of New York Press, 1989.

Hino, Shoun. "The Beginnings of bhakti's Influence on Advaita Doctrine in the Teachings of Madhusūdana Sarasvatī." In *Indian Philosophy and Text Science*, edited by Toshihiro Wada, 101–114. Delhi: Motilal Banarsidass, 2010.

Hirschler, Konrad. *The Written Word in the Medieval Arabic Lands: A Social and Cultural History of Reading Practices.* Edinburgh: Edinburgh University Press, 2012.

Holdrege, Barbara. *Bhakti and Embodiment: Fashioning Divine Bodies and Devotional Bodies in Kṛṣṇa Bhakti.* London: Routledge, 2015.

Holdrege, Barbara. "From *Nāma-Avatāra* to *Nāma-Saṁkīrtana*: Gauḍīya Perspectives on the Name." *Journal of Vaishnava Studies* 17.2 (2009): 3–36.

Holdrege, Barbara. "From Purāṇa-Veda to Kārṣṇa-Veda: The Bhāgavata Purāṇa as Consummate Śruti and Smṛti Incarnate." *Journal of Vaishnava Studies* 15.1 (2006): 31–70.

Hopkins, Steven P. "Extravagant Beholding: Love, Ideal Bodies, and Particularity." *History of Religions* 47.1 (2007): 1–50.

Hudson, D. Dennis. *Krishna's Mandala: Bhagavata Religion and Beyond.* Edited by John Stratton Hawley. Oxford: Oxford University Press, 2010.

Ingalls, Daniel H. H. "Foreword." In *Krishna: Myths and Rites*, edited by Milton Singer, v–xi. Honolulu: East-West Center Press, 1966.

Jayashanker, S. "Śree Raajaraajeśwara Temple, Thaḷipparamba." In *Temples of Kaṇṇoor District*, edited by S. Jayashanker, 132–138. Delhi: Controller of Publications, 2001.

Jha, Ganganath. *Pūrva Mīmāṃsā in Its Sources.* Benares: Benares Hindu University, 1942.

Jha, Ganganath, trans. *Tantravārttika.* Delhi: Sri Satguru Publications, 1983.

Jha, Govinda. *Umesh Mishra.* Translated by Jayakanta Mishra. New Delhi: Sahitya Akademi, 1995.

Joshi, S. D., and J. A. F. Roodbergen, eds. and trans. *Patañjali's Vyākaraṇa-Mahābhāṣya: Paspaśāhnika.* Pune: University of Poona, 1986.

Kachru, Sonam. *Other Lives: Mind and World in Indian Buddhism.* New York: Columbia University Press, 2021.

Kaicker, Abhishek. *The King and the People: Sovereignty and Popular Politics in Mughal Delhi.* New York: Oxford University Press, 2020.

Kamath, Harshita Mruthinti. "Praising God in 'Wondrous and Picturesque Ways': *Citrakāvya* in a Telugu *Prabandha.*" *Journal of the American Oriental Society* 141.2 (2021): 255–271.

Kane, P. V. *A History of Dharmaśāstra.* Vol. 1. Poona: Bhandarkar Oriental Research Institute, 1930.

Kane, P. V. "The Tantravārtika and the Dharmaśāstra Literature." *Journal of the Bombay Branch of the Royal Asiatic Society* (N.S.) 1 (1925): 95–102.

Kataoka, Kei. "Scripture, Men and Heaven: Causal Structure in Kumārila's Action-Theory of *bhāvanā*." *Journal of Indian and Buddhist Studies* 49.2 (2001): 10–13.

Keune, Jon. "Eknāth Remembered and Reformed: Bhakti, Brahmans, and Untouchables in Marathi Historiography." Ph.D. diss., Columbia University, 2011.

Keune, Jon. *Shared Food, Shared Devotion: Bhakti and the Equality-Caste Question in Western India.* New York: Oxford University Press, 2021.

Kinra, Rajeev. *Writing Self, Writing Empire: Chandar Bhan Brahman and the Cultural World of the Indo-Persian State Secretary.* Oakland: University of California Press, 2015.

Kirwan, Richard, ed. *Scholarly Self-Fashioning and Community in the Early Modern University.* Farnham: Ashgate, 2013.

Kiss, Csaba. "The Bhasmāṅkura in Śaiva Texts." In *Tantric Communities in Context*, edited by Nina Mirnig, Marion Rastelli, and Vincent Eltschinger, 83–105. Vienna: Austrian Academy of Sciences, 2019.

Kiss, Csaba. "A Sexual Ritual with Māyā in Matsyendrasaṁhitā." In *Śaivism and the Tantric Traditions: Essays in Honor of Alexis G. J. S. Sanderson*, edited by Dominic Goodall, Shaman Hatley, Harunaga Isaacson, and Srilata Raman, 426–450. Leiden; Boston: Brill, 2020.

Klostermaier, Klaus. "Calling God Names: Reflections on Divine Names in Hindu and Biblical Traditions." *Journal of Vaishnava Studies* 2.2 (1994): 59–69.

Krishnamachariar, M. *History of Classical Sanskrit Literature.* Madras: Tirumalai-Tirupati Devasthanam Press, 1937.

Krishnamacharya, V. "Adhikaraṇādarśa of Bābādeva." *Adyar Library Bulletin* 14.1 (1950): 49–55.

Krishnamurthy, R. *The Saints of the Cauvery Delta.* New Delhi: Concept Publishing, 1979.

Küçük, Harun. *Science without Leisure: Practical Naturalism in Istanbul, 1660–1732.* Pittsburgh: University of Pittsburgh Press, 2020.

Kunjunni Raja, K. *The Contribution of Kerala to Sanskrit Literature.* Madras: University of Madras, 1980.

Kunjunni Raja, K., ed. *New Catalogus Catalogorum.* Vol. 9. Madras: University of Madras, 1977.

Laden, Anthony Simon. *Reasoning: A Social Picture.* Oxford: Oxford University Press, 2012.

Lindquist, Steven. "Literary Lives and a Literal Death: Yājñavalkya, Śākalya, and an Upaniṣadic Death Sentence." *Journal of the American Academy of Religion* 79.1 (2011): 33–57.

Lorenzen, David. "Bhakti." In *The Hindu World*, edited by Sushil Mittal and Gene Thursby, 185–209. New York: Routledge, 2004.

Lutjeharms, Rembert. *A Vaiṣṇava Poet in Early Modern Bengal: Kavikarṇapūra's Splendour of Speech.* Oxford: Oxford University Press, 2018.

Mahadevan, T. M. P., ed. *Preceptors of Advaita.* Secunderabad: Sri Kanchi Kamakoti Sankara Mandir, 1968.

Maitra, Nabanjan. "The Rebirth of Homo Vedicus: Monastic Governmentality in Medieval India." Ph.D. diss., University of Chicago, 2021.

Malinar, Angelika. "Arguments of a Queen: Draupadī's Views on Kingship." In *Gender and Narrative in the* Mahābhārata, edited by Simon Brodbeck and Brian Black, 79–96. London: Routledge, 2007.

Malinar, Angelika. *The Bhagavadgītā: Doctrines and Contexts.* Cambridge: Cambridge University Press, 2007.

Malkovsky, Bradley. *The Role of Divine Grace in the Soteriology of Śaṁkarācārya.* Boston: Brill, 2001.

Mallinson, James. *The Khecarīvidyā of Ādinātha: A Critical Edition and Annotated Translation of an Early Text of* haṭhayoga. London: Routledge, 2007.

Matchett, Freda. *Kṛṣṇa: Lord or Avatāra? The Relationship between Kṛṣṇa and Viṣṇu.* Richmond: Curzon, 2001.

McCrea, Lawrence. "The Hierarchical Organization of Language in Mīmāṁsā Interpretive Theory." *Journal of Indian Philosophy* 28.5 (2000): 429–459.

McCrea, Lawrence. "Hindu Jurisprudence and Scriptural Hermeneutics." In *Hinduism and Law: An Introduction*, edited by Timothy Lubin, Donald R. Davis Jr., and Jayanth K. Krishnan, 123–137. Cambridge: Cambridge University Press, 2010.

McCrea, Lawrence. "'Just Like Us, Just Like Now': The Tactical Implications of the Mīmāṁsā Rejection of Yogic Perception." In *Yogic Perception, Meditation, and Altered States of Consciousness*, edited by Eli Franco, 55–70. Wien: Verlag der Österreichischen Akademie der Wissenschaften, 2009.

McCrea, Lawrence. "Playing with the System: Fragmentation and Individualization in Late Pre- colonial Mīmāṁsā," *Journal of Indian Philosophy* 36.5 (2008): 575–585.

Mesquita, Roque. "Die Idee der Erlösung bei Kumārilabhaṭṭa." *Wiener Zeitschrift für die Kunde Südasiens* 38 (1994): 451–484.

Mesquita, Roque. *Madhva's Unknown Literary Sources: Some Observations*. New Delhi: Aditya Prakashan, 2000.

Miller, Barbara Stoler. *Phantasies of a Love-Thief*. New York: Columbia University Press, 1971.

Minkowski, Christopher. "Advaita Vedānta in Early Modern History." *South Asian History and Culture* 2.2 (2011): 205–231.

Minkowski, Christopher. "I'll Wash Out Your Mouth with My Boot: A Guide to Philological Argument in Mughal-Era Banaras." In *Epic and Argument in Sanskrit Literary History: Essays in Honor of Robert P. Goldman*, edited by Sheldon Pollock, 117–141. Delhi: Manohar, 2010.

Minkowski, Christopher. "Nīlakaṇṭha Caturdhara and the Genre of Mantrarahasyaprakāśikā." In *Proceedings of the Second International Vedic Workshop*, edited by Y. Ikari. Kyoto, forthcoming.

Minkowski, Christopher. "Nīlakaṇṭha Caturdhara's *Mantrakāśīkhaṇḍa*." *Journal of the American Oriental Society* 122.2 (2002): 329–344.

Minkowski, Christopher. "Nīlakaṇṭha's Mahābhārata," *Seminar* 608 (2010): 32–38.

Minkowski, Christopher. "The Vedastuti and Vedic Studies: Nīlakaṇṭha on Bhāgavata Purāṇa X.87." In *The Vedas: Texts, Langauge, Ritual*, edited by Arlo Griffiths and Jan E. M. Houben, 125–142. Groningen: Egbert Forsten, 2004.

Minkowski, Christopher, Rosalind O'Hanlon, and Anand Venkatkrishnan, eds. *Scholar Intellectuals in Early Modern India*. London: Routledge, 2015.

Minkowski, Christopher, Rosalind O'Hanlon, and Anand Venkatkrishnan. "Social History in the Study of Indian Intellectual Cultures?" *South Asian History and Culture* 6.1 (2015): 1–9.

Mirnig, Nina. "'Rudras on Earth' on the Eve of the Tantric Age: The *Śivadharmaśāstra* and the Making of Śaiva Lay and Initiatory Communities." In *Tantric Communities in Context*, edited by Nina Mirnig, Marion Rastelli, and Vincent Eltschinger, 471–510. Vienna: Austrian Academy of Sciences, 2019.

Mishra, Adya Prasad. *The Development and Place of Bhakti in Śāṅkara Vedānta*. Allahabad: The University of Allahabad, 1967.

Mishra, Umesh. *History of Indian Philosophy*. Vol. 1. Allahabad: Tirabhukti Publications: 1957.

Mitra, Rajendralal. *Notices of Sanskrit Mss*. Vol. 8. Calcutta: Baptist Mission Press, 1886.

Monius, Anne. "Dance before Doom: Krishna in the Non-Hindu Literature of Early Medieval South India." In *Alternative Krishnas: Regional and Vernacular Variations on a Hindu Deity*, edited by Guy L. Beck, 139–149. Albany: State University of New York Press, 2005.

Mukharji, Projit Bihari. "Truth as Materio-Moral Practice: *The Calling of History* for Histories of Science." *Comparative Studies of South Asia, Africa and the Middle East* 36.2 (2016): 355–361.

Müller, Max, ed. *Rig-Veda-Sanhita with the Commentary of Sayanacharya*. Vol. 2. London: W. H. Allen & Co., 1854.

Mulsow, Martin. *Knowledge Lost: A New View of Early Modern Intellectual History*. Translated by H. C. Erik Midelfort. Princeton: Princeton University Press, 2022.

Muñoz, José Esteban. "Ephemera as Evidence: Introductory Notes to Queer Acts." *Women & Performance: A Journal of Feminist Theory* 8.2 (1996): 5–16.

Nampoothiry, E. Easwaran. "Contribution of Kerala to Advaitavēdānta Literature." *Vishveshvaranand Indological Journal* 22 (1984): 184–194.

Narasimhachary, M. "Introductory Study." In *Āgamaprāmāṇya of Yāmuna*, edited by M. Narasimhachary, 1–46. Baroda: Oriental Institute, 1976.

Narayanan, Vasudha. "Singing the Glory of the Divine Name: Parāśara Bhaṭṭar's Commentary on the Viṣṇu Sahasranāma." *Journal of Vaishnava Studies* 2.2 (1994): 85–98.

Naregal, Veena. "Language and Power in Pre-colonial Western India: Textual Hierarchies, Literate Audiences, and Colonial Philology." *The Indian Economic and Social History Review* 37.3 (2000): 259–294.

Natarajan, B. *Sri Krishna Leela Tarangini by Narayana Tirtha*. Vol. 1. Madras: Mudgala Trust, 1988.

Nelson, Lance. "*Bhakti* in Advaita Vedānta: A Translation and Study of Madhusūdana Sarasvatī's *Bhaktirasāyana*." Ph.D. diss., McMaster University, 1986.

Nelson, Lance. "Bhakti Preempted: Madhusūdana Sarasvatī on Devotion for the Advaitin Renouncer." *Journal of Vaishnava Studies* 6.1 (1998): 53–74.

Nelson, Lance. "*Bhakti Rasa* for the Advaitin Renunciate: Madhusūdana Sarasvatī's Theory of Devotional Sentiment." *Religious Traditions* 12.1 (1989): 1–16.

Nelson, Lance. "Krishna in Advaita Vedanta: The Supreme Brahman in Human Form." In *Krishna: A Sourcebook*, edited by Edwin F. Bryant, 309–328. Oxford: Oxford University Press, 2007.

Nelson, Lance. "Madhusudana Sarasvati on the 'Hidden Meaning' of the *Bhagavadgītā*: Bhakti for the Advaitin Renunciate." *Journal of South Asian Literature* 23.2 (1988): 73–89.

Nelson, Lance. "The Ontology of *Bhakti*: Devotion as *Paramapuruṣārtha* in Gauḍīya Vaiṣṇavism and Madhusūdana Sarasvatī." *Journal of Indian Philosophy* 32.4 (2004): 345–392.

Nelson, Lance. "Theological Politics and Paradoxical Spirituality in the Life of Madhusūdana Sarasvatī." *Journal of Vaishnava Studies* 15.2 (2007): 19–34.

Nemec, John. "Innovation and Social Change in the Vale of Kashmir." In *Śaivism in the Tantric Traditions: Essays in Honor of Alexis G. J. S. Sanderson*, edited by Dominic Goodall, Shaman Hatley, Harunaga Isaacson, and Srilata Raman, 283–320. Leiden; Boston: Brill, 2020.

Nicholson, Andrew. "Review of *The Lost Age of Reason: Philosophy in Early Modern India 1450–1700*, by Jonardon Ganeri." *Journal of the American Oriental Society* 133.1 (2013): 158–160.

Nicholson, Andrew. *Unifying Hinduism: Philosophy and Identity in Indian Intellectual History*. New York: Columbia University Press, 2010.

Nicholson, Andrew J. "Vivekananda's Non-Dual Ethics in the History of Vedānta." In *Swami Vivekananda: His Life, Legacy, and Liberative Ethics*, edited by Rita D. Sherma, 51–72. Lanham: Lexington Books, 2021.

Novetzke, Christian. "The Brahmin Double: The Brahminical Construction of Anti-Brahminism and Anti-caste Sentiment in the Religious Cultures of Precolonial Maharashtra." *South Asian History and Culture* 2.2 (2011): 232–252.

Novetzke, Christian. *The Quotidian Revolution: Vernacularization, Religion, and the Premodern Public Sphere in India*. New York: Columbia University Press, 2016.

Novetzke, Christian. *Religion and Public Memory: A Cultural History of Saint Namdev in India*. New York: Columbia University Press, 2008.

Nowicka, Olga. "Local Advaita Vēdānta Monastic Tradition in Kerala: Locating, Mapping, Networking." *The Polish Journal of the Arts and Culture* 1 (2019): 27–51.

O'Hanlon, Rosalind. "Letters Home: Banaras Pandits and the Maratha Regions in Early Modern India." *Modern Asian Studies* 44.2 (2010): 201–240.

O'Hanlon, Rosalind. "Performance in a World of Paper: Puranic Histories and Social Communication in Early Modern India." *Past and Present* 219 (2013): 87–126.

O'Hanlon, Rosalind. "Speaking from Siva's Temple: Banaras Scholar Households and the Brahman 'Ecumene' of Mughal India." *South Asian History and Culture* 2.2 (2011): 253–277.

O'Hanlon, Rosalind, Gergely Hidas, and Csaba Kiss. "Discourses of Caste over the Longue Durée: Gopīnātha and Social Classification in India, ca. 1400–1900." *South Asian History and Culture* 6.1 (2015): 102–129.

O'Hanlon, Rosalind, and Christopher Minkowski. "What Makes People Who They Are? Pandit Networks and the Problem of Livelihoods in Early Modern Western India." *The Indian Economic and Social History Review* 45.3 (2008): 381–416.

Oberhammer, Gerhard. "Review: *Prahlāda: Werden und Wandlungen einer Idealgestalt*." *Oriens* 17 (1964): 267–270.

Okita, Kiyokazu. *Hindu Theology in Early Modern South Asia: The Rise of Devotionalism and the Politics of Genealogy*. Oxford: Oxford University Press, 2014.

Olivelle, Patrick. *The Āśrama System: The History and Hermeneutics of a Religious Institution*. Oxford: Oxford University Press, 1993.

Olivelle, Patrick. "From *trivarga* to *puruṣārtha*: A Chapter in Indian Moral Philosophy." *Journal of the American Oriental Society* 139.2 (2019): 381–396.

Olivelle, Patrick. *Renunciation in Hinduism: A Medieval Debate*. Vol. 1. Vienna: University of Vienna Institute for Indology, 1986.

Ollett, Andrew. "Artha: Semantics versus Pragmatics." *The Indian Philosophy Blog*, April 9, 2016. https://indianphilosophyblog.org/2016/04/09/artha-semantics-versus-pragmatics/.

Ollett, Andrew, and Anand Venkatkrishnan. "Plumbing the Depths: Reading Bhavabhūti in Seventeenth-Century Kerala." *Asiatische Studien/Études Asiatiques* 76.3 (2022): 581–622.

Orsini, Francesca. "Tulsī Dās as a Classic." In *Classics of Modern South Asian Literature*, edited by Rupert Snell and M. P. Raeside, 119–141. Wiesbaden: Harrassowitz, 1998.

Owens, Emily. "Enslaved Women, Violence, and the Archive: An Interview with Marisa Fuentes." AAIHS, October 4, 2016. https://www.aaihs.org/enslaved-women-violence-and-the-archive-an-interview-with-marisa-fuentes/.

Packert, Cynthia. *The Art of Loving Krishna: Ornamentation and Devotion*. Bloomington: Indiana University Press, 2010.

Padoux, André, and Roger Orphé-Jeanty. *The Heart of the Yogini: The* Yoginīhṛdaya, *a Sanskrit Tantric Treatise*. Oxford: Oxford University Press, 2013.

Paramasivan, Vasudha. "Between Text and Sect: Early Nineteenth Century Shifts in the Theology of Ram." Ph.D. diss., University of California, Berkeley, 2010.

Pellegrino, Gianni. "'Old Is Gold!' Madhusūdana's Way of Referring to Earlier Textual Tradition." *Journal of Indian Philosophy* 43.2–3 (2015): 277–334.

Peterson, Indira Viswanathan. "Multilingual Dramas at the Tanjavur Maratha Court and Literary Cultures in Early Modern South India." *Journal of Medieval History* 14.2 (2011): 285–321.

Peterson, Jonathan. "The Language of Legitimacy and Decline: Grammar and the Recovery of Vedānta in Bhaṭṭoji Dīkṣita's *Tattvakaustubha*." *Journal of Indian Philosophy* 48.1 (2020): 23–47.

Peterson, P. *A Sixth Report in Search of Sanscrit Mss. in the Bombay Circle*. Bombay: Government Central Press, 1899.

Pollock, Sheldon. "Deep Orientalism? Notes on Sanskrit and Power beyond the Raj." In *Orientalism and the Postcolonial Predicament*, edited by Carol A. Breckenridge and Peter van der Veer, 76–133. Philadephia: University of Pennsylvania Press, 1993.

Pollock, Sheldon. *The Ends of Man at the End of Premodernity*. Amsterdam: Royal Netherlands Academy of Arts and Sciences, 2005.

Pollock, Sheldon. "Is There an Indian Intellectual History? Introduction to 'Theory and Method in Indian Intellectual History.'" *Journal of Indian Philosophy* 36.5 (2008): 533–542.

Pollock, Sheldon. *The Language of the Gods in the World of Men: Sanskrit, Culture, and Power in Premodern India*. Berkeley: University of California Press, 2006.

Pollock, Sheldon. "The Languages of Science in Early Modern India." In *Forms of Knowledge in Early Modern Asia: Explorations in the Intellectual History of India and Tibet, 1500–1800*, edited by Sheldon Pollock, 19–48. Durham: Duke University Press, 2011.

Pollock, Sheldon. "Mīmāṁsā and the Problem of History in Traditional India." *Journal of the American Oriental Society* 109.4 (1989): 603–610.

Pollock, Sheldon. "New Intellectuals in Seventeenth-Century India." *The Indian Economic and Social History Review* 38.1 (2001): 3–31.

Pollock, Sheldon. "Pretextures of Time." *History and Theory* 46.3 (2007): 364–381.

Pollock, Sheldon. *A Rasa Reader: Classical Indian Aesthetics*. New York: Columbia University Press, 2016.

Pollock, Sheldon. "The Revelation of Tradition: *śruti, smṛti,* and the Sanskrit Discourse of Power." In *Boundaries, Dynamics and Construction of Traditions in South Asia*, edited by Federico Squarcini, 41–61. London: Anthem Press, 2011.

Pollock, Sheldon. "Sanskrit Literary Culture from the Inside Out." In *Literary Cultures in History: Reconstructions from South Asia*, edited by Sheldon Pollock, 39–130. Berkeley: University of California Press, 2003.

Pollock, Sheldon. "The Social Aesthetic and Sanskrit Literary Theory," *Journal of Indian Philosophy* 29.1 (2001): 197–229.

Pollock, Sheldon. "The Theory of Practice and the Practice of Theory in Indian Intellectual History." *Journal of the American Oriental Society* 105.3 (1985): 499–519.

Prentiss, Karen Pechilis. *The Embodiment of Bhakti*. Oxford: Oxford University Press, 1999.

Raghavan, V. "Bopadeva." In *Ramayana, Mahabharata, and Bhagavata Writers*, edited by V. Raghavan, 122–134. New Delhi: Publications Division, Ministry of Information and Broadcasting, 1978.

Raghavan, V. *The Great Integrators: The Saint-Singers of India*. New Delhi: Publications Division, Ministry of Information and Broadcasting, 1966.

Raghavan, V., ed. *New Catalogus Catalogorum*. Vol. 1. Revised edition. Madras: University of Madras, 1968.

Raghavan, V., ed. *New Catalogus Catalogorum*. Vol. 2. Madras: University of Madras, 1966.

Raghavan, V. *The Power of the Sacred Name: Indian Spirituality Inspired by Mantras*. Bloomington: World Wisdom Press, 2011.

Raghavan, V. "The Sūta Saṁhitā." *Annals of the Bhandarkar Oriental Research Institute* 22 (1941): 236–255.

Raghavan, V. "Upanishad Brahma Yogin, His Life and Works," *Journal of the Madras Music Academy* 27 (1956): 113–150.

Rainā, Suvīrā. *Nāradīya evaṁ Śāṇḍilya-bhaktisūtroṁ kā tulanātmaka adhyayana: bhakti ke ādyapravartaka ācāryoṁ ke bhakti-sūtroṁ tathā unase prabhāvita bhakti sampradāyoṁ kā prāmāṇika vivecana*. Delhi: Eastern Book Linkers, 1989.

Ramanujan, A. K. "Three Hundred *Rāmāyaṇas*: Five Example and Three Thoughts on Translation." In *The Collected Essays of A. K. Ramanujan*, edited by Vinay Dharwadker, 131–160. New Delhi: Oxford University Press, 1999.

Rambachan, Anantanand. *Accomplishing the Accomplished: The Vedas as a Source of Valid Knowledge in Śaṅkara*. Honolulu: University of Hawaii Press, 1991.

Ram-Prasad, Chakravarthi. "Knowledge and Action I: Means to the Human End in Bhāṭṭa Mīmāṁsā and Advaita Vedānta." *Journal of Indian Philosophy* 28.1 (2000): 1–24.

Ram-Prasad, Chakravarthi. "Knowledge and Action II: Attaining Liberation in Bhāṭṭa Mīmāṁsā and Advaita Vedānta." *Journal of Indian Philosophy* 28.1 (2000): 25–41.

Rao, Ajay. *Refiguring the Rāmāyaṇa as Theology: A History of Reception in Premodern India*. London: Routledge, 2015.

Rao, Ajay. "The Vaiṣṇava Writings of a Śaiva Intellectual." *Journal of Indian Philosophy* 44.1 (2014): 41–65.

Rao, T. N. Bhima. "Samartha Ramdasi Maths in Tanjore." *The Journal of the Tanjore Maharaja Serfoji's Sarasvati Mahal Library* 17.3 (1964): 1–4.

Rao, Velcheru Narayana. "Purāṇa." In *The Hindu World*, edited by Sushil Mittal and Gene Thursby, 97–115. New York: Routledge, 2004.

Rao, V. Narayana, and David Shulman. *A Poem at the Right Moment: Remembered Verses from Premodern South Asia*. Berkeley: University of California Press, 1998.

Rao, V. Narayana, David Shulman, and Sanjay Subrahmanyam. "A Pragmatic Response." *History and Theory* 46.3 (2007): 409–427.

Rao, V. Narayana, David Shulman, and Sanjay Subrahmanyam. *Textures of Time: Writing History in South India 1600–1800*. Delhi: Permanent Black, 2001.

Ratié, Isabelle. "'A Five-Trunked, Four-Tusked Elephant Is Running in the Sky': How Free Is Imagination According to Utpaladeva and Abhinavagupta?" *Asiatische Studien* 64.2 (2010): 341–386.

Reich, James D. *To Savor the Meaning: The Theology of Literary Emotions in Medieval Kashmir*. New York: Oxford University Press, 2021.

Reinhart, Kevin A. *Lived Islam: Colloquial Religion in a Cosmopolitan Tradition*. Cambridge: Cambridge University Press, 2020.

Saha, Shandip. "Creating a Community of Grace: A History of the Puṣṭi Mārga in Northern and Western India, 1493–1905." Ph.D. diss., University of Ottawa, 2004.

Saith, S. S., ed., *Catalogue of Sanskrit Manuscripts in the Panjab University Library, Lahore*. Vol. 2. Lahore: University of the Panjab, 1941.

Salomon, Richard, ed. and trans. *The Bridge to the Three Holy Cities: The Sāmānya-praghaṭṭaka of Nārāyaṇa Bhaṭṭa's Tristhalīsetu*. Delhi: Motilal Banarsidass, 1985.

Sāmbaśivaśāstrī, K., ed. *A Descriptive Catalogue of the Sanskrit Manuscripts in H.H. The Maharajah's Palace Library, Trivandrum*. Vol. 2. Trivandrum: V. V. Press, 1937.

Sanderson, Alexis. "Atharvavedins in Tantric Territory: The *Āṅgirasakalpa* Texts of the Oriya Paippalādins and Their Connection with the Trika and the Kālīkula, with Critical Editions of the *Parājapavidhi*, the *Parāmantravidhi*, and the **Bhadrakālī-mantravidhiprakarana*." In *The Atharvaveda and Its Paippalāda Śākhā: Historical and Philological Papers on a Vedic Tradition*, edited by Arlo Griffiths and Annette Schmiedchen, 195–311. Aachen: Shaker Verlag, 2007.

Sanderson, Alexis. "How Public Was Śaivism?" In *Tantric Communities in Context*, edited by Nina Mirnig, Marion Rastelli, and Vincent Eltschinger, 1–48. Vienna: Austrian Academy of Sciences, 2019.

Sanderson, Alexis. "The Śaiva Age: The Rise and Dominance of Śaivism during the Early Medieval Period." In *Genesis and Development of Tantrism*, edited by Shingo Enno, 41–350. Tokyo: Institute of Oriental Culture, 2009.

Sanderson, Alexis. "The Saliva Literature." *Journal of Ideological Studies* 24 & 25 (2012–2013): 1–113.

Sanderson, Alexis. "Saivism and the Tantric Traditions." In *The World's Religions*, edited by Stewart Sutherland, Leslie Holden, Peter Clarke, and Fried helm Hardy, 660–704. London: Routledge, 1988.

Sanderson, Alexis. "Tolerance, Exclusivity, Inclusivity, and Persecution in Indian Religion during the Early Medieval Period." In *In Honoris Causa: Essays in Honor of Aver Sarkar*, edited by John Makin son, 155–224. London: Allen Lane, 2015.

Sankunni, Kottarathil. *Aitihyamaala: The Great Legends of Kerala*. Translated by Sreekumari Ramachandran. Kozhikode: Mathrubhumi Books, 2011.

Sarma, K. Madhava Krishna. "The Vedāntakautūhala of Kamalākarabhaṭṭa." *Poona Orientalist* 9.1–2 (1944): 70–72.

Sarma, K. V. "Raghunātha Navahasta and His Contribution to Sanskrit and Marathi Literature." *Vishveshvaranand Indological Journal* 7.1 (1969): 69–82.

Sarma, S. A. S. "*Paḷḷivēṭṭa*, or the 'Royal Hunt,' in Prescriptive Literature and in Present-Day Practice in Kerala." *Cracow Indological Studies* 16 (2014): 289–314.

Sastri, P. P. S. *A Descriptive Catalogue of the Sanskrit Manuscripts in the Tanjore Mahārāja Serfoji's Sarasvatī Mahāl Library*. Vol. 13. Srirangam: Vani Vilas Press, 1931.

Sastri, P. P. S. *A Descriptive Catalogue of the Sanskrit Manuscripts in the Tanjore Mahārāja Serfoji's Sarasvatī Mahāl Library*. Vol. 14. Srirangam: Vani Vilas Press, 1932.

Sastri, S. Kuppuswami, ed. *A Triennial Catalogue of Manuscripts Collected for the Government Oriental Manuscripts Library, Madras*. Vol. 3, Part 1: *Sanskrit C*. Madras: Superintendent, Government Press, 1922.

Sastri, S. Kuppuswami, ed. *A Triennial Catalogue of Manuscripts Collected during the Triennium 1919–20 to 1921—22 for the Government Oriental Manuscripts Library, Madras.* Vol. 4, Part 1: *Sanskrit C.* Madras: Superintendent, Government Press, 1927.

Sastri, Srikantha. "Advaitācāryas of the 12th and 13th Centuries." *Indian Historical Quarterly* 14 (1938): 401–408.

Sathaye, Adheesh. *Crossing the Lines of Caste: Viśvāmitra and the Construction of Brahmin Power in Hindu Mythology.* New York: Oxford University Press, 2015.

Sathaye, Adheesh. "The Scribal Life of Folktales in Medieval India." *South Asian History and Culture* 8.4 (2017): 430–447.

Schultz, Anna. *Singing a Hindu Nation: Marathi Devotional Performance and Nationalism.* Oxford: Oxford University Press, 2013.

Schwartz, Jason. "Caught in the Net of *Śāstra*: Devotion and Its Limits in an Evolving Śaiva Corpus." *Journal of Hindu Studies* 5.2 (2012): 210–231.

Schwartz, Jason. "Ending the Śaiva Age: The Rise of the Brāhmaṇa Legalist and the Universalization of Hindu *Dharma*." Ph.D. diss., University of California, Santa Barbara, 2023.

Schwartz, Jason. "Parabrahman among the Yogins." *International Journal of Hindu Studies,* 21.4 (2017): 345–389.

Sedgwick, Eve Kosofsky. "Paranoid Reading and Reparative Reading: Or, You're So Paranoid, You Probably Think This Essay Is about You," in *Touching Feeling: Affect, Pedagogy, Performativity,* edited by Eve Kosofsky Sedgwick, 123–152. Durham: Duke University Press, 2003.

Sela, Ori. *China's Philological Turn: Scholars, Textualism, and the Dao in the Eighteenth Century.* New York: Columbia University Press, 2018.

Şen, A. Tunç. "The Emotional University of Insecure Scholars in the Early Modern Ottoman Hierarchy of Learning." *International Journal of Middle East Studies* 53.2 (2021): 315–321.

Sen, Kshitimohan. *Medieval Mysticism of India.* London: Luzac & Co., 1936.

Shafir, Nir. "The Almighty Akçe: The Economics of Scholarship and Science in the Early Modern Ottoman Empire." *Osmanlı Araştırmaları/The Journal of Ottoman Studies* 58 (2021): 251–280.

Sharma, Arvind. "Is Anubhava a Pramāṇa According to Śaṅkara?" *Philosophy East and West* 42.3 (1992): 517–526.

Sharma, B. N. K. *History of the Dvaita School of Vedānta and Its Literature: From the Earliest Beginnings to Our Own Time.* Reprint edition. Delhi: Motilal Banarsidass, 2008 [1961].

Sharma, Krishna. *Bhakti and the Bhakti Movement: A New Perspective.* New Delhi: Munshiram Manoharlal Publishers, 1987.

Shastri, Haraprasad. "Dakshini Pandits at Benares." *Indian Antiquary* 41 (1912): 7–12.

Sheridan, Daniel P. *The Advaitic Theism of the Bhāgavata Purāṇa.* Delhi: Motilal Banarsidass, 1986.

Sheridan, Daniel P. "Śrīdhara and His Commentary on the Bhāgavata Purāṇa." *Journal of Vaishnava Studies* 2.3 (1994): 45–66.

Shulman, David. "Creating and Destroying the Universe in Twenty-Nine Nights." *New York Review of Books,* November 24, 2012.

Shulman, David. *More Than Real: A History of the Imagination in South India.* Cambridge: Harvard University Press, 2012.

Shulman, David. "Notes on Camatkāra." In *Language, Ritual and Poetics in Ancient India and Iran: Studies in Honor of Shaul Migron,* edited by David Shulman, 249–276. Jerusalem: The Israel Academy of Sciences and Humanities, 2010.

Singer, Milton. "The Rādhā-Krishna *Bhajanas* of Madras City." In *Krishna: Myths, Rites, Attitudes,* edited by Milton Singer, 90–138. Honolulu: East-West Center Press, 1966.

Skaria, Ajay. "'Can the Dalit Articulate a Universal Position?' The Intellectual, the Social, and the Writing of History." *Social History* 39.3 (2014): 340–358.

Skinner, Quentin. "A Reply to My Critics." In *Meaning and Context: Quentin Skinner and His Critics,* edited by James Tully, 231–288. Cambridge: Polity, 1983.

Skinner, Quentin. *Visions of Politics*. Vol. 1: *Regarding Method*. Cambridge: Cambridge University Press, 2002.

Smith, Bonnie G. *The Gender of History: Men, Women, and Historical Practice*. Cambridge: Harvard University Press, 1998.

Smith, Fred. "Purāṇaveda." In *Authority, Anxiety, and Canon: Essays in Vedic Interpretation*, edited by Laurie L. Patton, 97–138. Albany: State University of New York Press, 1994.

Smith, Fred. "Reviews: *The Bhaktimandākinī*." *Bulletin of the School of Oriental and African Studies* 76.3 (2013): 523–525.

Smith, Fred. *The Self Possessed: Deity and Spirit Possession in South Asian Literature and Civilization*. New York: Columbia University Press, 2006.

Soneji, Davesh. "Performing Satyabhāmā: Text, Context, Memory and Mimesis in Telugu-Speaking South India." Ph.D. diss., McGill University, 2004.

Soneji, Davesh. "The Powers of Polyglossia: Marathi *Kīrtan*, Multilingualism, and the Making of a South Indian Devotional Tradition." *International Journal of Hindu Studies* 17.3 (2014): 339–369.

Stainton, Hamsa. *Poetry and Prayer in the Sanskrit Hymns of Kashmir*. New York: Oxford University Press, 2018.

Stainton, Hamsa. "Wretched and Blessed: Emotional Praise in a Sanskrit Hymn from Kashmir." In *The Bloomsbury Research Handbook of Emotions in Classical Indian Philosophy*, edited by Maria Heim, Chakravarthi Ram-Prasad, and Roy Tzohar, 239–254. London: Bloomsbury, 2021.

Stearns, Justin. *Revealed Sciences: The Natural Sciences in Islam in Seventeenth-Century Morocco*. Cambridge: Cambridge University Press, 2021.

Stoker, Valerie. "Conceiving the Canon in Dvaita Vedānta: Madhva's Doctrine of 'All Sacred Lore.'" *Numen* 51.1 (2004): 47–77.

Stoker, Valerie. *Polemics and Patronage in the City of Victory: Vyasatirtha, Hindu Sectarians, and the Sixteenth-Century Vijayanagara Court*. Oakland: University of California Press, 2016.

Stoker, Valerie. "Vedic Language and Vaiṣṇava Theology: Madhva's Use of *Nirukta* in His *Ṛgbhāṣya*." *Journal of Indian Philosophy* 35.2 (2007): 169–199.

Taber, John. "Kumārila the Vedāntin?" In *Mīmāṁsā and Vedānta: Interaction and Continuity*, edited by Johannes Bronkhorst, 159–184. Delhi: Motilal Banarsidass, 2007.

Timalsina, Sthaneshwar. *Seeing and Appearance: History of the Advaita Doctrine of Dṛṣṭisṛṣṭi*. Aachen: Shaker Verlag, 2006.

Tubb, Gary. "*Śāntarasa* in the *Mahābhārata*." *Journal of South Asian Literature* 20.1 (1985): 141–168.

Unithiri, N. V. P. *Pūrṇasarasvatī*. Calicut: University of Calicut, 2004.

Unithiri, N. V. P., H. N. Bhat, and S. A. S. Sarma, eds. *The Bhaktimandākinī: An Elaborate Fourteenth-Century Commentary by Pūrṇasarasvatī on the Viṣṇupādādikeśastotra attributed to Śaṁkarācārya*. École française d'Extrême-Orient, Collection Indologie 118. Pondicherry: Institut français de Pondichéry, 2011.

Upadhyaya, Baldev. "A Devotional Drama in Sanskrit." *Indian Historical Quarterly* 12 (1936): 721–729.

Uskokov, Aleksandar. "The Black Sun That Destroys Inner Darkness: Or, How Bādarāyaṇa Became Vyāsa." *Journal of the American Oriental Society* 142.1 (2022): 63–92.

Uskokov, Aleksandar. "Deciphering the Hidden Meaning: Scripture and the Hermeneutics of Liberation in Early Advaita Vedānta." Ph.D. diss., University of Chicago, 2018.

Vajpeyi, Ananya. "*Śūdradharma* and Legal Treatments of Caste." In *Hinduism and Law*, edited by Timothy Lubin, Donald R. Davis Jr., and Jayanth Krishnan, 154–166. Cambridge: Cambridge University Press, 2010.

van Buitenen, Johannes. *Rāmānuja's Vedārthasamgraha: Introduction, Critical Edition, and Annotated Translation*. Poona: Deccan College Postgraduate and Research Institute, 1956.

van Buitenen, J. A. B. *Yāmuna's Āgama Prāmāṇyam*. Madras: Ramanuja Research Society, 1971.

van der Veer, Peter. "Does Sanskrit Knowledge Exist?" *Journal of Indian Philosophy* 36.5 (2008): 633–641.

Vaudeville, Charlotte. "The Cult of the Divine Name in the Haripāṭh of Dñāndev." *Wiener Zeitschrift für die Kunde Sudasiens* 12–13 (1968–1969): 395–406.

Veluthat, Kesavan. "Making the Best of a Bad Bargain: The Brighter Side of Kaliyuga." *Indian Historical Review* 41.2 (2014): 173–184.

Veluthat, Kesavan. "Religious Symbols in Political Legitimation: The Case of Early Medieval South India." *Social Scientist* 21.1–2 (1993): 23–33.

Venkateswaran, T. K. "Rādhā-Krishna *Bhajanas* of South India: A Phenomenological, Theological, and Philosophical Study." In *Krishna: Myths, Rites, Attitudes*, edited by Milton Singer, 139–172. Honolulu: East-West Center Press, 1966.

Venkatkrishnan, Anand. "Hidden Mūrtis: The Sanskrit Students of Radcliffe College." In *Modern Sanskrit: Dialogues across Times, Spaces, and Religions.* London: Routledge, forthcoming.

Venkatkrishnan, Anand. "Leaving Kashi: Sanskrit Knowledge and Cultures of Consumption in Eighteenth-Century South India." *The Indian Economic and Social History Review* 57.4 (2020): 567–581.

Venkatkrishnan, Anand. "Philosophy from the Bottom Up: Eknāth's Vernacular Advaita." *Journal of Indian Philosophy* 48.1 (2020): 9–21.

Venkatkrishnan, Anand. "Ritual, Reflection, and Religion: The Devas of Banaras." *South Asian History and Culture* 6.1 (2015): 147–171.

Venkatkrishnan, Anand. "Skeletons in the Sanskrit Closet." *Religion Compass* 15.5 (2021): 1–9.

Vila, Anne. *Suffering Scholars: Pathologies of the Intellectual in Enlightenment France.* Philadelphia: University of Pennsylvania Press, 2018.

Wallis, Christopher D. "To Enter, to Be Entered, to Merge: The Role of Religious Experience in the Traditions of Tantric Shaivism." Ph.D. diss., University of California, Berkeley, 2014.

Whatmore, Richard. *What Is Intellectual History?* Cambridge: Polity, 2015.

Wilson, Frances, ed. *The Bilvamaṅgalastava.* Leiden: Brill, 1975.

Wilson, Frances, ed. *The Love of Krishna: The Kṛṣṇakarṇāmṛta of Līlāśuka Bilvamaṅgala.* Philadelphia: University of Pennsylvania Press, 1975.

Wilson, Horace Hayman, trans. *Ṛig-Veda Sanhitā: A Collection of Ancient Hindu Hymns, Constituting the Second Ashṭaká, or Book, of the Ṛig-Veda.* London: W. H. Allen & Co., 1854.

Windisch, Ernst, and Julius Eggeling, eds., *Catalogue of the Sanskrit Manuscripts of the Library of the India Office.* Part 4. London: Secretary of State for India in Council, 1894.

Winternitz, Moriz, and A. B. Keith. *Catalogue of Sanskrit Manuscripts in the Bodleian Library.* Vol. 2. Oxford: Clarendon Press, 1905.

Woolf, Virginia. "The Strange Elizabethans." In *The Second Common Reader*, edited by Andrew McNeillie, 9–23. London: Harcourt, 1986 [1932].

Wright, Samuel. "History in the Abstract: 'Brahman-ness' and the Discipline of Nyāya in Seventeenth-Century Vārāṇasī." *Journal of Indian Philosophy* 44.5 (2016): 1041–1069.

Wright, Samuel. *A Time of Novelty: Logic, Emotion, and Intellectual Life in Early Modern India, 1500–1700 c.e.* New York: Oxford University Press, 2021.

Wujastyk, Dominik. "The Love of Kṛṣṇa in Poems and Paintings." In *Pearls of the Orient: Asian Treasures from the Wellcome Library*, edited by Nigel Allen, 87–105. London and Chicago: Serindia Publications, 2003.

Wujastyk, Dominik. "Rāmasubrahmaṇya's Manuscripts: Intellectual Networks in the Kaveri Delta, 1693–1922." In *Aspects of Manuscript Culture in South India*, edited by Saraju Rath, 235–252. Leiden: Brill, 2012.

Wulff, Donna. *Drama as a Mode of Religious Realization: The Vidagdhamādhava of Rūpa Gosvāmī.* Chico: Scholars Press, 1984.

Index

For the benefit of digital users, indexed terms that span two pages (e.g., 52–53) may, on occasion, appear on only one of those pages.

Tables are indicated by an italic *t* following the page number.

Abhinavagupta, 27–28, 45–46, 49n.43, 55–56, 57–58, 58n.68
Advaitamakaranda, 36–37, 82–83, 88–89
Āgamas, 17–18, 20–21, 27–28, 61–62, 101–2, 111–12, 116, 120–21, 198–99, 202–3
Ajāmila, 85, 104–6, 118–19, 200
alaṁkāraśāstra, 26–27, 34–35, 62–63
Āḻvārs, 20–21, 22–23, 177n.7
Amṛtataraṅgiṇī, 36–47, 61–62, 90–91, 114, 215–16
Arpaṇamīmāṁsā, 161–63, 175–76
arthavāda, 89–90, 94–95, 97–101, 104–7, 112–13, 119–20, 152–53
Ātman, 18–19, 36–37, 45–46, 59, 60, 61, 63, 64, 65, 68*t*, 114–15, 117, 118–19, 150, 189–90, 197–98

Banaras, 14–15, 31, 36–37, 121–24, 129, 130–31, 132, 134–40, 144–46, 148–50, 151–52, 153, 155–56, 163–64, 165–67, 168–74, 185–86, 196, 208–9, 218
Bhadrakāḷī, 72–74
Bhagavad Gītā, 5–6, 18, 20–21, 58, 107n.70, 126–27, 133–34, 143, 160, 161–62, 164–65, 200–1, 202n.97
Bhagavadajjukam, 211–12
Bhagavannāmakaumudī; *Kaumudī*, 36–37, 82–84, 87–132, 138–40, 144, 152, 167–68, 193–95, 208
Bhāgavata Māhātmya, 29, 153–54
Bhāgavata Purāṇa; Bhāgavata, 1–2, 15–17, 19–22, 24–28, 33–35, 36–47, 48–49, 51–53, 54–69, 71–72, 75–84, 85–93, 94–95, 102–3, 104–23, 131, 133–34, 137–40, 144–51, 152–60, 161–65, 171–73, 175–76, 180–86, 192, 196–97, 200–1, 202–5, 206–7, 208, 209–10, 214–17
Bhāgavatatātparyanirṇaya, 22–23
bhajana sampradāya, 30–31, 36–37, 87, 125–26
bhakti
  bhaktimārga, 151, 158–59, 183–85
  bhaktirasa, 26–28, 43–44, 46–47, 49, 51, 63, 64–66, 87, 90–91, 123–24, 166–67, 193–95
  definitions of, 2–3, 59–61, 67–69, 90–91, 139–40, 183–85, 187–91, 201–4, 206–7
  emotions of, 5, 19–22, 51–54, 138
  historiography of, 22–28, 29–32, 35, 133–34, 175–80
  movement, 85–86, 165–74, 180–81
  network, 79–84, 173–74
  practices of, 30, 67–69, 91–92, 140, 143, 152–53, 155, 173–74, 198–201, 204–5
  qua criticism, 3–8, 76–79, 171–73
  as religion, 2–3, 29, 67–69, 76, 92, 133–34, 140, 153–54, 157, 206–7, 208–9
Bhakti Sūtras, 175–87, 190, 191, 192, 193–99, 201–4, 205–6, 208
Bhakticandrikā, 175–76, 185–99
Bhaktikalpataru, 161–62, 166–67
Bhaktinirṇaya, 138–48, 152–60, 166–67, 175–76, 196–97, 199n.90
Bhaktirasāyana, 177–78, 185–86, 188–89, 191, 200–1
Bhāskararāya, 175–76, 179–80, 197–205
Bhavabhūti, 16, 47–48, 50–51, 211–13
bhōga, *bhōgī*, 64, 67–69, 68*t*
bhukti, 50–51, 53–54, 59, 69
Bilvamaṅgala, 81–82
  Bilvamaṅgalastava, 81–82
Bōdhēndra, 125–29, 199n.90
Brahma Sūtras, 18, 48–49, 48n.37, 106, 111n.82, 187–88, 193–96, 203–4
brahmajñāna, 141–42
Brahman, 18, 19–20, 38–43, 45–46, 47–49, 55–56, 59–60, 64–65, 68*t*, 99–100, 114, 115, 116, 117, 118–19, 127–29, 141–42, 150, 155–56, 183, 188–90, 193–95, 197–98, 203–4

Brahmanism
 Brahmanical, 3–8, 17–18, 21, 23–24, 29–30, 35, 43–44, 70–72, 74–75, 77–79, 87–88, 94–95, 102–3, 131, 133–34, 143, 144–46, 155–56, 168–73, 196
 Brahmin (caste), 6–8, 17–18, 27–28, 29–31, 34–35, 36–37, 69–79, 80, 85–86, 87–88, 123–24, 125–26, 130–32, 133–46, 151, 152–60, 165–74, 175–76, 196, 208–9
 discourse of, 23–24, 27–28, 159–60, 171–73
 provincializing, 6–8, 14–16
brahmavidyā, 114n.88, 191
Brahmēndra, 125–26, 127–29

Caitanya, 23–24, 25–26, 41–42n.18, 80–81, 82, 88–89, 121–24, 129, 165–66, 183, 207n.110
caste, 2–8, 12–15, 17–18, 29–30, 31, 33–34, 35, 69–80, 83–84, 85–86, 91–92, 96–97, 98–99, 118–20, 125–26, 127–30, 133–34, 137–38, 153–57, 160, 171–74, 196–97, 203–4, 209–10
colonialism, 12–14, 180–81
 precolonial, 12–14, 181–82, 201–2, 209–10
cultural history, 9–10, 30–31, 36, 69, 87, 123–24, 132, 137–38, 208, 213, 217–18

Dēvas, 31, 123–26, 133–39, 163–64, 165, 166–67, 168–74, 175–76, 193–95, 208, 209–10
 Anantadēva, 88n.16, 110n.78, 123–24, 130–31, 136–37, 138–51, 152–60, 167–68, 196–97, 198–99
 Anantadēva II, 136–37, 139–40, 161–62, 164n.88, 166–67, 168–69, 171–73
 Āpadēva, 136–37, 160–65
 Bābādēva, 161–62, 163–64
Dhanañjaya, 43–44, 46
dharma, 2–3, 17–18, 85–86, 92, 96–97, 96n.39, 104–5, 107n.70, 126–27, 133–34, 152, 160, 162, 171–73, 196, 200, 203–4
 dharmaśāstra, 91–92, 94–95, 96–97, 102–3, 107–8, 109, 136, 137–38, 139–40, 171–73
 varṇasaṁkara, 196
 varṇāśrama, 17–18, 75–79, 92
dīkṣā, 27–28, 82
Draupadī, 53, 53n.55, 195–96

Ēknāth, 5–6, 31, 136–38, 153, 155–56, 168–69, 171–73

Gadādhara, 82, 165–66
Gauḍīya Vaiṣṇavas, 22–23, 25–27, 30–31, 36–37, 38, 43–44, 80–81, 82, 87, 88–89, 121–25, 165–66, 183, 193–95, 196–97, 205–6

Gōpīnātha, 91–92
gōpīs, 52–53, 119–20, 131, 191, 200–1

Haṁsasandēśa, 47–48, 51–53
Harivaṁśa, 20–21, 50–51

intellectual history, 2–3, 6–8, 9–17, 30–32, 35, 41–42, 43–44, 65, 83–84, 113n.86, 133–34, 157, 159–60, 164–65, 175–80, 181–82, 183, 197–98, 207, 208
itihāsapurāṇa, 96–100, 104–5, 109, 116

Jīva Gōsvāmī, 22–23, 25–26, 41–42n.18, 80–81, 88–89, 110n.78, 121–23, 183n.34, 188n.49
jñāna, 18, 116, 143, 164–65, 175–80, 183–85, 187–90, 192
Jñāndēv, 5–6
Jñānēśvarī, 5–6

Kamalākara Bhaṭṭa, 158–59, 163–65, 197–98
karma, 18, 77, 92, 116, 155, 165, 183–85, 195–96
karmayōga, 160, 198n.85
kāvya, 43–44, 45–48, 53–54, 61–64, 90–91, 203–4
Kerala, 29–30, 33–38, 47, 52–53, 54n.58, 55–56, 58–59, 65n.88, 69–81, 82–84, 87–89, 91–92, 113–14, 115, 203–4, 208–9, 211–15, 217, 218
Kṛṣṇa, 19–22, 33–34, 35, 41–42, 46n.30, 47–48, 51–53, 54–56, 57–58, 63–64, 65, 69–71, 80–81, 82, 88–89, 92, 104–5, 109, 114–16, 127–29, 136–37, 144–50, 152–53, 166–67, 192–93, 194n.69, 198–99, 205
kṛṣṇabhakta, 144–50, 161–62
Kṛṣṇabhakticandrikā, 144–51
Kṛṣṇakarṇāmṛta, 37–38, 80, 81–82
Kṛṣṇānanda, 54–55, 70–71, 75
Kumārila (Bhaṭṭa), 17–18, 96–100, 104–5, 163–65, 196–97

Laghustuti, 54–55, 56–58, 65–66, 73–75, 77–79
Lakṣmīdhara, 34–35, 36–47, 61–63, 64, 65, 82–83, 87, 88–93, 94–95, 104–21, 126–29, 152, 216–17

Madhusūdana Sarasvatī, 126–27, 148–50, 155–56, 177–80, 185–86, 187, 188–90, 191, 193–95, 196–97, 206–7
Madhva; Mādhva, 22–24, 102, 118–19, 121–23, 124–25, 126–27, 129, 188–89, 193–95, 201–2
Mahābhārata, 17–18, 20–21, 55n.61, 65, 98–99, 102, 109–10, 119–20, 154, 185–86, 195–96

Mahant Rāmcaraṇdās, 206–7
māhātmya, 187, 188–89
Manōnurañjana, 144–51
mantra, 27–28, 49–50, 62–63, 81, 85–86, 89–90, 118–19, 120–21, 127–29, 167–68, 209–10
Mathurāsētu, 162n.82, 162n.83, 166–68
Mīmāṁsā; Mīmāṁsakas, 2–3, 16–19, 20–21, 29, 30–31, 61–62, 87, 89–90, 93–103, 104–13, 119–20, 123–24, 129, 135–37, 139–40, 152–66, 171–74, 175–76, 183–86, 196–98
Mīmāṁsākutūhala, 158–59, 164–65
Mīmāṁsānyāyaprakāśa, 136–37, 160, 161
Mīmāṁsā Sūtras (MS), 17–18, 96–153
Mughal, 12–14, 80–81, 134–36, 144–45n.33, 166–67, 166n.95, 196
mukti, 27–28, 53–54, 59–61, 69, 118–19
Muktimaṇḍapa, 134–36, 139–40, 169–71

Nāmasiddhānta, 85–86, 125–26
Nārāyaṇa Tīrtha, 125–26, 175–76, 177–78, 179–80, 183–203, 205–7
Nṛsiṁha, 88–90, 117–19
Nyāya, 101, 175–76, 191, 203–4
  Navya Nyāya, 88–89, 148–50, 165–66, 183

Pāñcarātra, 20–21, 34–35, 55–58, 101–2, 120–21, 198–99
Pārthasārathi Miśra, 99–100, 164n.88
Patañjali (grammar), 16, 75, 157n.66
Patañjali (*yōga*), 175–76, 193–95, 197–98
Prabhākara, 17–18
Prahlāda, 118–19
prasthānatrayī, 18–19
Pratyabhijñā, 27–28, 29, 34–35, 45–46, 47–48, 49n.43, 54–56, 57–58, 77–79
Puṇḍarīka, 88–89
purāṇa, 19–20, 30–31, 43–46, 61–63, 87, 90–91, 92, 93–95, 96n.40, 102–3, 104–13, 115, 119–20, 120n.108, 123, 129, 152–53, 168–69, 183–85
Pūrṇasarasvatī, 34–35, 36–37, 41–43, 47–55, 58n.69, 60n.74, 61–62, 64, 67–71, 75, 79–80, 82, 89, 91, 113–14, 217

Rāghavānanda, 34–35, 36–37, 41–43, 47, 51–52, 54–80, 82, 216, 217
Raghunātha Navahasta, 168–69
Rāmānuja, 22–24, 109–10, 121–23, 126–27, 180–81, 182, 192–95
Rāmārcanacandrikā, 167–68
Rāmatīrtha, 123–24, 138–39, 146, 155, 167–68
Rāmdās; Rāmdāsī, 125–26, 130, 168–71
rasa, 26–27, 42–47, 49–50, 63–66, 90–91
religion, 1–8, 14–16, 27–28, 29–30, 34–35, 47, 49, 67–79, 83–84, 85–86, 92, 120–21, 133–34, 140, 144–46, 153–54, 157, 180–81, 205–7, 208–10, 217–18

Śabara, 17–18, 96, 97, 106n.66
Śaiva; Śaivism, 16–17, 21–22, 23–24, 27–28, 29–32, 33–35, 37–38, 37n.7, 42–44, 47–48, 50–51, 53–62, 65, 67–70, 71–72, 74–75, 77–79, 81–84, 85–86, 89–92, 93, 94–95, 101, 111–12, 113–14, 120–21, 127–29, 131, 144–48, 175–76, 179–80, 185–86, 197–98, 201–3, 205–6, 207, 208, 209–10, 217
Śākta; Śakti, 27–28, 29–30, 34–35, 42–43, 47–48, 54–55, 56, 58–59, 65–66, 69–70, 72–75, 77–79, 80n.133, 127–29, 175–76, 179–80, 197–98, 201–6
samādhi, 42–43, 116, 117, 197–99
Sāṁkhya, 57–58, 142–43, 197–98
saṁkīrtana, 152–54
  singing the name of God, 25–26, 30–31, 36–37, 68*t*, 77–79, 85–86, 87–88, 92, 93, 104–5, 107–8, 111–13, 116–19, 120n.108, 121, 123–29, 130–31, 135–36, 139–40, 143–44, 152, 153–55, 157, 169–71, 173–74, 200–1, 202n.97, 204, 208–9
Śāṇḍilya, 180–82, 205–6
Śaṅkara, 24, 25–26, 27–28, 34–35, 48–49, 58–59, 67n.93, 69–70, 100–1, 104–5, 113–14, 121–23, 126–29, 160, 163–64, 167–68, 206–7
śāstra, 1–2, 5–8, 12–16, 28, 83–84, 175–76, 208–10
Siddhāntatattva, 123–24, 136–37, 138–40, 141
Smārta, 23–24, 34–35, 74–75, 207
smṛti, 17–18, 19–20, 61–62, 93–103, 115, 116, 120n.108, 152, 160
social history, 9–16, 32, 35, 74–75, 135–36, 165–74, 209–10, 214–15
śravaṇa, *manana*, and *nididhyāsana*, 48–49, 114–15, 117
Śrīdhara (Svāmī), 25–27, 36–38, 41–42, 43–44, 88–89, 105–7, 113–14, 118–19, 120n.108, 121–23, 139–40, 161–62, 179–80
Śrīvidyā, 27–28, 42–43, 51–52, 54–55, 127–29, 201–2, 204–6
śruti, 17–18, 19–20, 61–62, 94–95, 96, 101–3, 111, 116, 152
stōtra, 47–51, 55–56, 59, 60n.74, 61, 65–66, 80, 81
subaltern, 6–8, 12–14, 30, 71–72, 87–88, 133–34, 155–56, 196, 216–17

subtextual reading, 11–16, 32, 36, 67–69, 75–76

Tantra; Tantric; Tantrism, 27–28, 29–30, 34–35, 47–48, 54–55, 59, 61–63, 65, 66–67, 70–72, 77–79, 83–84, 85–86, 93, 130–31, 167–68, 175–76, 179–80, 197–98, 201–2, 205, 208–9

Upaniṣads, 18–19, 41–42, 54–56, 60, 77–79, 99–101, 102–3, 114, 115, 116, 117–19, 120–21, 123–24, 127–29, 141–43, 150, 163–64, 183–85, 192, 193–95, 200–1, 203–4
Utpaladēva, 27–28, 55–56, 58, 61, 77–79

Vaiṣṇava; Vaiṣṇavism, 16–17, 20–28, 29, 34–35, 37–38, 47–48, 51–52, 54–59, 61, 69–70, 75, 77–79, 80–81, 82–84, 85–86, 89, 92, 93, 94–95, 101–2, 113–14, 120–23, 144–48, 161–62, 165–69, 175–77, 179–80, 197–98, 201–4, 206–7, 214–15, 217
Vallabha; Vallabhācārya, 23–24, 80–81, 188–89, 207n.110
  Vallabha Sampradāya, 80–81, 82, 183, 196–97, 201–2
Vēdānta, 2–3, 16–17, 18–19, 20–21, 22–28, 29, 31, 34–35, 41–42, 48–49, 54–56, 58, 77–79, 80, 82–83, 107, 109–10, 113–25, 137, 142–43, 144–46, 148–50, 161, 163–65, 171–73, 175–76, 192, 193–96, 197–98, 211–13
  Advaita; Advaitins, 18–19, 21–22, 23–26, 27–28, 29, 30–32, 34–35, 36–70, 74–75, 77–79, 80, 81, 82–83, 87, 99–100, 105n.65, 113–29, 131, 135–36, 138–44, 160, 163–65, 167–68, 169–71, 175–80, 183–98, 205–7, 208–9, 217
  Dvaita, 22–23, 186n.46, 193–95
  Śrīvaiṣṇava; Viśiṣṭādvaita, 22–23, 35, 70–71, 101–2, 109–10, 118–21, 126–27, 129–30, 181–82, 192–95
Vēdānta Dēśika, 22–23, 101–2, 119–20
vernacular
  everyday; quotidian, 1–8, 15–16, 30–31, 72–73, 85–86, 87–88, 129–30
  language, 10–11, 14–15, 18–19, 30–31, 79–80, 82–83, 85–86, 131, 133–34, 137–138, 153, 155–56, 157–58, 171–73, 176–77, 206–7
vidhi, 89–90, 93–94, 97–99, 104–7
vikalpa, 107–8, 183–85
Viṣṇu Purāṇa, 20–21, 22–23, 24, 48–49, 58, 106, 107, 109–10, 111–12, 120–21
Viṣṇusahasranāma, 119–20
vivakṣitārtha, 93–94, 104–5
vyavasthā, 107–8

yōga
  as practice, 47–48, 67–69, 197–205
  as school, 31–32, 175–76, 197–206, 208–9
  Yōga Sūtras, 31–32, 175–76, 185–86, 193–95, 197–205
  Yōgasiddhāntacandrikā, 185–86, 197–205
yōgī, 67–69, 68*t*, 71–72, 77, 169–71